THE
Interpersonal Theory of Psychiatry

By HARRY STACK SULLIVAN, M.D.

Conceptions of Modern Psychiatry
The Interpersonal Theory of Psychiatry
The Psychiatric Interview
Clinical Studies in Psychiatry

Prepared under the auspices of

THE WILLIAM ALANSON WHITE PSYCHIATRIC FOUNDATION
COMMITTEE ON PUBLICATION OF SULLIVAN'S WRITINGS

Mabel Blake Cohen, M.D.   Dexter M. Bullard, M.D.
David McK. Rioch, M.D.   Otto Allen Will, M.D.
Helen Swick Perry, *Editorial Consultant*

HARRY STACK SULLIVAN, M.D.

THE
Interpersonal Theory
of Psychiatry

Edited by
HELEN SWICK PERRY *and* MARY LADD GAWEL
With an Introduction by MABEL BLAKE COHEN, M.D.

W·W·NORTON & COMPANY·INC·*New York*

THE WILLIAM ALANSON WHITE PSYCHIATRIC FOUNDATION
COMMITTEE ON PUBLICATION OF SULLIVAN'S WRITINGS

PRINTED IN THE UNITED STATES OF AMERICA
FOR THE PUBLISHERS BY THE VAIL-BALLOU PRESS
789

Contents

Editors' Preface   vii

Introduction, by Mabel Blake Cohen, M.D.   xi

PART I   Introductory Concepts

1. The Meaning of the Developmental Approach   3
2. Definitions   13
3. Postulates   31

PART II   The Developmental Epochs

4. Infancy: Beginnings   49
5. Infancy: The Concept of Dynamism—Part 1   62
6. Infancy: The Concept of Dynamism—Part 2   92
7. Infancy: Interpersonal Situations   110
8. The Infant as a Person   135
9. Learning: The Organization of Experience   150
10. Beginnings of the Self-System   158
11. The Transition from Infancy to Childhood: The Acquisition of Speech as Learning   172
12. Childhood   188
13. Malevolence, Hatred, and Isolating Techniques   203
14. From Childhood into the Juvenile Era   217
15. The Juvenile Era   227
16. Preadolescence   245
17. Early Adolescence   263
18. Late Adolescence   297

v

PART III   Patterns of Inadequate or Inappropriate
Interpersonal Relations

19. The Earlier Manifestations of Mental Disorder: Matters
Schizoid and Schizophrenic   313
20. Sleep, Dreams, and Myths   329
21. The Later Manifestations of Mental Disorder: Matters
Paranoid and Paranoiac   344

PART IV

22. Towards a Psychiatry of Peoples   367
Index   385

Editors' Preface

IN THE preparation of this first book from the unpublished lectures of Harry Stack Sullivan, the initial problem was one of selection from the wealth of material which Sullivan left. The most detailed statements of his later conceptual framework are found in five series of unpublished lectures which he gave in the Washington School of Psychiatry, and the William Alanson White Institute of Psychiatry, Psychoanalysis, and Psychology, in New York; the sixth series was terminated by his death in 1949. Fortunately, these lectures were recorded, and he also left behind two Notebooks outlining them, the first prepared in 1944–1945, and a revision dated 1946–1947. At the suggestion of David Mc Kenzie Rioch, M.D., a friend and colleague of Sullivan's, the present book has been limited mainly to a series of lectures which Sullivan gave in the Washington School of Psychiatry in the winter of 1946–1947, since this series represents the last complete statement which Sullivan made of his conceptions of psychiatry.

Sullivan's conceptions were not static; his lectures changed from year to year as his own ideas and formulations unfolded and developed. Yet each series which he gave presented a carefully organized approach to psychiatry via the developmental route— that is, he traced from earliest infancy to adulthood the development of the person, from this study arriving at certain conclusions as to mental disorder in later life. Thus, while the general framework of his thinking remained the same, in each series certain ideas were discarded and certain new ideas were woven in, often intricately. It is for this reason that it has seemed desirable to use his last complete statement as the basis for this book.

A few exceptions have been made, however. We have found it possible, mainly through the use of bracketed footnotes, to incorporate most of the new material which appeared in the unfinished lecture series which he began in 1948. In addition, we have occasionally relied on lectures from earlier years to clarify obscure passages or to enrich sections where the limitations of lecture time had obliged him to refer only hurriedly to ideas which he had elsewhere discussed in detail. We have also had to rely on earlier series to supply a few sections which were lacking because of mechanical failures of recording equipment. But in all such incorporations from other series, we have been guided by the outline in his last Notebook, since we did not wish to include formulations which he had, by 1946–1947, revised or abandoned, nor did we wish to change the emphasis of his own plan of presentation. All major incorporations of this kind are indicated in footnotes.

There is some difference in style between the earlier and later parts of the book. The chapters which deal with infancy represent, not primarily observations on the human infant, but hypotheses as to what must have occurred in the life of every person during these early months, in view of the given psychobiological equipment of the infant, the order of maturation of abilities, the inevitable impact of the culture, and the data of later life. For these lectures, in which he was often presenting inference rather than observation, Sullivan made full and careful notes, precisely wording many of the postulates which he wished to present; in lecturing, he often read from his Notebook, expanding and explaining it. But in the later lectures, when he was dealing with material that could be supported by observation and might be within the recall of his hearers, he spoke extemporaneously, from only outlined notes. Thus much of the material in the earlier chapters reflects Sullivan's writing style, which was at times complex; in the later lectures, Sullivan spoke in a more easy and colloquial vein. In editing the book, we have avoided any change of those statements which have been fully worded by Sullivan in writing. We have, however, had to do more stringent editing and reorganization in those places where Sullivan spoke extemporaneously, for the meaning and emphasis of his spoken statements did not always carry over in written form.

Many students have commented on the importance of Sullivan's Notebooks. In this series of lectures, Sullivan included, usually in the same wording, most of the statements which appear in his last Notebook. Where a formulation in this Notebook did not appear in the corresponding lecture, we have usually included it at the appropriate place, provided its omission seemed not to have been intentional. The titles of the Parts and Chapters of this book also conform, with very few changes, to Sullivan's Notebook headings. His use of quotation marks has not usually been changed in passages taken from his Notebook; his use of single quotation marks, to indicate special fringes of meaning which he attached to certain words or phrases, is particularly characteristic of all his writings.

One omission has been made in preparing this book: Sullivan devoted three lectures, following Part II, to a discussion of the work of the psychiatrist—in particular, the psychiatric interview. Since these overlap a separate lecture series on this specific topic, which will be published in another book, they have been omitted here.

The preparation of this book has represented collaboration in what Sullivan would have called the syntaxic mode, for many people have contributed generously of their time, money, and thought. The Sullivan papers were turned over to the Foundation, in which Sullivan worked and which is made up of his students and colleagues, by James I. Sullivan, who has been unfailingly helpful in the project of assembling the papers for publication. In order to finance the initial phases of the work of cataloguing and editing the papers, a $15,000 fund was set up by ninety-three of Sullivan's students and colleagues. Without this very practical demonstration, by those who knew Sullivan's work best, of their interest in seeing that it reached a wider audience, this book could not have been published.

In the editing of this book, Mabel Blake Cohen, M.D., has acted as psychiatric consultant, and she has been our chief adviser at all stages of the work. All of the members of the Committee on Publication of Sullivan's Writings have read the manuscript, approved its content, and offered criticisms.

At the time the Foundation came into possession of the Sullivan papers, it was Patrick Mullahy and Otto Allen Will, Jr., M.D., who first read through much of the material and impressed the Foundation with its richness and the importance of publishing it. And Mr. Mullahy has also read the final manuscript of this book and made many splendid suggestions regarding it. Many other students and colleagues of Sullivan's helped in the initial planning for the publication of the papers and contributed encouragement and momentum, notably Alfred H. Stanton, M.D. In the days when Sullivan was still lecturing, Mary Julian White, M.D., personally supervised the recording and transcribing of the lecture series on which this book is based; because of her planning, this is one of the finest and most complete sets of lectures available to the Foundation.

Among those who have read all or part of this book and made excellent suggestions are Robert A. Cohen, M.D., Philip A. Holman, and Stewart E. Perry. And finally, we are profoundly grateful to Katherine Barnard, Editor for Norton, who skillfully added the finishing touches to the book.

Grateful acknowledgment is made for permission to quote from the following published works: To the American Psychological Association for P. W. Bridgman's "Some General Principles of Operational Analysis" (*Psychological Review*, 1945, 52:246–249). To Beacon House, Inc., for Leonard Cottrell and Ruth Gallagher's *Developments in Social Psychology, 1930–1940* (1941). To the Thomas Y. Crowell Company for Seba Eldridge's *The Organization of Life* (1925). To Harcourt, Brace and Company, Inc., for Edward Sapir's *Language: An Introduction to the Study of Speech* (1921). To Hermitage House, Inc., for Patrick Mullahy's *Oedipus: Myth and Complex* (1948). To the Houghton Mifflin Company for Ruth Benedict's *Patterns of Culture* (1934). To the McGraw-Hill Book Company, Inc., for Kurt Lewin's *A Dynamic Theory of Personality* (1935). To Macmillan & Company, Ltd. (London), for Charles Spearman's *The Nature of 'Intelligence' and the Principles of Cognition* (1923). To The Macmillan Company (New York) for Bronislaw Malinowski's "Culture" and T. V. Smith's "Mead, George Herbert" (in the *Encyclopedia of the Social Sciences*). To the University of Illinois Press for Harry Stack Sullivan's "Tensions Interpersonal and International" (in *Tensions That Cause Wars*, edited by Hadley Cantril; 1950).

Helen Swick Perry
Mary Ladd Gawel

Introduction

THAT THE field of theoretical psychiatry is today in a state of healthy flux is due in large part to the impact of Sullivan's thinking. And his thinking was, in no small part, a product of his ability to see the relatedness of the social sciences. His use of an operational approach and field-theory concepts, his recognition that the psychiatrist is not merely an observer but quite specifically a *participant* observer, and his utilization of concepts derived from the anthropologist's analyses of other cultures—all these have introduced a more dynamic character into psychiatric practice and theory. And, conversely, the contributions of Sullivan's thinking to the social psychologist's frame of reference have influenced the latter to alter his concept of "normal" behavior in order to take account of some of the forces and influences from the past which had hitherto been the province only of abnormal behavior.

This book embodies Sullivan's latest conceptions. The most appropriate introduction to it is an attempt to identify and perhaps put somewhat into historical perspective those concepts which represent his most unique and valuable contributions to the field of psychiatry.

Looking back on the development of Sullivan's theories, I find it significant that one of his very early concerns was with the problem of communication. His association with Edward Sapir, an anthropologist primarily interested in linguistics and communication, forwarded and enriched Sullivan's own investigations in this field. His treatment of language, symbols, and communication in the present book is one of the most useful for psychiatrists that I have ever seen. Sullivan's interest gradually broadened from a consideration of communication between two or a few persons to include problems of communication between larger aggregates of people, and thus to include also problems of disturbed behavior in the social scene at large. And the UNESCO Tensions Project bears witness to Sullivan's interest in the application of his theory of personality to problems between nations.

This interest in communication is not a side branch but is basically related to the core of Sullivan's work. This core can be described as the psychiatry of interpersonal relations, or as the study of communication between persons, or as the operational approach to psychiatry in which the psychiatrist plays the role of participant observer. It rests on the propositions that: (1) a large part of mental disorder results from and is perpetuated by inadequate communication, the communicative processes being interfered with by anxiety; and (2) each person in any two-person relationship is involved as a portion of an interpersonal field, rather than as a separate entity, in processes which affect and are affected by the field.

Sullivan has not been alone in his interest in interactional psychiatry and the study of behavior in terms of field theory. He has been very much in step with the times. Modern social science, no less than modern physics, now considers field processes rather than isolating out single and separate units to study. Such scientists as George Mead, John Dewey, Ruth Benedict, Edward Sapir, Leonard Cottrell, Kurt Lewin, and Karen Horney have also been aware of the significance of the cultural setting in influencing personal development, and have recognized that what is studied is a field of interaction.

Sullivan's primary discipline was that of psychiatry rather than that of social psychology, and he has brought a psychiatrist's thinking and clinical experience to bear upon the problems of field psychology. His major work consisted of clinical investigation, which for him was inseparably connected with the therapeutic approach to patients. His broad theoretical structure began to take form only after he had spent almost twenty years in such clinical investigation. Approximately the first ten years of clinical work were spent in the intensive investigation of schizophrenia; his first paper on this subject appeared in 1924, and the publication of numerous other papers on schizophrenia reflected his continuing study. Beginning in 1931, when he entered private practice, he spent approximately ten years in the equally intense investigation of neurotic processes. Toward the end of this period the theoretical structure for which he is now best known began to emerge. At the same time, he began to turn his interest increasingly to the communication of his concepts to others, and the Washington School of Psychiatry began giving instruction under his leadership. In 1938 the journal *Psychiatry* was founded with Sullivan as coeditor, and in 1939 he delivered the series of lectures which were published in the following year as *Conceptions of Modern Psychiatry*. The present book reflects the further elaboration and refinement of his theory after that time.

What school of psychiatric thought does Sullivan belong to? The old controversy as to whether Sullivanian psychiatric theory is or is not psychoanalytic has, in my opinion, no validity. Sullivan was trained in the psychoanalytic school; he developed serious theoretical differences with some of Freud's original hypotheses; he accepted others, which are included in his own formulation, such as concepts of conscious and unconscious processes. In this he has been no different from the other major workers since Freud in the field of theoretical psychiatry (and under that general term I include psychoanalysis). The ongoing development of any science requires the refinement and alteration of old concepts and assumptions in the light of new findings. An unfortunate tendency to cultism, both in certain of Freud's students and in certain of Sullivan's, has created a picture of two watertight, competing theories of personality. A careful examination of Sullivan's work will reveal, first, that he did not interest himself in some of the phenomena that Freud studied, such as infantile sexual behavior or the detailed phenomena of hysterical processes; and, second, that Sullivan has observed and theorized about certain phenomena which were relatively neglected by Freud. The most important of these areas which were relatively neglected by Freud has to do with the particular patterns of interaction which occur between particular people. Sullivan's formulation is in contrast to Freud's earlier one, which located the person in a generalized environment in which he manifests generalized and predetermined biological needs rather than specific patterns of interaction. Thus Sullivanian psychiatry brings to the whole field of psychiatric theory a particular point of view and a set of observations which can be and should be integrated with what was known before, and which then should be used in the true scientific spirit for further development, rather than preserved intact in the spirit of discipleship.

In attempting to delineate some of Sullivan's major contributions to psychiatric theory, one might mention first his formulation of infantile and childhood experience. In order to develop successfully into a predictive science, psychiatry must know what the effects will be of a specific constellation of parental and other forces acting upon the constitutional matrix of a specific child. The dynamic patterns of interaction must be known both specifically and also generally, in terms of types or categories of pattern. Sullivan has contributed to progress in this direction in two main ways. First, he has attempted to conceptualize in a systematic way the nature of experience. Much of what is experienced by the infant prior to the development of language must be inferred, although some direct observations can be made on the child-mother relationship in the early months of life, by trained workers with special opportunities. Sullivan's conclusions are based in part on inference and in part on his clinical observations, especially of schizophrenics, since much of their psychotic experience partakes of the nature of experience in early infancy. Observation of infants such as that done by Margaret Ribble, David Levy, and others has tended to confirm the conclusions arrived at by Sullivan. In Sullivan's conceptualization, experience occurs in three modes, which he has called prototaxic, parataxic, and syntaxic. The lines of demarcation between the modes point up the crucial role of language in human experience: prototaxic refers to experience occurring before symbols are used; parataxic refers to experience characterized by symbols used in a private or autistic way; and syntaxic is used for experience which one person can communicate to another, for it is conceptualized in symbols which are defined alike by each. Each of these modes of experience is discussed and elaborated on in considerable detail in this book.

Sullivan's second important contribution to a theory of child development is the concept of dynamism. He defines dynamisms as "the relatively enduring patterns of energy transformation which recurrently characterize the interpersonal relations . . . which make up the distinctively human sort of being." In this context, pattern is defined as the envelope of insignificant particular differences. Each organism develops a variety of interwoven and overlapping patterns, in relation to the important zones of interaction with the environment (such as the oral and anal zones), and also in relation to the important needs (such as hunger and lust). These dynamisms are developed and patterned from early interpersonal experience and are then carried by the person into his subsequent interpersonal experience.

The interpersonal field, then, is made up of the interaction of a variety of dynamisms of two or more organisms. Some of these dynamisms are *conjunctive* (for example, the need for intimacy) and lead to an integration of a situation, with a resolution or reduction of tension; others, which involve anxiety, are *disjunctive* and lead to disintegration of the situation; sometimes a dynamism can be nonoperative, since there is no corresponding dynamism brought to the situation by the other person. The patterns of interaction are those established in earlier living; and to the extent that anxiety processes have entered into the formation of these patterns, they will be inappropriate and inadequate. One of the dynamisms complicated by anxiety is the "malevolent transformation," in which the need for tenderness has, under the impact of anxiety, been replaced by malevolent behavior. Sullivan has made a number of generalizations which are stated in the form of theorems; to some extent, these have a predictive value. To illustrate: the theorem of tenderness states that "the observed activity of the infant arising from the tension of needs induces tension in the mothering one, which tension is experienced as tenderness and as an impulsion to activities toward the relief of the infant's needs." The use of this type of generalization avoids the pitfalls of instinct theory, yet has the merit of bringing a wide variety of individual responses together into a meaningful category. However, Sullivan has by no means achieved a complete classification and systematization of the dynamic patterns of interaction, and there is no doubt that this point of view, if it proves sufficiently useful, will require expansion.

Much of what has been said so far has included by implication the fact that Sullivan made use of the concept of anxiety as the chief disruptive force in interpersonal relations and the main factor in the development of serious difficulties in living. Anxiety too has been defined operationally. Sullivan has made no attempt to say what anxiety *is*—he describes it in terms of its effects. Certainly it has its origins in the conditions of prolonged and complete human dependency in infancy: the urgency of the biological needs, and the fact that the efforts of a mothering person are necessary for their satisfaction.

"Now, in discussing anxiety, I have come to something that has nothing whatever to do with the physicochemical needs of the living young. The tension called anxiety primarily appertains to the infant's, as also to the mother's, communal existence with a *personal* environment, in utter contradistinction to the physicochemical environment." The need for relief of anxiety is called the need for interpersonal security. The tension called anxiety, in early experience, is differentiated from all other reductions in euphoria by the absence of anything specific, and consequently there is in the infant no capacity for action toward the relief of anxiety. "Therefore, there is, from the very earliest evidence of the empathic linkage, this peculiar distinction that anxiety is not manageable. Anxiety is a tension in opposition to the tensions of needs and to action appropriate to their relief. . . . Of all experience of the present, the experience of anxiety is the sort least clearly interpenetrated by elements of the past and the future; it is the least interpretable and productive of foresight."

The question of the method of communication of anxiety from mother to child has been left largely unanswered by Sullivan. He lumped such communicative experiences under the category of "empathy"; but by empathy he did not mean anything resembling extrasensory perception. He meant rather that the sensory pathways of communication from mother to child are, as yet, uninvestigated, and therefore cannot be adequately described.

A summing up of Sullivan's major contributions to psychiatry would not be complete if one omitted his clinical work itself. It was in the actual treatment of patients that his theory grew, with a constant return to the therapeutic situation for verification and further development. In fact, it is natural for one who knew and worked with Sullivan to think of him primarily as a clinician, since the teaching of the art and science of psychotherapy was one of his greatest skills. In supervising the work of a student psychiatrist, he would, after listening for an hour or so to a student's stumbling report on a patient, have a grasp of the patient as a person which was astonishing and clarifying. To cite but one example of the application of his theory to the practice of psychotherapy: in working with a patient, Sullivan always listened to the data with the question in mind, "Where is the flow of communication being interfered with by the threat of anxiety?" Such a point could be identified by noting where the patient shifted from a presumably significant subject; where the security operations of the patient began to intensify; or where various somatic accompaniments of anxiety began to appear. Having identified such a point of change, a therapist is then in a position to recall, or to inquire about, what was going on just prior to the shift. This technique, when grasped and correctly used, gives a precise and reliable method for identifying and investigating patterns of difficulty in living.

In the present book, the mental disorders per se are touched on but briefly, and principles of therapy only by implication. While later books in this posthumous group of Sullivan's writings will be concerned specifically with these topics, here the main concern is with the developmental approach to the understanding of human personality. However, the three chapters on mental disorders in Part III merit careful consideration, since they present in very condensed fashion many of Sullivan's ideas on the psychoses and on obsessional states. It is hardly necessary to mention that his contribution to the psychopathology and therapy of these conditions was outstanding. In the discussion published here, he has used the central theme of dissociation in presenting the psychoses. Thus, in acute schizophrenia, "not-me" processes are actually present in awareness; other conditions, such as paranoid states, represent a variety of methods for disposing of dissociated systems which have erupted into awareness, and therefore in a sense represent unfortunate outcomes of efforts at reintegration. Sullivan tentatively proposes that the severely obsessional person be thought of as showing evidence of the presence of serious dissociation: "the obsessional substitutions which make up such conspicuous and troublesome aspects of [the lives of severely obsessional people] are simply all-encompassing attenuations of contact which protect them from their abnormal vulnerability to anxiety."

And finally, it should be pointed out that Sullivan's psychiatric theory and his psychotherapeutic techniques were alike predicated on the assumption that human behavior is positively directed toward goals of collaboration and of mutual satisfaction and security, unless interfered with by anxiety. He never ceased to admire the marvelous capacity of the human being, and to use, implicitly or explicitly, as his frame of reference the idea that "we are all much more simply human than otherwise, be we happy and successful, contented and detached, miserable and mentally disordered, or whatever."

Mabel Blake Cohen, M.D.

PART
I

Introductory Concepts

CHAPTER
1

The Meaning of the
Developmental Approach

AFTER A good many years of effort at teaching psychiatry I have concluded that either certain appraisals of myself as a good teacher are entirely unfounded or the teaching of psychiatry is extremely difficult; and I think quite possibly both are the case. But the fabulous difficulty of teaching psychiatry, as I have seen it over the years, is that it is quite easy to learn certain things—that is, to get so you can talk about them—but it is extremely difficult to get any two people to mean just the same thing when they talk about what they have supposedly learned.

This difficulty is a result of the fact that psychiatry deals with living and that everybody has a great deal of experience in living. But no one lives in anything like the highest style of the art; and it is very disconcerting to notice how badly one lives in the sense of the extent to which fatigue and other discomforts are connected with one's most important dealings with other people. So it is not very easy to develop that type of objectivity about the subject matter of psychiatry which one can acquire about the works of a clock or the principles of physics or even the phenomena of *quantum meruit* in law.

We interpret everything that we hear in this field of psychiatry on a double basis and, unhappily, neither of the bases is very helpful: first, on the basis of what one presumes the data mean in terms of what one knows already, or half-knows; and secondly, on the basis of how this can be interpreted so that it does not increase one's feeling of discomfort and inadequacy in living—one's *anxiety*, an extremely important term which I shall later define.

Some psychiatrists have had a great deal of training in the area in which psychiatry can perhaps be most easily taught; namely, in the area of describing, as if they were museum pieces, those people who have such great difficulties in living that their situation would be apparent to all. This is the psychiatry of mental disorders; and what one learns about mental disorders by way of descriptive psychiatry is not very meaningful. It does of course provide the psychiatrist with justification for making a living; and he has a feeling of being worth while because he knows a good deal about what these un-understood beings are apt to look like for a long time to come. If the patients manage to change for the better, everybody is so pleased that no one wastes much time condemning the psychiatrist for his mistakes in prognosis.

But the kind of psychiatry I am talking about attempts to *explain* serious mental disorders; and it also is of some use in living in general. How to communicate this particular theory of psychiatry has puzzled and harassed me for a great many years, and I have finally come to the decision that the only approach is by the developmental route. In other words, if we go with almost microscopic care over how everybody comes to be what he is at chronologic adulthood, then perhaps we can learn a good deal of what is highly probable about living and difficulties in living. The success of this kind of teaching has not been impressively great. It has taken the collaborative work of a group of extraordinarily gifted people, including some of my most distinguished colleagues in the Washington and New York areas, to arrive at something of a consensus about one of the central theoretical formulations in the type of psychiatry that I am attempting to teach.

In understanding what I am trying to say you will have to discard the notion that it is something you have known all the time, which just happened to get well formulated or peculiarly formulated by me. We are really up against one of the most difficult of human performances—organizing thought about oneself and others, not on the basis of the unique individual *me* that is perhaps one's most valuable possession, but on the basis of one's common humanity.

Briefly, I shall proceed by examining one hypothesis after another, selecting those which seem to be the best theoretical formulations now available as to how, from birth onward, a very capable animal becomes a person—something very different from an animal; and as to how this transformation of a very gifted animal—who is always there but who cannot be defined because he is constantly being transformed—is brought about, step by step, from very, very early in life, through the influence of other people, and solely for the purpose of living with other people in some sort of social organization.

No matter what kind of social organization there is, everyone who is born into it will, in certain ways, be adapted or adjusted to living in it. If the person is very fortunate, he will be pretty well adapted to living in that social organization. If he is extremely fortunate, he may come to know almost by intuition, you might say—which simply means that it isn't clearly formulated—so much about living itself that he can move into a quite different social organization; and fairly rapidly—but by no means immediately—he may learn to live quite successfully in this new social organization. That sort of transfer is practically out of the question for a great many of the people that psychiatrists see as patients. They are not quite able to live adequately as people in the social organization that they have been trained to live in.

To repeat, no very simple explanation is adequate to communicate some of the instrumentalities that might be useful for improving one's own life and the life of others. The only way that has occurred to me of providing something more useful is by this careful following of that which is possible and probable from birth onward. When psychiatry is approached that way it does not become simple—far from it. Since we have six or seven, or even more, extremely refined channels of contact with events around us, our experience of various combinations of the functions of these channels becomes pretty complicated. And since most of human life is not by any means concerned merely with events in the physico-chemical universe, but is concerned also with matters of cultural definition—values, prejudices, beliefs, and so on—the actual complexity of the field becomes mathematically rather overwhelming. The best that I can hope to present are dependable frames of ref-

erence as a guide in exploring this complex field, and the conviction that I have had personally for many years, that the great
capabilities of the human animal do not fail to make sense when
given an adequate chance.

I would like to say—I think with no material fear of extrava-
gance—that I don't believe many psychiatrists have a very good
theoretic framework for thinking about difficulties in living, their
origin, their dependable manifestations, or their fairly certain improvements. I do not mean to imply that most psychiatrists are not
useful to people. But I am stressing the need for a genuinely scientific approach to cope with the rapidly multiplying inefficiencies,
inadequacies, misfortunes, and miscarriages of life which come
to the attention of the psychiatrist. When I talk about a scientific
approach I mean something about as far from empiricism as the
mind will go—something precise, something capable of formulation, with a varying range of probability. So far as I know, most
of the ways in which one goes about being a human being could
be very different from anything we have ever heard of. In other
words, the human organism is so extraordinarily adaptive that not
only could the most fantastic social rules and regulations be lived
up to, if they were properly inculcated in the young, but they
would seem very natural and proper ways of life and would be
almost beyond study. In other words, before speech is learned,
every human being, even those in the lower imbecile class, has
learned certain gross patterns of relationship with a parent, or with
someone who mothers him. Those gross patterns become the utterly buried but quite firm foundations on which a great deal more
is superimposed or built.

Sometimes these foundations are so askew from what I would
describe as good foundations for living in a particular society that
the subsequent development of the person is markedly twisted
from conventional development—that is, from the average in the
purely statistical sense, from the way in which most people live.
In those circumstances we recognize the results as psychoneuroses
or psychoses. But to make anything useful in the way of thought
about these psychoneuroses and psychoses and to develop any certainly helpful technique for dealing with these 'warped' people,
your thinking has to reach very much further back than the pre-

senting situation. The great difficulty is that in this reach-back you find that a large part of the person's living is not particularly different from yours. And this apparent identity between your living and his living confuses the fact that this living, while outwardly identical, may not be at all identical in meaning to you and to him. And so you cannot ignore those aspects of his living that seem quite natural or normal to you.

In attempting to formulate and teach a theoretic framework for psychiatry over the years it has seemed to me necessary to avoid as far as possible psychiatric neologisms. Of course, every science has to have its technical language. But since this is the study of living and since it has the difficulties which I have already stressed, why add to the certainty of confusion and the Tower-of-Babel phenomena by putting in a lot of trick words? For these trick words, so far as I can discover, merely make one a member of a somewhat esoteric union made up of people who certainly can't talk to anybody outside the union and who only have the illusion that they are talking to one another. Any experiment in the definition of most of the technical terms that have crept into psychiatry shows an extraordinary fringe of difference in meaning. For that reason, I think we should try to pick a word in common usage in talking about living and clarify just what we mean by that word, rather than to set about diligently creating new words by carpentry of Greek and Sanskrit roots.

If I succeed then in communicating my ideas—and to the extent that I succeed—I hope that psychiatrists may derive some benefit in formulating their professional and other dealings with people in rather general terms; such general terms will, I believe, permit further exploration in the direction of getting highly probable statements. There are people who want certainties; they want to be able to distinguish certainly between correct and incorrect propositions. That is a perfectly foredoomed goal in psychiatry. You see, we are not that simple. We have so much spare adjustive equipment that we really live for the most part with only shockingly poor approximations to what might be correct or incorrect.

All of us are afflicted by the fact that long before we can remember, certainly long before we can make brilliant intellectual formulations, we catch on to a good deal which is presented to us, first, by the mothering one and, then, by other people who have to do with keeping us alive through the period of our utter dependence. Before anyone can remember, except under the most extraordinary circumstances, there appears in every human being a capacity to undergo a very unpleasant experience. This experience is utilized by all cultures, by some a little and by some a great deal, in training the human animal to become a person, more or less according to the prescriptions of the particular culture. The unpleasant experience to which I am referring I call anxiety. And here I am making the first of a long series of references to the basic conception of anxiety, which incidentally I have set forth briefly in my paper, "The Meaning of Anxiety in Psychiatry and in Life." [1]

In discussing the concept of anxiety, I am not attempting to give you the last word; it may, within ten years, be demonstrated that this concept is quite inadequate, and a better one will take its place. But this concept of anxiety is absolutely fundamental to your understanding what I shall be trying to lay before you. I want to repeat that, because I don't know that I can depend on words really to convey the importance of what I am trying to say: Insofar as you grasp the concept of anxiety as I shall be struggling to lay it before you, I believe you will be able to follow, with reasonable success, the rest of this system of psychiatry. Insofar as I fail to get across to you the meaning of anxiety, insofar as you presume that I mean just what you now think anxiety is, I shall have failed to communicate my ideas.

Because a great many phenomena in the whole biological field are easier to understand if you trace them from their beginnings to their most complex manifestations, I would like to describe how I think anxiety begins in the infant. I do not know how early in life anxiety first manifests itself. It is not exactly a field that you can get mothers and children to cooperate in exploring. I have no doubt that as a great many other things vary from person to

---

[1] [Harry Stack Sullivan, "The Meaning of Anxiety in Psychiatry and in Life," *Psychiatry* (1948) 11:1–13. Also, see "Towards a Psychiatry of Peoples," *Psychiatry* (1948) 11:105–116. And "The Theory of Anxiety and the Nature of Psychotherapy," *Psychiatry* (1949) 12:3–12.]

person, so the precise data which have to do with being anxious vary from infant to infant. It is demonstrable that the human young in the first months of life—and I think it is true of some other young, but it is very conspicuous in the human young— exhibits disturbed performance when the mothering one has an 'emotional disturbance'—I am using that term quite loosely to mean anything that you think it means. Whatever the infant was doing at the time will be interrupted or handicapped—that is, it will either stop, or it will not progress as efficiently as before anxiety appeared.

Thus anxiety is called out by emotional disturbances of certain types in the significant person—that is, the person with whom the infant is doing something. A classical instance is disturbance of feeding; but all the performances of the infant are equally vulnerable to being arrested or impeded, in direct chronological and otherwise specific relationship to the emotional disturbance of the significant other person. I cannot tell you what anxiety feels like to the infant, but I can make an inference which I believe has very high probability of accuracy—that there is no difference between anxiety and fear so far as the vague mental state of the infant is concerned. Some of you may feel inclined to say, "Well, do infants have fear?" And that, of course, becomes a matter of, "Well what do you mean by fear?" But I would like to point out that if an infant is exposed to a sudden loud noise, he is pretty much upset; certain other experiences of that kind which impinge on his zones of connection with the outside world cause the same kind of upset. Almost anybody watching the infant during these upsets would agree that it didn't seem to be fun; the infant didn't enjoy it. There is no doubt that this—whatever you call it—develops, with no break, into manifestations which we in ourselves call fear, and identify in others as fear. I have reason to suppose, then, that a fearlike state can be induced in an infant under two circumstances: one is by the rather violent disturbance of his zones of contact with circumambient reality; and the other is by certain types of emotional disturbance within the mothering one. From the latter grows the whole exceedingly important structure of anxiety, and performances that can be understood only by reference to the conception of anxiety.

In this connection, I will venture to say that the sort of experience which the infant probably has as primitive anxiety, or primitive fear, reappears much later in life under very special circumstances—perhaps in everyone, but certainly in some people. These circumstances are fairly frequent in the earlier stages of what we call the schizophrenic disorders of living. In quite a number of people, they are not too infrequent in so-called dreams at disturbed times of life, perhaps more specifically in the adolescent era. In these circumstances, anything from a hint to perhaps a fairly full-scale revival of the most primitive type of anxiety arouses *uncanny emotion*.

By uncanny emotion—which is just a trick term, since it hasn't any divine warranties for existing—I refer to an indeterminately large group of feelings of which the most commonly experienced is *awe*. Perhaps some of you have experienced it on first hearing a huge pipe organ. Many people experience great awe on their first glimpse into the Grand Canyon. Everybody has had some experiences of awe. I couldn't begin to name all the different sorts of circumstances in which most people experience awe. The rest of the named uncanny emotions are less well known. I would number them as *dread*—dread in far more than the purely conversational sense—*horror*, and *loathing*. All of these uncanny emotions have a sort of shuddery, not-of-this-earth component which is, I believe, a curious survival from very early emotional experience, all of which can be thus characterized. If you think of an occasion in your own early life when you really experienced one of these uncanny feelings, of which, as I say, awe is much the most common, you will realize that it is as if the world were in some way different. If you try to analyze the experience, you may talk about your skin crawling, or this or that; at any rate, you know that it was very curious. I think any of you who recall an awe-inspiring incident will realize it could easily have been terribly unpleasant. True, many of you, perhaps, have never experienced awe to that extent; awe is certainly the mildest of the uncanny emotions. But if there were a great deal more of such emotion, you would be very far from a going concern as long as you had it. That is the nearest I can come to hinting at what I surmise infants undergo when they are severely anxious.

In attempting to outline this whole system of psychiatry, I want to stress from the very beginning the paralyzing power of anxiety. I believe that it is fairly safe to say that anybody and everybody devotes much of his lifetime, a great deal of his energy—talking loosely—and a good part of his effort in dealing with others, to avoiding more anxiety than he already has and, if possible, to getting rid of this anxiety. Many things which seem to be independent entities, processes, or what not, are seen to be, from the standpoint of the theory of anxiety, various techniques for minimizing or avoiding anxiety in living.

For years and years psychiatrists have been struggling to cure this-and-that distortion of living as it came up in patients. Some of these distortions have proven extraordinarily resistant. I am inclined to say, when I don't feel that too many people are hanging on my words, that some of the cures have probably just been the result of mutual exhaustion. And why has this been so? Well, the present indication is very strongly in the direction of the wrong thing having been tackled. There was nothing particularly wrong with that which was allegedly to be cured. It was a pretty remarkable manifestation of human dexterity in living.

Then what was the trouble? Was it susceptibility, vulnerability to anxiety which called out this alleged symptom? When you begin to look for the anxiety or the vulnerability to anxiety—which from the standpoint of this theory explains the occurrence of the symptoms—then the picture becomes quite different. Much more can be accomplished—much more has been accomplished—from this standpoint.

And here let me say that I would not dare to speak in this way on the basis of my own experience alone. The same things that make psychiatry slippery for others make it slippery for me; it is awfully easy to be deceived. But a much more practical psychotherapy seems to be possible when one seeks to find the basic vulnerabilities to anxiety in interpersonal relations, rather than to deal with symptoms called out by anxiety or to avoid anxiety. I would not state this so positively had it not been tested by a considerable number of my colleagues in their work over the years. Although the results have been quite impressive, this does not mean that psychiatry is getting so easy that we can do it for recreation. I will probably be an utterly forgotten myth long before psychiatry gets to be remotely like an easy job for anyone. But I think that a grasp of the concept of anxiety—and seeing where it fits into the development of a person's living—will save a great deal of psychiatric effort if one is a therapist, and prevent a great many commonplace stupidities if one chooses to use psychiatry in other ways.

CHAPTER 2

Definitions

Psychiatry as Interpersonal Theory

I THINK that there is no other field of scientific endeavor in which the worker's preconceptions are as troublesome as in psychiatry. To illustrate this I will give three definitions of psychiatry. The first and broadest definition would run something like this: Psychiatry is the preoccupation of psychiatrists; it is all that confounding conglomerate of ideas and impressions, of magic, mysticism, and information, of conceits and vagaries, of conceptions and misconceptions, and of empty verbalisms. That is the broadest definition of psychiatry and, so far as I know, a good many people are very far advanced students of that field.

Now there is a second definition which I was moved to make a good many years ago when I was attempting to find out what, if anything, I thought about psychiatry; and this is a polite definition for psychiatry of the prescientific era. This second definition sets up psychiatry as an art, namely, the art of observing and perhaps influencing the course of mental disorders.

The third definition of psychiatry, which is the one relevant here, may be approached by considering it as an expanding science concerned with the kinds of events or processes in which the psychiatrist participates while being an observant psychiatrist. The knowledge which is organized in psychiatry as a science is not derived from anything special about the data with which the psychiatrist deals. It arises not from a special kind of data but from the characteristic actions or operations in which the psychiatrist participates. The actions or operations from which psychiatric information is derived are events in interpersonal fields which include the psychiatrist. The events which contribute information for the development of psychiatry and psychiatric theory are events in which the psychiatrist participates; they are not events that he looks at from atop ivory towers. But of all the actions or operations in which the psychiatrist participates as a psychiatrist, the ones which are scientifically important are those which are accompanied by conceptual schematizations or intelligent formulations which are communicable. These, in turn, are those actions or operations which are relatively precise and explicit—with nothing significant left equivocal or ambiguous.

With the coming of the operational view, at least in the realm of physics, a certain interest has developed in whether there could be an operational approach to the field of psychology. A very interesting symposium, which includes a discussion of operationalism in psychology, is to be found in the *Psychological Review* for September 1945.[1] To this symposium, a very restrained contribution was made by the eminent philosopher and physicist, P. W. Bridgman. "A term," says Bridgman, "is defined when the conditions are stated under which I may use the term and when I may infer from the use of the term by my neighbor that the same conditions prevailed." I have found myself somewhat entertained by this very exact statement. I am going to define terms, you see, but I won't have succeeded, according to Bridgman. All I can certainly do is state what I intend by a term, but long experience has taught me that your intention in using that term may not necessarily be the same. That, if anything, shows how far psychiatry is from being scientific. In a great many of the discourses that I have heard as a psychiatrist, the speaker has not defined his terms, nor have I provided him with any basis for guessing the conditions which covered my use of those terms. Thus when I use some particular word with a rather heavy freight of conditions as to its usability, I hope that you will at least hear me out and see whether you can come to a similar use of that term, so that you will gradually understand

[1] ["Symposium on Operationism," *Psychological Review* (1945) 52:241–294. See especially P. W. Bridgman, "Some General Principles of Operational Analysis," pp. 246–249. (By permission of the American Psychological Association.)]

fairly well what I have to say. If you do not pay some attention to the way in which I take a word that you are thoroughly accustomed to and tuck it into a particular meaning—instead of a whole dictionary of meanings—then shortly we will be parting company for quite dissimilar goals.

Let me quote Bridgman further. "Terms used in a scientific context must be subject to the presuppositions of scientific enterprise. One of the most important of these is the possibility of checking or verifying the correctness of any statement . . . [and] for all essential purposes the definition may be specified in terms of the checking operations [by which one determines that this condition is satisfied]." In other words, it is important that the statements which are used can be checked as to their validity, not, needless to say, merely by the person who uses them, but by the person who hears them. Psychiatry as a scientific enterprise should consist of a great body of statements, the correctness of which could be thus checked. It does not come anywhere near that ideal yet. Many statements which will be made in the course of this formulation leave a good deal to be desired when viewed from this precise standpoint formulated by Bridgman. Yet if one is occupied not merely with taking exceptions, with misunderstanding, and so forth, but with studying the actual basis for these statements, it will be found that while many of them do not get past all the requirements of Bridgman's definition, they need but fairly simple operations and inference to come very close to it. In other words, they are not yet satisfactory statements, but they are not awfully far from satisfactory statements; and there are very real difficulties about making entirely satisfactory scientific statements in this particular area. That happens to be the case in practically all statements about, for instance, covert operations; it has to be the case with certain statements regarding the very early stages of personality development. And in these instances you might apply yourself to considering the probable correctness of the inference incorporated in the statement.

The history of this field includes two tributaries which I am inclined to mention at this point in an attempt to set up as precisely as possible the reason for the interpersonal approach. Needless to say, behind all this phase of psychiatry are the discoveries of Sigmund Freud.

The first tributary is the psychobiology of Adolf Meyer. Both the Freudian discoveries and the formulae of Meyer center their attention emphatically on the individual person, as the central unit of study. Some of you may be well acquainted with the system of psychiatry which Adolf Meyer developed and to which he applied the term psychobiology. By this organization of thought, Meyer made, in my opinion, a very important contribution to the understanding of living. Before Meyer's contribution, the grand divisions of knowledge included—in the upper reaches beyond biology—psychology and sociology; and psychology was something which pertained to the mind but with the clear implication that the mind rested on concomitant physiological substrates. So psychology was a purely scientific discipline that studied something that rested on something else.

Psychobiology—and I will abstract the definition, or lack of definition, of the field provided by Meyer—is the study of man as the highest embodiment of mentally integrated life. In other words, it is a more-or-less conscious integration, which makes use of symbols and meanings. This embodiment of mentally integrated life includes the peculiar phenomenon of subject organization by which one is able to think of oneself as if objectively. While certain statements of psychobiology may seem somewhat uncertain, Meyer has stated specifically and succinctly that psychobiology is concerned with the individual human organism as a primary entity. He says that although he likes to speak of persons and groups, the person is the agent of contact. The individual has to do the choosing of his interpersonal material. The person is an object with subject capacity.

In the days when psychobiology was coming into being as a very important member of the hierarchy of knowledge—to my way of thinking a vast improvement on psychology—another discipline was being born called social psychology, which was the second tributary to the interpersonal approach. Under provocation of some very original thinking by Charles H. Cooley, George Herbert Mead, at the University of Chicago, developed a formula of social psychology which included the development of the self—not too far removed from what I discuss as the *self-system*—on the basis of reflected appraisals from others and the learning of roles which one undertook to live or "which live one"—to use a not very closely related statement of Georg Groddeck. The social psychology of Mead was much less vividly and utterly centered on the unique individual person. It showed very clearly that the unique individual person was a complex derivative of many others. It did not quite serve for the purpose of psychiatry as here defined, because there was, you might say, no source of energy presented to account for shifts in roles, the energy expended in playing roles, and so on.

I want to refer now to a very condensed comment on the significant work of Mead in founding social psychology:

Although Mead's interests were wide and touched fruitfully the history and significance of science, the role of religion, the basis of politics and the claims of metaphysics, his central preoccupation was with the genesis of the self and the nature of mind. Mead took more seriously than most philosophers the task bequeathed to speculative thinkers by Darwin: the elaboration of a purely natural history of the psyche. He early enunciated the thesis . . . that the psychical is a temporary characteristic of the empirical interaction of organism and environment concomitant with the interruption of that interaction.

He thus set for himself the task of explaining the development of this discontinuous characteristic of a continuing process into a functional mind or self. The essentially active nature of the organism furnishes the basis for this achievement. The capacity of the human organism to play the parts of others (inadequately described, he thought, as imitation) is the basic condition of the genesis of the self. In playing the parts of others we react to our playing as well. When the organism comes to respond to its own role assumptions as it responds to others it has become a self. From roles assumed successively and simultaneously there arises gradually a sort of "generalized other," whose role may also be assumed. One's response to this generalized role is his individual self.[2]

Thus one can see a certain very striking convergence of thought in the psychobiology of Meyer and the social psychology of Mead, which is concerned with the evolution of the self.

There is another field which is very powerfully tributary to the

[2] [T. V. Smith, "Mead, George Herbert," *Encyclopaedia of the Social Sciences*; 10:241–242. (By permission of The Macmillan Company.)]

development of this theory, cultural anthropology, which is concerned with the study of the social heritage of man. I should like to refer, in this connection, to Malinowski; the briefest statement of his extremely helpful views appears in the *Encyclopaedia of the Social Sciences*. While I would like to say a good deal on this subject, I shall confine myself to one short quotation from Malinowski: [3] "In every organized activity . . . human beings are bound together by their connection with a definite portion of environment, by their association with a common shelter and by the fact that they carry out certain tasks in common. The concerted character of their behavior is the result of social rules, that is, customs, either sanctioned by explicit measures or working in an apparently automatic way." Among the latter type of customs are moral values, "by which man is driven to definite behavior by inner compulsion," to quote Malinowski again. Without considerable help from the student of cultural anthropology on such massive questions as language, for example, I believe that it is impossible at all readily to pass from the field of psychobiology and social psychology, as defined, to that of psychiatry as here defined.

And finally, I believe that there is also an absolutely necessary convergence of social psychology as the study of interpersonal interaction, and of psychiatry as the study of interpersonal interaction—a tautology which I hope you will forgive me. As a psychiatrist, I had come to feel over the years that there was an acute need for a discipline which was determined to study not the individual human organism or the social heritage, but the interpersonal situations through which persons manifest mental health or mental disorder. Approaching it from another viewpoint, Leonard Cottrell,[4] who has, I think, carried social psychology a long way,

[3] [Bronislaw Malinowski, "Culture," *Encyclopaedia of the Social Sciences*; 4:621–645; p. 622. (By permission of The Macmillan Company.)]

[4] [Leonard Cottrell and Ruth Gallagher, *Developments in Social Psychology, 1930–1940;* New York, Beacon House, Inc., 1941. See also Cottrell, "The Analysis of Situational Fields in Social Psychology," *Amer. Sociological Rev.* (1942) 7:370–387. In the former, Cottrell and Gallagher have this to say on Sullivan's amendment to Mead's work (see pp. 23–24): "In a brilliantly organized theory of personality development, Sullivan attempts to show the influences within a given culture which channelize awareness, the disciplines which actually repress the child's interest in certain objects and activities, and the cultural omissions which serve to blind him to certain meanings by

came to the conclusion that investigations in social psychology had to be made within the frame of reference of interpersonal situations.

In my attempt to outline such a field, I discovered that it seemed to be the field in which the activity—the actions and the operations—of a psychiatrist could be given communicable conceptual schematization, and, therefore, seekable scientific meaning.

It is, I believe, perfectly correct to say with Bridgman ". . . I act in two modes . . . . my public mode . . . and in the private mode, [in which] I feel my inviolable isolation from my fellows. . . ." [5] Psychiatry studies, as I see it, activity in the public mode and also that part of activity in the private mode which is not in any sense inviolably isolated. Let me say that insofar as you are interested in your unique individuality, in contradistinction to the interpersonal activities which you or someone else can observe, to that extent you are interested in the really private mode in which you live—in which I have no interest whatever. The fact is that for any scientific inquiry, in the sense that psychiatry should be, we cannot be concerned with that which is inviolably private. The setting up of the psychiatric field as a study of interpersonal relations is certainly necessary if psychiatry is to be scientific; furthermore, by this simple expedient of so defining psychiatry, we weed out from the serious psychiatric problems a great number of pseudo-problems—which, since they are pseudo-problems, are not susceptible of solution, attempts at their solution being, in

---

withholding the tools of awareness. These objects of the child's perception, but not his apperception, enter to complicate the patterns of verbal response which he learns along the way. When the discrepancy between his verbal self-other patterns and these 'parataxic' or dissociated elements becomes so great as to cause serious anxiety, we have all the symptoms of a neurosis. . . .

"If we accept Mead's analysis of the way in which meaning emerges from an incorporated verbal structure of rights and duties, Sullivan's work suggests an important amendment. The meaning that is borne by verbal interchange in interpersonal relations can be completely distorted by the dissociated elements which are at work to set the tone and color of the situation. It is impossible to know the intentions of another fully; but it becomes easier to approximate this understanding when you are aware of the subverbal reaction tendencies in your own behavior which you would otherwise unwittingly project on the situation, and when, at the same time, you are aware of the meaning of certain tensions and irrelevant motions which are complicating the verbal response of the other."]

[5] [Work cited.]

fact, only ways of passing a lifetime pleasantly. Let me repeat that psychiatry as a science cannot be concerned with anything which is immutably private; it must be concerned only with the human living which is in, or can be converted into, the public mode.

Thus as psychobiology seeks to study the individual human being, and as cultural anthropology, which has been a powerful tributary to social science, seeks to study the social heritage shown in the concerted behavior of people making up a group, so psychiatry—and its convergent, social psychology—seeks to study the biologically and culturally conditioned, but *sui generis*, interpersonal processes occurring in the interpersonal situations in which the observant psychiatrist does his work.

Man the Animal and Human Experience

Man is born an animal. Man, the animal, is known only as newborn. The processes which convert man, the animal, into something else begin to become effective in a very short time after birth. It is safe to infer that man, the animal, if he continued to exist as such, would be found to be an exceedingly gifted member of the biological series, and especially gifted in the evolution of his central integrative apparatus, which has provided unique capabilities of three sorts: (1) in the interrelation of vision and the prehensile hands—the greatest tools of interrelation other than the mouth; (2) in the interrelation of hearing and the voice-producing apparatus, which is so exquisitely refined as to permit that fantastic evolutionary development, language; and (3) in the interrelation of these and all other receptor-effector systems in an exceedingly complicated forebrain, which permits operating with many kinds of abstracts of experience.

There is abundant evidence that the human animal is not able to look after himself for a long time after birth; and that the abilities that characterize him are matured serially over a term of no less than ten to twenty years. The human animal is utterly dependent at birth and, diminishingly but still greatly, dependent on the tender cooperation of the human environment for five or six years after birth. The human animal is furthermore characterized by a remarkably long period during which various biological capabilities mature in turn.

It is likewise clear that the inborn potentialities which thus mature over a term of years are remarkably labile, subject to relatively durable change by experience, and antithetic to the comparatively stable patterns to which the biological concept of *instinct* applies. The idea of 'human instincts' in anything like the proper rigid meaning of maturing patterns of behavior which are not labile is completely preposterous. Therefore, all discussions of 'human instincts' are apt to be very misleading and very much a block to correct thinking, unless the term *instinct*, modified by the adjective *human*, is so broadened in its meaning that there is no particular sense in using the term at all.

Excluding the outcomes of hereditary or developmental disasters to which the term, idiot, is correctly applied, the individual differences in inborn endowment of human animals are relatively unimportant in comparison with the differences of the human animal from any other species of animal—however spectacular the differences between humans may seem against the background of life histories in any particular culture area. This problem of human differences is basic to a simply delusional interest in personality and the uniqueness of personality; because this is so troublesome, so preoccupying to some otherwise very capable students of so-called human nature, I wish to put plenty of emphasis on whatever individual differences there are. At the same time, I want to warn you that in psychiatry as a study of interpersonal relations, all these individual differences are much less important than are the lack of differences, the similarities in the arts for instance, the parallels in the manifestation of human life wherever it is found.

If we exclude instances of identical twins, we may assume that each human animal is somewhat different from every other one, with respect to matters of organization as a living creature, and with respect to functional activities concerned with living in the biologically necessary environment. I need scarcely remind you of such differences as hair color and texture and its distribution over the body surface; in the color of the iris; in skin pigmentation; in blood group and type; and in size and shape of sundry items such as fingers, nose, and ears. I could go on almost indefinitely on the differences, which may be described as varying from the obvious to the recondite, between one particular biological organization and another.

Rather more impressive for the student of interpersonal relations are the hereditary or at least inborn differences in function of (1) the visual receptor with respect to light frequencies; (2) the hearing receptor with respect to sound frequencies; (3) anatomical differences reflected in the possibilities of sundry dexterities, including speech; and (4) differences in the complex of factors underlying the activities which are measured by the Binet type of 'intelligence tests.'

It is commonly but quite erroneously supposed by those not really informed in the field that man shows a typical response to light waves of frequencies within the so-called visible spectrum. Although it is true, statistically, that one can apply the visual sensitivity or color sensitivity curve of a thousand people to the next hundred thousand, one finds that the color sensitivity of a particular retina, when it is mapped with great care, does not precisely approximate the statistical curve. So there are differences—and for all we know there may be rather notable differences, particularly, for example, in the Chinese. I don't know whether their added kink in the occipital zone does affect vision, but I surmise it does. Most likely it does not affect vision in the area of color sensitivity; yet it may do so even there—we are not too sure.

Besides this, there are great individual differences in response to light intensity—for instance, the particular time when the rods take over in dim illumination—and those differences are particularly impressive in that they vary with the health, nutrition, and other conditions of the person concerned; such variations may be quite significant in certain special circumstances affecting the survival of the person concerned, as, for example, in night flying and even in night driving of an automobile.

These variations in the distance receptor for light are trifling compared with the differences in the auditory receptor for air waves. Here too we have a fairly typical curve of sensitivity arrived at by statistical method and this curve applies to a great many data of individual hearing. Individual variation from these statistical curves is very much greater than is that in the field of color vision. As a matter of fact, hearing is a fairly simple function of age: in most people the curve changes at perhaps an imperceptible velocity up to a certain age; and then there is a more or less steady diminution with time in acuity of hearing. Differences here can be more readily observed so that we know that the heard word is quite notably different for some people than it is for others. Moreover, there are pathological variations, due to early disease and injury, which are much more frequent than is the case in the visual receptor area, and have much more insidious effects on the world as experienced. Dexterity, too, is notoriously variable among different people; we are all aware, for example, of the utility of long fingers if one is to be a pianist, or the handicap of a cleft palate if one wants to be an orator.

But the differences that have been most talked about over the past two decades, sometimes with great enthusiasm, are the remarkable range of intelligence factors, intellectual endowments, and so on, which vary, as you well know, from the low-grade imbecile to the genius, if genius can be considered a function of intelligence; by genius I mean those people who have really outstanding ability to see the relatedness of events, which seems to be the ultimate of the measurable intelligence factors. We all know that it is much easier to explain things to some people than it is to others; and all too many of us are very free in classifying people as to whether they are bright or dull, clever or stupid. Enough of an indeterminately great number of inborn factors have already been discovered to justify one in feeling that one's own animal substrate is certainly uniquely individual. Moreover, we already know something of the durable effects that may arise from defects of interchange with the optimum physicochemical environment, as in the case of the deficiency diseases.

Another field of difference, which is of even more interest to the psychiatrist, is the differences, the presumably inborn differences, in the rate of maturation of one's capabilities. Then there are differences arising from factors of the character of health, accidental injury, and diseases, already indicated in the case of hearing, but needless to say, applying in many other fields.

All these differences which I have so far mentioned are differences in inborn potentialities and individual development histories of human animals as underlying human beings. Now I would like to consider differences in nongenetic factors, elements, circumstances, or influences that determine human career-lines in terms of satisfaction or frustration of needs, and the enhancement or depreciation of self-regard. One of these factors is language. And while I shall not at the moment discuss language as determining differences in human career-lines, I should like to provide some background for later consideration of this by quoting from Edward Sapir's *Language:* [6]

[Language is a] purely human and noninstinctive method of communicating ideas, emotions, and desires by means of a system of voluntarily produced symbols . . . [which] are, in the first instance, auditory and . . . produced by the so-called "organs of speech." . . . the essence of language consists in the assigning of conventional, voluntarily articulated, sounds, or of their equivalents, to the diverse elements of experience. . . . The elements of language, the symbols that ticket off experience, must . . . be associated with whole groups, delimited classes, of experience rather than with the single experiences themselves. Only so is communication possible, for the single experience lodges in an individual consciousness and is, strictly speaking, incommunicable. To be communicated it needs to be referred to a class which is tacitly accepted by the community as an identity. . . .

[This field of language includes much more than the basic] cycle of speech, [which] in so far as we may look upon it as a purely external instrument, begins and ends in the realm of sounds. . . . the typical course of this process may undergo endless modifications or transfers into equivalent systems without thereby losing its essential formal characteristics.

The most important of these modifications is the abbreviation of the speech process involved in thinking. This has doubtless many forms . . . . it is well known what excellent use deaf-mutes can make of "reading from the lips" as a subsidiary method of apprehending speech. The most important of all visual speech symbolisms is, of course, that of the written or printed word . . . [in which] each element (letter or written word) in the system corresponds to a specific element (sound or sound-group or spoken word) in the primary system.

There are still more complex transfers, of which Sapir mentions the Morse telegraphic code and the different gesture languages such as those "developed for the use of deaf-mutes, of Trappist monks vowed to perpetual silence, or of communicating parties

[6] [*Language, An Introduction to the Study of Speech*; New York, Harcourt, Brace and Co., 1921; see pp. 7–23.]

that are within seeing distance of each other but are out of ear-shot," as, for example, the flag language used in the Signal Corps. Sapir continues:

> There is no more striking general fact about language than its uni-versality . . . . we know of no people that is not possessed of a fully developed language. . . . The fundamental groundwork of language—the development of a clear-cut phonetic system, the specific association of speech elements with concepts, and the delicate provision for the formal expression of all manner of relations—all this meets us rigidly perfected and systematized in every language known to us. . . .
> Scarcely less impressive than the universality of speech is its almost incredible diversity. . . . [This universality and diversity of speech force us] to believe that language is an immensely ancient heritage of the human race. . . . It is doubtful if any other cultural asset of man, be it the art of drilling for fire or of chipping stone, may lay claim to a greater age. I am inclined to believe that it antedated even the lowliest developments of material culture, that these developments, in fact, were not strictly possible until language, the tool of significant expression, had itself taken shape.

Here then is a field not biologically given, or the result of accidents to biologically given equipment, but of human trans-mission. This transmission is from other people and takes place by other than biological genetic processes or by disturbances of the physicochemical transfer which makes up the basic life processes. This is, as Sapir says, a field almost infinitely diversi-fied, and is a symbolic way of referring to all the classes of experi-ence and all the relationships which man under sundry circum-stances has come into contact with.

There are also differences which lie in the general field of culture more or less exterior to language, which is perhaps the most im-portant field of culture, but is by no means the exclusive field of culture. I have mentioned the extremely helpful work of Malinow-ski. I should also like to refer to the work of Ruth Benedict who has this to say about the nature of culture and its place in living:

> . . . The inner workings of our own brains we feel to be uniquely worthy of investigation, but custom, we have a way of thinking, is be-haviour at its most commonplace. As a matter of fact, it is the other way around. Traditional custom, taken the world over, is a mass of detailed behaviour more astonishing than what any one person can ever evolve in individual actions, no matter how aberrant. Yet that is

a rather trivial aspect of the matter. The fact of first-rate importance is the predominant rôle that custom plays in experience and in belief, and the very great varieties it may manifest.

No man ever looks at the world with pristine eyes. He sees it edited by a definite set of customs and institutions and ways of thinking. . . . John Dewey has said in all seriousness that the part played by custom in shaping the behaviour of the individual as over against any way in which he can affect traditional custom, is as the proportion of the total vocabulary of his mother tongue over against those words of his own baby talk that are taken up into the vernacular of his family. . . . The life history of the individual is first and foremost an accommodation to the patterns and standards traditionally handed down in his community. From the moment of his birth the customs into which he is born shape his experience and behaviour. By the time he can talk, he is the little creature of his culture, and by the time he is grown and able to take part in its activities, its habits are his habits, its beliefs his beliefs, its impossibilities his impossibilities. Every child that is born into his group will share them with him, and no child born into one on the opposite side of the globe can ever achieve the thousandth part. There is no social problem it is more incumbent upon us to understand than this of the rôle of custom. Until we are intelligent as to its laws and varieties, the main complicating facts of human life must remain unintelligible.[7]

From my discussion of all these varied factors of human difference, one might think, at first glance, that these differences should be the subject of our study. We will attempt, however, to study human similarities. And we will not study people as such, but what they do, and what can be fairly safely inferred as to why they do it.

One of the most inclusive biological and psychobiological terms with which we have already had several contacts is *experience*, for which I shall offer the following defining statement:

Experience is anything lived, undergone, or the like. Experience is the inner component of events in which a living organism participates as such—that is, as an organized entity. The limiting characteristics of experience depend on the kind of organism, as well as on the kind of event experienced.

Experience is not the same as the event in which the organism

[7] [Ruth Benedict, *Patterns of Culture;* Boston: Houghton Mifflin Co., 1934; pp. 2–3.]

participates; when I look at and see a frog, my experience of the frog—my perception of the frog—is not the frog. The frog, if he is a 'real' frog—which is by no means necessary—has reflected a particular pattern of light which then existed; my eyes have undergone the impinging of this particular pattern of light; sundry different 'internal changes' have ensued, including the identification of the 'inner' data with the concept, frog.

In other words, there is a relatively 'outer' object, giving rise to something which 'puts me in contact with' it, as we say; and there is a very complex, relatively private or 'inner' bundle of changes of state here or there, to which I may refer as the act of perceiving, which results in the *percept.* Nothing in the present state of our acquaintance with the universe suggests any necessary correspondence between the perceived characteristics of a course of events like the frog as frog and the ultimate 'real' characteristics of this course of events.

Failure to take into account the interpolated act of perception leads to a multiplicity of pseudo-facts and pseudo-problems, as witness the fact that even a competent philosopher—I think it was Charles Morris—in setting up a theory of signs, comments on the fact that we wink, close the eye, before an approaching object strikes the cornea. This is quite typical of a wide variety of approximations in common speech—however allegedly scientific this common speech is—which literally mislead one quite gravely. Actually, of course, a pattern of reduced illumination, moving in a certain fashion which has already been interpreted by previous experience, touches the cornea.

Charles Spearman used the word *sentience* to refer to the primary data out of which we come to have information.[8] I should

---

[8] [*Editors' note:* See, for instance, Charles Spearman's discussion of sentience and experience in *The Nature of 'Intelligence' and the Principles of Cognition* (London: Macmillan and Co., 1923; in particular, pp. 36–47): ". . . All knowing inevitably begins with sensory experience. . . . Between the material thing and the perceptual experience there has intervened a long, complicated, and often loosely linked chain of events that are extremely unlike either the conscious percept at their near end or the material thing disappearing at the far end. . . . Percepts, by the time they have become amenable to ordinary introspection, are already far removed from what is here mainly at issue, namely, the *initial* effect of sensory stimulation upon consciousness; they have already behind them an eventful history, not only

like to offer here a theory of sentience and any other primary data of experience—and of the phenomenology of memory—as being the totality of significant states of the organism related to the impinging of events.

In my example about the frog, I have tried to emphasize the importance of the act of perceiving, which is interpolated between whatever outside reality is and what we have in our minds. What we have in our minds begins in experience, and experience for the purpose of this theory is held to occur in three modes which I shall set up, one of which is usually, but by no means certainly, restricted to human beings. These modes are: the *prototaxic*, the *parataxic*, and the *syntaxic*.[9] I shall offer the thesis that these modes

---

on previous occasions in the person's life, but even on *the very occasion itself*. . . . The initial (and for the most part unintrospectable) mental effect of sensory stimulation will be taken by us to be indeed sensation in the strict meaning of a state . . . . for which, perhaps, 'sentience' is a better term. . . ."]

[9] [*Editors' note:* We are indebted to Patrick Mullahy for permission to quote his definition of Sullivan's three modes of experience (Patrick Mullahy, *Oedipus, Myth and Complex;* New York: Hermitage Press, Inc., 1948; pp. 286–291):

"All experience occurs in one or more of three 'modes'—the prototaxic, parataxic, and syntaxic. As the Greek roots of this horrendous term indicate, the *prototaxic mode* refers to the first kind of experience the infant has and the order or arrangement in which it occurs. . . . According to Sullivan's hypothesis all that the infant 'knows' are momentary states, the distinction of before and after being a later acquirement. The infant vaguely feels or 'prehends' earlier and later states without realizing any serial connection between them. . . . He has no awareness of himself as an entity separate from the rest of the world. In other words, his felt experience is all of a piece, undifferentiated, without definite limits. It is as if his experiences were 'cosmic.' . . .

"As the infant develops and maturation proceeds, the original undifferentiated wholeness of experience is broken. However, the 'parts,' the diverse aspects, the various kinds of experience are not related or connected in a logical fashion. They 'just happen' together, or they do not, depending on circumstances. In other words, various experiences are felt as concomitant, not recognized as connected in an orderly way. The child cannot yet relate them to one another or make logical distinctions among them. What is experienced is assumed to be the 'natural' way of such occurrences, without reflection and comparison. Since no connections or relations are established, there is no logical movement of 'thought' from one idea to the next. The *parataxic mode* is not a step by step process. Experience is undergone as momentary, unconnected states of being.

". . . The child gradually learns the 'consensually validated' meaning of

are primarily matters of 'inner' elaboration of events. The mode which is easiest to discuss is relatively uncommon—experience in the syntaxic mode; the one about which something can be known, but which is somewhat harder to discuss, is experience in the parataxic mode; and the one which is ordinarily incapable of any formulation, and therefore of any discussion, is experience in the prototaxic or primitive mode. The difference in these modes lies in the extent and the character of the elaboration that one's contact with events has undergone.

The prototaxic mode, which seems to be the rough basis of memory, is the crudest—shall I say—the simplest, the earliest, and possibly the most abundant mode of experience. Sentience, in the experimental sense, presumably relates to much of what I mean by the prototaxic mode. The prototaxic, at least in the very early months of life, may be regarded as the discrete series of momentary states of the sensitive organism, with special reference to the zones of interaction with the environment. By the term, sensitive, I attempt to bring into your conception all those channels for being aware of significant events—from the tactile organs in, say, my buttocks, which are apprising me that this is a chair and I have sat on it about long enough, to all sorts of internunciatory sensitivities which have been developed in meeting my needs in the process of living. It is as if everything that is sensitive and centrally represented were an indefinite, but very greatly abundant, luminous switchboard; and the pattern of light which would show on that switchboard in any discrete experience is the basic prototaxic experience itself, if you follow me. This hint may suggest to you that I presume from the beginning until the end of life we undergo a succession of discrete patterns of the momentary state of the organism, which implies not that other organisms are impinging on it, but certainly that the events of other organisms are moving toward or actually effecting a change in this momentary state.

The full implication of these and many other terms cannot

language—in the widest sense of language. These meanings have been acquired from group activities, interpersonal activities, social experience. Consensually validated symbol activity involves an appeal to principles which are accepted as true by the hearer. And when this happens, the youngster has acquired or learned the *syntaxic mode* of experience."]

appear until I have sketched a series of phases gone through by
the newborn human being—in my language, a potentially mature
person. I shall therefore shortly begin to trace the developmental
history of personality, which, as you will see, is actually the developmental history of possibilities of interpersonal relations.

CHAPTER
3

Postulates

Three Principles Borrowed from Biology

I WANT at this point to mention three principles which are a part of my logical philosophy or theory and are woven into my system of thought. These three principles, which I have borrowed from the biology of Seba Eldridge,[1] are the principle of communal existence, the principle of functional activity, and the principle of organization. It is by dealing with applications of these principles that all basic phenomenology of life can, at the biological level, be thrown into meaningful reference. The principle of communal existence refers to the fact that the living cannot live when separated from what may be described as their necessary environment. While this is not as vividly apparent at some of the higher levels of life as it is at the lowest, because storage capacities somewhat disguise the utter dependence on interchange in the higher organisms, the fact is that the living maintain constant exchange through their bordering membranes with certain elements in the physicochemical universe around them; and the interruption of this exchange is tantamount to death of the organism. Thus by the principle of communal existence I mean that all organisms live in continuous, communal existence with their necessary environment. I will not develop the principle of organization, since it scarcely needs any particular emphasis; and the principle of func-

[1] The first time that I encountered these principles succinctly stated was in a book by Eldridge entitled *The Organization of Life* [New York: Thomas Y. Crowell Company, 1925], and it is from this source that I have borrowed them. Although this book sets up some excellent general considerations, it goes on to more or less vitalize a particular doctrine of life which at least is not popular at this time.

tional activity is, of course, the most general term for the processes which literally make up living.[2]

From a consideration of these three principles, it is possible to think of man as distinguished from plants and animals by the fact that human life—in a very real and not only a purely literary or imaginary sense—requires interchange with an environment which includes culture. When I say that man is distinguished very conspicuously from other members of the biological universe by requiring interchange with a universe of culture, this means, in actual fact, since culture is an abstraction pertaining to people, that man requires interpersonal relationships, or interchange with others. While there are apparent exceptions, which I shall later mention, it is a rare person who can cut himself off from mediate and immediate relations with others for long spaces of time without undergoing a deterioration in personality. In other words, being thus cut off is perhaps not as fatal as for an animal to be cut off from all sources of oxygen; but the lethal aspect of it is nonetheless well within the realm of correct referential speech, and is not merely a figure of speech or an allegory.

The One-Genus Postulate

I now want to present what I used to call the one-genus hypothesis, or postulate. This hypothesis I word as follows: We shall assume that *everyone is much more simply human than otherwise*, and that anomalous interpersonal situations, insofar as they do not arise from differences in language or custom, are a function

[2] [*Editors' note:* The other two principles were described by Eldridge as follows: "At every stage of the interaction between organism and environment . . . a complicated set of responses comes into play. . . . These processes of interaction between the organism and the environment, including the interactions between component parts of the organism and *their* environments, constitute what is termed functional, or physiological, activity. . . . A third property of the organism is that of organization itself. The term connotes not only the structure of the organism statically regarded, but the variability of this structure, both in the individual and in the race. . . . This property might also be conceived as the organization, in matter, of the physiological processes, together with the tendency of this organization to vary. Or, to vary our terms again, it is the morphological property in vital activity, the property which has manifested itself in countless forms of life in the past, and is destined to take countless other forms in the future" (p. 2).]

of differences in relative maturity of the persons concerned. In other words, the differences between any two instances of human personality—from the lowest-grade imbecile to the highest-grade genius—are much less striking than the differences between the least-gifted human being and a member of the nearest other biological genus. Man—however undistinguished biologically—as long as he is entitled to the term, human personality, will be very much more like every other instance of human personality than he is like anything else in the world. As I have tried to hint before, it is to some extent on this basis that I have become occupied with the science, not of individual differences, but of human identities, or parallels, one might say. In other words, I try to study the degrees and patterns of things which I assume to be ubiquitously human.

Heuristic Stages in Development

I would like at this point to set up a heuristic classification of personality development which is very convenient for the organization of thought. These heuristic stages are: infancy, childhood, the juvenile era, preadolescence, early adolescence, late adolescence, and adulthood or maturity.

Infancy extends from a few minutes after birth to the appearance of articulate speech, however uncommunicative or meaningless. *Childhood* extends from the appearance of the ability to utter articulate sounds of or pertaining to speech, to the appearance of the need for playmates—that is, companions, cooperative beings of approximately one's own status in all sorts of respects. This ushers in the *juvenile era*, which extends through most of the grammar-school years to the eruption, due to maturation, of a need for an intimate relation with another person of comparable status. This, in turn, ushers in the era that we call *preadolescence*, an exceedingly important but chronologically rather brief period that ordinarily ends with the eruption of genital sexuality and puberty, but psychologically or psychiatrically ends with the movement of strong interest from a person of one's own sex to a person of the other sex. These phenomena mark the beginning of *adolescence*, which in this culture (it varies, however, from culture to culture) continues until one has patterned some type of performance which satisfies one's lust, one's genital drives. Such patterning ushers in *late adolescence*, which in turn continues as an era of personality until any partially developed aspects of personality fall into their proper relationship to their time partition; and one is able, at *adulthood*, to establish relationships of love for some other person, in which relationship the other person is as significant, or nearly as significant, as one's self. This really highly developed intimacy with another is not the principal business of life, but is, perhaps, the principal source of satisfactions in life; and one goes on developing in depth of interest or in scope of interest, or in both depth and scope, from that time until unhappy retrogressive changes in the organism lead to old age.[3]

I shall try to outline my theory by exhausting the easily conceivable possibilities of each of these stages of development, showing the beginnings of things wherever they are either observable or fairly safely inferable, beginning at birth and moving toward at least chronological adulthood.

Euphoria and Tension

In our thinking we need, besides biological or human postulates, certain concepts that are borrowed from other fields of human activity, including a few from the field of mathematics. The one I particularly want to mention at this time is the idea of limits, and the notion of the absolute. I use absolute constructs every now and then in thinking about interpersonal relations. That is, I attempt to define something I know does not exist by extrapolation from extreme instances of something that does exist. These ideal constructs or polar constructs are useful for clear discussion of phenomena which fall more or less near one of these polar absolutes.

The two absolutes that I want to present at the moment are absolute *euphoria* and absolute *tension*. Absolute euphoria can be defined as a state of utter well-being. The nearest approach to anything like it that there is any reason for believing one can observe might occur when a very young infant is in a state of deep sleep.

---

[3] [*Editors' note:* The definitions of these heuristic stages have been incorporated here from another of Sullivan's lectures, given in 1945, on *The Psychiatric Interview.*]

Absolute tension might be defined as the maximum possible deviation from absolute euphoria. The nearest approach to absolute tension that one observes is the rather uncommon, and always relatively transient, state of terror.

Now, it is a peculiarity of life that the level of euphoria and the level of tension are in reciprocal relation; that is, the level of euphoria varies inversely with the level of tension. And now I am going to make—partly, I suppose, for my own amusement—a frank and wholehearted reference to mathematics. This reciprocal relation may be expressed by saying that y is a function of x, and the relationship is $y = 1/x$.

Those of you who remember the conversion of the mathematical formula $y = 1/x$ into numerical representation will perhaps recall that y has a boundless limit when x equals zero and that, however much the value of x is increased, y never reaches zero. That is, the limits—zero for the one and infinity for the other—are never actually observed. This is just another way of saying that absolute euphoria and absolute tension are constructs which are useful in thought but which do not occur in nature. These absolutes are approached at times, but almost all of living is perhaps rather near the middle of the trail; that is, there is some tension, and to that extent the level of euphoria is not as high as it could be.

While euphoria need not trouble us very much, tensions are a very important part of our thinking.[4] On this matter of tensions, I should like to include here an excerpt from an article of mine:

In any discussion about personality considered as an entity, we must use the term *experience*. Whatever else may be said about experience, it is in final analysis experience of *tensions* and experience of *energy transformations*. I use these two terms in exactly the same sense as I would in talking about physics; there is no need to add adjectives such

---

[4] I would refer anyone who is deeply interested in the philosophical justification of the concept of tension to a paper by Albert Dunham ["The Concept of Tension in Philosophy," *Psychiatry* (1938) 1:79–120], in which he discusses the philosophy of the concept of tension, and also to the works of Kurt Lewin, who set up the earliest, I think, systematic treatment of the concept of tension in explaining human behavior. [See Kurt Lewin, *A Dynamic Theory of Personality*, translated by Donald K. Adams and Karl E. Zener; New York: McGraw-Hill, 1935.] However, Kurt Lewin's conceptions are by no means identical with those that I am about to unwind.

as 'mental'—however 'mental' experience itself may be conceived to be.

In the realm of personality and culture, tensions may be considered to have two important aspects: that of tension as a potentiality for action, for the transformation of energy; and that of a *felt* or wittingly noted state of being. The former is intrinsic; the latter is not. In other words, tension *is* potentiality for action, and tension *may* have a felt or representational component. There is no reason for doubting that this contingent rather than intrinsic factor is a function of experience rather than of tension *per se*, for it applies in the same way to energy transformations. They, too, *may* have felt or representational components, or transpire without any witting awareness.[5]

$$
\text{EXPERIENCE is of } \begin{cases} \text{tensions} \\ \text{energy transformations} \end{cases}
$$

$$
\text{occurs in 3 modes} \begin{cases} \text{prototaxic} \\ \text{parataxic} \\ \text{syntaxic} \end{cases}
$$

$$
\text{TENSIONS are those of } \begin{cases} \text{needs} \begin{cases} \text{general} \\ \text{zonal} \end{cases} \\ \text{anxiety} \end{cases}
$$

$$
\text{ENERGY TRANSFORMATIONS are} \begin{cases} \text{overt} \\ \text{covert} \end{cases}
$$

Yet the undergoing of tensions and of energy transformations, however free the events may have been from any representative component, is never exterior to the sum total of *living* and in many instances not beyond the possibility of some kind of *recall*—indication as of the dynamically surviving, actual past, with detectable influence on the character of the foreseen and dynamically significant neighboring future.[6]

[5] When I mention felt components of tension or energy transformation, I am talking about experience in the later two modes—the parataxic and the syntaxic—because, as I have insisted repeatedly, it is practically impossible to get anything into consciousness for discussion about experience in the prototaxic mode; for all I know, when a tension exists in a person and is wholly unnoted, that may merely mean that it is felt in the prototaxic mode. But this doesn't make very much difference because there is no way of demonstrating that it is so; it is purely for theoretical perfectionism, if you please, that I bring this to your attention.

[6] [Statement by Sullivan, in *Culture and Personality*, edited by S. Stansfeld Sargent and Marian W. Smith (Proceedings of an Interdisciplinary Conference held under auspices of The Viking Fund, Nov. 7 and 8, 1947); New York: The Viking Fund, Inc., 1947.]

Returning now to my account of the development of the human animal in becoming a person, I have suggested that euphoria may be equated to a total equilibrium of the organism, which we know never exists, but which is approached in those time intervals or instants when tension is at its minimum. In the very young infant these intervals occur when the breathing cycle has started on its lifelong course; when there is no deficiency of body temperature, of water supply, and of food supply (in the stomach usually); and when no noxious events are impinging on the so-called periphery of what will later be called awareness.

The Tension of Needs

The tensions that episodically or recurrently lower the level of the infant's euphoria and effect the biologic disequilibration of his being are *needs* primarily appertaining to his communal existence with the physicochemical universe. Now very early in life we need assume nothing except a communal existence with the physicochemical universe; but when we make that assumption we must be very clear in realizing that the infant is not himself adequately equipped to maintain that absolutely necessary communal existence. There has to be a mothering one; while I know no inherent difficulty about this being a wolf or an ape, as the historic myths have it, the brute fact is that we have no authentic or verifiable account of anyone who has been raised by wolves, apes, or the like —if we did have, we might know a little more about the human animal.

The relaxations of these episodic or recurrent tensions which disturb the equilibrium of the infant's being are, of course, equilibrations with specific respect to the source of disequilibrium, whether it be lack of oxygen, lack of sugar, lack of water, or lack of adequate body temperature. And the relaxation of the tensions called out by lacks of this kind I call *satisfaction* of the specific need which was concerned.

I will mention at this time—and the immediate relevance of this will gradually appear—that satisfactions can be defined by noting the biological disequilibration which actions, that is, energy transformations, of the infant have served to remedy. In other words, a need, while it is in a broad biological sense disequilibrium, acquires its meaning from the actions or energy transformations which result in its satisfaction.

When I speak of the actions or energy transformations of the infant which serve to remedy biological disequilibration or to satisfy needs, it may be fairly easy to see how the infant's breathing movements serve to remedy his oxygen needs and how sucking movements serve to remedy his sugar and water needs. It may not be quite so evident how any activity of the infant serves his need for maintaining body temperature, for example. But those who have dealt with newborn infants know that they are quite audible, once they are going concerns, if they are not covered with insulating material that reduces heat loss. The outcry is the initial action of the infant which is directed toward the remedy of the need for reduced heat loss; and the reduction of the heat loss, the experience of adequate internal temperature, is a satisfaction of that need.

The alternation of need and satisfaction gives rise to experience or, if you will, *is* experience—needless to say, in the prototaxic mode. The need—that is, the felt discomfort of the disequilibrium, the specific tensional reduction in euphoria—begins to be differentiated in terms of the direction toward its relief, which amounts to increasingly clear foresight of relief by appropriate action. It need scarcely be said that this foresight is the experience of the neighboring future—and this experience, too, must occur in the prototaxic mode in very early infancy, because there is no other basis for experience. What I am saying in essence is that the first successful activity of an infant—such as breathing to relieve anoxia —begins to define the nature of the need for oxygen, which, before that, is undifferentiated, and also begins to define the nature of extreme tension, or almost complete absence of euphoria. Thus beginning with the first activities of the infant, the first transformations of energy that are associated with the diminution of need and its ultimate extinction for the time being, the personality develops what is later clearly identifiable as the foresight function. A great many truths, which will gradually appear, are wrapped up in that statement, but the one that I wish to note now is that this does imply something of the neighboring future.

By and large any experience that can be discussed—that is, any experience in the syntaxic or parataxic mode—is always interpenetrated by elements of the near past, sometimes even the distant past, and by elements of the near future—anticipation, expectation, and so on. These elements are powerfully influential in determining the way that tensions are transformed into activity—that is, the way in which potentiality in the tension becomes action.

The comparatively great influence of foresight is one of the striking characteristics of human living in contrast to all other living. The whole philosophical doctrine of representation might, if one wished, be wrapped up in this statement that successful action creates or is identified with—I might use any number of vague words that don't quite convey what I mean here—foreseen relief.

I want to quote next a section by Kurt Lewin on environmental structure and needs:

The life-space of the infant is extremely small and undifferentiated. This is just as true of its perceptual as of its effective space. With the gradual extension and differentiation of the child's life-space, a larger environment and essentially different facts acquire psychological existence, and this is true also with respect to dynamic factors. The child learns in increasing degree to control the environment. At the same time—and no less important—it becomes psychologically dependent upon a growing circle of environmental events. . . . For the investigation of dynamic problems we are forced to start from the psychologically real environment of the child. In the "objective" sense, the existence of a social bond is a necessary condition of the viability of an infant not yet able itself to satisfy its biologically important needs. This is usually a social bond with the mother in which, functionally, the needs of the baby have primacy.[7]

From recasting similar considerations concerning the relationship of the very young human and the necessary environment, it becomes possible to draw out a general principle which I used to call a theorem. This principle or theorem is designed to be an especially compact and meaningful way of expressing one of the basic derivatives from this approach.

My theorem is this: *The observed activity of the infant arising from the tension of needs induces tension in the mothering one, which tension is experienced as tenderness and as an impulsion to activities toward the relief of the infant's needs.* In other words,

[7] [Work cited; pp. 74–75.]

however manifest the increasing tension of needs in an infant may be—and we will study a very important manifestation of that tension in the energy transformations of the cry—the observation of these tensions or of the activity which manifests their presence calls out, in the mothering one, a certain tension, which may be described as that of tenderness, which is a potentiality for or an impulsion to activities suited to—or more or less suited to—the relief of the infant's needs. This, in its way, is a definition of tenderness—a very important conception, very different indeed from the miscellaneous and, in general, meaningless term 'love,' which confuses so many issues in our current day and age.

The manifest activity by the mothering one toward the relief of the infant's needs will presently be experienced by the infant as the undergoing of tender behavior; and these needs, the relaxation of which require cooperation of another, thereon take on the character of a general *need for tenderness*.

To sum up: The tension called out in the mothering one by the manifest needs of the infant we call *tenderness*, and a generic group of tensions in the infant, the relief of which requires cooperation by the person who acts in the mothering role, can be called *need for tenderness*. As I have said, I regard the first needs that fall into the genus of the need for tenderness as needs arising in the necessary communal existence of the infant and the physicochemical universe.[8]

Even though the needs which I include when I speak of the generic need for tenderness are direct derivatives of disequilibrium arising in the physicochemical universe inside and outside the infant—that is, making up the infant and the necessary environment—nonetheless these generic needs all require cooperation from another; thus, the need for tenderness is ingrained from the very beginning of things as an interpersonal need. And the complemen-

---

[8] The only nonphysicochemically induced need that is probably somewhere near demonstrable during very early infancy and which certainly becomes very conspicuous not much later than this, is the *need for contact*, by which I mean just about what the word ordinarily means. The very young seem to have very genuine beginnings of purely human or interpersonal needs in the sense of requiring manipulations by and peripheral contact with the living, such as lying-against, and so on. But, when I talk as I do now of the first weeks and months of infancy, this can only be a speculation which need keep no one awake nights worrying over whether it is justified.

tary need of the mothering one is a need to manifest appropriate activity, which may be called a general need to give tenderness, or to behave tenderly; and this, whatever tensions and energy transformations may be mixed up in it, is again interpersonal in kind, if not in all details.

So far I am saying—in what may seem a very complicated way—that because the infant is practically absolutely dependent on the intervention of others, or a particular other, for survival and for the maintenance of the necessary interchange, the mother behaves tenderly and helps in the relieving of sundry recurrent disequilibria. There is a reason for the complexity of the explanation, if only to emphasize that this is not merely a business of the nourishing of the young as if by a good incubator.

The Tension of Anxiety

But now I pass to another broadly important statement, where there is much less chance for confusion over whether things are interpersonal or impersonal. This again I call a theorem: *The tension of anxiety, when present in the mothering one, induces anxiety in the infant*. The rationale of this induction—that is, *how* anxiety in the mother induces anxiety in the infant—is thoroughly obscure. This gap, this failure of our grasp on reality, has given rise to some beautifully plausible and perhaps correct explanations of how the anxiety of the mother causes anxiety in the infant; I bridge the gap simply by referring to it as a manifestation of an indefinite— that is, not yet defined—interpersonal process to which I apply the term *empathy*. I have had a good deal of trouble at times with people of a certain type of educational history; since they cannot refer empathy to vision, hearing, or some other special sense receptor, and since they do not know whether it is transmitted by the ether waves or air waves or what not, they find it hard to accept the idea of empathy. But whether the doctrine of empathy is accepted or not, the fact remains that the tension of anxiety when present in the mothering one induces anxiety in the infant; that theorem can be proved, I believe, and those who have had pediatric experience or mothering experience actually have data which can be interpreted on no other equally simple hypothetical basis. So although empathy may sound mysterious, remember that there is much that sounds mysterious in the universe, only you have got used to it; and perhaps you will get used to empathy.

Everything that I have discussed before coming to anxiety is a function of the biologically necessary communal existence of the infant, barring only the hint I have given of a need for contact with the living. Now, in discussing anxiety, I have come to something that has nothing whatever to do with the physicochemical needs of the living young. The tension called anxiety primarily appertains to the infant's, as also to the mother's, communal existence with a *personal* environment, in utter contradistinction to the physicochemical environment. For reasons presently to appear, I distinguish this tension from the sundry tensions already called needs by saying that the relaxation of the tension of anxiety, the re-equilibration of being in this specific respect, is the experience, not of satisfaction, but of interpersonal *security*.

The tension called anxiety, as early experienced in the prototaxic mode, is differentiated from all other reductions in euphoria by the *absence* of anything specific—you will recall that, when speaking of tensions of needs, I referred to *specific* sources of disequilibration, such as the lack of oxygen, water, or sugar. Because of the absence of anything so specific in anxiety, there is a consequent lack of differentiation in terms of the direction toward its relief by appropriate action. There is in the infant no capacity for action toward the relief of anxiety. While needs, as already suggested, begin to be, as it were, recognized or experientially represented in terms of the first of the infant's actions associated with their relief, the relief of anxiety has none of that aspect. No action of the infant is consistently and frequently associated with the relief of anxiety; and therefore the need for security, or freedom from anxiety, is highly significantly distinguished from all other needs from its very first hypothetical appearance.

Perhaps I should expand this idea somewhat so that its meaning becomes less obscure. At an indeterminately early age the tensions which appear in the infant connected with his relationship to the physicochemical environment tend to be relatively localized and marked with the prototype of what later we call emotional experience. Thus the experience connected with the need for water, or the tension associated with this need, begins to take on specific character. The same is true of the need for heat, the need for sugar, and, as I will develop at very considerable length presently, the need for oxygen. This more or less specific character of the connected experience, this mark, if you please, which characterizes the experience, permits the differentiation of activity suited to or appropriate to the relief of these needs. To leap a great many years of development, as an adult you *know*, for example, when you are hungry; that is, you can differentiate the experience connected with tensions due to your need for food, or due to the liver's resistance to giving up food until it has a new supply in prospect. You, by the mark of this particular experience, think, "I am hungry," and seek a restaurant or consider sponging a meal off of someone. This is the differentiation of appropriate action for the relief of a tension on the basis of the specific character of the experience that you are having.

Now my point is that anxiety, in contradistinction to these other tensions, has nothing specific about it; it does not gradually get itself related to hypothetical but reasonably probable contractions in the stomach, or dryness of the throat, or what have you. It does not have any specific characteristics of that kind, and consequently there is no basis in the experience of early anxiety for any differentiation, or clarification, of action appropriate to the avoidance or relief of anxiety. Therefore, I say that the infant has no capacity for action toward the relief of anxiety.

As I have said, human beings manifest needs for sundry more or less specific satisfactions. Converted into this language, the need for interpersonal security might be said to be the need to be rid of anxiety. But anxiety is not manageable: It comes by induction from another person; the infant's capacity for manipulating another person is confined, at the very start, to the sole capacity to call out tenderness by manifesting needs; and the person who would respond to manifest need in the situation in which the infant is anxious is relatively incapable of that response because it is the parental anxiety which induces the infant's anxiety—and as I shall explain shortly, anxiety always interferes with any other tensions with which it coincides. Therefore, there is, from the very earliest evidence of the empathic linkage, this peculiar distinction that anxiety is not manageable.

Anxiety is a tension in opposition to the tensions of needs and to action appropriate to their relief. It is in opposition to the tension of tenderness in the mothering one. It interferes with infantile behavior sequences—that is, with the infant's growing effectiveness in his communal existence with the physicochemical environment. It interferes, for example, with his sucking activity and doubtless with his swallowing. In fact, one may say flatly that anxiety opposes the satisfaction of needs. Of all experience of the present, the experience of anxiety is the sort least clearly interpenetrated by elements of the past and the future; it is the least interpretable and productive of foresight. In other words, because of the factors that I have been discussing and various others, the explanatory identifying elements of the past and the foresight of relief in the future, which are so important in accounting for activities or energy transformations in any particular situation, are, in this realm of anxiety, the easiest to overlook and the hardest to find.

Everywhere else the differentiation, however fantastic, of needs and the choosing of appropriate actions directed toward their relief—or even very inappropriate actions but allegedly, you might say, directed toward their relief—show the effect of the past and, even at a very early stage, the element of anticipation of the near future. In anxiety, however, because there is no lever with which to begin such differentiation, it is hard to get experience of anxiety in the past to fit into interpreting present instances of it, and anxiety can almost be said to cut off foresight. Now that is very loosely expressed. But at least one can say that the more anxious one is, the less the distinguished human function of foresight is free to work effectively in the choice, as we call it, of action appropriate to the tensions that one is experiencing.

The capacity to experience anxiety is not an exclusively human capacity, but the role of anxiety in interpersonal relations is so profoundly important that its differentiation from all other tensions is vital. I shall, therefore, next review the probabilities as to the infant's tensional history up to and including the occurrence of the earliest experiences of anxiety. In this process I shall touch particularly upon the seeming, and perhaps very real, relationship of terror and anxiety. But this will be with the earnest hope that no one will think that I am saying that anxiety is terror. What I am instead attempting to say is that of all the experiences which are differentiated on the basis of specific marking, the only one that comes within gunshot of the experience of primitive anxiety is terror, which, I have already hinted, is the closest approach to absolute tension that one can imagine.

PART
II

The Developmental Epochs

Infancy: Beginnings

Ways of Dealing with the Tension of Fear

THE FIRST great danger to the newborn is that of anoxia, depriva-
tion of oxygen in contact with the tissues. This danger becomes
acute with the separation of the newborn infant from the maternal
circulation and continues, intensifying very swiftly thereafter, until the successful institution of the breathing cycle by which air
flows in and out from thenceforth. Recurrence of this danger of
anoxia at any time in life is accompanied by an extraordinary form
of fear to which we refer as terror. Occasions of danger other than
the failure of oxygen supply may call out terror, but from very
early in extrauterine life any interference with freedom of the
bodily movements which are concerned with the cyclic alternation of negative and positive pressure in the lungs calls out general
activity of the infant or older person which is suggestive in appearance of what we later in life would unquestionably call rage
behavior. However, when I speak of activity of the infant which
is suggestive of what we later see in people who are enraged, I
am not, like the old behaviorists, asking you to picture rage as one
of the primitive emotions. I am suggesting that the most certain
way of terrifying anybody at any time in his life is to interfere
rather quickly with his supply of air. Choking, submersion in carbon dioxide or other oxygen-free gases, and so on, are extremely
terrifying experiences. A peculiarity of the danger of anoxia is
that not only does anything which impedes breathing tend to call
out severe fear which rapidly becomes terror and this sort of behavior which is seen in the infant as screaming and kicking and so
on, but, if the oxygen starvation progresses, the organism is so

built that there will be general convulsions, convulsive releases
of undifferentiated motor impulses, before death actually happens.

Fear, from its mildest to its most extreme form, that of terror,
is to be considered to be the felt aspect of tension arising from
danger to the existence or biological integrity of the organism.
Such dangers are, in general, those of anoxia—oxygen starvation,
which I have just been discussing; of thirst—water starvation; of
starvation for carbohydrates and other chemical foodstuffs; of
subcooling; of molar injury to the body—that is, massive injury
to the body; and of impairment or failure of sundry vital factors.
Circulatory failure is probably the same old danger of anoxia and,
if at all rapidly deepening, is very apt to be accompanied by terror.

If you think of fear from a rather adult standpoint, you will notice that there are four generic patterns for dealing with or relaxing the tension of fear. And if you will forget infancy entirely for
the moment and think of yourself in a fear-provoking situation,
such as being threatened by an oncoming enemy in a warfare situation, you will realize that one of the patterns for dealing with fear
is to remove or destroy the fear-provoking circumstances. Another
is to escape from the fear-provoking circumstances. A third, not so
immediately self-evident, is to neutralize the fear-provoking circumstances. To describe the fourth generic pattern I shall use a
word which is rather misleading: the fourth pattern is to *ignore*
the fear-provoking circumstances. If you consider even the ordinary risks to our somatic organization, such as traffic hazards
and other hazards of transportation, you will immediately realize
that when I speak of *ignoring* the danger, I am referring to pretty
complicated processes. For example, even if a person knows that
the risk incurred in crossing busy streets is fully as great as the risk
incurred in traveling in airplanes, it is obvious that he must ignore a
great deal of this risk inherent in crossing streets when he is going about his daily business; yet actually to say that the risk is
ignored implies, as I say, something pretty complicated.

As to the other patterns for dealing with fear, removing or de-
stroying the source of a danger is fairly evident. The classical way
of handling fear is to get away from that which is feared, to escape
it. In certain circumstances one can neutralize fear. Thus, for example, if you are dealing with a person who is given to violence,

you can neutralize the danger of his violence if you can impress him with the equal probability of your successful use of violence; and another way, of course, is to ignore him.

The vigorous motor activity which is called out by restraint of the infant's freedom of respiratory movements may be effective in removing or escaping from the restraining circumstances. This effectiveness may be direct, or it may be mediate by way of calling out mothering activity. Now some people have doubts as to the propriety of using so-called teleological arguments in which the goal is supposed to cause, in a certain curious fashion, the phenomena discussed. And so I shall defer, as long as I can, any attempt to make use of so-called teleological explanations. In a great many ways, many of the details of the equipment of the human animal can readily be discussed from this teleological standpoint, but they can also be considered as the result of evolutionary change controlled by survival value. Thus if you will think, not of a human infant, but of a kitten or a puppy, you will realize that one of the encompassing risks to this infant dog or cat is that, when it is under the mother for purposes of reducing heat loss, it will be cut off from communal existence with the atmosphere by the body of the mother. When this happens, the sort of vigorous movement which is called out fairly early in oxygen privation serves to apprise the mother of the danger to the puppy or kitten. In the same way, if a human infant is threatened with anoxia because a blanket is cutting off his oxygen supply, here again vigorous movements, which may ultimately become convulsive discharges, will have a very strong likelihood of calling out mothering activity, of displacing this obstruction, or of displacing the infant to the point where contact with the air can be renewed. Since we store less oxygen than we do water and sugar, very extensive provisions for insuring a practically continuous contact with the circumambient atmosphere have had great survival value for the human animal and in fact for all the higher animals.

As I have said, the vigorous movements which are called out by oxygen hunger, and which look like performances of older children in rage, are effective in escaping from the restraining influences or circumstances bearing on the oxygen supply, either directly—in the example I have spoken of, by getting out from under a blanket—or mediately, by way of calling out mothering activity. The audible vibratory air movements which accompany the institution of the breathing cycle—the birth cry—are the first instance of infantile activity which evokes the tensions of generic tenderness in the mothering one. Crying remains for some time the most effective infantile behavior appropriate to the relief of fear. To the extent that the tender acts of the mothering one are correctly addressed to removing the disturbing circumstances, this crying, which is heard by the infant, is experienced as adequate and appropriate action. In many other instances, while it may not bring immediate relief of the danger causing the tension of fear, it at least brings tenderness in the course of what might be described as random efforts on the part of the mothering one, which are closely, or reasonably closely, identified with the relief of the fear-evoking danger.

Since I want to forestall, as far as I can, any possible reservations to these thoughts, I shall here take up the question of the hearing of the infant's crying by the infant. The middle ear and the Eustachian tube are filled with fluid, at least in many infants, for a little while after birth, and under those circumstances it might be quite difficult to demonstrate that an infant can hear someone playing a piano ten feet away. But while air is a comparatively elastic medium which carries sound waves quite nicely, water, saline solution, and so on are relatively inelastic media which carry vibrations still better. Now since vibration occurs in the neighborhood of the larynx, as in crying, and is reflected and refined in the neighborhood of the opening of the Eustachian tube well back in the throat, the only question about an infant's hearing his own crying is whether the auditory division of the appropriate nerve is functionally adequate at birth. Since it can be demonstrated that that nerve is functionally adequate before birth, it seems to me perfectly possible to speak of even the birth cry as being heard by the infant; certainly very soon after the institution of the breathing cycle, the infant hears himself cry. Thus you will realize that, since we are talking about a very primitive type of experience, it is quite as credible to talk about the experience of the newborn infant as it is, for example, to talk about the experience of an amoeba—and the experience of an amoeba is something that can safely be set up as an hypothesis to account for certain observable facts.

From the standpoint of the infant's prototaxic experience, this crying, insofar as it evokes appropriate tender behavior by the mothering one, is adequate and appropriate action by the infant to remove or escape fear-provoking dangers. Crying thus comes to be differentiated as action appropriate to accomplish the foreseen relief of fear.

Anxiety as a Threat to the Organism

Let us now consider the case of the anxious infant—the infant suffering anxiety induced by anxiety on the part of the mother. Anxiety does not arise from danger to the communal physico-chemical interchange or to the organization of the infant's body. It arises by induction from the anxiety of the mother. It is a func-tion of the necessary interpersonal communality with someone ma-ture enough to cooperate in the complex activities needed for the relief of the infant's physicochemical needs. I would like to repeat that dangers calling out fear can be handled in four ways, at least by adults. But if you will now think of anxiety, which is originally induced by anxiety in the mothering one, you will immediately see that, not only in infancy but for the rest of life, the circum-stances conducive to anxiety cannot be removed, nor destroyed, nor escaped. Some of you may think that an adult can remove or destroy the source of anxiety by killing the person who makes him anxious, or escape it by leaving town; but later on in my dis-cussion it will become apparent that the source of anxiety is not so easily handled. Certainly there is no possibility of the infant's doing anything to remove or destroy the source of the infantile anxiety, nor is there any escaping it.

Crying in relation to infantile anxiety is often ineffectual or worse. It often increases the anxiety of the mothering one, and thereby increases the anxiety of the infant. This is partly because of the direct induction of more anxiety in the infant when anxiety increases in the mother, and partly because the anxiety of the mother interferes with her competence to manifest tenderness and par-ticularly with her competence to do the right thing, you might say, to cooperate in the infant's escaping dangers, and so on. There isn't any right thing to do with infantile anxiety except for the mother to cease to be anxious. Anxiety interferes with both the mother's cooperation and the infant's behavior patterns for the relief of his need, which calls out fear when it is not relieved; thus if the infant has some need at the same time that he becomes anxious, there is then in the infant a double handicap, because not only is he anxious, but also a need is being left unresolved and is, therefore, presumably increasing. The act of crying itself—that is, the production of the audible vibrations which make up the cry—is a reductive modification of freedom of expiring breath, and, in fact, as the crying becomes violent, may also represent an interference with inspiring breath. Thus any intensification of crying, such as one would expect when the crying reflects both the danger of need and infantile anxiety induced by the mother's anxiety, may incur the danger of interference with the oxygen exchange. And this, added to everything else, rapidly aggravates fear in the direction of terror. Now as I have said before, this particular type of restraint in the communal existence of the infant—marked interference with breathing—calls out a vigorous type of molar activity on the part of the infant which suggests what is later quite properly called rage behavior. It is an actual fact of pediatric experience that sometimes this combination of unsatisfied need, anxiety in the infant, and succeeding threat to the respiratory freedom progresses to the point that the infant is blue, cyanotic, which means that there is nothing like enough oxygen in the circulating blood, and also progresses into general convulsions called spasms by most people, I believe. Now here is a picture, which, I trust, clearly shows the relative inappropriateness and inadequacy of the infantile behavior for the relief of anxiety. For the source of the anxiety is, at this stage of development, solely anxiety in the mothering one—that is, in the significant, relatively adult personality whose cooperation is necessary to keep the infant alive.

This picture may seem to suggest that when this coincidence of needs and anxiety occurs, things rapidly progress in a fashion which becomes thoroughly dangerous for the survival of the infant. To a certain extent that is true, but if this were the whole story, there would probably be no extant specimens of our particular species. I can perhaps best suggest what happens by describing the way the heart is protected from any dangerous or fatal activities of the apparatus which slows and regulates—that is, evens—the cardiac rhythm. This is the so-called vagus influence, which not only slows the heart, but can actually stop the heart from beating—a fatal performance if it were prolonged. In order to prevent this, an apparatus manifests itself which enables the heart to escape from inhibition. Thus while the vagus influence may stop the heart for a little while, the heart then escapes and hurries to make up for lost time in circulating oxygen and foodstuffs. Similarly in the development of terror connected with infantile anxiety, we have dynamisms (I shall use this word instead of apparatus) which protect the infant from the otherwise extremely dangerous kind of coincidence I have described. The exact meaning of dynamism I shall exemplify later when we have more to work on.

The Dynamisms of Apathy and Somnolent Detachment

There are dynamisms which are called out by these emergency situations both in very early life and in later life. In the infant, one of these dynamisms manifests itself particularly in saving the infant from this geometrical progression, so to speak, of disaster called out by unsatisfied need, anxiety, and the resulting interference with breathing which provokes terror, the maximum state of tension. The dynamism which intervenes in the type of situation that I have described—which is quite often aggravated continuously by the mounting anxiety of the mothering one—is part of the adaptive capabilities of man and of some, at least, of the higher animals. It is the possibility of becoming apathetic, of manifesting under certain circumstances the condition which we call *apathy*. In apathy all the tensions of needs are markedly attenuated. You will remember that I have previously set up a discrimination between two tensions: the tension of needs, which can be satisfied, and which can be experienced as fear of a danger of the need; and the tension of anxiety, which is brought about by the interpersonal situation. The latter can be said to be the need for interpersonal security, and it is very distinct from the need for interchange with the physicochemical environment—for preserving the integrity of the bodily organization and the smooth working of its vital processes. I have now said that in the state called apathy the tension of all needs is markedly attenuated. I am not too sure about the relationship of apathy and anxiety. It is a recondite problem, and I shall tell you almost at once how I have, at least provisionally, resolved it.

But first I want you to consider the anxious and terrified infant, who may be described as a shrieking, kicking infant, and to consider how apathy intervenes to markedly attenuate the infant's tensions—that is, not actually to obliterate them, but to greatly reduce them. Let us say that the tensions were, in this particular example, first, a need for food, then, because feeding was impaired by the mother's anxiety, ultimately a need for both food and oxygen. Apathy reduces the tension of these needs; in states of apathy, however, the needs are not abolished, but are merely markedly attenuated, and there is usually enough of the tension of needs to maintain organic life. That is, apathy does not ordinarily so attenuate needs that one will calmly or apathetically starve to death, die of thirst, undergo devastating injury, or the like. But this is true only in the absence of any extraordinary danger in the physico-chemico-biological sphere; as long as apathy prevails, there is no possibility of an adequate tensional response to an acute or extreme danger. I am adding this not because it pertains immediately to our discussion of the infant, but because I want you to realize that apathy as an escape from this pyramiding of tension, which culminates in terror—an extremely expensive state—is not nearly as charmingly efficient and safe as is the apparatus for the escape of the heart from inhibition. In the latter, the apparatus always works if the person is well enough to survive the stoppage of the heart, as is almost invariably the case; but in the case of the infant, terror when mixed with anxiety might easily lead to death. Thus the vulnerability of the infant in this process of getting to be a person is somewhat greater than is the vulnerability of the heart in the example which I have cited.

To get back to my resolution of the problem of the relationship between apathy and anxiety, I would like to set up provisionally the term *somnolent detachment* as the protective dynamism called out by prolonged severe anxiety, in contradistinction to apathy as the protective dynamism called out by unfulfilled needs. I do not know whether the dynamism of somnolent detachment is manifested early in infancy—and it is impossible, so far as I have yet been able to find, to devise any procedure which would settle that question—but certainly later in life something corresponding to apathy intervenes in anxiety if it is severe and prolonged. The difference in actual appearance between the young when apathetic and the young involved in somnolent detachment is nil. There is no objective difference. But since a good deal of our speculation and inference about the very early stages of life comes from following backward from later clearly discriminable states to their first manifestations, we are, I think, entirely justified in saying that from the beginning these escape or safety devices are entitled to different names. Apathy is called out by unsatisfied, extremely aggravated needs; somnolent detachment is called out by inescapable and prolonged anxiety. That is, somnolent detachment, since anxiety is induced by interpersonal situations, is the safety device which attenuates the susceptibility to the interpersonally induced tension of anxiety. It suffices, at this stage of our consideration of developmental history, to observe that the intervention of these, as it were, safety dynamisms attenuates the infant's disturbed condition to a point at which a very important change of state of awareness occurs, and the infant sleeps.

Tension of the Need for Sleep

I have spoken several times of awareness without defining it. Let me say that the state of awareness has to be inferred about the infant; presently we will have some data which will make awareness more than just a "given." But one can safely say that from practically the first hour of extrauterine life, there are two phases of existence: one, awareness, which anyone should be able to accept provisionally, and the other, the state of sleep.

Now sleep as a phase of living is quite as important, and in some ways just as intricate, as is waking. In man and in the higher animals, at least, the *phasic* variation of living between waking and sleep is necessary for the continuation of life. Apathy and somnolent detachment may from this standpoint be regarded as dynamisms that insure life despite grave interference with the ability to fall asleep. Most of the life of the infant is spent in the phase of sleep. Roughly the division of life between sleeping and waking varies inversely with developmental age. But this reciprocal relationship (remember that inverse variation is a reciprocal relationship) is a complex function which is by no means as simple as my former example of the inverse relationship between tension and euphoria. We may say, however, that no other significant factor being concerned, the portion of the life of the infant spent in sleep varies inversely with the developmental age of the infant. It should be noted that at the start of extrauterine life, the developmental age and the chronological age are nearly or very nearly equivalent. But this one-to-one relationship disappears quite early in life; in fact, every day the infant lives, there is a less close correspondence between developmental age and chronological age as measured by a calendar or a clock.

This whole topic of needs, anxiety, and sleep will come up again and again and will be developed more as we go on. But since I am still trying to set forth a consideration of the developmental epoch of infancy, I shall, after making a few more remarks, defer any further development of the subject of sleep.

I have already pointed out that living has two phasic variations, sleeping and waking. But living in the phase of sleep is not a state of tensionless euphoria. The more one 'needs sleep,' the more intense becomes the particular tension state which is the disequilibrium of being that is relaxed or remedied by sleeping; so sleep has the relation to this particular tensional state that satisfaction, let us say, of the need for sugar has to the need for sugar. By this statement, which I trust has been adequate, I have brought you to the third and last of the great genera of tensions which pertain to human living: In addition to the tensions of needs and the tensions which we call anxiety, induced by disturbance of interpersonal relations, we have here the tensions concerned with the phasic state of living which is called sleep. We shall presently discover that the tensions of needs and of anxiety are oppositional to the tensions of sleeping. None of these tensions are of the same genus; they are very significantly different.

I have discussed at some length the differences, which appear very early in the infant, in the tension of anxiety as compared with the tension of needs. The handicaps of language being what they are, I would like to review what I have been saying. I have chosen to use one word, *needs*, to refer to tensions primarily connected with the physicochemical requirements of life, with the avoiding of injury, and with the maintenance of internal, if you please, functional activities of various kinds. I have labeled all these *tensions of needs* and discriminated them from the *tension of anxiety*, which does not directly pertain to the physicochemical universe, but pertains instead to the relationship of the infant with the relatively adult person whose cooperation is necessary for the survival of the infant. And finally I would say that there is a third great type of *tensions which pertain to sleeping* in contrast with waking. While, as I have said, a certain amount of sleep in a certain span of time is necessary for the survival of man and some, at least, of the higher animals, this necessity is distinctly different from the needs for oxygen, sugar, water, heat, and so on; and it is certainly different from the extremely disturbing tensions of anxiety. So it is that when I use the locution *need for satisfaction*, I shall be using *need* as a technical term, because a need in the technical sense can be satisfied. When I talk about the *need for interpersonal security*, I shall be talking about anxiety; and when I talk about the *need for sleep*, I shall be talking about a third genus of tension not readily to be related to the other two grand divisions of tension. I am reviewing these points so that we will be secure in our use of language.

At this stage of our consideration of the first year of developmental history, infancy, I have, I trust, shown that the infant has physicochemically conditioned recurrent needs, the satisfaction of which—aside from breathing—requires interpersonal cooperation, which cooperation can be called tenderness. The manifestation of this tender cooperation for the relief of the infant's needs is disturbed, interfered with, by anxiety in the mothering one. This anxiety in the mothering one not only interferes with her tender cooperation with the infant, but also induces anxiety in the infant. That anxiety in the infant interferes, in turn, with his part of the cooperation for the satisfaction of his needs, such as sucking, swal-

lowing, and so on. Now the continuing tension of these unsatisfied needs, along with the tension of anxiety itself, interferes in
turn with the biologically necessary sleeping which the infant must
do an extraordinarily large part of the time or else die. But this
phasic change from waking to sleeping is protected from the pil-
ing up of needs and anxiety by the infant's ability to become apathetic.

Now, clearly, I have not quite solved the problem of anxiety,
but in my discussion of the anxious infant you observed that it
was the appearance of terror, or the movement toward terror, that
made the situation extremely aggravated. The dynamism of apathy
attenuates fear to the point that it does not interfere with going
to sleep. I realize that I am leaving the matter of anxiety somewhat
at loose ends here. In general, we can say, however, that after a
mothering one has had the experience of an infant going into
what looks like rage behavior—perhaps becoming cyanotic from
screaming, perhaps having spasms—the maternal anxiety is enormously relieved once the infant begins to quiet down and goes to
sleep. Since the maternal anxiety has diminished, it is difficult to
say anything concrete about the relief of the infant's anxiety. The
probability is that even a mother who was made intensely anxious,
for example, by a telegram bringing bad news portending most
unpleasant consequences for the future, will be so distracted from
the threat of mere future trouble by an infant in a condition resembling rage that when apathy spreads over the infant and he
becomes quieter and moves toward sleep, the anxiety of the mother
provoked by the so-called rage behavior of the infant naturally
diminishes quite rapidly.

Now there is one more thing I want to touch on briefly here.
The physicochemical growth rate—the rate of organizing physico-
chemical-biological structures—is very high in the earlier phases
of extrauterine life, as illustrated by the very rapid relative increase in weight of the infant, which means that physicochemical
substances have been built into the infant from the outer world.
Since this rate is very high in the earlier phases of extrauterine
life, any considerable period of lifetime spent in the state of apathy
is of grave moment. In this connection, I should like to call atten-

tion to the work of Margaret Ribble,[1] who has done some excellent observational work on underprivileged infants and whose data I respect very highly. She has described the syndrome of infantile apathy which, once it is well established, provides a very unfavorable outlook for the infant's survival. In other words, if the circumstances of interpersonal collaboration or cooperation which keep an infant alive are so much disturbed that the infant has to have recourse to apathy during quite a large part of his waking life, then the infant perishes.[2] Thus apathy, while it is lifesaving, as I hope I have shown, is something which, if it is used very much, literally starves the infant in all ways, and the infant perishes.

[1] [Margaret A. Ribble, "Clinical Studies of Instinctive Reactions in New Born Babies," *Amer. J. Psychiatry* (1938) 95:149–158.]

[2] This outcome of apathy is not nearly so likely later on; the way in which apathy can make people perish later in life is by making them unable to escape sudden or rapidly oncoming dangers.

Infancy: The Concept of Dynamism–Part 1

Zones of Interaction

I AM NOW beginning to lead up rather directly to the very important concept of dynamism, although I shall not reach that goal for a while yet. In the meantime, we will learn something more about the concept of anxiety and all that is implied in this concept, which is quite basic to this whole way of looking at psychiatry, and also about the prototaxic, parataxic, and syntaxic modes of experience.

We have seen that, from the very beginning of the breathing cycle, the infant has a whole list of needs, activities, and satisfactions, and that delays in satisfactions constitute dangers to early infantile survival and as such are sources of augmented tension to which we refer as fear. Throughout all this list, crying is adequate and appropriate action toward the relief of the fear, because it brings into being the circumstances necessary for the satisfaction of the particular need which is involved. So far as the infant is concerned, in these very early weeks of life, the cry effects (1) the relief of anoxia by starting the breathing cycle; (2) the relief of thirst and hunger by 'producing,' in a certain sense, the nipple in the infant's lips, from which the infant sucks relief-giving substance which is swallowed; (3) the relief of subcooling by preventing excessive heat loss; and (4) the removal of noxious physical circumstances, such as a restraint of bodily freedom of movement, painful local pressures, and the like. The cry is functional activity of the infant, principally appertaining to (besides the breathing cycle) the head end of the alimentary tract. The infant's part in relief of thirst and hunger also centers here, in the sucking and swallowing activity.

The receptor-effector organ complex which is here concerned —that is, the audible-sound-producing and hearing apparatus, the nipple-investing, nipple-holding, and sucking apparatus, and the neuro-glandular-muscular complexes concerned in breathing, crying, and the transporting of foodstuffs—all this is an instance of what we call a *zone of interaction* in the communal existence which is necessary for the survival of the infant. It is evident that the actual interchange of oxygen and carbon dioxide occurs in the pulmonary respiratory epithelium, and that the actual interchange of water and foodstuffs occurs far from the mouth; in other words, the tissues actually concerned in communal existence with the physicochemical environment, only begin in what we shall call the *oral zone*—or, in the case of oxygen, only begin and end in the oral zone. But, physiologically considered, the oral zone is a remarkable organization which can be divided for purposes of discussion into three types of apparatus: (1) receptor apparatus, which I have already touched on—organization of special sense apparatus, such as sight, special tactile sensitivities, gustatory or taste sensitivities, and olfactory or smell sensitivities; (2) eductors, of which I have not yet spoken; and (3) effectors, which are ordinarily muscles and glands. Now what are the eductors? The eductors, a word borrowed from Spearman,[1] are the elaborate apparatus, a large part of it in the brain, which pertains to the central and other nervous systems, and which—in a sensible and use-

---

[1] [*Editors' note:* Spearman uses the word *eduction* in an endeavor to reduce cognitive events to a set of ultimate laws. Sullivan uses the word as the mid-process between the receptors and effectors. According to Spearman, "an item in thought or perception is said to be 'educed' from other items there when derived from these by their very essence or nature" (Charles E. Spearman, *Creative Mind;* London: Nisbet and Co. Ltd., Cambridge Univ. Press, 1930, p. 34). Spearman discriminates between eduction and *apprehension of experience;* for example, "I-see-red" would represent apprehension of experience, in Spearman's terms. But while knowing, according to Spearman, must begin in such actually occurring experience, it extends further, for relations and correlates are *educed* from the bare presenting experience. (*The Nature of 'Intelligence' and the Principles of Cognition;* London: Macmillan and Co., 1923. See Chapters IV, V, VII, and XXI.)]

ful fashion, as it were—connects what impinges on the receptors with the activity of the effectors.

Now in all the zones of interaction that I shall discuss, it will be possible, from the standpoint of physiology—that is, from the standpoint of the effective functional activity of the organized creature—to observe the functioning of the receptors, the eductors, and the effectors, the eductors making what is received useful for life.

The oral zone is a remarkable organization of these three different kinds of apparatus; these apparatuses are concerned with the maintenance of the breathing cycle, the acquiring or rejecting of fluids and solids, and the utterance of those audible sounds basically important in interactions in the interpersonal field. The zone of interaction may then be considered to be the end station in the necessary varieties of communal existence with the physicochemical world, the world of the infrahuman living, and the personal world.

Processes in and pertaining to these zones of interaction must have a great deal to do with the occurrence of experience, with the perduring evidence, in other words, of living. So far as experience is, or effects, useful durable change in the functional activities of the living organism, it must relate backward and forward—that is, in phenomena of recall and foresight—to the zone of interaction to which it is primarily related, however much more widespread its relationship may actually be or become. Here is a discrimination of what *must* be the case from what *may* be the case.

As I have said several times, there is a good deal of evidence to show that all the way down to the level of the amoeba there is actually favorable—that is, profitable—durable change from experience. It must be that experience is related to the particular part of our communal existence and functional activity with the necessary environment from which the experience rose. If experience were not so necessarily related, it would not, needless to say, produce durable and favorable change in the particular functional activity. So I say that experience either *is* the useful durable change, or that it *brings about* the useful durable change in the function of the living organism.

From the data of later life, I hold that experience takes special color from, or is especially marked with reference to, the zone of interaction which is primarily concerned in its occurrence; and I believe that there is no necessity to make any particular change in this general statement when a very young infant is concerned in contradistinction to a grown person. In other words, the zone of interaction which is involved in a particular course of events gives a particular kind of mark, or color, to the experience which the living creature undergoes. For example, if I put salt in my mouth, or, to say it another way, if sodium chloride impinges upon me at the right place—namely, in my mouth—it tastes salt, and former experiences with salt are recalled to the extent of my identifying this as a salty taste; if there seems to be a good deal of that which tastes salt, I can foresee that I shall presently be thirsty, and therefore take steps to provide water with which to wash it down and otherwise make it useful instead of harmful when it is inside me. Now salt applied to an open wound is an experience, I assure you, but it has no marks in any sense relating it to the oral zone. Therefore, although sodium chloride is still the thing which has impinged upon me, because it has impinged upon a different zone of interaction with the environment, the experience of sodium chloride impinging upon me is an extraordinarily different thing; and instead of my having the experience of the ingestion of an absolutely necessary foodstuff which is identified as such, I have the experience of very severe pain due to a particular problem of fluid distribution, hypertonic solution, and so on, in my wound.

I make this rather obvious digression to illustrate what I really mean when I say that experience as experience, whatever else it may be, has color-reference back to, you might say, or some special type of marking which refers it to, a zone of interaction. Now the place where the real interaction between sodium chloride and my organism takes place is a long way from the place where the sodium chloride impinges significantly upon my organism. Thus even in this simple example you see that the oral zone in connection with sodium chloride, common salt, has much significance for me, although the point at which sodium chloride is of the most vital and absolute necessity for my continued survival begins several feet from there—and exists throughout all the tissues of the body, salt being an imperative necessity for the carrying on of the complex physicochemical arrangements by which we live. So the zone of

interaction, the end station of a particular type of communal existence, has striking psychiatric importance, that is, striking importance for the human organism in a large and total sense.

While experience is experience of the living of the organism, and
is total rather than local or partial in character, it is primarily the
experience of particular events impinging upon one or more of the
zones of interaction, which are end stations of the living organism.
Note that the zone of interaction is not to be equated with any particular fixed tissue organization; it is not quite as static as the mouth,
nose, pharynx, and larynx are in the anatomical person. Thus not
alone in man, but well down the biological series, if because of a
misfortune in genetic constitution, or an injury or misfortune in
development, a creature is born with an unusual defect, or comes
to suffer the destruction of part of the apparatus of a zone of interaction with the necessary environment, then quite frequently
other apparatus can be modified—chiefly the eductor apparatus,
the central nervous system. And so the zone of interaction, defined
from the standpoint of that which impinges upon it, becomes functional again, although the biological apparatus, the histological apparatus, if you please, is very different. An internationally famous
instance of this is the development in Helen Keller of quite adequate zones of interaction with personal environment, despite very
grave and extensive destruction of apparatus which, if you think
of zones of interaction in terms of apparatus, you might expect
would destroy completely the possibilities for such interaction.

The Role of Anxiety in the Beginning
Differentiation of Experience

Crying, as I have said, is adequate and appropriate action of the
hungry infant in that it frequently 'produces' the nipple-lips experience and its satisfaction-giving consequents of sucking, swallowing, and so on. Now crying is adequate and appropriate action
for the relief of the infant's hunger, not because it *invariably* gets
him fed, but because it *frequently*, so far as he is concerned, leads
to that change which is the nipple between his lips, which is the
instituting or initiating step in the procedure of sucking and swallowing, which in the end relieves or at least diminishes the hunger.
This lips-nipple experience, which we are sure the infant has, gen-

erally produces the fluid sucked and swallowed, the arrival of which is closely related to the relaxation or reduction of the tension of need for water and food.

Now one of the things I most detest in the German language is the production of words that take a printed line, by compounding other words. Unhappily, in trying to throw some light on the essentially simply inferable living of the infant, I have had to resort to compound hyphenated words. The one which provokes my distress at the moment is crying-when-hungry. Crying-when-hungry has no necessary relatedness, in the infant's experience, with crying-when-cold, crying-when-pained, or crying-under-any-other-circumstances. If crying-when-hungry frequently initiates the necessary circumstances for the relief of hunger and thirst, it comes to mean, in a primitive, prototaxic way, something like what I may suggest by the word sequence: "Come, nipple, into my mouth." It is a vocal gesture with reasonably dependable power of so manipulating what will later be called reality that the nipple complies. In other words, crying-when-hungry, so far as infantile experience can go, has power to manipulate quite ungraspable aspects of something-or-other, later lumped as reality, so that the nipple dutifully appears.

The most refined study of the sound waves which make up crying-when-hungry need show no 'objective difference' whatever from the sound waves making up crying-when-cold, for example. The two may not only sound alike, but in the physical acoustic sense may be the same, may have a one-to-one correspondence in every measurable sense; that is, the pattern of progression of sound waves, if duly recorded on a cathode-ray oscillograph, may be absolutely identical in every characteristic that can be measured through such a device. And yet, from the infantile standpoint, crying-when-hungry and crying-when-cold will not be in any sense the same thing.

The same kind of physical acoustic correspondence often appears when one says *whole* and *hole*. The so-called objective facts do not have significance with respect to the meaning, to the speaking person, of the (as we say) two different words. He may never have discovered that his two words are homonyms or homophones. We may say, under these circumstances, that he has not differentiated the homophonous character of the two words. As long as the use of either of these two homophones generally proves adequate to his needs, it is of no great importance to his living to discover that the two words, very different in dictionary meaning, sound alike—that is, are experienced by the hearer as quite exactly the same. Until something has called for such differentiation, our person may well believe that he "sounds different," as he might put it, when he utters "hole" from the way he sounds when he says "whole." In general, the matter will never have occurred to him, never have been the subject of what I shall later discuss as *observation, identifying,* and *valid formulation* of two different, but acoustically identical, verbal acts. I trust that I have illustrated, by this discussion of two homonymous or homophonous words, how, from the standpoint of the physics of sound, or from the study of linguistic process in actual operation, two very different words are utterly the same. Their difference, which comes out nicely when written words are substituted for them (remember that written words are symbols for spoken words) is a difference in the use to which they are put—that is, their usefulness as tools, their meaning to the user, what they are good for.

In the same way, the infant's crying-when-hungry, however utterly indistinguishable outside, you might say, it is from crying-when-cold, is an entirely different performance so far as the infant and his experience go. Thus one's actions, however they may impress the observer, are most importantly defined by what they are 'intended' for—that is, they are determined by the general pattern of motivation that is involved, by what is significant to the person concerned, quite irrespective of any impressions an observer may have.

A great many mistakes are made in psychiatry as a result of overlooking this fact. Some of these mistakes are very devastating indeed, such as the ancient superstition that the performances of the schizophrenic are essentially unpsychological. Few more sad combinations of words could be spouted. The truth is that however the performance of a Javanese head-hunter might look to a clerk in a Wall Street financial institution, the clerk's opinions would have only recreational or conversational value; they would be of exceedingly little importance with respect to head-hunters in Java.

The infant's experience of crying-when-hungry comes very early to relate backward and forward—that is, as recall and as foresight—to the 'producing' of the lips-nipple experience with its desired consequents of sucking and swallowing. I have said that crying-when-hungry *frequently* produces the nipple and the possibilities of relief. I want now to discuss two special instances in which this very early magical potency of vocal behavior goes wrong, as it were. Before I do that, I wish that you could rid yourself of any preconceptions about magic. I would like to suggest that when we speak of *magical potency* we are likely to mean—I think it may be adequately stated this way—that we have an exceedingly inadequate grasp on all that is actually happening. When you do something that works, it is like turning on the electric lights by flipping a switch. The lights come on magically because you flipped the switch—that is, if you don't know anything in particular about electricity and electric circuits, it seems magical; if the lights don't come on, that's extraordinary, indicating that something must be wrong somewhere. But if you know enough to guess *where* something may be wrong, you are pretty well acquainted with reality. I might add—perhaps slightly to parallel the relationship of the infant's crying-when-hungry and getting food—that even though sometimes when you flip a switch the lights don't come on, the fact that they generally have will probably lead you to flip switches in the future when you want light; and you will remain convinced that there is considerable potency in flipping a switch when you want light, even though it hasn't always worked. And so it is with a great deal in life.

I want particularly now to discuss very early experience of this sort of *infrequent* event. The first is the failure of the crying-when-hungry, arising from (as we see it) the absence of the necessary, more adult person who actually (in our sense) is the provider of the nipple. To digress for a moment, it is well to remember that the very young infant has no grasp on those phases of reality which we call independent persons, with or without nipples, and with or without milk to run through those nipples; this is utterly exterior to any reasonable supposition about very young infants. Now let us assume that the infant happens to be surrounded only by male persons—perhaps the mother is out doing some shopping or whatever. Crying-when-hungry therefore does not produce, in its usual magical fashion, the nipple in the mouth, which is the initiatory stage of infantile activity which satisfies hunger and thirst. In this case crying-when-hungry is continued until the nipple is produced, or until mounting fear has called out apathy and the infant finally sleeps. Crying-when-hungry then recurs as soon as the infant awakens. Now this is the beginning of a very important train of events with which we have dealings throughout life.

The other special instance which I wish to discuss is that in which anxiety is a complicating factor. We shall take a case in which the crying-when-hungry has produced the nipple, but this success, preliminary to sucking and the satisfaction of hunger and thirst, is complicated by the interference of the anxiety which has been induced in the infant because of or by anxiety in or pertaining to the person who carries the nipple in actuality. The satisfaction-giving consequents on the production of the nipple under these circumstances do not follow. Investing the nipple with the lips, sucking, swallowing, or any or all of these and other parts of the accessory behavior of nursing may be disordered by the coincidence of anxiety in the infant, induced by the mothering one's anxiety, with the infant's crying-when-hungry. The infant may produce the nipple in the magical fashion that has become frequent enough to be the normal expectation, as you might describe it—the proof of the power of crying-when-hungry—but this time something is very wrong.

The first of the special instances which I have mentioned—that is, crying-when-hungry when there is nobody to rally around tenderly—is a very early experience of the occasional inadequacy or powerlessness of otherwise generally appropriate and adequate behavior for the manipulation of what later will be called reality. The infant cries when hungry, and nothing happens except the development of processes in the infant which culminate finally in apathy and sleep, with the recurrence of crying on awakening. As I have said, this is a very early instance of a type of situation which recurs more or less frequently throughout life, in which a generally appropriate and adequate series of acts—that is, behavior—proves to be inadequate, and proves to have no power to bring about that which this behavior is ordinarily entirely sufficient to produce. This sort of experience, the experience of unexpected powerlessness, as we may call it, is an event infrequent enough to be quite exterior to expectation; in other words, it is an exception to something to which we are accustomed, an exception to the many times we have done something and the right result has come of it.

The accompaniments of these experiences of powerlessness are various. The significance of such experiences of powerlessness probably increases for some time after birth, until one has developed adequate ways of handling such experiences, and by adequate I mean personally adequate in the sense of avoiding very unpleasant emotion. The very early experiences would, if they continued long enough, unquestionably produce very marked effects on the developing personality of the infant, but here the intervention of the dynamism of apathy tones off, as it were, these instances of powerlessness, somewhat after the fashion that the old magic lanterns produced vignettes—you remember, something would fade out gradually, and later something would gradually come in. And so the intervention of the apathy processes, to which I have already referred, prevents a serious complicating effect from the relatively infrequent instances of the infant's powerlessness to produce the nipple by the cry.

I hope that I have made it clear that, even very early in life, frequent success has a very powerful influence in determining the character of foresight. I believe that I will not mislead you if I talk quite loosely and say that, given a pressing need which is increasing, it is not strange that the extremely young infant does not accumulate negative instances; and in any case the accumulation of negative instances is less apt to be significant because apathy has a sort of fade-out effect on things, and the chances of success upon the resumption of crying after sleep are pretty fair. Thus the relatively frequent, rather consistent success stamps in the magical power of the cry; and the occasional failures, due to the absence of the mother, and so on, do not greatly impair this growing conviction of what we would much later call a cause-and-effect relationship, which could be expressed—putting a great many words into the mouth of a very early infant—as, "I cry when I suffer a certain distress, and that produces something different which is connected with the relief of the distress."

This relief need not absolutely always occur for such convictions of relationship in the universe to become firmly entrenched in the infant. If this seems doubtful, let me say that one of the most conspicuous things we see, in the intensive study of personality, is the fantastic ease with which unnumbered negative instances can be overlooked for years in the area of one's more acute personal problems. It may even be that under certain circumstances, although not in very early infancy, a success which is purely an accident—that is, which is so exceedingly complex that it may be regarded as pure chance—may give rise to firm conviction that there is a vital causal relationship involved, and that if one could only do the right thing again it would produce the desirable result with which it was originally associated only by the merest and most terribly complex chance. So the erasing effect of negative experience is not very impressive, even from extremely early in life.[2]

Now what I have said thus far concerns the first of the special instances in which the infant's crying-when-hungry fails—the instance in which the provider of the nipple is absent. The second of the special instances, on the other hand, the case where anxiety is induced in the infant along with the showing up of the nipple, is to the infant an utterly different sort of experience. The ade-

---

[2] [*Editors' note:* The preceding three paragraphs are taken from Sullivan's 1948 lecture series, which was interrupted by his death. Earlier he had discussed these experiences of powerlessness as belonging generically to the field of the uncanny emotions—awe, dread, loathing, and horror. Sullivan remarked in his 1948 lecture, "Since this lecture series was originally prepared, I have changed my mind about uncanny emotion, about which I have done some fairly active thinking in the recent past. . . . It used to be very depressing to discover that I didn't agree with myself from one year to another, but ultimately I have found it rather encouraging. At least it gives me a chance to re-emphasize to you that psychiatry is a developing field, in which, perhaps, it is not to one's vast discredit that one does not become entirely and rigidly crystallized in the defense of what is an archaic idea. . . ."]

quate and appropriate crying-when-hungry has produced the nipple, but in the process has evoked anxiety; I am talking entirely from the standpoint of the infant, who is unable to discriminate anxiety as induced by the mother's anxiety—in fact, all of this is exterior to the clear understanding of the infant. But as mother draws near with her nipple—in other words, as from the infantile standpoint this mighty power of crying-when-hungry is about to bring results—lo, there comes the very severe drop in euphoria, in the general feeling of well-being, which is anxiety. Thus in this instance, while crying-when-hungry has produced the first step in the business, the nipple in the mouth, it has also brought anxiety —very severe tension which interferes with behavior activity in satisfaction of the need for water and food. What this must be like in infantile experience is suggested when I say that under these circumstances crying-when-hungry has produced a *different* nipple; the nipple now produced is not the same nipple, so far as the infant is concerned. The lips-nipple configuration is something new, and is anything but the satisfying lips-nipple configuration ordinarily produced; in fact, it is one that will not work, that is anything but relieving. It is, to use an exceedingly broad term in one of its exceedingly early relevancies, an evil eventuality which has arisen in connection with the oral zone of interaction, although we, in contradistinction to the infant, know that the anxiety has no primary or necessary relationship to the oral zone. On the contrary, the first time anything like this happens, it is perfectly certain that the anxiety in the mother which induced anxiety in the infant did not have any relation to the infant's taking nourishment. Afterward her anxiety may have something to do with the difficulties about feeding that characterized the first time she was anxious with her infant. But this is utterly outside the experience of the infant, and a matter of no consequence whatever in thinking about his experience, because the infant cannot differentiate the source of the anxiety. The anxiety is just there, and is extremely unpleasant; nothing that generally went right *does* go right, and the experience which unquestionably occurs— that is, the conjunction of nipple and lips—may actually be so clearly different that the infant rejects this particular nipple, will not hold it in his mouth, and therefore does not suck it.

Anxiety relates to the whole field of interpersonal interaction; that is, anxiety about *anything* in the mother induces anxiety in the infant. It doesn't need to have anything to do with the infant or the nursing situation. For example, as I mentioned before, a telegram announcing something of very serious moment to the prestige or peace of mind of the mother may induce a state of anxiety in her which induces anxiety in the infant; the infant's anxiety shows, so far as she is concerned, in this unexpected and exceedingly unsatisfactory difficulty in getting the infant to nurse. Now looking at it from the infant's standpoint, we can infer with certainty only that in this particular circumstance the outcome of ordinarily appropriate and adequate behavior when hungry—namely, crying-when-hungry—has produced the wrong nipple, a very evil situation with very unpleasant and unsatisfactory consequences.

Now oral rejection, in which the infant will not invest and hang on to the nipple, is not an appropriate and adequate way to deal with this particular evil or bad nipple. It does not in any way diminish or favorably affect the anxiety, which is induced by the mother's anxiety. In fact, if the mother is capable of noticing what's going on, and observes that the infant now rejects the nipple, avoids it, and will not hold and suck it, this will probably aggravate the mother's anxiety, adding a new anxiety, which will tend to aggravate the infant's anxiety. So mere rejection (you will remember that when first I spoke of the oral zone, I suggested that it accepted and rejected certain things) of this bad or anxiety-toned nipple is not adequate or appropriate: it doesn't reduce the anxiety, it certainly doesn't satisfy the need for food, and therefore it is a very perduring instance of the relationship of anxiety to living.

Now let me invite your attention briefly to something which I hope to express better later on. Even though anxiety is experience, and, as such, is total, and even though it has no necessary relationship to any particular zone of interaction, anxiety can be, as we put it, erroneously associated with a particular zone of interaction. For example, it may be erroneously associated with the mother's nipple, and consequently with the oral zone, since the nipple is significant to the infant only in connection with the oral zone at this very early stage—the infant has no interest in nipples except the nipple in the mouth or in the immediate proximity of the mouth. If the circumstances are something like those I have just discussed in my example of the mother made anxious by a telegram, there is no possibility of the infant's discriminating the irrelevance of his behavior in the oral zone of interaction, in rejecting the nipple, from something quite properly related to that zone of interaction as profitable experience—that is, extending backward and forward as recall and foresight. Now if you begin to grasp this aspect of anxiety-laden, or anxiety-colored, details of behavior, you will begin to have a hint of what a devastating complication of development frequent experiences of anxiety can be.

Here we have inferred what I believe perfect logical necessity requires: beginning discrimination by the infant of an actual nipple as two very different nipples, one conventional and desirable, the other evil and connected with, you might almost say, unending trouble. The more I talk about anxiety, the more you will see that this first appearance of anxiety which I have discussed is not so very different from an enormous number of the very troublesome results of anxiety in human living.

Signs, Signals, and Symbols in Early Experience

As I continue to build up data on which to support the statement of the concept of dynamism, we shall find the infant beginning to move out of the prototaxic and into the parataxic mode of experience, and perhaps the meaning of these modes may become more clear.

We have seen that recurrent physicochemical needs in the communal existence of the infant cause tension, the felt aspect of which later will be called the experience of, say, hunger and thirst. The experience of hunger includes the recall and the foresight of experiencing the satisfaction of hunger through adequate and appropriate behavior pertaining to one or more zones of interaction. This satisfactory, satisfaction-giving, adequate, and appropriate behavior *can be said* [3] to achieve a foreseen goal. The fore-

---

[3] By this I mean that it is perfectly appropriate to think in those terms if one has first thought in more valid terms before plunging into, for instance, the matter of "goal-directed behavior." Whenever I use these locu-

seen goal in this particular case is the satisfaction of hunger by means of crying-when-hungry and by means of the nursing behavior sequence which follows when crying-when-hungry has produced the nipple. The felt tension of hunger calls for crying-when-hungry. The nipple thus frequently evoked comes to be differentiated as the first significant step in satisfaction—the nipple comes to *mean* foreseen satisfaction. The tactile and thermal sentience arising from it in the region of the oral zone of interaction, and presently the organization of visual sentience about the nipple, comes to be a *sign* that satisfaction of hunger will follow. The novel terms I have introduced here are *goal* (which idea will not be developed for the present), *meaning*, and *sign*. The nipple is a *sign* that satisfaction of hunger will follow except when crying has evoked the evil or bad nipple with its aura of anxiety; and this latter eventuality, which we know is the case when the mother is anxious, comes to mean foreseen increasing distress.

At this point I wish to mention the term *prehension*, which I have used for a good many years. By prehension I mean what might be called the most rudimentary form of perception; in other words, the infant prehends the nipple-in-lips experience well in advance of his perceiving the nipple as something existing and durable and relatively independent of the lips. Prehension, in this sense of the very most rudimentary sort of perception, is a word that I like to use to remind you always that that which is prehended is important to the prehender, but is not, in any sense, the sort of full-blown experience that we ordinarily mean when we speak of *perceiving* something. Perception grows out of prehension, one might say, and, for all I know, this rudimentary process is always present behind perception; but as I go on with this idea, you will begin to see why I want a word that is less rich in meaning than is perception.

Thus the oral-tactile and the oral-thermal prehension, the visual

---

tions—such as *in a way of speaking*, or *it can be said*—I am suggesting that what I have previously attempted to communicate is more generally valid than the particular term that follows. There are a great many things that can be said which are all right in the particular universe or subuniverse of discourse in which they occur; but we are attempting to build up from more or less definitely indisputable evidence a particular referential language, so I shall attempt to indicate when I am not being exact in my language.

prehension, and the increasingly general tension associated with, or coincident with, the evocation of the bad nipple constitute a sign that evil consequences will follow. This sign and meaning aspect of experience is an exceedingly important one; from the study of this aspect of early experience we shall arrive presently in the exceedingly important field of language behavior. A sign is a particular pattern in the experience of events which is differentiated from or within the general flux of experience (at this stage of life, prototaxic experience); and this differentiation occurs in terms of recall and foresight of a particular frequent sequence of satisfaction or of increasing distress. The sign, as a pattern of experience, is a differentiation of frequently coincident elements in prototaxic experience of recurrent needs and satisfactions, and of recurrent anxiety or fear. A not uncommon eventuality in the infant's nursing behavior is the escape of the nipple from investiture by the lips—the incidents when the infant 'loses hold of' the nipple. Experience of the abrupt cessation of oral-tactile sentience arising from the presence of the nipple in the lips comes very early to be the signal for cessation of the sucking behavior; and it is the signal for the appearance of behavior which we can call searching for the nipple, with or without a resumption of crying-when-hungry. Here I have spoken of an abrupt cessation of certain inflowing 'stuff of sensation,' becoming or being a signal for a change of behavior. And let me say at this point that signals are a particular kind of signs. We will later discover that there are two major kinds of signs, of which the first, the one we have just discussed, is the signal.

At this point it is necessary for me to make rather a long digression on various matters which may be in your mind, to the confusion of or confounding of what I am attempting to communicate. And so at this point I invite you to notice that we are discussing prototaxic experience, not behavior as a nonrepresented aspect of neuro-muscular-glandular organization of the infant. I am not talking about the biology of nursing or neurophysiology when I speak of the abrupt cessation of influx over the afferent channels being a signal for a change in musculoglandular action. Of course, the neuro-muscular-glandular organization and the degree of its functional maturation at a particular time set limits to the possibility of experience. Such processes involving 'outer' and 'inner' factors are the raw materials out of which is made up the living of the living organism—the momentary states and the succession of momentary states of the organism which are the prototaxic experience of the organism; and the prototaxic experience includes the ultimate elements of all reference to the past and the neighboring future. Of course there are afferent impulses carried over sensory nerves, and the central integrating nervous system, and motor and secretory nerves going out to the mouth, and so on; but if you will realize that in addition to all that, there is *experience* and that we are dealing with experience, then perhaps you will understand what seemed to necessitate this digression.

Survival value may be a useful concept for accounting for the biological equipment of the infant. This sort of thinking, however, is exterior to our interest. Our concern is the formulation of psychiatrically significant aspects of human life, to which end we are now considering the processes by which the newborn human animal becomes a person. Our concern is not with the patterns of excitation in the central nervous system, and the abrupt or gradual changes in these patterns; rather we are concerned with an all-inclusive aspect of the dynamic organism-environment complex —the enduring influence of the tensional history of the organism's living on the present and the near-future living of the organism, to which we refer as more-or-less elaborated experience. The series of significant states of the organism-environment complex, all but the first elements of which include factors of the past and future—factors of history and potentiality, as it were, which make up the mnemic series—includes also secondary elements which are the organization or the elaboration of experience. The sign is such an organization or elaboration of experience; but, as such, it is also a part of living, so that signs, and behavior conditioned by signs, are experience. In the same way, that out of which they were elaborated, from which, we might say, they were evolved, is more primitive, or less elaborated experience. An experience is always the experience of an organism. Signs exist 'in' experience and not "outside in objective 'reality.' "

The comment which I have made—namely, that signs exist 'in'

experience and not somewhere else—may seem to be saying that the sign is a subjective rather than an objective "reality." In this and in much that I have said thus far it may seem that I am expressing, however obscurely, the 'philosophy' of "idealism," in contrast or as opposed to the 'philosophy' of "realism." I suggest that these and all other tangential issues be held in abeyance for the present and that you observe only that the meaning intended to be conveyed by the term, sign, is all that is immediately relevant. I believe that you will ultimately discover that discriminations of the nature of subjective versus objective, ideal versus real, and so on, are all quite irrelevant to an understanding of the theory which I am here attempting to set up.

Now, returning to our nursing infant, let us consider another frequent eventuality, the 'failure to get milk out of' a particular nipple—that is, failure to produce or to continue the experience of milk-to-be-swallowed by sucking a particular nipple or nipplelike object. This eventuality is a signal for relaxing the 'hold' on the nipple and searching for a different nipple, perhaps with crying-when-hungry. If the same nipple, now unproductive of milk, is 'found,' it is invested, sucked, but quickly relinquished. There is in this eventuality experience of the kind which will lead to the differentiation of a third class of nipples. So far we have had good and bad nipples, the bad one being the nipple of an anxious mother. The third class of nipples is that of nipples neither good nor bad, but *wrong,* in the sense of incorrect, in the further sense of unsuitable and useless in the satisfaction of hunger.

In the nursing behavior of very young offspring of some of the mammals with more than one pair of teats, such as dogs, cats, cows, and mares, we observe clearly another set of facts which is sometimes indicated in human nursing and occasionally very clearly observable—namely, the differentiation of preferred nipples, doubtless dependent on experience factors which are related to ease or difficulty of investing and 'holding,' or on factors of productivity in terms of returns on the effort of sucking. These are teats good and correct, but better or worse in terms of the oral experience in the satisfaction of hunger and thirst. This is so striking in some instances that, although along with multiple teats there usually go multiple births and there are as many puppies as there are mother's teats, or close to the same number, some of the teats will be large and blunt, or obtuse, and they will be so neglected that those breasts actually are in danger of caking. Clearly they give milk—as a matter of fact, not uncommonly they are more productive than some of the others; but, to talk in adult objective language, they are hard to hold, they slide out of the puppy's mouth very readily, and probably they take up so much space in the mouth that they make sucking somewhat more difficult than when only a small area of the lip surface is used in investing the nipples.

These sundry experiences with the nipple or teat may be listed as encounters with

(A-1) the good and satisfactory nipple-in-lips which is the sig-nal—the uncomplicated signal—for nursing, and

(A-2) the good but unsatisfactory nipple-in-lips which is a sig-nal for rejection until the need of hunger is great enough to make this good but unsatisfactory nipple acceptable.

(B) the wrong nipple-in-lips—that is, one that does not give milk any longer—which is a signal for rejection and search for another nipple, and

(C) the evil nipple, the nipple of an anxious mother which, so far as the infant is concerned, is a nipple preceded by the aura of extremely disagreeable tension—anxiety—which is a signal for avoidance, often even the avoidance of in-vesting the nipple with the lips at all. So the signal might be converted into rather adult words by saying it is a signal for not-that-nipple-in-my-lips.

Groups A and B—encounters with good satisfactory and good unsatisfactory, and with wrong nipples—are experiences primarily of the oral zone of interaction; group C, on the other hand—the encounter with the anxiety-invested nipple—is experience of anx-iety as an evil which has been evoked by the oral-zone behavior of crying-when-hungry. When one keeps in mind the delayed functional competence of the human visual apparatus and the con-dition of mammalian young which are "born blind"—that is, with-out the eyelids being opened—it is evident that experience in groups A and B is built out of the following types of sentience: vibratory and aural sentience arising from the crying-when-hungry; tactile, thermal, and kinesthetic sentience from the lips area; kinesthetic sentience from the sucking and swallowing performances; and tactile and gustatory sentience from the transportation of the milk across the tongue and through the pharyngeal passage. This is the sort of influx from the impinging events of which the nipple-in-lips is the prehension. As visual sentience is added to these experiences, and permits clear visual experience of something more than moving patterns of light and shade, nipples good and satisfactory can often be distinguished at a distance from nipples good but unsatisfactory. But there is no visually discriminable difference between the bad nipple of anxiety and the objectively identical nipple which on another occasion is good.

Discriminating differentiation of good and satisfactory, good and unsatisfactory, and wrong—that is, useless—nipples, is the first of an exceedingly important field of useful additions to behavior—in this case, behavior in the relief of hunger and thirst. It is peculiarly significant in the elaboration of behavior more appropriate and dependably adequate than the initial magically appropriate and adequate crying-when-hungry. The important idea to be grasped here is that the infant is beginning to acquire useful additions to his behavior, and that these useful additions are those which are more appropriate because they are less 'magical' and more dependably adequate than the preceding behavior which in the beginning was crying-when-hungry. And the elaboration of this more useful behavior comes about by the *identifying of differences* in what we call perceived objects. The extremely useful improvements of behavior in nursing which we are now discussing have as their raw material the discrimination of these sundry kinds of nipples, including the very awkwardly identical—that is, so far as visual sentience can go—good nipple and nipple of anxiety. From our standpoint, which has nothing to do with the infant, it is the same nipple, but carried in one case by a tender mother and in the other case by an anxious one. To repeat, the useful additions to the infant's behavior arise by identifying the difference in what we call perceived objects—that is, important, more-or-less independent aspects of the infant-environment complex—whether objectively of the infant or of the environment. It is necessary in thinking about this stage of human development to realize that while toes, fingers, and so on, can be identified even to the point where one finger is distinguished from another—actually the thumbs are the things that come in for special attention—still these are, to the infant, independent perceptual objects. Even though they, from our adult standpoint, 'belong to' the infant, the probability is that toes, and particularly big toes, are just as independent to the infant as mothers and nipples for some time after the infant's visual receptor has combined its activities with other receptors concerned in the oral zone.

If I may digress again for a moment, I would like to comment on the fact that there are some rather startling coincidences in the make-up of the central nervous system, although I do think that biological and neurophysiological terms are utterly inadequate for studying everything in life. The most astonishing example that I can think of offhand is the coincidence in a receptor area of the afferent inflowing impulse nerves from around the middle of the lips in immediate juxtaposition to afferent nerve endings from the thumbs and also the neighboring side of the index finger. Now there is a day coming doubtless, long after we will all have been embalmed in history, when it will be possible in some fashion to translate these interesting and exciting coincidences in, say, the realm of neuroanatomy into some of what we have to learn in a quite different universe of discourse—namely, psychology, so-called psychobiology, and psychiatry. Although it is important to remember that that which is 'given' in structure sets limits to what may be possible in behavior and, even more broadly, in experience, we actually will very seldom be discussing structurally given things. When we are, I will make particular effort to invite attention to the fact that here does seem to be a correlation of 'somatic' organization with psychiatrically important phenomena. I hope that you will not try to build up in your thinking correlations that are either purely imaginary or relatively unproven, which may give you the idea that you are in a solid, reliable field in contrast to one which is curiously intangible; such a feeling of reliability is, I think, an illusion born out of the failure to recognize that what we know comes to us through our *experiencing* events, and is

therefore always separated from anything really formed or transcendentally real by the limited channels through which we contact what we presume to be the perduring, unknown universe.
So if a person really thinks that his thoughts about nerves and
synapses and the rest have a higher order of merit than his thoughts
about signs and symbols, all I can say is, Heaven help him.

I shall now return to my discussion of the independent aspects
of the infant-environment complex, which are identified as similar
perceived objects, but among which differences come to be identified. This identifying of differences among perceived objects is
the precursor, in two senses, of any *re*-cognition: it is a precursor
in the sense that it invariably antecedes recognition; and it is a
precursor in all acts of recognition, because the differences evoke
references to the past, in the process of which the experience of
similar differences is effective in causing what we lump under the
term *I recognize*.

The infant's identifying eventually progresses to the point where
he is able to generalize experience that is marked with the characteristics of several zones of interaction as experience pertaining
to *one* recurrent pattern of sentience from the distance receptors,
which pattern is frequently evoked by the infant's crying (whether
it be crying-when-hungry, crying-when-cold, or whatever). When
he has progressed to this point, he has begun to experience living
in an elaboration which is beyond the prototaxic mode. We might
say that he is experiencing the good mother in the parataxic mode.
Generalizing, then, is a particular development in the identifying
of differences; it is, we might say, what is left of things that are
similar when the differences have been identified. In other words,
the forms of experience are generalized so that things in common
in them, as well as all their sundry differences, are in perception
as useful experience. These influxes of experience are marked by
any one of several zones of interaction. Perhaps I can make all this
clear by putting it in another way. We know from our ivory tower
that the same mothering one, the *same* mother, produces, for instance, a nipple when the infant is hungry, produces blankets
when the infant is cold, produces dexterous manipulation when the
infant is on a safety pin that is open, and, needless to say, changes
the diapers when that is a most suitable and timely activity. Al-

though we, from our objective superiority, know that the *same mother* does all this, it is necessary to study what can be inferred with some certainty as to what goes on in the infant: Originally all these needs which the mother cooperates in meeting are marked or colored by the zone of interaction with the environment in which the sentience related to the need and its satisfaction had its origin; thus, we have already set up the difference, objectively invisible and indetectable, between crying-when-hungry, crying-when-cold, and so on. Now we come to the infant's ability to generalize, to detect the factors in *common* in the 'cooperating' person (who, needless to say, is not perceived in that elaborate fashion); all of this is generalized experience arising from, and distinguished by, more than one zone of interaction. Furthermore, this experience is generalized as pertaining to one recurrent pattern of sentience of the eyes and ears, the distance receptors, which is frequently evoked by crying-when-hungry, by crying-when-cold, and so forth, which in turn is generalized as *crying*. Thus the infant is generalizing also about crying, progressing from all these different kinds of perhaps identical-sounding crying, to crying as a generalization of what is identical or what is *not different* in these various vocal operations of crying. We might speak of this as analytic synthesis because it eliminates differences and finds that which is common to very important aspects of the infant-environment complex which are necessary for life. When we come, in living, to the point where this sort of synthesis is taking place, we encounter a degree of elaboration of experience which is removed from what I have thus far discussed—namely, experience in the prototaxic or earliest mode, in which one, as it were, 'lives one's living.'

The identifying of differences can make very useful contributions to behavior in the satisfaction of needs; and the generalizing of experience so that the significant common factors mixed in with the differences are identified or connected with one recurrent pattern of experience, primarily mediated by the distance receptors, elevates the complexity or elaboration of experience from the prototaxic to the parataxic mode of experience. I hope that it begins to be clear why I have set up these modes of experience—the prototaxic, the parataxic, and the syntaxic. The prototaxic mode, as I have suggested, is a very early form of, and presently a very strikingly odd form of, living as a living being.

On any given occasion, the experience of vision by and large takes place before there is contact with tactile, thermal, kinesthetic, gustatory, or olfactory end organs; the auditory experience takes place in the same way, as soon as the infant develops and hears sounds other than his own crying. In the same way, experience with anxiety, like experience through the distance receptors, begins before there is contact with any of the contact receptors—that is, begins before the anxious mother and her nipple reach the infant's mouth—but not, you remember, before light waves reach the infant's eyes or sound waves reach the infant's ears from the mother. Since anxiety has in common with the function of these distance receptors the fact that it begins before there is any contact with a nipple, any 'profiting' by the experience with the nipple of anxiety *must be* by wave discriminations, primarily referable to the functional activity of the auditory and visual distance receptors, a process which is more inclusive than seeing the nipple and its immediate adnexa. The nipple and the breast and the arrangement of clothing, and so on, of an anxious mother need be in no physically discriminable sense at all different from those of the tender nonanxious mother. And so, if there is to be any *useful* addition to behavior with respect to anxiety, it must arise by discriminating something not pertaining to that which really matters at this stage—namely, the nipple, nursing, and so on. Yet the functional activity of the distance receptors, hearing and sight, gives no gross clues to success or failure of crying-when-hungry in bringing to the infant the carrier of the good nipple, the good mother, in contrast to the most unpleasant experience of bringing to the infant the carrier of the nipple of anxiety, the bad mother, with her foreshadowing aura of anxiety.

Differentiation of the 'appearance'—that is, of distance receptor data—of the bad mother from that of the good mother is a complex refinement of visual and auditory perception which is called into being under the driving force of what we may call a desire to avoid anxiety, an inhering 'preference' for relative euphoria. To give a little hint of what I am talking about here, it may be useful for me to refer to my bitch and her puppies. While it is unfortunately true that dogs are so organized and so reared that they suffer anxiety provoked by anxious or tense people around them, still, by and large, the experience of the evil nipple or the nipple of anxiety by puppies is rare. But there comes a time in the life of the puppy, which in many respects I think is importantly connected with the development of his teeth, when nursing does not seem to be quite the right thing to encourage, and the mother then provokes in the puppies puppy-anxiety; I surmise that this includes very real elements of fear, since the mother has no hesitancy in inflicting pain in discouraging further nursing behavior.

I mention this to stress the statement previously made, which I would now like to repeat. Differentiation of the 'appearance' (and I hope you will notice that appearance is not the exact word here because it includes distance reception by the ear) of the bad mother from that of the good mother is a complex refinement—a visual and auditory perception which is called into being by the driving necessity of protecting one's euphoria, one's feeling of well-being, from anxiety, so far as one can. And since there is no gross perceptible difference, this differentiation can only be accomplished by a refinement. Thus there comes into being the first instance of another class of signs of which the current instance is the discrimination of what we may call *forbidding gestures*, presently to be referred to the perceived mothering one who has been fused into one, by this generalizing process, out of the earlier, separate, perceived objects, the good mother and the bad mother. This matter of the infant's refined discrimination of what we call forbidding gestures first applies to the mother and thereafter applies throughout life to practically all significant people—that is, those people who come to have an important place in his living, in other words, his interpersonal relationships. The discrimination of heard differences in the mother's vocalization and seen differences in the postural tensions [4] of the mother's face, and perhaps later of differences in speed and rhythm of her gross bodily movements in coming toward the infant, presenting the bottle, chang-

[4] Of course, postural tensions are not seen—the skin is seen—but I am talking about the configuration of the face, the appearance of the face as determined by the postural tensions of the so-called expressive muscles of the head.

ing the diapers, or what not—all these rather refined discriminations by the distance receptors of vision and hearing are organized as indices frequently associated with the unpleasant experience of anxiety, including the nipple of anxiety instead of the good nipple. As such indices, these discriminations, the organization of the data of these discriminations, become *signs of signs*—signs for other signs of avoidance, such as the nipple when the mother is anxious. So these discriminations by the distance receptors become signs of categories of signs, one might say, which so frequently follow that it suffices for the establishment of this relation. And signs of signs we call symbols. Thus while signals are rather simply related to behavior, symbols are more complexly related, in that they refer to sundry signals which affect behavior. And those symbols which we call forbidding gestures mean anxiety interfering with behavior in the satisfaction of a need.

To the mothering one, the heard crying of the infant is a sign that the infant is experiencing a need or is anxious. It signalizes the infant's generic need for tenderness, for some one or more of the sundry procedures required as cooperation in the satisfaction of the infant's needs or for the relief of his anxiety. The audible components of a whole series of different magic acts of the infant, his crying-when-hungry, crying-when-cold, and the like, evoke tender behavior of the mothering one and mean to her the infant's need for tenderness of one kind or another.

To be more exact about what the infant's crying is and does, one may say that his heard crying is physically a special pattern of sound waves which are emitted by his mouth and received by the mother's ears, and that this crying communicates the infant's need by, as we may say, being thus *interpreted* by the mother. The single generic meaning which might be phrased as 'baby needs tenderness' exists not 'in' the infant but 'in' the mother. This illustrates the relationship of a sign and its interpreter. In the language of Charles Morris, "any organism for which something is a sign will be called an *interpreter*." [5] The expression "organism

[5] [Charles Morris, *Signs, Language and Behavior*; New York: Prentice-Hall, Inc., 1946, p. 17.
Editors' note: At this point in the lecture, Sullivan added: "Incidentally, in my old age it is my unhappy fate that I can refer to nothing in the way of elaborate statements of views and ideas with which I find myself perfectly

for which" would be more suitably expressed, from my standpoint, as *organism 'in' which*. The sign interpretation evoked by experiencing the sign is educed by the experiencing organism from the present or actual encounter with the sign, on the basis of past and foreseen experience. Living with road signs, red and green lights, telephone bells, and the like makes it easy to overlook the absolute dependence of signs, as significant details of human experience, on the persons who thus interpret their encounters with the corresponding nonsignatory physical events.

Thus I would like to wean you somewhat from the very easy idea that a sign can exist irrespective of any organism to, for, or in which it is a sign. That is all right if you are trying to arrange automobile traffic on a chart, or by means of laws and statutes. But in developing a theory of personality you must remember that signs *are* signs only when there is an interpreter to attach meaning to a body of otherwise physical phenomena.

The infant acts to relieve a particular need, and the audible component of his act is experienced by the mother as a sign that he needs tender cooperation in satisfying some need, or for the relief of anxiety. Now as the infant's ability to prehend visible aspects of his surroundings grows, he comes to differentiate two signs in this connection: the sign of impending satisfaction (the appearance of and approach of the good mother), and the sign of trouble (the appearance of and approach of the bad mother). As the organization of his experience progresses, the infant comes to foresee that by his crying *in general* he will accomplish the appearance, approach, and satisfying cooperation of the good mother, or the appearance and distressing approach of the bad mother, in which latter eventuality, he will then cry to be rid of her and of her attendant anxiety.

Now here I am discussing how *any* crying of the very young infant is a sign to the mother, if she hears it, that the infant needs tenderness. From the infant's standpoint, as he gets his visual and auditory receptors into good working order by developmental

---

in harmony. I should have mentioned this before in quoting from my greatly esteemed late friend Sapir, as well as Cottrell and Benedict and others. I believe that many of you will find Morris' book very valuable in clarifying thought, although I have already expressed considerable difference with its beginning presentation."]

process in his organization, he begins to differentiate two signs of what is about to happen, namely, success or disaster; and as this progresses a little further he cannot fail—from mere frequency of instances, or absence of frequent negative instances—to notice that any crying he does brings either the sign of forthcoming satisfaction or relief, or the sign of the disaster of anxiety. So his crying can in a way now take on sign aspects, in that he is using it in, or it is fitting into, a pattern of adequate and appropriate behavior, which he observes. His own heard crying is coming to mean that he is experiencing a need and is acting to evoke the sign that satisfaction will follow, or perhaps the unwelcome sign of anxiety and increasing distress which calls for a different act of crying—crying to be rid of the bad mother. To the infant, the prehended— that is, primitively perceived—good mother is the symbol of forthcoming satisfaction; and the prehended bad mother is the symbol of anxiety and increasing distress. Generically, tender cooperation is meant by the good mother; urgently increased need for tenderness is meant by the bad mother and by the forbidding gestures which are gradually differentiated as her distinguishing perceived characteristics.

I have already attempted to indicate that there is no visual difference between a good and satisfactory nipple on the mother's breast and the same nipple when the mother is anxious. But so far as the infant's experience is concerned, these nipples are extremely different and call for entirely different treatment or behavior; and because they cannot readily be distinguished by vision, as in the case with some other things, there is, owing to the particular evolutionary history of the human animal, a distinct need to find some clues by which one can be oriented. Now I am using very adult language. If, to speak now of my puppies, their mother has one teat which is very large and also has a lot of black on it, whereas some nice handy teats are just pink, that makes it doubly simple for a puppy, when he can see, to recognize the unsatisfactory character of this large nipple, which is hard to hold although it is otherwise good. We are very strongly oriented by vision, when we can use it, that being a characteristic of the human animal beyond doubt. Where the visual sentience is grossly the same— but the objects concerned are terribly different, in that the one is a good thing and gives satisfaction, while the other is a minor disaster and must be avoided—under those circumstances, other clues are looked for. As I have said before, all this discussion of nipples applies, of course, a little later to the carriers of the nipple, the good and the bad mother, who, however, again are visually grossly identical. More refined discrimination is called for and becomes possible, including the discrimination of differences in the audible aspects of the good and the bad mother, as well as discriminations in the facial expression—that is, the results of postural tensions in the face—of the good and the bad mother. Now speaking objectively, which is charmingly simple and very apt to be misleading, we would say that the mother sounds and looks different when she is anxious from the way she sounds and looks when she is not anxious. These differences are the possible distance clues, we might say, to whether one has got what one wants or whether one has got the wrong thing, namely, the bad mother. This discrimination of good and bad mothers, like the discrimination of good and bad nipples, is, at this particular developmental period, just as real as is your discrimination of a person sitting next to you.[6]

[6] [*Editors' note:* In his 1948 lecture series, Sullivan developed this idea somewhat differently:

"Initially nothing like an extended visual grasp of the mother exists, although it unfolds fairly rapidly. So far as gross visual data are concerned, there is no particular difference between the good mother and the bad mother as a visual percept. There are, however, certain refined differences, but even before these become significant, other aspects of the distance contact with the mother have shown in all likelihood quite material refinements. Those that are associated with the good mother require no vast attention, but anything that gives warning of, or differentiates the bad mother—the source of anxiety—will, because of the extremely disagreeable nature of anxiety, get as much attention as can be given it. And the distance data in that field are heard data, vocal and tonal details, and so on.

"In particular, restrictions on the tonal scope of the voice probably are the first forbidding gestures that are built into the separate personification of the bad mother in contrast to her physically identical counterpart, the good mother. It is clear in dealing with domesticated animals, and it is certainly very clear in later phases of human life after infancy, that a great deal of what might be called 'the way the wind blows' is conveyed tonally; it has nothing in particular to do with verbal content, but is instead a matter of how verbal content is expressed, and the like. So the first forbidding gestures, and among the world's most dependable forbidding gestures that human beings ever differentiate in the interest of avoiding anxiety and pain,

I particularly want to note here that the forbidding gestures are, so to speak, pared or peeled off from the bad mother, and become occasional characteristics of an unspecified mother at a later stage of development; by that time these forbidding gestures, these audible and visible differences in the mother, are becoming signs in themselves of impending anxiety. This is a hint of how entities originally quite different to the infant—different because their functional significance is quite different, although we objectively say they are the same thing—are gradually fused in the infantile perception as the same or similar things. But that can happen only when there is a refinement of differentiation so that the infant is able to separate out the very important functional differences of the different nipples, for example, from his experience with the common carrier of the nipple.

I am here attempting to set before you a course of development based on what *must* be, to account for the useful and necessary things that are done by the infant. Even though many of us as adults spend most of our time doing things that seem, at least to our friends, utterly useless, nevertheless it is an extreme and, I believe, completely unjustifiable use of inference to reach a conclusion that the infant does a great many useless and troublesome things.

---

are undoubtedly changes in an accustomed voice. To the infant, in all likelihood, it is not a question of changes in a voice, but of two different accustomed voices. But from then on, there are few things more effective at changing the immediate integration of interpersonal situations than certain tonal tricks which come to us very, very naturally because they are, in a very real sense, the second oldest thing that has been very important in our experience with producing, hearing, and interpreting the voice."]

CHAPTER
6

Infancy: The Concept of
Dynamism—Part 2

The Integration, Resolution, and Disintegration
of Situations

WE SHALL now consider the infant's success or misfortune in bringing about the appearance, approach, and cooperation of the good mother in connection with the satisfaction of a need. To start again with the conception of euphoria disturbed by tension, it is evident that the recurrent tension of a physicochemical need— felt, say, as the need for food—may be considered as a tendency to bring about juncture of the good and satisfactory nipple and the infant's lips, which juncture is in turn a situation necessary for nursing behavior and the satisfaction of hunger. Since the nipple is a thing that is only there now and then, I shall turn that statement around, and say that the nipple-in-lips situation, originally evoked by crying-when-hungry, is the concatenation of events which is required for beginning and continuing nursing behavior until hunger and thirst shall have been satisfied.

Work—in physical terminology, not in the popular or personal sense—is done in effecting the nipple-in-lips situation, in maintaining it, and in remedying more-or-less accidental interruption of it until hunger is satisfied, whereupon the transformations of energy which make up this work cease. Now work, or transformations of energy, is actually functional activity, which is one of the three fundamentally important aspects of all living. We may say that the tension felt as hunger tends to *integrate* the nipple-in-lips situation and to maintain this integration of the nipple and the infant's mouth as long as the tension itself continues. Considering the infant's hunger and certain other needs as the generic need for tenderness to the extent that their satisfaction requires the cooperation of an older person, we may say that the sundry tensions underlying this need for tenderness generically tend to integrate, and to maintain the integration of, sundry interpersonal infant-mother situations which are manifestly necessary for the survival of the infant. From this standpoint, the satisfaction of a need is the ceasing of an integrating tendency to manifest itself in work.

I am now reviewing from a different standpoint all the elements, ideas, and facts which I have touched upon—needs and their satisfaction, signs and their meaning, and the whole story of the very early behavior of the infant beginning with the simplest thing, namely, the nipple-in-lips situation brought about from the infant's standpoint by crying-when-hungry—in order to shed more light on what I am presenting. Thus I say that from this standpoint of the interpersonal situation, we have to consider a tension, which includes the felt tension of a need, as a tendency to integrate a situation necessary and appropriate to the satisfaction of the need; and since the infant in the early months is practically wholly incapable of getting along without a mothering one, his needs manifest themselves, even from his very earliest activities, as tendencies to integrate particular types of necessary situations with the mothering one. And from this standpoint the satisfaction of a need, the relaxation of the tension underlying the felt aspects of a need, can be said to represent the ceasing, the ending, the temporary abeyance of an integrating tendency manifesting itself in the work of maintaining the interpersonal situation. The situation brought into being by the integrating tendency lapses with cessation of the work done in its maintenance; and since the situation was necessary and adequate for the satisfaction of a need, we may say that the satisfaction of this underlying need has *resolved* the related interpersonal situation. Now you will come presently to see why I talk of situations being resolved when there is no longer any integrating tendency to maintain them.

I have been discussing the tensions of needs from the standpoint of their being integrating tendencies, tendencies to integrate appropriate and necessary situations which happen to be interpersonal. Consider now the case in which the mother is or becomes anxious, thus inducing anxiety 'in' the infant. It is evident that anxiety generically tends to interfere with the integration of the interpersonal situation necessary for the satisfaction of a need, and that if anxiety appears at any time in the course of a situation toward resolution, it will tend to disintegrate any such situation. Now I make a careful distinction in using the term *resolution* of an interpersonal situation. It is something very different indeed from the *disintegrating* of that situation. When a situation resolves itself, it ceases to exist for the time being—and actually ceases to exist at all, because it will be a new situation when the same need integrates something very like it again. This resolution or ending of an interpersonal situation comes about by the relaxing of the tension of need, by the achieving of satisfaction of the need, whereas the situation may be prevented from being integrated, or may be disintegrated—torn apart—by the occurrence of anxiety. If anxiety comes, instead of a suitable object for integration, it makes 'impossible' the integrating of a suitable situation.

Let us assume, for example, that the infant is nursing away right merrily when something makes the mother notably anxious. That anxiety, as I have long since mentioned, immediately induces, in some fashion, anxiety in the infant. Then all sorts of difficulties occur, such as letting go of the nipple, cessation of search for the lost nipple, actually repelling the nipple if it is brought near the infant's lips, and even regurgitation instead of the swallowing of milk. Now there is an important fringe of behavior connected with nursing to which I have not previously referred; I shall hint at it by saying that in certain circumstances the infant may even, on the eventuality of anxiety, act as though he were being restrained when he is held in the necessary proximity to the breast so that the nipple can be invested. This may lead to the kind of miscellaneous activity, which can in a vague way be regarded as phylogenetically evolved, by which the infant escapes situations imperiling the oxygen supply.

Now, if we consider all that can follow on the occurrence of anxiety in the mother while the infant is nursing, we will have a better impression of the difference between the resolution of an interpersonal situation when, as it were, there is no earthly reason for its continuing, and the disintegration of that situation while there is still plenty of reason for its continuing. The fact is that the nipple of an anxious mother will still give milk, and that even though anxiety appears in the midst of nursing there is still a need for food; in other words, there is plenty of tension to keep up the nursing behavior, but the interpersonal situation is destroyed—it breaks up. Here is the difference between the disintegration of an interpersonal situation and its resolution by ceasing to have any rationale, any reason for existence, for the time being.

I have already discussed needs as integrating tendencies. I now invite attention to the fact that anxiety is a disjunctive or disintegrative tendency in interpersonal relations, which opposes the manifestation of any integrative tendency in the work of creating and maintaining an interpersonal situation; anxiety so modifies the transformations of energy making up the functional activity of the infant that work is now done to escape from, or to avoid, the interpersonal situation which corresponds to the significant need. Anxiety opposes the type of work which reflects the activity of an integrating tendency; anxiety opposes those transformations of energy which manifest themselves in the investing and holding of the nipple, in the sucking activity, in the transporting and swallowing, and in sundry accessory activities which I will deal with presently. All these things are, as I say, opposed by a disjunctive tendency, of which anxiety is the present outstanding instance before us. We shall see later that, so far as interpersonal relations are concerned, anxiety is almost always, but not quite always, an outstanding ingredient in breaking up interpersonal situations which otherwise would be useful in the satisfaction of the needs of the person concerned. It is evident that the eventuality of anxiety in no way relaxes the tension of need, but only opposes it.

If we think of a particular need as a tendency to integrate a situation in which activity is directed toward the goal of satisfactory resolution of the situation, we are considering a *vector* quality in the conception of integrating tendency. We can then picture anxiety as exactly opposed to the directional component of any need with the satisfaction of which it collides. I would like to remind you of the conception of vector, which might be defined as magnitude plus direction. Now the element of direction is the very significant thing in the conception of vector. My justification for talking about vectors at this time is that an interpersonal situation is not to be considered as something static, like, for example, the situation of objects on the table before me. Statics hasn't very much to do with living.

The interpersonal situation integrated by the infant's hunger plus the mother's need to express tenderness is characterized by a direction toward the goal of satisfying the infant's hunger, and the situation manifests this direction toward the goal by the fact that activity goes on which clearly achieves that goal. Now this directional element applies to the type of consideration of need which is implied by describing the need as an integrating tendency —that is, a tendency to bring about and maintain a situation, which in turn implies change toward the resolution of that situation, which happens, from another viewpoint, to coincide with the satisfaction of the need which started the whole business.

If you think of this direction of activity toward a goal, which is implied by the tension of need, then you can think of anxiety as exactly, that is, at 180 degrees, opposed to the vector quality of the need. If you think in terms of vector addition, as it is used in physical theory, you will remember that in the parallelogram of force, one vector goes off in one direction, and another goes in another direction, and the resultant vector is accurately depicted as the diagonal of the completed parallelogram. If you think in these terms, you will realize that anxiety—which complicates, by exact opposition, the manifestation of an integrating tendency in some particular direction—can mean only a *reduction* of, or a *reversal* of, the transformations of energy concerned in the action in the situation; that is, anxiety results in *less* activity toward the goal of satisfaction, or it results in activity *away* from the achievement of that goal. Anxiety added to, let us say, hunger during the nursing situation means therefore not that something new, a diagonal, comes out of these two things. Instead, the net result is either that, although nursing goes on, there is much *less* activity; or that something which is diametrically *opposed* to nursing, to the satisfaction of the need for hunger, occurs.

Now we will come later to many situations in life where two opposing vectors *do* add up to produce a third—where there is opposition to a certain type of activity, and, somewhat in accord with the physical pattern of the parallelogram of force, a new direction of the activity results. This new vector represents, from the physical standpoint, the discharge of both integrating tendencies, which occurs, however, by the integration of a *different* situation, in which action toward resolution, the achievement of a goal, is again evident. But in the very early situation where the infant is, at least for our purpose of discussion, activated by a single need—the need for food—the appearance of anxiety results, not in a new direction of activity, but in either a reduction of nursing activity, or in the complete disintegration and avoidance of a situation suitable for nursing. And this, as I have said, can be represented in physics by drawing two vector qualities 180 degrees apart, the resultant being either a reversal of motion that was previously present, or a very marked reduction in its acceleration. While this collision of a need, which may be thought of as an integrating tendency, with anxiety has but two possible outcomes from this standpoint—very much reduced velocity, you might say, or a reversal of direction—at the same time there is more tension now involved than was concerned in the need alone. In other words, vector considerations are perfectly all right to account for activity; but a much more intricate field, namely, tensor considerations, applies to the disturbances of euphoria which are, needless to say, much greater when two opposing tensions collide than when only one of them exists.

I have now begun to talk in terms familiar to the physicist—a course which I shall pursue somewhat further in discussing the terms, work and energy. You may recall that energy is sometimes defined as the capacity for doing work; or, more carefully, as that which diminishes when work is done, by an amount equal to the work done. You may be wondering whether I shall presently be considering something like a special "mental" energy. The answer to that question is this: Energy, when I mention it, is energy as conceived in physics, and as such has two basic forms—potential and kinetic. And work, as I use the term, is conceived in its physical meaning, not something you detest but have to do for a living.

I think that it might be useful to mention at this point one of the simplest illustrations of the discrimination of potential from kinetic energy in the realm of physics, since my use of the term, potential, in any of these discussions is pretty close to the physical meaning of the term. Imagine a simple pendulum, such as you can make by attaching a plumb bob or a watch or something or other to a string and tying the other end of the string to a nail so that the watch, plumb bob, or what not, is in free space, as it is called. If you then set it to swinging, you will find that at the end of its lateral motion it stops; for an instant it stands still. It swings in one direction, pauses instantaneously, and starts swinging back. All of the energy of the pendulum is potential at the moment of its fullest swing, when it is still; but if you should ever let such a pendulum hit you on the head, you would realize that there must have been quite a good deal of potential energy in it at that moment. So potential does not mean imaginary, or something of that kind, any more than electrical potential—which is another use of the same term—is imaginary, as putting your finger on a 33,000-volt circuit would clearly suggest to you by its consequences.

The Concept Itself: Background and Implications for Psychiatry

REVIEW OF TRIBUTARY CONCEPTS

By blend of the various considerations which I have now discussed I have arrived at the point of being able to set up—I hope with some clarity—an exceedingly important conception in this theory of psychiatry. This conception is the conception of dynamism, which is, I think, a vast improvement over the ancient idea of mental mechanisms and the like.

First I would like to review some of the conceptions we have discussed which play their parts in my conception of dynamism. We have held that any living organism may be considered in terms of three ultimate factors: its communal existence with a necessary environing medium; its organization; and its functional activity. We have said that man, the person, may be considered as an organism requiring in its necessary environing medium other persons, with whom functional activity occurs, and some part of the world of culture which is implicit in personality, and which becomes organized in the person himself.

We have introduced as fundamental terms in the analysis thus far the concepts of experience, of euphoria, and of recurrent tensions of two kinds, tensions of need and tensions of anxiety, with some mention of a third kind of tension which we will discuss *in extenso* later—tensions of sleep. We have discussed these recurrent tensions as manifest in awareness as felt components, and, in relation to the environing medium, as integrating or disjunctive tendencies with respect to situations in which activity—that is, behavior—addressed to the satisfaction of needs can occur. We have indicated that the relaxation of tensions, with the relief—that is, satisfaction—of their felt components requires, in the early phases of postnatal life, tender cooperation, additional to the behavior of the infant in crying-when-hungry, crying-when-cold, and the like. We have generalized the infant's needs as those for oxygen; for water; for foodstuffs; for body temperature; and, more vaguely, for bodily integrity and freedom, and adequate physiological process, these latter perhaps being susceptible to statement as the need to be free of pain and the need to be free of restraint of bodily movement. We digressed at this point to consider the fact that delayed relaxation of naturally increasing tension, which endangers life, is attended by the appearance of the felt tension of fear, which has its particular type of crying, crying-when-afraid; and that this tension of fear could reach a maximum with the felt component called terror and activity of the sort which later in life would appropriately be called rage behavior.

We have indicated that, since the satisfaction of all the infant's needs requires tender cooperation of another, all of them may be considered as implying, at the interpersonal level, a need for tenderness. But the satisfaction of this need for tenderness, and the concurrent satisfaction of the particular tension primarily concerned, is definitely interfered with by anxiety. We have considered in some detail the relation of the infant's crying to the occurrence of tender cooperation necessary for the satisfaction of the infant's needs, and subsequently, the breathing and nursing activities, which, as it were, begin in and around the mouth. This introduced us to the conception of the zone of interaction in the communal existence of the infant with environments physicochemical and interpersonal, with particular emphasis on the oral zone, including the hearing of the infant's audible productions. The meaning of the infant's perhaps 'objectively' identical crying-when-hungry, crying-when-cold, and the like, was mentioned; all of the infant's crying communicates to the mother the infant's need for tenderness, but has no such initial general meaning to the infant, as these various forms of crying are experienced by him. That is, in the infant's experience, his various types of crying initially have no general meaning of a need for tenderness, although they all mean that to the mother.

I have said that we have considerable reason for believing that experience in its simplest, least elaborate form—that is, prototaxic experience of some momentary state of the organism—carries, as an inevitable feature of the experience itself, indication of the zone of interaction where whatever was experienced has impinged; thus, experience from the lips is definitely marked with its origin in that area and is inherently different from experience from the fingertip. Prototaxic experience is, in a way, an enduring record of the total state of the organism, including the impinging events, or rather their effects on the zone of interaction impinged with.

We then considered a number of practically inevitable eventualities in the infant's early nursing behavior, and inferred from a number of these something of their meaning in the development of the infant's experience of living. From this came a consideration of the very important conception of signs in their two basic types: the signal and the symbol, the latter being a sign of other signs, or of whole categories of signs. In addition to the previously suggested signal character of crying-when-hungry, crying-when-cold, and the like, as heard and otherwise experienced by the infant, we inferred the occurrence of four different signals which must evolve from experience of the nipple in conjunction with the lips—or, in the case of the fourth signal, in forceful disjunction with the lips; these four signals are the good and satisfactory nipple-in-lips, the good but unsatisfactory nipple-in-lips, the wrong nipple-in-lips, and the evil nipple-in-lips. The differentiation of signs of other signs or categories of signs—that is, symbols—was illustrated by reference to the early prehension of the good mother and her anxiety-evoking counterpart, the bad mother, with subsequent differentiation of the forbidding gestures which significantly characterize her.

We stressed at this point the basic relationship of a sign and the possessor or interpreter of the sign, warning against the error of objectifying the observable characteristics of anything as identical with, or necessarily related to, its signatory reality as a particular pattern in the infant's, or other organism's, experience of events. In this connection you may recall my comment about road signs, which objectively are pieces of tin on stakes, presenting patterns of reflection, but which are seen by the eye as patterns to which meaning is attached, particularly if your previous experience has included learning to drive a car and to avoid the police in so doing. The piece of tin on a stake which is stuck along the road is a sign in the police sense, but that piece of tin on a stake, and the letters on it, is a sign in our sense only insofar as it evokes its appropriate meaning in the person who perceives it. The *person* has the sign.

This point of the relationship of sign and the interpreter of the sign was developed by reviewing the communication to the mother of the infant's need for tenderness by the audible components of several different actions of the infant, which are experienced by him as behavior in the satisfaction of several needs, and for the relief of anxiety—and which are only presently to be generalized by him as evoking the good mother, or exorcising the bad mother when she unfortunately is 'produced' by crying or other activities. The nipple-in-lips was then considered from the standpoint of its constituting a situation necessary for the occurrence of nursing behavior and the satisfaction of hunger and thirst, the tension of which underlying needs could be conceptualized as recurrent forces which integrate these necessary, actually interpersonal, situations, and which perform work in maintaining them for the duration of their recurrent utility. We then reviewed anxiety from this dynamic standpoint and saw that it is not an integrating tendency, but a disjunctive one which, when coincident, exactly opposes, in the vector sense, the force of any integrative need.

Having thus come to a useful statement in the realm of the transformation of physical energy, which is the only kind of energy

I know, and the vector characteristics of two of the three genera of basic tensions (sleep not yet concerning us), I shall proceed now to a statement of the concept of dynamism.

STATEMENT OF THE CONCEPT OF DYNAMISM

Let me begin by saying that the present view of the universe, as held by a great majority of mathematicians, physicists, and other scientists, makes the discoverable world a dynamism. This is implied in the fundamental postulate that the ultimate reality in the universe is energy, that all material objects are manifestations of energy, and that all activity represents the dynamic or kinetic aspect of energy. A doctrine in which force and the conception of energy—which underlies the conception of force—is the ultimate conception or postulate would naturally be a conception of dynamism, a dynamism of the universe. Whitehead, among the philosophers, has conceived the universe as an organism,[1] and certainly there is no difficulty in seeing living organisms as particular dynamisms. Living organisms are often multicellular organizations, and the sundry kinds of living cells which in a sense compose the organism are themselves usefully conceived as dynamisms, or as subdynamisms, one might call them, which are dynamically regulated in their living in accordance with the living of the organism as a whole. Malignancies, the sarcomatous and the carcinomatous evils which befall some organisms, may be regarded as instances of the escape from such dynamic regulation of some cells of the organism which, because they have escaped this regulation, become capable of destructively independent living. They become, as it were, destructively independent dynamisms, which invade the regulated cellular structure and organization of the host organism, or the host dynamism. The unnumbered subdynamisms, the individual cells, are organized into numerous systems of dynamisms such as the kidneys, the excretory-secretory structures of the intestines, the lungs, the heart, the blood, and what not; these systems of cellular dynamisms are in turn integrated into the total dyna-

[1] [*Editors' note:* See Alfred North Whitehead, *Process and Reality;* New York: The Macmillan Company, 1929. Whitehead states, "This doctrine of organism is the attempt to describe the world as a process of generation of individual actual entities, each with its own absolute self-attainment" (p. 94), and earlier, "An actual entity is a process, and is not describable in terms of the morphology of a 'stuff'" (p. 65).]

mism of the organism so that the whole thing makes up a vast unitary system, as it may be called from the standpoint of unregenerated biology. This total dynamism of the organism cannot, however, be separated from its necessary environmental milieu without ceasing to be a living organism.

This consideration of the organism as a dynamism and made up of subdynamisms is, to some extent, illustrated by the fact that the cornea of the eye, and even the heart and other organs, can in many cases go on manifesting living, and can be perfectly capable of transplantation elsewhere without dying, even though the carrying organism has died. Thus, the major, the total dynamism, may come to an end, but some of the subsidiary dynamisms making up, in a very dynamic sense, this totality do not necessarily expire immediately.

In general, we can say that the ultimate entities usefully abstracted in the study of the morphology, or organization, of living organisms is this living dynamism, the cell. Similarly, the ultimate entity, the smallest useful abstraction, which can be employed in the study of the functional activity of the living organism is the *dynamism* itself, *the relatively enduring pattern of energy transformations which recurrently characterize the organism in its duration as a living organism.* That is perhaps the most general statement that I can make about the conception of dynamism; it reaches far beyond the realm of psychiatry, certainly throughout the realm of biology, perhaps in the thinking of some people much further. The sundry dynamisms of interest to the biologist are all concerned with energy transformations making up functional activity in the communal existence of the organism with its necessary environment, through factors of its organization. The dynamisms of interest to the psychiatrist are the relatively enduring patterns of energy transformation which recurrently characterize the interpersonal relations—the functional interplay of persons and personifications, personal signs, personal abstractions, and personal attributions—which make up the distinctively human sort of being.

THE DEFINITION OF PATTERN

I spoke, just now, of *relatively enduring patterns*, and since this term will be repeated time and again in this presentation, it may be well at this point to say a few words about the word *pattern* itself. I shall give you a definition of pattern for which I believe I am the sole authority, a situation which always awakens very great suspicion on my part. *A pattern is the envelope of insignificant particular differences.* Taxonomy, the science of classification, which is particularly important in the biological field, deals chiefly with patterns. A particular fruit may properly be called an orange if the differences in characteristics of the specimen under consideration do not, when compared with the defined ideal orange, differ in a significant degree from the defined characteristics: size, shape, verrucosity or wartiness of the skin, surface reflectance of light waves, and even such morphological details as septation—that is, how many parts it is divided into by septa in the pulp—thickness of the rind, and number and viability of contained seeds. Yet all these may vary within fairly wide limits and still their variation, or any combination of variations, does not significantly extend beyond the defined pattern, orange. Physicochemical characteristics which underlie the taste of the fruit and the smell of the fruit have a place in the pattern of its characteristics; these too may vary considerably, and you still have an orange. But *significant* variation in some of these characteristics—that is, variation which goes beyond the pattern, orange—makes the specimen under consideration some other member of the botanical world, such as a lemon or a kumquat.

Another example of insignificant particular differences may be found in the realm of hearing, which is exceedingly rich in patterns. For instance, Mozart's Quartet in F Major is experienced as that particular pattern of music despite many errors which may be made in a particular performance of it, and despite the fact that the instruments may not be very well tuned, or may, in fact, be rather strikingly out of tune. The Quartet in F Major is a pattern of musical experience, and as such can exist in spite of a good many insignificant variations in a particular performance. But the experience of these variations may become more pronounced as the result of that peculiar misuse of human ingenuity called "swinging" the classical compositions; even here one can sometimes recognize the musical pattern of a beloved masterpiece, although the current atrocity may have varied from the pattern to a point where it is not, in any musically significant sense, the masterpiece, but is a vulgarism somewhat related to it. Now here is an instance where, in my opinion, the changes deliberately introduced by the re-composer have in a very significant way destroyed that which existed before, so altered its pattern that it is ridiculous to call it what an earlier composer did. But even under these circumstances, subpatterns in the masterpiece will often stand out so vividly that they evoke a recollection of the pattern as a whole, and it suddenly dawns on us, if we have not been warned in advance, that the dubious aesthetic pleasure that we are undergoing is someone's tortured revision of some particular composition.

Heard language is entirely a matter of sound patterns. The phonemes out of which spoken words are composed or compounded are patterns of sound which do not differ too much from a culturally defined mean. The sounds out of which we build up our English words, for example, are a certain set of culturally defined areas in the continuum of possible sound variation, which can be conceived to have a certain mean which could be determined by research as, I suppose, the statistically most common area of sound that speakers of that particular phoneme in English used. But in the continuum of sound one can get a considerable distance away from this mean without causing the average hearer any difficulty whatever in spotting exactly what phoneme you were using. Culture establishes what areas of this continuum of audible sound shall be a phoneme of a particular language, and if I knew all about the phonemes of all the languages, now used or unearthed from the past, I wouldn't be vastly surprised to discover that an indefinitely large number of articulated sounds have been utilized in the establishment of the patterns which make up the phonemes of one language or another.

Not only are phonemes sound patterns approximating a culturally established norm, but words themselves are patterns of phonemes which adequately approximate a culturally established pattern. For example, I suppose many of you have a certain amount of appreciation, if not respect, for the word psychiatry, but I wonder how many of you are equal to "ps-heeatrea." [2] My venerated colleague, Adolf Meyer, during a visit with a European colleague, caught on to the fact that when this man, who spoke

[2] [Editors' note: This is a phonetic approximation of the Greek ψυχιατρεια.]

excellent English, spoke of "ps-heeatrea" he was referring to their common preoccupation. The joy that the old man had in this correct pronunciation of a word derived from the Greek fixed this example of a variation in word pattern in my mind.

I am harping on this to invite your attention to the great significance of the pattern of phonemal succession, and the stressing of some part of this pattern, which together make up the word. And incidentally, words, contrary to naive impressions, do not exist in dictionaries, any more than road signs exist by the side of the road. A word—that is, a word per se rather than a symbol of a word—exists, like a sign, in them that have it. Since these words are acquired by hearing them, in finding that one can imitate them, and so on, they prove to be fantastically useful in producing the illusion, at least, of communication; and in some cases —and particularly, I hope, in the present case—communication by words is not too bad. But it is patterns of sound, stress, and so on that make up the words.

It is quite probable that an acoustical recording would show your pronunciation of any word relatively commonly used in your speech to be quite different in the morning, once you have fully wakened from sleep and are feeling very fresh and energetic, from your pronunciation of that same word late in the evening, when you are much in need of sleep and are feeling fairly fatigued, if not somewhat alcoholic. These acoustically recordable sounds that you emit in saying commonplace words would be astonishingly different in the details which can be recorded by the use of physical apparatus. Yet, unless fatigue was quite extreme, or the alcoholism was marked enough to interfere with the fine movements of your throat and mouth, these pronunciations, different as they were, would sound no different whatever to you, and would be equally and precisely of the same intelligibility to the hearer. Of course, it is possible for fatigue to be sufficient to seriously impair the production of words, so that their articulation would be considered defective, and their intelligibility impaired; this happens when the words, or the syllables, or even the phonemes, especially in the case of a person who originally learned some other language, cease to fall within the limits of insignificant variation.

From this very long discussion of taxonomy, music, and words, I trust that you see that there is something, at least, in my defining a pattern as the envelope—the limit in a tridimensional or multidimensional sense—of insignificant particular differences. As long as the congeries of particular differences is insignificant, then whatever is being discussed fits the pattern, which pattern, you might say, gives it its meaning, its authenticity, or its identity.

DYNAMISMS IN PSYCHIATRY

Organisms begin by reproduction; grow; mature; resist, or repair the damage caused by, some of the noxious influences which they encounter; reproduce themselves; and, in the higher manifestations of life at least, degenerate and come to an end in death. The patterns of energy transformation which characterize their life span are only *relatively* enduring. These patterns appear, in the higher forms of life at least, by maturation; they are changed variously by growth and by favorable or unfavorable influences; and perhaps in no two recurrent manifestations are they identical in all discoverable particulars. The dynamisms which interest us are relatively enduring patterns which manifest, in some cases at least, postnatal origin by maturation, and in all cases change by experience in the occurrence of which they are a significant factor. To put this very crudely, we might say that dynamisms grow or degenerate as a result of their recurrent manifestations, but that is really a pretty mystical idea. We can be more sure of what we are talking about when we say that dynamisms are modified by experience, which has in a significant sense been brought about by their manifestation.

The thing I particularly want to emphasize about dynamisms at this point is that their manifestation in the living of the organism is, in the sense that we originally used the term, *experience* of the organism. And in a sense which will later become a little clearer, this experience of the organism is particularly related to the manifestation of the particular dynamism at work and is striking, although the change in the dynamism is insignificant from the standpoint of a pattern. It will presently appear that while these changes are insignificant so far as the pattern is concerned, they can be very significant so far as living is concerned. I reiterate this notion of a pattern to emphasize the idea that a conception such as pattern can remain valid, even though, in a long stretch of duration, the objectively observable manifestations may be quite different.

We have commented somewhat on the growth of the infant's experience by the differentiation, from the general flux of his prototaxic experience, of particular useful patterns of sentience, which is the crude stuff of perception. These patterns, which I call signs, soon come in most instances to generalize various items of experience, marked or colored by various zones of interaction. To explain further: While a given experience in the early infant is not ordinarily marked by more than one zone of interaction— although sometimes it may be—the signs come quite frequently to generalize various experiences marked, respectively, by various zones. This generalizing of experiences marked by various zones, often including vision and hearing, becomes experience in the parataxic mode. For example, when sentience arising from vision and hearing is, in a certain sense, combined with experience arising, let us say, in the tactile or thermal perceptive or kinesthetic organs of sentience around the lips, then we have an elaboration of experience which extends beyond what is meant by prototaxic experience— the earliest type of experience—and is, in fact, experience in the parataxic mode. The "usefulness" of the earliest signs resides in their facilitating the satisfaction of needs, which they accomplish by functioning in recall and foresight. These signs modify the integrating tendency responsible for their occurrence in the subsequent integrating and maintenance of particular interpersonal situations; and these situations include the activity toward satisfaction which is implied in the conception of a situation integrated by an integrating tendency.

The dynamisms of particular interest to psychiatry are of two genera: those conceptualized with primary reference to the sundry recurring tensions which manifest themselves as integrating, disjunctive, and isolating tendencies; and, on the other hand, those conceptualized with primary reference to the energy transformations characteristic of particular zones of interaction. Dynamisms of the first kind will be exemplified in our subsequent consideration, for example, of *fear;* of the anti-anxiety system which is called the *self-system*—the system involved in the maintenance of felt interpersonal security; and of *lust*, which is my particular term for certain tensions of or pertaining to the genitals, and which has an excellent historical background. Dynamisms of the second kind will be exemplified in the discussion of, for example, the *oral dynamism*. Any observable behavior may be said to manifest concomitant activity of dynamisms of both sorts, as does the phasic change in awareness concerned in sleep.

I have already stressed the pattern element of dynamism, and the fact that a dynamism is a relatively enduring pattern of energy transformation. I have attempted to hint that even though such a pattern is relatively enduring, there is nothing static about it, but that change, however insignificant, is brought about by each recurrent manifestation in living of this recurrent pattern. I have tried to get at how this change in a dynamism—its growth or degeneration, if you please—can be conceptualized. I have talked about the very early signs educed by the infant in connection with the infant's living, and have shown that these signs are "useful" in that their function in recall and foresight facilitates, makes easier, hastens (depending on what the significant criterion is) the integration of situations in which an underlying need can be satisfied. Thus I have hinted that dynamisms can and do 'include' (I am dubious about this use of a geographical word) signs and symbols, and I have attempted to give you some notion of how the accumulation of signs, the elaboration of experience into signs, facilitates life and also affects the dynamisms concerned.

I have brought forward for your consideration two grand divisions, two genera, of dynamisms that are useful conceptions. One conceives the dynamism with primary reference to the tensions which recurrently disturb the euphoria of the living creature and manifest themselves in interpersonal relations as integrating, disjunctive, or isolative tendencies of a particular sort. The second concept of the dynamism, which is equally important, is on the basis of primary reference to the energy-transformation characteristics of particular zones of interaction. We shall consider these dynamisms further as we go along.

CHAPTER 7

Infancy: Interpersonal Situations

The Concept of Personality

WE SHALL now extend somewhat our consideration of the communal existence of the human being with the necessary environments—the physicochemical environment, the environment of infrahuman living, and the environment of other people. The concept of zones of interaction as end stations in this interaction or interpenetration has already been indicated at the start of our consideration of the concept of dynamism, and we may now say further of these zones of interaction that they may be conceived, in part, as molar physiological structures, in which there occur transformations of energy specifically concerned with the functional activity of the organism in maintaining its necessary communal existence. But these structures are structures in the activity of which there arises specific experience of the organism, always in the prototaxic mode, although it is sometimes elaborated, as, for instance, in the occurrence of signs. This experience in turn influences the subsequent manifestations of the integrating tendencies concerned in the particular functional activity, and thus introduces factors of recall and foresight, of functional history and adaptation to a foreseen goal, which is commonly meant by anticipation. These factors of recall and foresight, of functional history and adaptation to a foreseen goal, can scarcely be called details of physiological structure; but they are, nonetheless, certainly important details of the actual organism as it goes on living, and, when the organism concerned is a human being, we call them details of personality. In the present particularist sense, when we are talking as if the infant were a complete discrete entity, *personality is the*

relatively enduring pattern of recurrent interpersonal situations
which characterize a human life.

The concept of *interpersonal situation* necessary for the occurrence of activity in the satisfaction of a need is of fundamental
importance in psychiatric theory. The nipple-in-lips, our first
example of such an interpersonal situation, is integrated and maintained by the infant's need for water and food and the mother's
need to give tenderness in this connection. The infant's oral zone of
interaction and, generally, the mother's mammary zone of interaction are the details of the two personalities which are principally
concerned in the integration of this nipple-in-lips situation. The
infant's experience of the relevant oral behavior, and the mother's
experience of nursing the infant are just as significantly a part of
any particular nursing situation as are the physiological structures
which are involved. In the ever-expanding world of the infant, it
comes to be the nipple, which is a discernible characteristic of the
good mother, with which he is orally integrated. In the world of
the mother, it is the lips of the more-or-less personified particular
infant with which her nipple is invested. The infant's personification of the good mother is the prehended pattern of her participation in recurrent nursing situations and integrations of other
needful sorts which have been resolved by satisfaction. She—the
infant's personification of the good mother—symbolizes forthcoming satisfaction of the sundry needs—that is, she symbolizes in
turn the integration, maintenance, and resolution of situations that
include her, through appropriate and adequate activity on the infant's part.

The Organization of Personifications

In what I have just said, I have introduced the idea of *personification*, which derives its importance from the fundamental
importance of the interpersonal situation in understanding the phenomena with which psychiatry deals. Here, in discussing the personification of the good mother, which is formed early in infancy,
we start out on the long course of attempting to understand personifications and their dynamic role. As I have said, the infant's
personification of the good mother is the pattern that he in a primitive way perceives as the pattern of her participation in recurrent

nursing situations and other sorts of integrations called into being by his needs, which situations have been resolved with satisfaction. Foresight, as I have said before, pertains to that which has happened, and foresight about the good mother pertains to things that have gone well. Thus the infant's personification of the good mother symbolizes the forthcoming satisfaction of the sundry needs, or, to say the same thing in a different way, symbolizes the integration, maintenance, and resolution of the situations that are necessary for the infant's appropriate and adequate action in satisfaction of his needs.

Now this personification is not the 'real' mother—a particular living being considered as an entity. It is an elaborate organization of the infant's experience. The mother's personification of the infant is not the infant, but a growing organization of experience 'in' the mother, which includes many factors only remotely pertaining to dealing with this particular 'real' infant. It is important to understand that the infant's personification of the mother is composed of, or made up from, or organized from, or elaborated out of, what has occurred in the infant's relation to what you might call the 'real' mother in satisfaction-giving integrations with her. And the mother's personification of the infant—which was sometimes rather rudimentary in the days when it was thought that the soul joined the infant at the age of seven months or so, before which I presume the infant could be called *it* instead of *he* or *she*—is not the infant and is not merely an abstract of the events that the mother has encountered when integrated with the infant; it includes also much that is only remotely related to dealing with this particular baby. The mother's personification of "her" infant, may, if he be her seventh offspring, have much less to do with experience with this infant than with the first and second of her babies. Her previous experience, in any case, would influence her experience arising in sundry dealings with this particular baby. The mother's personification of the infant includes experience when the infant is anxious as well as when he is not. It includes experience when the infant is sleeping as well as when he is awake. It includes the observation of growth changes in the infant, and a perhaps richly formulated expectation of changes yet to come. That which the personified infant signifies to or symbolizes 'in' the mother is clearly more than forthcoming satisfaction of the need to give tenderness, or to participate in the integration, maintenance, and resolution of situations integrated by the infant's immediate needs.

The mother is, as we say, a carrier of social responsibilities with respect to her child. Part of what he symbolizes to her is her recognition of these responsibilities. What these responsibilities are varies somewhat from one family group to another in any particular community, or in any particular culture area. The degree to which these social responsibilities are effectively discharged may vary greatly in the same mother with respect to different children and with respect to the same child at different times. That these responsibilities will have no effect on the rearing of the child is, if not inconceivable, at least extremely improbable. Thus when I speak of the factors which are only remotely related to dealing with the particular 'real' infant, but which nonetheless enter into and are a part of the mother's personification of the infant, I include the very extensive, very important element of the mother's responsibility to the social order of which she is a member or in which she has a part. The recognized social responsibilities which the personified infant symbolizes for the mother have something— often a great deal—to do with the situations in which the infant prehends the bad mother, and out of his experience in such situations he organizes his personification of the bad mother.

Anxiety, as a phenomenon of relatively adult life, can often be explained plausibly as anticipated unfavorable appraisal of one's current activity by someone whose opinion is significant. When it is apparent that someone is anxious in talking with us, we might ask, "What would I think were you to speak freely what is in your mind?" And very often the other person might say, "You would think less of me," or "You would be shocked at me," or something of the sort. Now that is a typical rationalization of anxiety. By rationalization we mean giving a plausible and often exceedingly inconsequential explanation. And so I say that anxiety in relatively adult people can often be explained plausibly as anticipated unfavorable appraisal of one's current activity. A mother loaded with these social responsibilities which inhere in her from her membership in a social group may come to expect criticism of her mothering activities by her husband, his mother or sister, her mother or sister, the nurse, or anyone else who observes her handling of the baby. In many instances this known or presumed disapproval, this real or fancied faultfinding with respect to her care for her offspring makes her anxious. Unless, for instance, I have very considerable and well-founded esteem for something that I do, another person's criticism of what I do, or even the suspicion that the other person feels critical toward me for what I do, is tantamount to my being anxious. Therefore, unless the mother is very clear on the social responsibilities she is undertaking to discharge, certain that she is doing at least an averagely good job at it, and clear on the reasons why other people might differ about it and criticize her for it, any criticism of her handling of the baby, any suspected critical attitude toward her handling of the baby, is apt to make her anxious. And when you remember that anxiety in the mother induces anxiety in the infant, you will understand that the induced anxiety of the infant makes him more difficult and worrisome to care for, so that his behavior may seem to justify disparagement of the mother's work with him.

The implications of this sort of vicious circle underlie the psychiatrist's interest in the dynamic composition of the family group in which a patient's infancy was spent. When I was a young psychiatrist attending conferences of very capable staff members, I would hear accounts of mental patients which sometimes went back to the great-grandparents of the patient. These accounts included details about which ones of the ascendants had gone to mental hospitals, and which ones had gone to jails, and which ones had gone to posts on university staffs, and so on. And it all ended rather nicely in a woman who married a man and bore this patient, and had a difficult or an easy labor. And the infant had or had not had a feeding difficulty (that preoccupation didn't show up when I was such a young psychiatrist, but shortly afterward), and then after a while the infant learned to walk and talk and cease to wet himself. And presently all this wonderful array of rumor and data evolved into his being before us as a mental patient. In subsequent years we got more and more interested in doing something for this mental patient so that he might cease to be a mental patient and become a member of society, to his chagrin or delight as the case might be. And then we found that we could omit the study of a good deal of this inscrutably complex heredity—about which, at best, the patient would probably have very few useful views—because out of all the rumor and data there was very little which would help us to find out why he had curiously distorted views on a good many people in his environment. Eventually we got to the point of guessing that anxiety had a lot to do with the patient's problems. But then the question was how to explain the peculiarities of anxiety. And it is from experience with the difficulties in this work of cure or treatment—a much more satisfactory concern than the mere chronicling of the patient's family history—that we finally got back to studying the development of the anti-anxiety system in human personality. Now in this presentation I am attempting to suggest how anxiety begins—what factors are influential in the beginning of anxiety in the natural history of a given person. It reaches back very, very far, and this is the reason why it is important to know the composition of the family group in which the infant spent his first months.

Consideration of the composition of the family group may indicate that persons other than the mother have exerted great influence on the earliest phase of developmental history, long before these other persons enter into significant, direct, interpersonal relations with the infant. Moreover, in a good many instances some person other than the mother does have recurring, significant, direct, interpersonal relations with even the young infant. Occasionally there is a so-called wet nurse, and not infrequently there is a nurse or an older sister who does part of the work of caring for the infant's needs in situations integrated by the nurse or sister. Any such surrogates in the mothering function also personify the infant to some extent, and these personifications of the infant include as important factors the surrogate's experience and expectations with regard to infants as a class and this infant in particular.

It may be that one of these surrogates in the mothering function will have come to manifest the peculiar expectations with respect to others to which I shall presently refer as *malevolence*. This malevolent person may behave toward the infant in ways quite other than giving tender cooperation in satisfying the infant's manifest needs; she may instead hurt and otherwise provoke fear in the infant. Since the malevolent behavior is also apt to be accompanied by anxiety and to induce anxiety in the infant, the infant's prehensions of such a surrogate come to be organized as experience of the bad mother. Let us take, for example, the situation of our mother with seven children of which the seventh is the baby now under discussion. Let us suppose that the first-born and the second-born were girls and that the first-born girl, after a fashion not uncommon in eldest children, is very difficult and is out of the house a good deal. The second-born girl is mother's helper, has had plenty to do, has felt very much rebuffed and neglected for years, and has come to be mischievous, as her aunt might call it. And now with the arrival of the seventh baby, mother's helper takes over a good part of the absolutely necessary relatively adult cooperation in looking after the baby. Now that will not include giving the baby pap, but it may certainly include keeping the baby covered, and changing the diapers, and so on. Insofar as mother's helper is malevolent—something that we will come to understand presently —the tenderness theorem will not apply in simple fashion to her dealings with the baby. And frequently or occasionally, in looking after the infant's needs, mother's helper will be rough, sound unpleasant, hurt the baby, and generally discompose him. But she will not do these things with a feeling of complete sweetness and light, because mother's helper will know quite clearly that if any of these minor atrocities to the infant were observed by mother or by someone else who told mother about them, mother's helper would get her ears boxed, or something of that kind. Now the anticipation by mother's helper of possible retribution for these little mischievous acts toward the baby is, in a sense that will presently become clear, tantamount to her being anxious as well as malicious. Under those circumstances, what the baby gets in the way of experience includes anxiety as well as fear, and that experience is, very early in infancy, the same experience that the infant has in his relation to his mother when she is anxious; therefore all such experience is organized in the rudimentary infantile personification of the bad mother. When compelling circumstances necessitate the delegation of an important part of the mothering to a malevolent surrogate, some considerable number of the infant's contacts with the mother are also apt to involve anxiety, for she can scarcely "be at peace with herself" about the mothering which her baby is receiving. There thus come to be two or more persons who recurrently induce anxiety in the infant, his prehensions of whom are organized in a single early personification of the bad mother.

It is also evident that a surrogate in part of the mothering function may be both tender and relatively free from anxiety, as may be the mother herself. In this case the infant organizes prehensions of two or more people in his earliest personification of the good mother. And in such cases, where the mother has a very good mother's helper—good in the sense of having no serious interference with the manifestation of tenderness toward the baby—then the mother will be reasonably comfortable about the mothering which her baby is receiving, and both the mother and her helper will be relatively free from anxiety. Therefore, when one or the other of these people is with the infant, the infant will have considerable experience of tender cooperation in the satisfaction of his needs and relatively little experience of anxiety. Under those circumstances, at the very start of the personifying process in early infancy there is a personification of the good mother in which the experience (from our point of view) comes from experiences with two people, but is not so differentiated by the infant.

These two of several not too uncommon instances should suffice to indicate the possible complexity of the infant's beginnings of personification, out of which beginnings will evolve his sequential personifications of the significant people who are visually and audibly differentiable within the flux of his experience. I have hinted several times thus far that as the data from the visual and the hearing receptors grow in utility in foreseeing and integrating satisfaction-giving situations, and in foreseeing and avoiding anxiety-provoking situations, differences in the persons concerned tend to appear. I have not yet said so, but I presume that differences in 'actual' persons associated with anxiety are noted by the infant before he notes differences in people involved in his getting satisfactions; the reason for this is the extremely undesirable character of anxiety and the importance of getting away from it. Perhaps in middle infancy or toward the latter part of infancy, as the infant progresses to the point where this distance data—data obtained by sight and by hearing—begins to be differentiated, its differentiation with respect to people who make the infant anxious (the mother, or the mother and a malevolent mother's helper) is on the basis of characteristics which are identical in kind, in functional significance, with those which we later call *forbidding gestures*. These forbidding gestures consist of tonal and other modifications of speech, and differences in facial posture and so on, of the mothering one.

Now I have emphasized in my two examples, first, of an anxious mother and a malevolent mother's helper, and, second, of a calm and tender mother and mother's helper, that since experience objectively related to two people may be combined in the infant's beginning personification of the bad mother, or of the good mother, this personification might be called *complex*. From our standpoint, it is complex in that it has one personification for characteristics that we would attribute objectively to two people. The meaning of this complexity deserves more than passing consideration. There is no reason for supposing that "useless" signs are organized within the infant's experience. The organization into one sign of experience with two people who regard themselves as distinct is an early instance of an exceedingly important ability which is by no means restricted to man alone in the biological series. And this organization into one sign of experience with two (to themselves) different people is *anything but* an instance of an unfortunate something which one might call "confusion." To think that the infant "confuses," in one rudimentary personification, details of his experience with two people, the mother and the surrogate, is literally to foreclose any possibility of understanding personality development. On the contrary, the infant differentiates experience arising in his encounters with one (from our point of view) identical person in organizing two rudimentary personifications, those of the good and the bad mother.

Some of you may wonder how I know this—in other words, what higher source of information I have as to what the infant of, let us say, less than the age of six months experiences. I only hope that you have been patient in your anticipation, strong in the belief that perhaps I would eventually give you a clue, which I will now attempt to do.

The probable correctness of this particular inference—that the infant differentiates his experience with a 'real' mother into two personifications, that of the good mother and that of the bad mother—is suggested by the course of developmental events in which we can participate with increasing sureness from late in infancy onward. In other words, from later data—the implication of which is quite certain—I make inferences regarding what can be observed in the young infant that seems closely and logically related to these later data, even though the actual events at this early stage are beyond participant observation, and therefore beyond a type of knowledge which is very convenient to have. It may seem that such use of inference is dangerous or even bad, but it would be exceedingly difficult to explore any new field if one did not use inference which extended from what is reasonably certain, both as to datum and implication, into the unexplored periphery of the new field. And so, in setting up this doctrine of the very earliest events in personification, I have to extend inference from what can be participated in later, backward to where it, to my way of thinking, can reasonably be inferred to begin.

The infant's differentiating and organizing of what is primarily prototaxic experience into the more complex elements of experience that I name signs, arises from a combination of two sets of factors. One of these factors is the *possibility* of thus organizing experience. It is always well to be that rudimentary in your thinking; there has to be a demonstrable possibility of something before it is reasonable to do very much with it. That there is a possibility that an infant under six months can organize signs can be, I believe, validated from careful observation of almost any six-month-old infant. So I believe that the possibility of thus organizing experience is demonstrable. I may say that it is not confined to the human, but extends, to my knowledge, as far as colts and puppies. Besides the possibility, which must be present, there has to be the factor of *functional utility* of such signs in the integration of situations necessary for the securing of satisfaction and, very soon after the beginning of life, the avoiding or minimizing of anxiety. This is the implication of my reference to "useful" and "useless"—terms which can easily be misleading. But keep in mind that when I say that a sign is "useful," and that "useless" signs are not organized in the early phase of life, what I am referring to is *functionally* useful, in the sense of facilitating some functional activity which is vital in the business of satisfying needs or avoiding anxiety. It is solely in this connection that these two dubious words—useful and useless—get into our thinking here, and I trust that the great number of other possible meanings will not creep into your thought. The point is that what the infant differentiates and organizes out of his primarily prototaxic experience is *useful* additions to his integrating tendencies, and as I have said before, these useful additions function in recall and foresight.

To repeat, there is no reason for supposing that useless signs are organized within the infant's experience. Thus there is no differentiation of a tender real mother from a tender mother's helper in the situations in which the infant satisfies his needs, for the very reason that such differentiation would in no way facilitate the satisfaction of needs in the very early months of life. And in the same way, in these earlier months of life no facilitation of the avoiding or minimizing of anxiety (mainly avoiding at this stage) would be accomplished by differentiating between an anxious mother and an anxious and malevolent mother's helper. What happens to the infant is, to all intents and purposes, identical, whether the mother or the mother's helper is involved; the only 'objective' which makes any sense is to avoid anxiety, and since anxiety is induced, it makes very little difference what the person who induces it looks like or thinks herself to be.[1]

[1] [*Editors' note:* In Sullivan's 1948 lecture series he worded this somewhat differently:
"What the infant can, with reasonable probability, be believed to do rests primarily on his biological capabilities for doing it, but rests practically on the usefulness of doing it. And all that is particularly useful in the extremely dependent phase of life—early infancy—is the improvement of differentiation of those interpersonal situations that work, and those interpersonal situations that miscarry dreadfully by producing anxiety.
"In the beginning, all relations, with whatever people, which are a part of the satisfying of the infant's needs blend into a single personification which I call the good mother, to name it something; and all experience, with however many persons, which results in severe anxiety blends into a single personification which I call, to call it something, the bad mother. And the growth of differentiation, as the distance receptors begin to be more efficient and better related to one another and to the rest of the organism, is, I believe, primarily for the purpose, one might say, of becoming alert to those mis-

The young infant does not differentiate insignificant details of experience, but only the pattern, beyond whose limiting envelope events are significantly different. Forthcoming satisfaction is most significantly different from anxiety, and in the earliest months the identity of the particular person who signalizes the forthcoming satisfaction is of no moment whatever in the integration by the infant of the necessary interpersonal situation and the infant's activity in its resolution.

And here I would like to remind you of the start of this discussion by noting that even our initial example of an interpersonal situation, namely, the nipple-in-lips, is integrated and maintained doubly, in a duplex fashion, by the infant's need for water and food, and by the mother's need to give tenderness in this connection. And here I am saying that, in the earliest months of life, the infant's part in forthcoming satisfaction—his part of the integration of the nipple-in-lips, and his activity in maintaining this integration and in resolving it by having secured enough water and foodstuff for the satisfaction of his needs—has no use for, is in no way facilitated by, the inclusion of data which might seem quite significant to you or me in looking at the situation. If the carrier of the nipple gets it in the right place, within the prehensile ability of the infant's mouth, this, *provided* that the situation is free from anxiety, is tantamount to the complete integration of the satisfaction-giving situation. And that is the case in the earliest months with all the interpersonal cooperation which is necessary

---

carriages of things which will bring anxiety—that is, among the various things which can be perceived and organized as experience, the infant becomes alert to those that can be classed as forbidding gestures. Anything he can pick up, from the vague entities moving around him, which can be learned to be a precursor of anxiety is so incorporated. The infant learns to make this differentiation, not because he has any great skill at warding off anxiety, but because anxiety is extremely unpleasant and represents a major miscarriage of living, whereas in the rest of the infant's living the worst that can happen is that a lot of time may elapse between the appearance of need and its satisfaction. But there the device of apathy comes in to give one a rest, so that one can start over with renewed vigor at the end of the repose. However, with anxiety there is no possibility of resting or doing anything else except suffering. Thus I believe that the growth of differentiation—in the sense of refined learning, however unrefined it may be in its beginning—probably is in this area of how to get the first clues to the probability of anxiety, just as if that would be very helpful to the infant, because anxiety is such an extremely unpleasant experience."]

for the survival of the human young. There are no significant differences at the beginning, unless the carrier of whatever is needed —the relatively adult person—is anxious, in which case, as I have already stated, action and satisfaction are impaired or reversed and the infant suffers the misery of anxiety. And it is for this reason that I infer with considerable security the initial organization of two complex signs in the infant's experience, the good and the bad or anxiety-carrying mother.

Thus I have now set up for our consideration the idea that the infant is bound to have two personifications of any mothering person, barring the most incredible good fortune, and that the infant in the earliest stages of life need have only two personifications for any number of people who have something to do with looking after him. So far as the more adult persons in the infant's unknown world are concerned, each one of them is bound to have a different personification of the infant. By this time, I trust it is completely clear that personifications are not, in some metaphysical sense, the organism or the person that is personified.

Nursing as an Interpersonal Experience

The experience involved in becoming a person may be said to begin as a function of the first nursing. Prototaxic experience connected with the institution of breathing and the maintenance of body temperature probably precedes this, but it is in connection with frequently recurring activity of the oral zone that sentience, presently to be elaborated into primitive personifications, has its origin. The extraphysiological factors in the nursing situation are a growing personification of the good mother by the infant, and one or more personifications of the infant by the mother. The good mother begins as a discrimination or differentiation of the good and satisfactory nipple. That is, it is differentiated as a pattern of experience, very significantly different from the nipple of anxiety. The personification grows by the discrimination of the sundry classes of nipples that I have talked about, other than the anxiety-invested nipple, and sentience originating in distance receptor apparatus is added to the initial, more purely oral data. And by this I refer to the oral dynamism, which more or less pertains to the mouth but at this very early stage also includes the auditory channel, because all that is heard is the infant's production. Very early in life the auditory zone begins to split off as a zone of interaction in its own right. In the course of events, the sundry classes of nipples become an important part of the pattern of experience which is the personification, good mother; but even this part of the personification has expanded to include sentience from extraoral zones as remote as the prehensile hands, the buttocks, and the feet. The nursing situation still includes as its central detail the nipple-in-lips, its oldest core, as elaborated by additional data with discrimination of various classes of nipples and so on; but it now shows patterning of activity by the hands and so forth.

There may be evident discrimination between what we might call nursing-when-recumbent and nursing-when-erect. Observable accessory movements show relatively durable differences in the two cases. I am now talking of the development of personality in the infant, let us say, under six months of chronologic age. By this time there have already appeared ways of using the arms and hands, the legs and feet, and so on, in connection with the mother's body, clothing, and so forth, when nursing, which we call accessory movements. In the human, these do not, so far as I can guess, have very much to do with the getting of milk out of the nipple, but they do tend to fall into pattern, that is, they get to be, as we can very recklessly say, habitual accompaniments of nursing. And even at this early age the accessory movements—which presumably supply sentience that is organized into the personification of the good mother and makes up part of the infant's experience of the nursing behavior—show certain differences when the mother happens to be nursing while lying down in comparison with when she is nursing sitting up. And these accessory movements, particularly those of the arms and hands, are not merely something that coincides with nursing, but actually are details of behavior which may persist as patterns of activity years after a person has ceased to nurse at the breast. Some of these movements show up in states of fatigue, preoccupation, and so on, as curious manneristic movements.

More than the infant's oral zone and the mother's mammary zone is now significantly concerned in the integration of the nursing situation. And more than milk, the warmth of the mother's body, some olfactory sentience, and so forth—which were concerned in the earlier nursing—enter now into the recurring nursing experience. There are now several other important factors of sentience. For example, there is that of the infant's hands; the good mother as integrated by the infant in the nursing situation now includes elements to be grasped, pushed, pulled, rubbed, and otherwise encountered by the sensitive palmar and plantar surfaces—that is, the palms of the hands and the soles of the feet—as well as the elements of what is seen and heard in connection with the nursing situation. Insofar as all of these are sentience recurrently associated, for the infant, with the nursing situation, they can be presumed to be items in that which is personified as the good mother—which, you will remember, is anything but an appreciation of the mother as an adult human being as another adult might see her.

In some of the mammals with accessory nursing behavior, this behavior has very striking relationship to the breast, but where human beings are concerned, I think it is quite as common for a nursing infant to be toying with some of the mother's hair as to be toying with the mammary zone of her body. The fact that the accessory movements of the human infant may have very little to do with the actual mechanics, you might say, of getting milk into the mouth does not, however, lessen the real contribution of these movements to the growing personification of the source of milk, the good mother.

Zonal Needs and General Needs

Factors of biological organization which provide energy for transformation in the several zones of interaction now manifest themselves in these zones as dynamisms, and there are manifest needs to suck, to feel, to manipulate orally and with the hands, and so forth. We have already spoken of two genera of dynamisms which are of peculiar interest to psychiatry: the second of these consisted of dynamisms conceptualized with primary reference to the energy transformations characteristic of particular zones of interaction. Up to now—that is, through, let us say, the second or third month of the extrauterine life of the infant—we have considered the need for water and food which is satisfied in the nursing situation as a dynamism, an integrating tendency, which, so far as the infant is concerned, is manifested in the appropriate and adequate action. But now we have progressed to the point where we are speaking of the oral zone itself as a dynamism, and as a dynamism it manifests needs to suck, just as the hands manifest needs to feel, and to manipulate, and so on; and incidentally the oral zone also does considerable manipulation. We can speak of the oral zone and the manual zone as being in the service of another class of dynamisms—namely, the needs; but these zones, themselves considered as dynamisms, show zonal needs, of which the need to suck is a particular instance.

Now it is true of these zonal needs that they must suffice quantitatively for the resolution of situations which are integrated by general needs—that is, needs for oxygen, for water, for food, and so on; but it is equally true that the zonal needs often, if not always, exceed this necessary quantitative aspect. And the quantity concerned here is the quantity of energy which is provided in the zone of interaction for transformation in the shape of doing the work of interchange which is centered in this zone. In other words, quite early in development, the partition of energy to be transformed in the oral zone, for example, may be greater than the energy needed for the satisfaction of the needs for water and food; and this excess manifests itself in the maintenance of activity which is not needed for the satisfaction of the great general need for food and water, but begins to be the need for exercise, we might call it, of the particular zone of interaction concerned. Thus, quite early in life, the energy provided for transformation in the act of sucking may be in excess of that which is transformed in sucking for milk, and the surplus manifests itself as a need to suck which is in no sense necessarily associated with a nipple, much less with getting milk from the nipple.

Years ago a very important contribution to the probability of this whole approach to psychiatric theory was provided by the work of Dr. David M. Levy dealing with this very point, which appeared first in his study of the relation of thumbsucking to the ease with which milk was obtained from the nourishing nipple.[2] If

[2] [David M. Levy, "Fingersucking and Accessory Movements in Early Infancy: An Etiologic Study," *Amer. J. Psychiatry* (1928) 7:881-918.]

it was very easy to satisfy the need for food by sucking, then there was a great deal of sucking of other things; and the upper extremities particularly and the lower extremities to some extent provide the infant with things that can be invested by the lips and sucked. Further development of Dr. Levy's basic research in this connection was extended as far as the pecking behavior of chickens. There again it was found, under an experimental setup, that if it was extremely easy for these little birds to get a sufficiency of food, then they pecked themselves and each other, and, in fact, in some cases practically denuded each other of feathers in order to discharge the zonal need—that is, to transform the energy, provided for the securing of food by activity of the oral zone, which was in excess of the needs for food.[3]

Thus quite early in life the zones of interaction begin to be conspicuous as dynamisms in their own right, with more-or-less fixed partitions of the total vital energy for transformation in each zone; and energy is transformed only in doing work. Therefore, there is a zonal need to suck, and so on, which is quite supplementary, you might say, to the general need for food, even if necessarily related to it. If the zonal need is not adequate to the provision of food, that is a very serious business. But if the zonal need is in excess of what is required for the securing of food and water, then there is behavior for the discharge of the tension of the oral zone which is in excess of that required for the securing of food and water. The oral zone, parenthetically, is very well provided with energy for transformation, and the oral needs, in contrast to general needs, have very considerable importance in understanding personality development. So much for this consideration.

The Anal and Urethral Zones in Interpersonal Experience

Now let us look at two other important zones of interaction in the communal existence of the infant, namely, the *anal zone* and the *urethral zone*. These end stations pertain to the expulsion of food residues and excess water. The general need concerned may

[3] [David M. Levy, "A Note on Pecking in Chickens," *Psychoanalytic Quart.* (1935) 4:612–613. "On Instinct-Satiation: An Experiment on the Pecking Behavior of Chickens," *J. General Psychol.* (1937) 18:327–348.]

be called the need to be rid of more-or-less solid and of liquid waste products concerned with the communal existence and functional activity of the organism. The tensions underlying these needs are felt as the recurrent need to empty the rectum and the urinary bladder; and in the experiencing of these felt needs, tensions in two systems of neuromuscular organs are of central importance. Now, you will note that there is somewhat of a distinction here in the method of development of thought. When I spoke of the need for food and water, I did not specify any organ as of central importance in the felt need; but perhaps because the anal and urethral zones are eliminatory zones, where waste is 'thrown out,' and because of various other considerations that will be discussed, these zones and their felt needs can actually be broken down into meaningful reference to neuromuscular apparatus. Perhaps chiefly by virtue of improved survival value, the mammalian bodily organization has come to provide for the intermittent discharge of these waste products, and, especially in the case of the less fluid and much more viscous feces, for their spatial separation from the body integument.

At this point I am introducing into this discussion a group of inferences derived from my own observations, not, so far as I know, supported by observations, investigations, or experiments by anyone else, and certainly not supported by an adequate body of observation and experiment by me. I wish particularly to stress the element of provisions for the spatial separation, the separation in space, of the organism and the expelled feces. As in the case of the food and water needs of the infant, so also in the ridding of himself of the urine and feces, there is requisite the cooperation of a relatively mature mothering agency, to convey the infant away from coverings wetted by the extruded urine, and to remove the feces from the infant's body surface and from his proximity. The removal of feces entails the cleaning of soiled areas, particularly the mucocutaneous junction at the anus.

The character of the covering tissue on what we often think of as the inside of our body is, in general, very different from the covering of what we ordinarily think of as the outside of our body. Now when I speak of what is "thought of" as the inside, I am not talking about the actual, beyond-any-perchance inside.

The nasal spaces, the mouth, and the gastrointestinal tract are in a very practical sense outside the body; but they are so circumscribed by and contained in the body, for such very special purposes of the body, that the covering or membrane which separates them from what is not of the body is quite different in character from the skin and nails and hair and so on, which appear on the unquestionable outside. The particularly significant details that I wish to mention as characterizing these quasi-inside coverings are that they secrete mucus and that they have ciliary apparatus for moving things, and so on. The mucous membranes join the skin, and the place of joining is always a zone of interaction in the communal existence of the organism, although there are zones such as the ear where no such mucocutaneous junction is presented to the outer world. Where there are mucocutaneous junctions, there are really extraordinary risks to the integrity of the organism—owing to peculiarities of joining blood supplies, and one thing and another—and almost invariably there is a rich supply of receptor organs, as if to aid in protecting these comparatively delicate carpentries of two different kinds of covering membranes. The mucous membrane lining the alimentary tract ends in the anus—that is, its distal part is the anal orifice, the anus; and there, as at the lips, is a junction of mucous membrane and skin. And it is in connection with this anal end of the alimentary tract that there occurs a peculiar segregation of receptors which, while they are not in a strictly technical sense distance receptors, might be called anticontact receptors.

As I have said, the removal of feces through cooperation of the mothering agency entails the cleaning of soiled areas, particularly this mucocutaneous junction in the anus. End organs of afferent (that is, receptor) nerve channels carrying intelligence, or the basis of intelligence, inward in this anal region provide a peculiarly important part of the sentience which is marked or colored by origin in the anal zone of interaction. And this particular component of the anal sentience has this aspect, which I have just mentioned, of a quasi-distance quality, in that it determines the separation of the organism and the actual fecal mass—and by determines I do not mean that it brings it about, but that it shows whether this separation is or is not the case. In the intervals between their elimination, the feces are accumulated in a section of the alimentary canal, the tension of the muscular walls of which exert pressure against the innermost of three anal sphincters, and this pressure gives rise to the felt need to defecate. Sphincters are more or less ring-shaped muscular organs which appear where it is necessary to close a canal, and the sphincters of interest here are this set of three anal sphincters and two urinary sphincters. Incidentally, the upper end of the alimentary canal has an organization of muscle that is quite like a sphincter, which is called the *orbicularis oris*. This again is a sort of ring-shaped assembly of muscular tissue, although its precise shape is concealed by the refinements of the mouth form; its functional activity is very much more refined than that of the other sphincters and is combined with that of other muscular structures, because there is seldom occasion for any sphincter action at the oral end, except possibly when you are blowing brass wind instruments.

As I have said, the pressure of the muscular walls of the rectal part of the alimentary canal against this inner of three sphincters gives rise to the felt need to defecate. Now we must distinguish between the rectum, which is a storing space primarily, and the anal canal, which runs from the innermost sphincter through the middle sphincter, past the outer sphincter to the anus. This canal is so organized that it has to be emptied of any feces admitted into it, and gives rise to vivid sentience as long as this emptying has not been accomplished. This vivid sentience, arising from the end organs with which this canal is provided, is a particular type of discomfort, occurring when that canal is no longer being merely traversed by fecal matter, but has some in it that has to be expelled.

In later life, the expulsion of feces other than those actually in the anal canal tends to cease unless the extruded mass actually leaves contact with these quasi-distance receptors in the anus, and the detachment of each fecal mass from contact with these receptors favors the admission of another mass into the anal canal until the act of defecation has been completed. Now this is the area of data which may be proven by investigation to be erroneous, but about which I believe I have adequate basis for this presentation. It is literally true that the separation of a fecal mass from contact with the anus is necessary for ordinary completion of the act of defecation. This may seem to you a very trivial matter, but it is actually vastly more significant for theory than is a great deal that has been taught quite solemnly.

Appropriate and adequate activity of the infant in satisfying the need to defecate consists in the relaxing of the anal sphincter apparatus and the coordinate increasing in the tension of the muscular walls of the rectal canal as the anal canal empties itself. Indefinitely early in life, perhaps from the very beginning, the factor of separation from the feces begins to be important and contributes something to the experience of tenderness which is organized by the infant in his personification of the good mother.

The urine is handled by a somewhat similar combination of a cavity with muscular walls, the pressure from tension in which is exerted against the innermost of two sphincters. The canal from this first to the second sphincter must, like the anal canal, be emptied, and gives rise to vivid sentience until this has been accomplished, excepting during the actual flow of urine. Now this sentience is suspended during the actual transfer of masses which have passed the first sphincter en route to the last, and becomes significant only when that normal, functionally perfectly useful process is interrupted or is about to end. At those times, these intersphincter parts of the eliminatory canals cause vivid sentience which has the pattern of arising from their nonempty state, and disappearing when they are empty. They have ample muscular provisions for bringing about the emptying, which automatically happens unless something materially interferes. The most striking difference in the apparatus for being rid of the urine and the apparatus for being rid of the feces is that in the former there is one less sphincter.

With respect to the urinary excretory apparatus, there are important differences in the morphological organization of the male and the female, arising from the fusion of some parts of the more external reproductive apparatus with a part of the urine channels. These differences are of no special moment in the earlier stages of developmental history, and may be ignored in the stage of infancy. The urethra, the canal for the urine from the bladder to the outside, ends in an unusual mucocutaneous junction, respectively at the end of the erectile penis in the male, or in the vulva in the neighborhood of the erectile clitoris in the woman. The lining of the urethra joins with a specialized epithelium which is supplied with peculiarly characterized receptor end organs, the great import of which will appear only later in life when the development of the lust dynamism has begun through appropriate maturation.

The more significant components of sentience pertaining to the intermittent discharge of the urine arise from, first, the deeper, intersphincter part of the urethra; secondly, the distal part of the urethra; and thirdly, the surfaces closely associated with the urethral orifice. You will notice that I have not mentioned any component of pressure against the inner sphincter, which is another area of significant difference from the anal apparatus. It is the increasing pressure of the fecal mass forced by the walls of the rectum against the inner sphincter of the anal canal which is ordinarily recognized as the need to defecate. So far as the need to urinate is concerned, however, this is, so far as I know, quite unexceptionally related to the permitting of a small amount of urine to pass the inner sphincter, whereupon it strikes this peculiarly sensitive intersphincter region and gives rise to an urgent desire to urinate. To what extent pressure against the urinary sphincter may be a component of experience in this particular, I do not know, but it is very much less striking than in the anal situation.

There are significant differences in the earliest manifestation of these two excretory functions, such that the need for cooperation with respect to the urine—that is, for tenderness in connection with the satisfaction of the need to urinate—may be chiefly an aspect of body temperature protection, quite different from that assumed to be the case with regard to the feces. The urine is an aqueous saline solution, rich in dissolved nitrogenous waste products, of which urea is very conspicuous. It is usually sterile so far as bacteria and other lower organisms are concerned; in other words, it is not, as you might put it, infected with bacteria, yeasts, molds, and so on. It is entirely an excretory secretion, its quantity and contents being determined by such vital factors as the electrolyte balance of the body fluids and the nitrogen metabolism. The feces, on the other hand, consist of excretory secretion and unassimilable material taken in as, or with, food. Its composition, even its consistency, varies between wide limits. It is an excellent pabulum for the growth of a great variety of lower organisms—bacteria, fungi, and yeast—the metabolic products of which may be thoroughly noxious, not only to the infant, but to adults. This becomes increasingly true with the introduction of food substances other than the mother's milk and the corresponding dilution of the previous excretory secretions. In other words, when alimentation is proceeding perfectly in the infant, that which comes out does not include cellulose, and so on, but is only mucus and the secretion of the excretory elements of the alimentary canal; but as soon as alimentation goes wrong, incompletely digested milk and so on is added to this; and later on, when eating consists of more than milk, and indigestible substances are mixed in with the digestible, these in turn are mixed with the excretory secretions in making up the feces.

The alimentary canal is a digestive, absorbing, and excretory channel. Enzymes secreted into it at several points bring about chemical transformations productive of substances which can be usefully absorbed in aqueous solution and otherwise. Chemical changes of the kind that are here significant are a joint function of time and temperature, as is the absorptive function itself. The rate at which the food mass is transferred from the oral to the anal zones is of very real importance for survival, and the extent to which this permits adequate absorption of the useful products of digestion is a complex function of motility, water content, and osmotic tensions. In general, the intestinal contents, after the first weeks of extrauterine life, tend to be formed masses by the time they are ready for expulsion, but fluid stools may be produced under certain circumstances throughout the whole span of life.

The mothering functions necessary for the survival of the infant are, with respect to the urine, relatively simple. Besides attention to the continued excretion of this waste matter, there is chiefly the requirement that the infant shall not remain in contact with the urine long enough to interfere with the control of his internal temperature, or the damage of his integument, his neighboring skin, by maceration or soaking. Mothering with regard to the feces is quite another matter. Its prompt removal is indicated. The anal orifice needs to be cleaned, and the feces need to be inspected for the indices which they provide as to the adequacy of the alimentary function, necessary indeed to life and growth. This discrimination between the mothering function regarding the urine and the mothering function regarding the feces is important. Suppression of the urinary excretion would be a very grave problem, but beyond making sure that this does not occur, the mothering function is only to see that the infant is not wet—which would interfere with the maintenance of body temperature, the radiation of heat and one thing and another, and, if prolonged, would lead to unfortunate change in the skin. But with the feces, which are extraordinarily apt to undergo bacterial putrefaction, fungus growth, and so on, it is quite another matter. I have already mentioned that there are some facts which suggest that for completion of fecal expulsion, ideally the removal of the extruded feces from contact with the anal orifice is indicated. And because the very swiftly growing body of the infant is chiefly made up of what comes to him through successful working of the alimentary function, any hints of disturbance of that function are timely warnings of what may be very serious trouble; among the hints which anybody can discover is the character of the feces.

The anal zone of interaction thus necessarily comes to involve factors of an interpersonal character from very early in life. The functional activity centering in the anal zone often becomes involved in the manifestations of infantile anxiety, especially when the mothering one is made anxious by these details of her mothering function. By this I refer to those who find it extremely difficult to deal with the infant's soiled diapers, and so on. Here, as in the case of other needs which we have considered, anxiety manifests itself in direct vector opposition to the satisfaction of the need to defecate. Its occurrence tends to bring about retention of the feces, with increased tension of need to be rid of them. Now it is quite true that the vicissitudes of evolution have protected us from the possibility of complete suppression of the expulsion of feces because of anxiety. But the presence of anxiety tends to prolong the retention; at the same time, the more there is in the rectum, the more the pressure that is normally expressed against the internal sphincter, and the greater the need to be rid of the rectal contents. How anxiety interferes with the whole field of sentience in these two activities in the elimination of waste will become more evident presently. But we should note at this particular time that the water content of the feces is in large measure a function of the time which the food mass is retained in the alimentary canal, and the water content is the principal factor in determining the consistency of the feces. In other words, the longer the feces are retained, other factors being equal, the firmer is the consistency of the feces, and there is a point at which the feces may become so firm, and there may be such a quantity of them coalesced into a mass, that the expulsion is actually an occasion of pain—so that there may be very real suffering in connection with their transit through the anal canal. Therefore, insofar as anxiety tends to bring about retention of the feces, anxiety connected with recurrent needs to defecate may come to be—in, let us say, the fourth, fifth, or sixth month of infantile life—associated with pain in the procedure which would normally be the satisfaction of the need to defecate. Now this pain does not remove the satisfaction of defecating, but pain is never attractive, crazy ideas about sadism-masochism notwithstanding. And so one of the striking influences of anxiety, in connection with this particular zone of interaction with the environment, is that it can lead to actual physical suffering in connection with the satisfaction of the need to empty the bowels.

CHAPTER
8

The Infant as a Person

The Infant's Differentiation of His Own Body

THE ORAL zone, as I have already suggested, is an independent dynamism in the sense that while it is the principal zone of interaction in satisfying the infant's need for water and food, it also manifests an excess over needs of the energy partitioned to it; this excess appears as a need to suck, to manipulate with the lips, and so forth, quite irrespective of the need or satisfaction of hunger and thirst. In this case, there occurs what is somewhat uncertainly called 'pleasure' in the various activities which characterize the zone.

By the age of six months the infant is manifesting a variety of zonal needs and some related sign processes. Maturation has been proceeding at a great rate. The eyes, for example, converge in the way that is necessary for binocular vision and the visual appreciation of distance. That does not mean that by the age of six months the infant is particularly good at judging distance. But by the age of six months, that particular coordinate activity of the two eyeballs has matured so that the *fovea centralis*—the center of most acute vision in each retina—is pointed at the particular object being looked at. In addition, coordinate activity of two or more zones of interaction is now frequent. For some time the eyes have been turned toward sources of sound, and by the age of six months the whole head is turned in that direction quite frequently. Hand and arm movement is well developed and serves to convey to the mouth anything that is grasped. This coordination of hands and mouth is a very outstanding aspect of early coordination of two zones of interaction. The infant in these early months literally moves in such fashion as to carry anything that he can retain in his hand to his mouth, where it is tinkered with, sucked, and manipulated generally. Thus thumbs, fingers, toes, and all manner of portable objects have been explored and exploited by the mouth.

As a consequence of this manual-oral coordination, the discrimination of an exceedingly important pattern of experience begins—the differentiation of the infant's body from everything else in the universe. Perhaps this will become clearer if we compare this experience to the infant's differentiation of nipples into good and satisfactory, good and unsatisfactory, and wrong nipples; this differentiation of the nipples is primarily an *intrazonal discrimination*—that is, an organization of sentience which arises primarily within the oral zone; the eyes gradually contribute, although in the beginning they are not yet differentiated as an important zone of interaction. But in manual-oral coordination we are talking about *differentiation that is based on sentience from more than one zone.* Since the baby gets no milk when he sucks his thumb, one might think that the thumb would thus tend to fall into the class of wrong nipples—however suitable for satisfying the zonal need to suck; but the thumb is uniquely different from any nipple by reason of its being *in itself* a source of zonal sentience. *The thumb feels sucked.*

The recurrent multizonal sentience here concerned is in many ways significantly different from the recurrent multizonal sentience in which distance receptors participate with the contact receptors of the oral zone, of the fingers, or of the anus. The latter group of multizonal sentience provides experience for the growing personification of the good mother, as I have explained at some length, and for certain uncomfortable variants which contribute to the personification of the bad mother. The infant's appropriate activity—although it is often adequate for the evocation of the good mother, the good and satisfactory nipple, the good mother's satisfaction-insuring cooperation—is not uniformly effective. Sometimes it is, at least for a time, wholly ineffectual. Sometimes it miscarries badly, and the bad mother appears, approaches, and results in anxiety and, in some cases, in actual pain.

But the infant's appropriate activity to secure the thumb-in-lips situation, once it has been patterned, is always adequate, unless it is opposed by anxiety. Of course, a certain amount of what we shall later discuss as trial-and-error learning is necessary for the infant to be reasonably sure of getting the thumb into the mouth, but, as the neuromuscular apparatus matures, it comes to be pretty dependable. It fails only when the infant is anxious. But in this case it is a failure which is not organized as such, but is instead part of the growing system of experience 'with' anxiety—that is, the experience of being anxious. And when the infant is anxious, anxiety is so much more conspicuous than are the matters opposed by anxiety that failures of this kind are not organized as failures of the activity to create the thumb-in-lips situation. In this thumb-in-lips situation there are *no* failures organized as such in the infant's experience; and the uniform success of this performance is thus significantly distinguished in multizonal experience by its invarying approximation to its foreseen achievement. This is in contrast to the activity with respect to producing the mother and getting food, being cleaned, being covered, and so on, which even though adequate and appropriate may on occasion fail. Needs are differentiated, so far as the infant is concerned, by their foreseen satisfaction. Foreseen satisfaction of hunger may, at least temporarily, miscarry rather badly. But foreseen satisfaction of the zonal need to suck when the thumb-in-lips situation is that which is appropriate is *invariably* followed by the achievement of the satisfaction. So here is an important distinction between this situation and all those previous situations which were obviously relevant and significant to the infant.

By the time the infant is six months old, grasping, the kinesthetically sensed [1] transporting by the hand to the mouth, and the oral sucking and other manipulation of anything thus presented to the mouth—all these are well advanced, along with visual and other accompanying sentience in many cases. But in the infant's experi-

---

[1] By "kinesthetically sensed" I refer to those types of receptor processes which acquaint us with the position of our joints and so on, or, more specifically, the position of joint surfaces and tension against joint surfaces and so on, and by which, after we have had a great deal of experience, we learn where our extremities are. The movement of these surfaces gives us our acquaintance with, or sentience about, the geometry of the body. Getting the thumb into the mouth involves learning how the elbow, the wrist, and other joints feel, or having prototaxic experience which is effective in bringing about adjustments of muscular movement, and so on.

ence, of all that which is thus grasped, transported, and manipulated, only the parts of his own body which he can get into his mouth, generally his thumb, uniformly and invariably feel sucked and orally manipulated. Thus of all the things which are transported to the mouth, which in actual fact amounts to practically everything which can be moved, the thumb is the only one that feels sucked at the same time that the mouth 'feels sucking.'

Now it is true that the hand feels a variety of events connected with the oral manipulation of sundry objects transported to the mouth, but these manual experiences and their coincident oral experiences are of a relatively wide variety. The hand feels all sorts of things—a ball, a block, or the rods of the crib, let us say. The hand may feel the ball or the block, or something of that kind, at the same time that the mouth is feeling the ball or the block, but the feeling in the hand and the feeling in the mouth, so far as we have any reason to suppose at this time, are not particularly connected with an object. There is sentience from the hand, and this does add up in the course of time to a great deal of acquaintance with objects; and there is very vivid sentience from the lips and mouth, which also adds up to a great deal of acquaintance with objects. But there is no particular reason for thinking of these as being either necessarily or probably organized into any unitary conception of the particular object. This is entirely the contrary of the experience with the thumb-in-lips. All these feelings of the hand with objects other than the thumb which are presented to the mouth combine in the organization of sentience about living among portable objects, so to speak; but the invariant coincidence of the manual-tactile sentience and the sundry oral elements of sentience is not present in these cases.

There may be frequent occasions of fairly sustained coincidence of manual sentience from grasping a nursing bottle and oral sentience from manipulating its attached nipple, but the relation of felt oral and manual needs, and the foresight of satisfaction by activity to integrate the appropriate situation is by no means invariably successful. And this situation of nursing bottle and nipple—by the age of six months or shortly afterward, the infant can grasp and hold the bottle and keep the nipple in approximation to the mouth—does really depend on somebody's providing the nursing bottle, and on the bottle's remaining within reach if it is dropped, which events are by no means invariable concomitants with the infant's wanting the bottle. As a matter of fact, infants very commonly have to go to the same length to get the nursing bottle that they do to get the milk-giving nipple of the mother —that is, they have to cry—and by the age of six months they often cry plenty without anything happening. So while there is the invariant relationship of the foreseen satisfaction connected with the thumb-in-lips, there is anything but this invariant relationship connected with any situation in which there is something intermediate, as it were, between the hand and the lips. The thumb-in-lips is dependable, and is independent of evoking the good mother; the infant can bring it into being, as it were, without cooperation—in isolation from any of his personifications, whether of the good mother or the bad mother. While he cannot live by sucking his thumb, and cannot thus satisfy recurrent needs for food and water, he has matured and profited enough by the organization of his experience to be self-sufficient in respect to satisfying this particular oral zonal need which, as I have said before, generally exceeds in its available transformable energy that which is required for the necessary nursing behavior.

The relatively invariant coincidence of felt need, foresight of satisfaction by adequate and appropriate activity, and independence of cooperation by an at least dimly prehended other person in securing the anticipated satisfaction—all these will come presently to be an important part of a master pattern of experience to which reference is made by the use of the word "my," and more particularly "my body," and, by the sophisticated, "my mind" or even "my soul." Bear in mind that I am for the moment omitting experiences in which anxiety opposes—to the point of preventing—adequate and appropriate activity, which as I have said tends to bring about the organization of experience-with-being-anxious, or experience-while-being-anxious, or anxiety-colored experience, and therefore does not add to the organization of data about the need and its satisfaction. The thumb-in-lips situation is the first we have encountered in which two zonal needs are satisfied by one adequate and appropriate activity that the infant can perform without cooperation of a chronologically more mature person—in which there is no need for evoking the good mother and no danger, at this particular stage, of evoking the bad mother. It is the first situation in which there is an *invariant* coincidence of the felt need and the foresight of its satisfaction by certain activity which is always adequate and appropriate, with the satisfaction of the two zonal needs.

This is a pattern of experience, or it is a kind of experience that will be organized in a pattern. This is an extremely important pattern, for it is the pattern which will evolve, with further experience throughout years and years, into a symbol—a very complex, meaningful, and rich sign; and this sign is the organization of data to which one refers as "my body" and which may include, in a certain less exact sense, practically anything to which "my" is applied seriously. I am not, of course, suggesting that the infant's experience in sucking his thumb and feeling it sucked immediately blossoms out into a considerable formulation of his body. But it is the point of departure for this formulation; it is the type of experience, or the type of activity sequence, which is more or less paradigmatic of experience which will presently be said to include "my body." And for various reasons which will concern us later, it is this pattern, "my body," which has so much to do with the very firmly entrenched feelings of independence, of autonomous entity, if you please, which have been a great handicap to the development of a grasp on interpersonal relations, and which are behind what I have for many years called the delusion of unique individuality.[2] The importance of trying to see how this extraordinary pattern of experience characterized by "my" comes into being, why it has to be as it is, and how it appears as early as perhaps the sixth month of extrauterine life, is that it gives us some idea of how extremely troublesome it is to strip off, from this grand division of experience, the later elaborations which are vicious and misleading in complicating human interpersonal relations. Any important central development of experience that begins so early has roots which are extremely difficult to get at rationally or to formulate.

[2] [*Editors' note:* See Sullivan's paper, first given as a lecture in 1944 and published posthumously with minor revisions, "The Illusion of Personal Individuality," *Psychiatry* (1950) 13:317-332.]

To sum up briefly the beginnings of this experience, by mid-infancy the hands are exploring all reachable parts of the infant's life space and are encountering a variety of objects which fall into two grand divisions, the self-sentient and the non-self-sentient. The thumb is the classical example of what I mean by the self-sentient. It is discovered not by the hand but by the mouth, or rather by hand-mouth cooperation. The mouth feels the thumb, and the thumb feels the mouth; that is self-sentience. This, as I have said, is the point of departure for an enormous development. But the hands, not in connection with the mouth, proceed to contribute a great deal of sentience which is elaborated in this same general field, and the basis of elaboration is that some of the things which the hands encounter are not only felt by the hands but feel the hands, although many of the things that the hands encounter are felt by the hands but do not feel the hands. Prehension about the former (the self-sentient) becomes additional pre-information or information which will presently be organized as the conception of the body; and prehension about the latter (the non-self-sentient) will presently, but distinctly later, be part of the elaborate group of conceptions and misconceptions which is external reality—that which is outside the body.

One might glibly say that the infant is now 'learning about' his own body. But this objective language, by which one might describe in general terms what the infant is doing as something observed, is extremely misleading, so far as contributing to the study of development of personality is concerned. A great deal of what might be read into the infant's behavior cannot, for the best reasons on earth, be the case from the infant's standpoint.

The Influence of Anxiety on the Infant's Acquaintance with His Body

The infant's acquaintance with that which is infant—that which is self-sentient, which feels as well as is felt—does not proceed very far in most directions before it encounters very powerful influences brought to bear by the more mature persons making up the infant's objectively verifiable world. The reason for the infant's not even being free to get acquainted with his own body is a blend of two things, one of which we have touched on at some length before: first, the social responsibility carried by the mothering one to take her infant and turn out a decent, acceptable human being; and, second, a variety of beliefs entertained by the mothering one, some of which may be valid—that is, pretty good approximations to something inhering in the universe and, in particular, in the raising of infants.

One of these bodies of social responsibility and belief soon begins to interfere with the thumb-in-mouth situation. The tendency of the manual zone is not only to grasp and transport to the mouth, but also to pull, and tinker, and so on. Because of this effect of the manual zone on things that it contacts, and because of the present eruption of teeth, it is believed—and, I have no doubt, correctly in some instances at least—that too much of this thumb-in-mouth or hand-in-mouth will result in an aesthetically unfortunate, and perhaps even digestively unfortunate, distortion of the teeth, such that if it is not interfered with, the baby will presently have what is called buckteeth. And this would necessitate expensive, tedious, and, to the child, very unwelcome orthodontic intervention for the sake of beauty. So it becomes to many mothering ones important to do something about the infant's initial venture in self-sufficiency—thumb-sucking. And as time passes, a varying degree of anxiety, identifiable to the infant as the undergoing of forbidding gestures and so on, is brought to bear to interfere with the infant's very important discovery that his body is, in a curious sense, invariably dependable. Thus the infant's activity in satisfying, by sucking his thumb, excess zonal needs pertaining to the mouth is apt to be brought under stern prohibition by the mothering one. So far as I know, this stern prohibition does not ever appear immediately, and even if it did, the infant would suck his thumb when the mother was not around. Thus the thumb-in-lips experience invariably takes places; we do not expect to find an infant who has not sucked his thumb. Nothing less than restraint apparatus to keep the hand away from the mouth would prevent an infant from doing so, and it is quite possible that the result of such very early restraint would be anything but a human being as we like to think of one. Thus there always occurs this discovery by the infant of what might presently be called by a variety of names such as self-sufficiency or (and this name is much more distressing to me) autoerotic perfection. But, as I have said, it is only a matter of time in most cases before this discovery by the infant becomes subject to strong pressure from the carrier of culture who is looking after the infant, lest there be evil effects from it.

By the exploration of the hands, as I have said, many things besides the mouth are discovered—among them, the feet, the umbilicus, the anus, and the external genitals. So far as I have yet detected in my very casual contact with infant-rearing, most mothering ones see nothing the matter with the infant's feeling of the umbilicus; by the time the infant has sufficient dexterity of the upper extremities to do so, the umbilicus will presumably be very nicely healed, and, therefore, there is no great risk of fatal infection. And since one of the deeply ingrained motor patterns seems to be a general motion of curling up, it is quite early that, for instance, a foot and a hand are brought into contact with each other; and that is all right from the mother's point of view.

But an equally convenient kind of exploration, from a geometrical standpoint—namely, feeling of the perineal region, the anus and the external genitals—is, in the estimation of the mothering one, a very different matter indeed. As I suggested before, there is a certain reason, probably ingrained in the organization of the human being, for keeping a certain distance from at least stale feces. Particularly in the northwestern European culture, if a culture area may be so described, the idea of the noxious character of the feces and even the noxious character of the anal region is very strikingly implanted. The hand manipulating the anus, as any mother knows, will shortly be the hand that is in the mouth; thanks to the great development of the doctrine of germs and to the doubts about physical and sexual purity and cleanliness— which are written into the so-called Christian underpinnings of Western culture, built in turn on the Jewish foundations—many mothers feel that a finger conveying anything from the perineal region to the mouth would be disastrous. Thus any exploration of the fecal mass by the hands of the baby, or any tinkering around the area that is touched by the fecal mass, frequently is extremely repellent to the mothering one. And even if these things are not so regarded by the mothering one, she will know that they are so regarded by a large number of other people. Thus the sooner she can get her young to leave that part of the body alone, the better for their standing as potential members of the community in which they live. And, therefore, while in a good many cases there is some pretty strong forbidding of much sucking of the thumb, there is almost invariably pretty strong forbidding of any tampering with the expelled feces or the anal orifice itself.

The social responsibilities and beliefs pertaining to the place of lust in life are somewhat different from those which apply to the expelled feces and the anal orifice itself, although they are all too frequently confused—that is, literally welded together. These beliefs and social responsibilities—the dangers to public decorum and personal standing in the community which presently will relate to what one does with and about one's genitals and other people's genitals—lead to the necessity for strong forbidding on the part of the mothering one of the infant's explorations of the external genitals by the hand.

Thus anxiety, and all sorts of blended feelings in which anxiety is an element, can be evoked in the mothering one with regard to the culturally strong taboos about feces—and even dirt, insofar as it comes to have a more or less fecal connotation—and about handling, or even looking at, the external genitals. The extent to which anxiety in the mothering one, and blended emotions in which anxiety composes an important part, can attach to these two fields of activity is very widely variable. On the one hand, the mothering one's attitude can be what I would say is simply necessary for the infant's becoming a person suitable for life in his particular community—that is, a gradual discouragement of interest in the extruded fecal mass and in the sentient anus, which feels as well as is felt, and in the genitals, which similarly feel as well as are felt. The mother may discourage this from very clear consideration of the customs and beliefs and interests which are acceptable in the community and in the community as she presumes it will develop by the time her young participate actively in it. On the other hand, the mothering one's attitude may be a state of practically sustained, very severe anxiety because baby handles his penis, let us say, or a state of sustained and severe anxiety over his getting his hands soiled with feces. This sometimes amounts to what a psychiatrist without previous acquaintance with the behavior would call frank, severe mental disorder—that is, major psychosis on the part of the mothering one. And this attitude can very successfully obliterate, by inducing intolerable anxiety in the infant, any possible chance of his catching on to what is happening. Thus the social responsibilities and beliefs of the mothering one are apt to interfere to a startling extent with the infant's very dependable, independent, appropriate and adequate action for the satisfaction of purely zonal needs. This may lead to all sorts of efforts by the mothering one—forbidding gestures which get more and more unpleasant, if not actually the inculcating of pain or the use of incredible orthopedic interferences—which are apt to be enforced to segregate out these zones of "ownness" as belonging to that queer thing which we shall shortly discuss as the area of personality called *not-me*.

Thus the development of the pattern of experience which will presently be manifest as the very extensive symbol organization called "my body" gets a good many additions and limitations from the mothering one who may be the embodiment of culture, prejudice, mental disorder, or what not; and so I believe it perfectly safe to say that no one can become a person with just a mature attitude toward his body—in other words, simply with that degree of information which can be acquired by the use of human abilities as they mature.

The Learning of Facial Expressions

Lest we lose track of a great deal that is going on by mid-infancy —that is, by the age of six to eight months—I want to call attention to another very important type of interpersonal process which has been at work. And the interpersonal process involved in the learning of facial expressions is closely related to the experience of "my body" and might be called one of the vicissitudes of ownness.

We are provided with muscular apparatus, fixed to the bones and cartilages of the head, which is capable of doing a great many useful and necessary things for the survival of the underlying animal and therefore of the person. Many of these muscular structures are immediately under a comparatively thin layer of covering—skin and some fatty tissue, and so on. The effector aspect of these muscles—the nerve centers and the muscular tissue itself—

is capable of a very striking manifestation of postural tonicity. A great many of the skeletal muscles are also capable of this postural tonicity but in a much less refined fashion. This postural tonicity has no immediate reference to, shall I say, the simplest function. For instance, the simplest function of these muscles in my arm is to pull up my arm, and they are ordinarily, except when I am asleep or under general anesthetic, maintaining a posture so they can immediately pull, if properly innervated; that is, when I am resting my hand on my thigh, these muscles do not just go flabby and hang down, so to speak. Instead, they come to rest in a posture which permits me immediately to move my forearm when I tighten these muscles. We speak of that as a postural tension, and, in the case of the arm muscles and many others, this postural tension is essentially a sort of active resting condition, so that immediate results can be brought about if there are to be changes in geometry.

With a good many of these effector structures around the face, the postural tensions are much more differentiated than in the case of the arm. And, while it is true that a person who is so mad that he could bite a tenpenny nail, as the expression has it, will be maintaining very high postural tension in his masseter or biting muscles, still these extreme examples of what we call emotional expression, or expressive postures, are not anywhere near easily equated with preparation, or resting preparedness for action, of these muscles. There is actually an enormous amount of change in the appearance of the surface of the face that can be brought about by shifting the pattern of postural tensions in a great many muscles in the face.

By mid-infancy, solely because of contact with the mothering one and any other significant people, the infant has learned certain patterns of postural tension of the face that are right and wrong. Among the most important of all these learnings is the coordination of posture and change of posture—that is, the expressive movement—of the face which is ordinarily called smiling. It might be thought, and in fact I am sure that for many years it has been taught, that we are born with instincts, or something of that general class, for smiling, and, I suppose, for expressing all sorts of things from respectful admiration to frank disgust. But that charmingly simple idea undergoes a little damage when we lift our eyes from our own community and bring them down on the very young in a strikingly alien culture area, such as, for example, Bali or one of the Micronesian Islands in the period before the war and the diffusion of Western culture. In these places, oddly enough, some human beings seem not to have the instinct to smile in the sense that we know it, but instead an instinct to smile in a very different way, so different that you wouldn't recognize it as a smile until you noticed what the others did in a similar situation. The point is that man has an unending, a numerically enormous, number of possible resting states of the face, and a still more enormous number of transitions in resting states of these so-called expressive muscles. Thus a truly astounding number of so-called expressions is possible, and it is by the organization of initially prototaxic experience, later elaborated further into combinations of sentience from various zones, that the infant gradually picks out from this numerical multitude rough approximations to what the culture-carriers esteem as expressions. That is literally the way that a great deal of our facial expression comes into being.

Facial expressions are always a blend of both postural tensions and motion. That is to say, a fixed frown, for example, rapidly loses its capacity to communicate to anyone, and becomes recognized as a feature. But prescribed changes from certain momentarily fixed postural tones to certain other momentarily fixed postural tones has immense and dependable communicative capacity for those who know each other—that is, for denizens of the same or approximately the same culture. These expressions are learned —and this learning is by trial and error under the influence of anxiety or the absence of anxiety. Insofar as there is success, there is nothing forbidding, no discouraging disturbance of euphoria. Insofar as things fail there is a disturbance of euphoria, again because of the social responsibility, and the expectation of the development of intelligence, and all sorts of things which the mothering one has about the infant. Thus people literally learn to express their emotions by trial-and-error approximations under the influence of anxiety. Now I am not talking here of how the infant looks very early in life when he is crying, but I am talking about how the infant looks when he is crying by the time he is twelve months old, by which time his crying shows a good deal of influence by the expectations, the use of minor forbidding gestures, the anxiety, and so on of the mothering one.

The Learning of Phonemes

I am now going to touch briefly on another type of learning which manifests itself in mid-infancy, and which I shall presently discuss in more detail. Provided the underlying human animal has not had any genetic or pathological misfortunes, by the sixth to eighth month a form of learning appears which is a manifestation of human potentialities of simply overwhelming importance in subsequent life: this is not trial-and-error learning under the influence of anxiety, but it is trial-and-error learning by human example or by human model. Here it is not the anxiety-tinted or euphoria-protecting attitude of the mothering one which determines success, but it is the infant's already developed coordination of two zones of interaction. We have touched upon one development of coordination which does not have human example— namely, the getting of the thumb into the lips. That appears to be arranged by a rather astounding connection in the central nervous system in the human and certain closely related species, the mouth being an enormous source of data in the early acquaintance with reality. But the coordination of two zones that I am now referring to is a coordination in which, when we first mentioned it, we did not separate the zones—this was when we spoke of the infant's hearing his own crying. I am now talking about hearing as an independent zone of interaction. The delicate coordination of sound production with activities of the hearing zone is now proceeding by maturation, and the infant is now 'experimenting' [2] in approximating sounds heard, needless to say, from others. There is no need for the infant to approximate sounds heard from himself—they are there, they always have been there. One of the first things we mentioned was the birth cry, which I suggested that the infant heard, but that was probably heard by bone conduction or anyway by solid conduction. But now I am talking about the long process of learning by trial and error from example, by

[2] When I use such words as "experimenting" in talking about the infant, you must understand that this is all illusory language and that I don't mean quite what you might find in the dictionary.

which the infant begins to approximate sounds *made by him* to sounds *heard by him*. And this development, which originally appears in rather curious noises commonly called gurgling and cooing, proceeds in the next few months through babbling to the actual close approximation of those particular stations in the continuum of sound which are the phonemes out of which the speech of the people significant to the infant is constructed. Now this cannot occur if the infant cannot hear, and it could not occur if the infant were living in an utterly mute and silent environment. But, barring these circumstances, as early as the eighth month after birth the coordination of the ear-receptor and the voice-producing apparatus is already beginning to manifest itself in what are literally the preliminaries to acquiring the capacity to make the right phonemal sounds, out of which all the stupendous structure of language will presently have its being.

CHAPTER
9

Learning: The Organization of Experience

I NOW want to take up an area of very great importance which I have never gotten very well under control. It is undoubtedly a field which requires multidisciplined thinking, and some of the people who could perhaps add most valuably to such a multiple approach are, unhappily, people who feel that psychiatrists have no business in this neighborhood—a form of craft-union antagonism which, I trust, will gradually fade into history. The topic I now wish to discuss is learning—that is, the organization of experience.

So far, the processes of maturation of the underlying animal have not yet included any of the more or less epoch-marking developments which will later concern us—such as the acquisition of language, in contrast to the very few sounds that are identified by others as words; the need for compeers with whom to interact; and the other maturations that mark off the eras of personality development. But still there has been a truly astounding series of maturations of the underlying capabilities, and by the end of the ninth month the infant is manifesting pretty unmistakable evidence of processes which are of the pattern of, or are rudimentary instances of, a very great deal of that which is peculiarly the human way of life. Maturation has progressed, thereby bringing into being capabilities of the underlying human animal for becoming a human being, and experience has been organized in the opportunities which are provided both by the cooperation with the mothering one, and by the rather incidental physical environment of objects and the like.

Thus by the end of the ninth month of infancy there are organizations of experience which are manifested in recall and foresight in many of the categories of behavior that make up the fully human type of living. Needless to say, these organizations are imperfectly developed. But the point is that they are manifested in patterns which make it highly probable that the rudiments of a large area of human living are already organized by the end of the ninth month. These organizations appear as growth of the dynamisms concerned, both with respect to the integration and maintenance of suitable situations, and with respect to the vector quality (the appropriateness and adequacy) of behavior in the resolution of the various situations—that is, with respect to the achievement of satisfaction as a goal. To say this a little differently, the close observation of situations, as early as the end of the ninth month, shows that there is considerable organization of experience which can be called the development of the appropriate dynamisms for integrating and maintaining situations, and for the choice—and I am using that word very broadly—of the appropriate and adequate energy transformations or activities for the achievement of the resolution of the situation—that is, for the satisfaction of the need which is involved.

This growth may be considered to result from sundry learning processes which rest on the necessary basis of serial maturation of capacities of the underlying animal, coupled with the opportunity for manifesting the ability concerned; in most cases the opportunity still involves an element of cooperation with the mothering one—that is, it is interpersonal. First, one always has to have the maturation of the capability; and secondly, one must have appropriate and useful experience, so that the ability, the actually demonstrable transformations of energy in activity addressed to the goal, appears; and experience of the type that we can call learning processes has a very great deal to do with the latter.

Learning by Anxiety

I am now going to set up a heuristic classification of the processes of learning. The first of all learning is, I think, beyond doubt in immediate connection with *anxiety*. I have already tried to suggest, and will again and again suggest, that severe anxiety probably contributes no information. The effect of severe anxiety reminds one in some ways of a blow on the head, in that it simply wipes out what is immediately proximal to its occurrence. If you have a severe blow on the head, you are quite apt later to have an incurable, absolute amnesia covering the few moments before your head was struck. Anxiety has a similar effect of producing useless confusion, and a useless disturbance of the factors of sentience which immediately preceded its onset, a phenomenon which is so striking that in later life the great problem of psychotherapy is very often centered on this very matter of getting the patient to see just when anxiety intervened, because that area is disturbed in such a way that it is almost as if it had not been.

Less severe anxiety does permit gradual realization of the situation in which it occurs, and there is unquestionably, even from very early in life, some learning of an inhibitory nature; that is, the transfer of attributes of "my body" to the "not-me" aspect of the universe. But regardless of all these refinements, the first greatly educative influence in living is doubtless anxiety, unqualified.

Vastly more important, in fact perhaps astoundingly important in its relation to our coming to be human beings acceptable to the particular society which we inhabit, is the next process of learning, which is learning on the basis of the *anxiety gradient*—that is, learning to discriminate increasing from diminishing anxiety and to alter activity in the direction of the latter. As I have said before, this notion of gradients can perhaps be illustrated by the distribution of amoebae in the water near, let us say, a hot spring. The conduction of heat in the water will result in a temperature gradient from extremely high, utterly beyond the temperature limits of life, down to a temperature lower than that in which the amoebae live most successfully. There is a certain optimum temperature for the growth of the amoebae, and at that point the concentration of amoebae will be very high. But because of peculiarities in the amoebae, or peculiarities in physical space which can hold only a certain number of amoebae, the concentration of amoebae will grade off both ways. There will be some amoebae in a rapidly declining triangle, we might say, toward the hotter water, and there will be some, perhaps the more underprivileged amoebae, trailing off as a tail into the colder water. What attenuates the concentration of amoebae, particularly in the direction of the hot water, is their avoidance of temperatures which are intolerable to their processes, which is no more mysterious than anything else that goes on in any of the living. Since these amoebae are influenced by that particular manifestation of energy called heat, they rise to a maximum very rapidly at a certain distance from the hot water, and decline to a minimum rather more slowly in the direction of the cold water.

Very early in human life there begins to be discrimination as to when euphoria is diminishing—that is, when one is getting more anxious; and this is really the discrimination of a gradient. The all-or-nothing character of anxiety and euphoria has disappeared very early in life—in fact, I doubt that it ever existed—and an immense amount of what is human behavior in any society is learned simply on the basis of this gradient from anxiety to euphoria. For example, the satisfaction of rubbing the anal region with the finger, let us say, might carry such rapidly increasing anxiety under certain circumstances—namely, in the presence of the mothering one, the social censor—that really quite early in life there might be learning about this. The infant might learn, first, that this is not to occur when the mothering one is around, which is, more or less, learning by pure anxiety; and secondly, that the peculiar circumstance of fiddling with this area through a blanket —even though the infant does not recognize the blanket as such— seems much less strikingly characterized by very rapidly mounting anxiety. And so, presently, direct manipulation of the anus may be restricted to periods of somnolence; or, if the impulse is quite strong, some mediate performance may be engaged in.

Now, if I make myself at all clear, you will realize that I am indicating here the formulation for a type of process of really staggering importance; I have never found a satisfactory name for this process, and therefore still use the good old term of the most traditional psychoanalytic standing—*sublimation*, the long-circuiting of the resolution of situations, chiefly those pertaining to zonal needs—a long-circuiting which proves to be socially acceptable. However, in considering this stage of infancy, one should not think in terms of impulses, social acceptability, and so on, but should realize that the actually describable and intelligible factor is the anxiety gradient, and that learning by the anxiety gradient often includes irrational tricks that permit satisfaction without encouraging notable anxiety. Needless to say, this begins at a time when anything like consensually valid formulation is simply inconceivable.

[Thus the infant] learns to chart a course by the anxiety gradient. Simple performances which would relax the tension of some needs have to be made more complicated in order that one may avoid becoming more anxious. Before he is very many months of age, the child will be showing full-fledged *sublimation*, in the sense of quite unwittingly having adopted some pattern of activity in the partial, and somewhat incomplete, satisfaction of a need which, however, avoids anxiety that stands in the way of the simplest completely satisfactory activity. . . . Whether it recurs in the second or the fifty-second year of chronological age, sublimation is, unwittingly, not a matter of conscious thought of a communicable sort, but rather the outcome of referential processes in the parataxic mode, in the service of avoiding or minimizing anxiety. . . .[1]

This unwitting development, which is the pattern of sublimation, becomes an important element in learning to be human—that is, in learning to behave as one should behave in a given society.

Other Learning Processes

The next important learning process is learning by *trial and success* of techniques for the relief of the tensions of needs. For example, in order to satisfy the zonal need to suck, the infant learns how to get the thumb into the proper position in the mouth. That is literally done by trial movements of the extremities, aided by a certain amount of visual sentience and a good deal of kinesthetic sentience. There are quite a number of misses and some hits, the hits being successes in getting the thumb into the mouth; and it is these successes that become stamped in as 'habits'—although 'habit' has many unfortunate connotations. In other words,

---

[1] [*Editors' note:* All the quotations in this chapter, including this one, are from Sullivan's "Tensions Interpersonal and International: A Psychiatrist's View," in *Tensions That Cause Wars,* edited by Hadley Cantril; Urbana, Ill.: Univ. of Ill. Press, 1950, pp. 95–98.]

the successes are the patterns of sentience and effector impulse which work.

Thus while unnumbered of the manipulative attempts of the infant's hands, for example, fail—which is, perhaps, in infancy not too astounding—some of them succeed. And again, diligent study of the infant shows that a success has a really remarkable fixing power. In other words, that which works, however wrongly designed, is very apt to become part of the activity resources of the person, which is true even in adult life. And so, second only to learning by the anxiety gradient is the learning of how to do things by trial and success.

In late infancy and from then on through life, an important process of learning is by *rewards and punishments*. Probably this kind of learning exists earlier in infancy, but this is more difficult to be sure of, since there it would have to depend on empathic factors.

The rewards which encourage learning in the very young probably begin with *fondling*, pleasure-giving manipulation of the child. They take in general the pattern of a change from relative indifference to the child to more or less active interest in and approval of whatever he seems to be doing. The need for "audience response" becomes conspicuous remarkably early in human life.

The punishments are commonly the inflicting of *pain*, the refusal of contact or of attention, and of course, the inducing of anxiety—a very special punishment. I know of no reason why punishment should be undesirable as an educative influence excepting it be anxiety-ladened. Pain has a very useful function in life and loneliness and the foresight of enforced isolation, the "fear of ostracism," is bound to be an important influence from early in the third stage of development.

The next very important learning process is *trial-and-error learning by human example*, or from human example. I have already mentioned this in discussing facial postures; smiling, as I have said, appears pretty early, while a number of other instances of this kind of learning can invariably be observed in late infancy—that is, very definitely under the age of eighteen months, and probably by the age of twelve months. In this kind of learning, unlike the manipulative learning, the error is important. The success is, you might say, just too good to be important. When success is achieved, the problem is finished. Success in manipulation, on the other hand, has the effect of immediately stamping in a pattern of behavior. But the error in this particular way of learning—learning from human example—is to be kept clearly in mind. It is what one observes as part of the content of consciousness, in those who are mature enough to communicate clearly their experience.

[Not only is this kind of learning probably exemplified in the patterning of facial expressions, but] it is certainly the chief agency in the acquisition of *language*. The phonemes of any system of speech have simply nothing to do with any but cultural necessity. The child learns to approximate from among an indeterminately great variety of vocal sounds that he utters, the particular sound-areas that are used by the significant people around him. In the same way, he picks up the patterns of tonal melody in their speech; often being able to reproduce the tonal, melodic, progressions of speaking well in advance of his "use" of any word.

The only other very important process in learning that I know of is the very refined process which Spearman called the *eduction* [2]—more or less the pulling out—of relations. This comes to be a highly complex capacity, rather strikingly, but by no means exclusively, restricted to the human. It is a capacity—of the most infinite complexity—of our nervous systems which enables us to get more and more to see relations which endure in nature and therefore are to a truly remarkable degree dependable. Spearman built up tests for superior intelligence which depended practically entirely on the capacity to educe, or to grasp, an increasingly complex series of relations which characterize the world as known.

The first instances of this sort of learning to live are purely matters of inference, but it is entirely reasonable to believe that some of the elementary mechanical-geometric relations pertaining to "parts" of a very important preconceptual "object," presently to be named *my body*, are prehended quite soon after birth.

And this process of educing relations can be observed in the infant in certain rudimentary aspects of his interpersonal relation with the mothering one before the use of words.

Every important process in learning which I have been able to formulate is illustrated, at least in rudiment, before speech. I would like to emphasize again the fact that beyond any perchance,

[2] [*Editors' note:* See Chapter 5, footnote 1.]

as early as or before the end of the tenth month in many instances, so much learning of sounds by trial and error, or from human example, appears that the baby sounds to a person at a little distance as if he were talking to himself. This is a truly amazing instance of human ability. I would like to remind you that in your dealings with friend and foe, stranger and intimate acquaintance, modifications and stresses in the tonal patterns of your remarks can do things which no words qua words could do. When you see how very early and how extremely important this form of learning is, and how basically important are the things which are learned, oh, so long before communicable thought can take place, you may perhaps feel a little more impressed with the importance of the phase of infancy.

CHAPTER 10

Beginnings of the Self-System

Three Aspects of Interpersonal Cooperation

WE HAVE got our human animal as far, in the process of becoming a person, as the latter part of infancy, and we find him being subjected more and more to the social responsibilities of the parent. As the infant comes to be recognized as educable, capable of learning, the mothering one modifies more and more the exhibition of tenderness, or the giving of tenderness, to the infant. The earlier feeling that the infant must have unqualified cooperation is now modified to the feeling that the infant should be learning certain things, and this implies a restriction, on the part of the mothering one, of her tender cooperation under certain circumstances.

Successful training of the functional activity of the anal zone of interaction accentuates a new aspect of tenderness—namely, the additive role of tenderness as a sequel to what the mothering one regards as good behavior. Now this is, in effect—however it may be prehended by the infant—a *reward*, which, once the approved social ritual connected with defecating has worked out well, is added to the satisfaction of the anal zone. Here is tenderness taking on the attribute of a reward for having learned something, or for behaving right.

Thus the mother, or the parent responsible for acculturation or socialization, now adds tenderness to her increasingly neutral behavior in a way that can be called rewarding. I think that very, very often the parent does this with no thought of rewarding the infant. Very often the rewarding tenderness merely arises from the pleasure of the mothering one in the skill which the infant has learned—the success which has attended a venture on the toilet chair, or something of that kind. But since tenderness in general is becoming more restricted by the parental necessity to train, these incidents of straightforward tenderness, following the satisfaction of a need like that to defecate, are really an addition—a case of getting something extra for good behavior—and this is, in its generic pattern, a reward. This type of learning can take place when the training procedure has been well adjusted to the learning capacity of the infant. The friendly response, the pleasure which the mother takes in something having worked out well, comes more and more to be something special in the very last months of infancy, whereas earlier, tenderness was universal when the mothering one was around, if she was a comfortable mothering one. Thus, to a certain extent, this type of learning can be called learning under the influence of reward—the reward being nothing more or less than tender behavior on the part of the acculturating or socializing mothering one.

Training in the functional activity of the oral-manual behavior —that is, conveying things by the hand to the mouth and so on— begins to accentuate the differentiation of anxiety-colored situations in contrast to approved situations. The training in this particular field is probably, in almost all cases, the area in which *grades of anxiety* first become of great importance in learning; as I have already stressed, behavior of a certain unsatisfactory type provokes increasing anxiety, and the infant learns to keep a distance from, or to veer away from, activities which are attended by increasing anxiety, just as the amoebae avoid high temperatures.

This is the great way of learning in infancy, and later in childhood—by the grading of anxiety, so that the infant learns to chart his course by mild forbidding gestures, or by mild states of worry, concern, or disapproval mixed with some degree of anxiety on the part of the mothering one. The infant plays, one might say, the old game of getting hotter or colder, in charting a selection of behavioral units which are not attended by an increase in anxiety. Anxiety in its most severe form is a rare experience after infancy, in the more fortunate courses of personality development, and anxiety as it is a function in chronologically adult life, in a highly civilized community confronted by no particular crisis, is never very severe for most people. And yet it is necessary to appreciate that it is anxiety which is responsible for a great part of the inadequate, inefficient, unduly rigid, or otherwise unfortunate performances of people; that anxiety is responsible in a basic sense for a great deal of what comes to a psychiatrist for attention. Only when this is understood, can one realize that this business of whether one is getting more or less anxious is in a large sense the basic influence which determines interpersonal relations—that is, it is not the motor, it does not call interpersonal relations into being, but it more or less directs the course of their development. And even in late infancy there is a good deal of learning by the anxiety gradient, particularly where there is a mothering one who is untroubled, but still intensely interested in producing the right kind of child; and this learning is apt to first manifest itself when the baby is discouraged from putting the wrong things in the mouth, and the like. This kind of learning applies over a vast area of behavior. But in this discussion I am looking for where things are apt to start.

Training of the manual-exploratory function—which I have discussed in connection with the infant's getting his hands near the anus, or into the feces, or, perhaps, in contact with the external genitals—almost always begins the discrimination of situations which are marked by what we shall later discuss as *uncanny emotion*. This uncanny feeling can be described as the abrupt supervention of *severe anxiety*, with the arrest of anything like the learning process, and with only gradual informative recall of the noted circumstances which preceded the extremely unpleasant incident.

Early in infancy, when situations approach the 'all-or-nothing' character, the induction of anxiety is apt to be the sudden translation from a condition of moderate euphoria to one of very severe anxiety. And this severe anxiety, as I have said before, has a little bit the effect of a blow on the head, in that later one is not clear at all as to just what was going on at the time anxiety became intense. The educative effect is not by any means as simple and useful as is the educative effect in the other two situations which we have discussed, because the sudden occurrence of severe anxiety practically prohibits any clear prehension, or understanding, of the immediate situation. It does not, however, preclude recall, and as recall develops sufficiently so that one recalls what was about to occur when severe anxiety intervened—in other words, when one has a sense of what one's action was addressed to at the time when everything was disorganized by severe anxiety—then there come to be in all of us certain areas of 'uncanny taboo,' which I think is a perfectly good way of characterizing those things which one stops doing, once one has caught himself doing them. This type of training is much less immediately useful, and, shall I say, is productive of much less healthy acquaintance with reality, than are the other two.

Good-Me, Bad-Me, and Not-Me

Now here I have set up three aspects of interpersonal cooperation which are necessary for the infant's survival, and which dictate learning. That is, these aspects of interpersonal cooperation require acculturation or socialization of the infant. Infants are customarily exposed to all of these before the era of infancy is finished. From experience of these three sorts—with rewards, with the anxiety gradient, and with practically obliterative sudden severe anxiety—there comes an initial personification of three phases of what presently will be *me*, that which is invariably connected with the sentience of *my body*—and you will remember that *my body* as an organization of experience has come to be distinguished from everything else by its self-sentient character. These beginning personifications of three different kinds, which have in common elements of the prehended body, are organized in about mid-infancy—I can't say exactly when. I have already spoken of the infant's very early double personification of the actual mothering one as the good mother and the bad mother. Now, at this time, the beginning personifications of *me* are *good-me*, *bad-me*, and *not-me*. So far as I can see, in practically every instance of being trained for life, in this or another culture, it is rather inevitable that there shall be this tripartite cleavage in personifications, which have as their central tie—the thing that binds them ultimately into one, that always keeps them in very close relation—their relatedness to the growing conception of "my body."

Good-me is the beginning personification which organizes experience in which satisfactions have been enhanced by rewarding increments of tenderness, which come to the infant because the mothering one is pleased with the way things are going; therefore, and to that extent, she is free, and moves toward expressing tender appreciation of the infant. Good-me, as it ultimately develops, is the ordinary topic of discussion about "I."

Bad-me, on the other hand, is the beginning personification which organizes experience in which increasing degrees of anxiety are associated with behavior involving the mothering one in its more-or-less clearly prehended interpersonal setting. That is to say, bad-me is based on this increasing gradient of anxiety and that, in turn, is dependent, at this stage of life, on the observation, if misinterpretation, of the infant's behavior by someone who can induce anxiety.[1] The frequent coincidence of certain behavior on the part of the infant with increasing tenseness and increasingly evident forbidding on the part of the mother is the source of the type of experience which is organized as a rudimentary personification to which we may apply the term bad-me.

So far, the two personifications I have mentioned may sound like a sort of laboring of reality. However, these personifications are a part of the communicated thinking of the child, a year or so later, and therefore it is not an unwarranted use of inference to presume that they exist at this earlier stage. When we come to the third of these beginning personifications, *not-me*, we are in a different field—one which we know about only through certain very special circumstances. And these special circumstances are not outside the experience of any of us. The personification of not-me is most conspicuously encountered by most of us in an occasional dream while we are asleep; but it is very emphatically encountered by people who are having a severe schizophrenic episode, in aspects that are to them most spectacularly real. As a matter of fact, it is always manifest—not every minute, but every day, in every life—in certain peculiar absences of phenomena where

---

[1] Incidentally, for all I know, anybody can induce anxiety in an infant, but there is no use cluttering up our thought by considering that, because frequency of events is of very considerable significance in all learning processes; and at this stage of life, when the infant is perhaps nine or ten months old, it is likely to be the mother who is frequently involved in interpersonal situations with the infant.

there should be phenomena; and in a good many people—I know not what proportion—it is very striking in its indirect manifestations (dissociated behavior), in which people do and say things of which they do not and could not have knowledge, things which may be quite meaningful to other people but are unknown to them. The special circumstances which we encounter in grave mental disorders may be, so far as you know, outside your experience; but they were not once upon a time. It is from the evidence of these special circumstances—including both those encountered in everybody and those encountered in grave disturbances of personality, all of which we shall presently touch upon—that I choose to set up this third beginning personification which is tangled up with the growing acquaintance of "my body," the personification of *not-me*. This is a very gradually evolving personification of an always relatively primitive character—that is, organized in unusually simple signs in the parataxic mode of experience, and made up of poorly grasped aspects of living which will presently be regarded as 'dreadful,' and which still later will be differentiated into incidents which are attended by awe, horror, loathing, or dread.

This rudimentary personification of not-me evolves very gradually, since it comes from the experience of intense anxiety—a very poor method of education. Such a complex and relatively inefficient method of getting acquainted with reality would naturally lead to relatively slow evolution of an organization of experiences; furthermore, these experiences are largely truncated, so that what they are really about is not clearly known. Thus organizations of these experiences marked by uncanny emotion—which means experiences which, when observed, have led to intense forbidding gestures on the part of the mother, and induced intense anxiety in the infant—are not nearly as clear and useful guides to anything as the other two types of organizations have been. Because experiences marked by uncanny emotion, which are organized in the personification of not-me, cannot be clearly connected with cause and effect—cannot be dealt with in all the impressive ways by which we explain our referential processes later—they persist throughout life as relatively primitive, unelaborated, parataxic symbols. Now that does not mean that the not-me component in adults is infantile; but it does mean that the not-me component is, in all essential respects, practically beyond discussion in communicative terms. Not-me is part of the very 'private mode' of living. But, as I have said, it manifests itself at various times in the life of everyone after childhood—or of nearly everyone, I can't swear to the statistics—by the eruption of certain exceedingly unpleasant emotions in what are called nightmares.

These three rudimentary personifications of *me* are, I believe, just as distinct as the two personifications of the objectively same mother were earlier. But while the personifications of me are getting under way, there is some change going on with respect to the personification of mother. In the latter part of infancy, there is some evidence that the rudimentary personality, as it were, is already fusing the previously disparate personifications of the good and the bad mother; and within a year and a half after the end of infancy we find evidence of this duplex personification of the mothering one as the good mother and the bad mother clearly manifested only in relatively obscure mental processes, such as these dreamings while asleep. But, as I have suggested, when we come to consider the question of the peculiarly inefficient and inappropriate interpersonal relations which constitute problems of mental disorder, there again we discover that the trend in organizing experience which began with this duplex affair has not in any sense utterly disappeared.

The Dynamism of the Self-System

From the essential desirability of being good-me, and from the increasing ability to be warned by slight increases of anxiety—that is, slight diminutions in euphoria—in situations involving the increasingly significant other person, there comes into being the start of an exceedingly important, as it were, secondary dynamism, which is purely the product of interpersonal experience arising from anxiety encountered in the pursuit of the satisfaction of general and zonal needs. This secondary dynamism I call the *self-system*. As a dynamism it is secondary in that it does not have any particular zones of interaction, any particular physiological apparatus, behind it; but it literally uses all zones of interaction and all physiological apparatus which is integrative and meaningful from the interpersonal standpoint. And we ordinarily find its ramifications spreading throughout interpersonal relations in every area where there is any chance that anxiety may be encountered.

The essential desirability of being good-me is just another way of commenting on the essential undesirability of being anxious. Since the beginning personification of good-me is based on experience in which satisfactions are enhanced by tenderness, then naturally there is an essential desirability of living good-me. And since sensory and other abilities of the infant are well matured by now—perhaps even space perception, one of the slowest to come along, is a little in evidence—it is only natural that along with this essential desirability there goes increasing ability to be warned by slight forbidding—in other words, by slight anxiety. Both these situations, for the purpose now under discussion, are situations involving another person—the mothering one, or the congeries of mothering ones—and she is becoming increasingly significant because, as I have already said, the manifestation of tender cooperation by her is now complicated by her attempting to teach, to socialize the infant; and this makes the relationship more complex, so that it requires better, more effective differentiation by the infant of forbidding gestures, and so on. For all these reasons, there comes into being in late infancy an organization of experience which will ultimately be of nothing less than stupendous importance in personality, and which comes entirely from the interpersonal relations in which the infant is now involved—and these interpersonal relations have their motives (or their motors, to use a less troublesome word) in the infant's general and zonal needs for satisfaction. But out of the social responsibility of the mothering one, which gets involved in the satisfaction of the infant's needs, there comes the organization in the infant of what might be said to be a dynamism directed at how to live with this significant other person. The self-system thus is an organization of educative experience called into being by the necessity to avoid or to minimize incidents of anxiety.[2] The functional activity of the

[2] Since *minimize* in this sense can be ambiguous, I should make it clear that I refer, by minimizing, to moving, in behavior, in the direction which is marked by diminishing anxiety. I do not mean, by minimize, to "make little of," because so far as I know, human ingenuity cannot make little of anxiety.

self-system—I am now speaking of it from the general standpoint of a dynamism—is primarily directed to avoiding and minimizing this disjunctive tension of anxiety, and thus indirectly to protecting the infant from this evil eventuality in connection with the pursuit of satisfactions—the relief of general or of zonal tensions.

Thus we may expect, at least until well along in life, that the components of the self-system will exist and manifest functional activity in relation to every general need that a person has, and to every zonal need that the excess supply of energy to the various zones of interaction gives rise to. How conspicuous the 'sector' of the self-system connected with any particular general need or zonal need will be, or how frequent its manifestations, is purely a function of the past experience of the person concerned.

I have said that the self-system begins in the organizing of experience with the mothering one's forbidding gestures, and that these forbidding gestures are refinements in the personification of the bad mother; this might seem to suggest that the self-system comes into being by the *incorporation* or *introjection* of the bad mother, or simply by the introjection of the mother. These terms, incorporation or introjection, have been used in this way, not in speaking of the self-system, but in speaking of the psychoanalytic superego, which is quite different from my conception of the self-system. But, if I have been at all adequate in discussing even what I have presented thus far, it will be clear that the use of such terms in connection with the development of the self-system is a rather reckless oversimplification, if not also a great magic verbal gesture the meaning of which cannot be made explicit. I have said that the self-system comes into being because the pursuit of general and zonal needs for satisfaction is increasingly interfered with by the good offices of the mothering one in attempting to train the young. And so the self-system, far from being anything like a function of or an identity with the mothering one, is an organization of experience for avoiding increasing degrees of anxiety which are connected with the educative process. But these degrees of anxiety cannot conceivably, in late infancy (and the situation is similar in most instances at any time in life), mean to the infant what the mothering one, the socializing person, believes she means, or what she actually represents, from the standpoint of the culture being inculcated in the infant. This idea that one can, in some way, take in another person to become a part of one's personality is one of the evils that comes from overlooking the fact that between a doubtless real 'external object' and a doubtless real 'my mind' there is a group of processes—the act of perceiving, understanding, and what not—which is intercalated, which is highly subject to past experience and increasingly subject to foresight of the neighboring future. Therefore, it would in fact be one of the great miracles of all time if our perception of another person were, in any greatly significant number of respects, accurate or exact. Thus I take some pains at this point to urge you to keep your mind free from the notion that I am dealing with something like the taking over of standards of value and the like from another person. Instead, I am talking about the organization of experience connected with relatively successful education in becoming a human being, which begins to be manifest late in infancy.

When I talk about the self-system, I want it clearly understood that I am talking about a *dynamism* which comes to be enormously important in understanding interpersonal relations. This dynamism is an explanatory conception; it is not a thing, a region, or what not, such as superegos, egos, ids, and so on.[3] Among the things this conception explains is something that can be described as a quasi-entity, the personification of the self. The personification of the self is what you are talking about when you talk about yourself as "I," and what you are often, if not invariably, referring to when you talk about "me" and "my." But I would like to make it forever clear that *the relation of personifications to that which is personified is always complex and sometimes multiple;* and that *personifications are not adequate descriptions of that which is personified.* In my effort to make that clear, I have gradually been compelled,

[3] Please do not bog down unnecessarily on the problem of whether my self-system ought to be called the superego or the ego. I surmise that there is some noticeable relationship, perhaps in the realm of cousins or closer, between what I describe as the personification of the self and what is often considered to be the psychoanalytic ego. But if you are wise, you will dismiss that as facetious, because I am not at all sure of it; it has been so many years since I found anything but headaches in trying to discover parallels between various theoretical systems that I have left that for the diligent and scholarly, neither of which includes me.

in my teaching, to push the beginnings of things further and further back in the history of the development of the person, to try to reach the point where the critical deviations from convenient ideas become more apparent. Thus I am now discussing the beginning of the terrifically important self-dynamism as the time when —far from there being a personification of the self—there are only rudimentary personifications of good-me and bad-me, and the much more rudimentary personification of not-me. These rudimentary personifications constitute anything but a personification of the self such as you all believe you manifest, and which you believe serves its purpose, when you talk about yourselves one to another in adult life.

The Necessary and Unfortunate Aspects of the Self-System

The origin of the self-system can be said to rest on the irrational character of culture or, more specifically, society. Were it not for the fact that a great many prescribed ways of doing things have to be lived up to, in order that one shall maintain workable, profitable, satisfactory relations with his fellows; or, were the prescriptions for the types of behavior in carrying on relations with one's fellows perfectly rational—then, for all I know, there would not be evolved, in the course of becoming a person, anything like the sort of self-system that we always encounter. If the cultural prescriptions which characterize any particular society were better adapted to human life, the notions that have grown up about incorporating or introjecting a punitive, critical person would not have arisen.

But even at that, I believe that a human being without a self-system is beyond imagination. It is highly probable that the type of education which we have discussed, even probably the inclusion of certain uncanny experience that tends to organize in the personification of not-me, would be inevitable in the process of the human animal's becoming a human being. I say this because the enormous capacity of the human animal which underlies human personality is bound to lead to exceedingly intricate specializations—differentiations of living, function, and one thing and another; to maintain a workable, profitable, appropriate, and adequate type of relationship among the great numbers of people that can become involved in a growing society, the young have to be taught a vast amount before they begin to be significantly involved in society outside the home group. Therefore, the special secondary elaboration of the sundry types of learning—which I call the self-system—would, I believe, be a ubiquitous aspect of all really human beings in any case. But in an ideal culture, which has never been approximated and at the present moment looks as if it never will be, the proper function of the self-system would be conspicuously different from its actual function in the denizens of our civilization. In our civilization, no parental group actually reflects the essence of the social organization for which the young are being trained in living; and after childhood, when the family influence in acculturation and socialization begins to be attenuated and augmented by other influences, the discrete excerpts, you might say, of the culture which each family has produced as its children come into collision with other discrete excerpts of the culture—all of them more or less belonging to the same cultural system, but having very different accents and importances mixed up in them. As a result of this, the self-system in its actual functioning in life in civilized societies, as they now exist, is often very unfortunate. But do not overlook the fact that the self-system comes into being because of, and can be said to have as its goal, the securing of necessary satisfaction without incurring much anxiety. And however unfortunate the manifestations of the self-system in many contexts may seem, always keep in mind that, if one had no protection against very severe anxiety, one would do practically nothing—or, if one still had to do something, it would take an intolerably long time to get it done.

So you see, however truly the self-system is the principal stumbling block to favorable changes in personality—a point which I shall develop later on—that does not alter the fact that it is also the principal influence that stands in the way of unfavorable changes in personality. And while the psychiatrist is skillful, in large measure, in his ability to formulate the self-system of another person with whom he is integrated, and to, shall I say, "intuit" the self-system aspects of his patient which tend to perpetuate the type of morbid living that the patient is showing, that still, in no sense, makes the self-system something merely to be regretted. In any event, it is always before us, whether we regret or praise it. This idea of the self-system is simply tremendously important in understanding the vicissitudes of interpersonal relations from here on. If we understand how the self-system begins, then perhaps we will be able to follow even the most difficult idea connected with its function.

The self-system is a product of educative experience, part of which is of the character of reward, and a very important part of which has the graded anxiety element that we have spoken of. But quite early in life, anxiety is also a very conspicuous aspect of the self-dynamism *function*. This is another way of saying that experience functions in both recall and foresight. Since troublesome experience, organized in the self-system, has been experience connected with increasing grades of anxiety, it is not astounding that this element of recall, functioning on a broad scale, makes the intervention of the self-dynamism in living tantamount to the warning, or foresight, of anxiety. And warning of anxiety means noticeable anxiety, really a warning that anxiety will get worse.

There are two things which I would like to mention briefly at this point. One is the infant's discovery of the unobtainable, his discovery of situations in which he is powerless, regardless of all the cooperation of the mothering one. The infant's crying for the full moon is an illustration of this. Now even before the end of infancy, it is observable that these unattainable objects gradually come to be treated *as if* they did not exist; that is, they do not call out the expression of zonal needs. This is possibly the simplest example of a very important process manifested in living which I call *selective inattention*.

The other thing I would like to mention is this: Where the parental influence is peculiarly incongruous to the actual possibilities and needs of the infant—before speech has become anything except a source of marvel in the family, before it has any communicative function whatever, before alleged words have any meaning—there can be inculcated in this growing personification of bad-me and not-me disastrous distortions which will manifest themselves, barring very fortunate experience, in the whole subsequent development of personality. I shall soon discuss some typical distortions, one of the most vicious of which occurs in late infancy as the outcome of the mothering one's conviction that infants have *wills* which have to be guided, governed, broken, or shaped. And when, finally, we come to discuss concepts of mental disorders we will have to pick up the manifestations of a few particularly typical distortions, in each subsequent stage from the time that they first occur.

CHAPTER
11

The Transition from Infancy to Childhood: The Acquisition of Speech as Learning

The Consistency and Sanity of the Parental Efforts at Education

IN LATE infancy, there are increasing efforts by the parents, principally the mothering one, to perfect the socialization, or the beginning socialization, of the infant. In this socialization process, I wish to emphasize the element of *frequency* in the infant's experience, which is important in any relatively inadequate creature's learning of complex entities, or acquiring of complex patterns of behavior—and this is more and more the situation which the infant is really in. And along with the element of frequency, the element of *consistency* must be grasped as very important; consistency may be considered a function of frequency, insofar as consistency means repetition of a particular pattern of events, just as inconsistency means a reduced frequency of a pattern of events or a greater variety of patterns of events. Many of the difficulties which show up from the end of the first year of life onward may prove to be the accumulating results of inconsistencies in the efforts of the acculturating parent to teach the infant what is what. The extent to which the parent fails to provide anything like an invariant pattern of events takes on very great significance at the time when the child is using speech as his outstanding acquisition, say, in the third year of life; but it is improbable that the parental influence which is strikingly inconsistent at that time was anything like wholly consistent at, say, the end of the first year of life. Therefore, it is rather difficult to say just when deviations in the consistency and frequency of interpersonal events begin to bear on the development of personality.

Now besides the elements of consistency or inconsistency, frequency or infrequency, in the interpersonal events to which the infant is subjected, there is also to be considered another element, which I call, in the absence of a better word, the *sanity* of the educational efforts. By sanity I mean the parental modification of these efforts in accordance with the infant's capacity for observation, analysis, and elaboration of experience at a given time. Let me mention a few negative examples which possibly will illustrate what I am driving at.

One instance might be described as the doctrine of the will, which is a result of parental misinformation—all too easy to acquire and to retain in this civilization. Now I cannot at this time discuss *in extenso* the roots from which arises the illusion that we have a more-or-less all-powerful, or at least magically potent, will. But I do wish to invite your attention to the disastrous effects of treating a year-old baby as if he were being willfully troublesome. No matter what any of us may believe about the will, I think that most of us would not push the idea of the powerful will so far as to include the twelfth month of life after birth. But some parents do, and become involved in all sorts of curious, if not subpsychotic, attempts to guide, direct, break, manage, and so on, the self-willed infant.

My second example of, shall I say, insanity in the socializing influences brought to bear from the twelfth month onward is one which is much less conspicuously based on unutterable misconceptions of personality development. This is the subjection of the infant to a person, to a mothering one, who regrets the fact that the infant must grow up, and in a good many ways encourages him to stay put. Thus she provides experience, rewards, and anxiety in a fashion that works against the process of maturation in her offspring, and will presently, unless something changes radically in their relationship, literally be trying to keep the child young.

Another example of what I would consider a lack of sanity of educative effort is the idea that the infant must be clean and dry by, let us say, the age of fifteen months, an achievement of which the mother is insufferably proud. I have encountered pretty dependable evidences of a history of early training of this kind in quite a number of gravely—in fact, quite hopelessly—disordered people. I believe that I am correct in saying that the only way one could get an infant of fifteen months to be clean and dry would be by setting up terrific anxiety barriers to the development of anything like practical, useful, helpful feelings about the perineal area in the evolution of the concept "my body" and all its relationships to the concept "me."

In a very much more considerable number of disturbed, disordered personalities, I have uncovered another vicissitude of early training which can be regarded as not sane, and which I have already discussed; this is what I used to call the primitive genital phobia, where the parent is fearsomely upset by the infant's tinkering with the external genitals. Before the end of infancy, well before there is any speech behavior, all sorts of incredible orthopedic devices—marbles in the pajama back, bandages, and this and that—are sometimes used to prevent this supposedly dreadful component of the infant's manual exploratory performances. Insofar as such training occurs before the genital sentience is well integrated into experience, it can only be incredibly unrelated to anything that is any good to us in later life. Even insofar as it comes after the special sentience of the genitals—which you must remember is quite limited until the lust dynamism has matured —there too it represents, as it were, a hole punched in the totality of "my body," and is responsible for certain peculiarities encountered in later life, such as desiring to be masturbated by somebody else but having a dreadful time if one masturbates oneself, and so forth. Such easily misunderstood intricacies of the later so-called sex life are the outcome of quite seriously deviated personality development beginning before childhood.

Now these instances of "insanity" that I am laying before you may be generalized under a topic I have previously touched on —namely, the parental expectations about the infant, which are a part of the personification of the infant existing in the mothering one. Even in this realm of pure expectation on the part of the parents, a peculiar viciousness may appear as the infant approaches the end of infancy, by which time the infant has acquired, to a certain extent, expressive posturings of the face, the so-called expressions of pleasure and displeasure, and so on, and has lost much of the peculiar lineaments which are the rule at birth and a few months afterward. So it is that, in certain families and with certain mothering ones, the expectations about the infant now begin to take on color on the basis of whom the infant is alleged to look like, and whom the infant is now detected to be showing signs of "taking after." And the person whom the infant is supposed to look like, or take after, may be either a real parent or relative or even a mythological ancestor. In certain situations, these fancied resemblances in looks or in behavioral rudiments are very much more important, in the formulation of behavior by the mothering one, than are the infant's looks or behavior as they might be observed by someone with scientific detachment. Where parental expectations bring about this kind of situation, certain accidental events actually begin to take precedence over, and thereby interfere with, certain learning processes that were already started, which I shall touch on presently.

Overt and Covert Processes

I want now to develop further some points that I have not developed adequately as I went along. As I have discussed recall and foresight previously, the discussion has centered around the influence of past experience on living, if that past experience has recurred frequently enough—or has been otherwise sufficiently marked by importance—for it to be organized into signs. The function of organized experience in present behavior can be called, in part, the manifestation of sign processes in recall and foresight. Up to the ninth or tenth month the observer has nothing to work on other than inference, in convincing himself of the importance of this organized experience. It is not subject to clear, objective demonstration, but has to be inferred from what can be observed.

Now at this point I wish to make a perduring distinction—a distinction that will be important from infancy to the end of living —between what can be observed by a participant observer, and what can never be so observed but must always be the result of inference from that which is observed. And this is the distinction between *overt processes* in interpersonal relations and *covert processes*.[1]

A great deal that I have described thus far has concerned covert processes, and has been arrived at as a result of inference. As soon as speech behavior appears, it begins to be what it forever after will be, a wonderfully good index to the probability of the correctness of the inference. Moreover, in the latter months of infancy, there are better grounds for making certain inferences about the covert processes because of the beginning manifestation of the phenomenon of *delayed behavior*. I have spoken earlier of how the tension of anxiety acts in direct vector opposition to needs. It is now possible to observe in the young that needs themselves rather unmistakably manifest a certain hierarchical organization. Sometimes hunger takes precedence over something else that is going on, and behavior calculated to satisfy hunger—or behavior in the pursuit of the satisfaction of hunger—interrupts, as it were, something else that was going on; but, when the hunger is satisfied, instead of sleep supervening, the interrupted activity is resumed again, and has apparently been waiting in a sort of quiescent state until the more potent motivation worked itself out or was satisfied. Occasionally one will see, when the interrupted activity is resumed, that there has actually been some change in its situational pattern. It is to be inferred from this observation that something has certainly been going on in connection with the delayed or interrupted motivation, at the same time that the more potent motivation was moving on to satisfaction. Such inferred activity I call covert activity, in contradistinction to that which is clearly manifest.[2]

---

[1] I did not always use these terms; at one time I talked about implicit processes instead of covert ones. I have now abandoned the word implicit, because it has picked up so many shades of meaning which are troublesome or irrelevant to what I am attempting to communicate that some other word in common use has seemed more desirable. The discrimination of covert, as against overt, serves just as nicely.

[2] As a matter of fact, I have picked up a good deal of data which suggest that it may be possible to infer covert processes from delayed behavior manifested by the infant even before the age of six weeks. If these data are correct, they mean that covert symbol operations in connection with zonal

Thus by the end of infancy and on the threshold of childhood, one does see what can only, I think, be explained as the continuation of symbol operations behind a screen, one might say—the screen being the presenting activity, the energy transformation connected with the satisfaction of a stronger need. It is as if some sign processes had been going on during the period that behavior in the satisfaction of an intercurrent need was in progress, and the whole thing had progressed covertly. This sort of thing one can see in oneself very well, the most distinguished example being perhaps the phenomenon of how greatly puzzled one may be about some problem in the afternoon or evening, and how perfectly lucid one may be about the same problem early next morning after one has slept on it.

Now these covert processes might be taken to be extremely private, and also not at all directly susceptible to the type of social patterning, of educative change, which most certainly applies to quite a substantial part of the overt behavior of the year-old infant. In origin, however, these covert processes have been derived from the organization of experiences which were essentially interpersonal, however little the personification of the other person may have developed in the infant. Perhaps the only time when it is not possible to recognize covert processes as interpersonal phenomena is when a kind of synthesis of interpersonal events has taken place —as might often happen in these processes—by which one has arrived at new conclusions by combining old experiences in a new fashion; when that has happened there may seem to be no direct connection with specific interpersonal events.

As I further develop the topic of the self-system and its function, it will become clear, I believe, that many covert processes which were all right at the age of, let us say, twelve months, have been rigidly excluded from the repertory of the older person, chiefly by dint of learning under the guidance of anxiety; and that any possibility of the appearance of these covert processes promptly brings out a degree of anxiety that is ordinarily sufficient to interfere with their appearance.

---

and general needs show up in a rudimentary form amazingly early in the postnatal life of the human young.

The Learning of Gesture and Language

Of the learning that goes on from the end of the first year, the immediately and vastly important congeries is the acquisition of overt behavior which belongs to what might well be called two grand divisions of interpersonal communicative behavior, namely, those of gesture [3] and of language. In order to suggest the great importance of the gestural performance of speech, I might point out that it is only in quite restricted fields of living—for example, when a scientist is being a good scientist—that language behavior is stripped of gestural components. Most people would find such rigidly defined language behavior rather more soporific than communicative.

The learning of gestures, by which I include the learning of facial expressions, is manifested by the infant, certainly well before the twelfth month, in the learning of the rudiments, one might say, of verbal pantomime. And this learning is, in good measure, learning by trial-and-error approximation to human example. Quite recently I observed the most amazing instance of this, in my exceedingly limited experience. My most recent full-time nurse was delivered, now about eleven months ago, of a robust infant whom I saw for the first time, after my fashion of interest in infants, within the last month. During this visit I was utterly amazed to notice that under our conversation the infant was carrying on a very interesting conversation of his own. I discovered that what had caught my attention was the beautiful tonal pattern. Only perhaps fifty percent of the sounds were, I would say, good phonemal stations in the English language, but the melody, the pattern of tone, was speech; it was what our speech would be like if speech were not articulate. In other words, before this infant was twelve months old, he had, by trial-and-error learning from what he heard—he was being raised in a very vocal home—

[3] [*Editors' note:* Sullivan used "gesture" in a somewhat broader sense than is usual; in other lectures, and in other parts of this lecture, it becomes clear that by gesture he included, not only facial expressions and pantomime with other parts of the body, but also the melody, rhythm, and emphasis of speech. In other words, by gesture he referred to the "expressive," as opposed to the "denotative" aspects of speech—terms which he used in the 1948 lecture series.]

gotten the melodic progression of speech very nicely within his competence, so that there was nothing obviously infantile in it. It was so startlingly like speech that I could distinguish it only by careful listening, and only after I listened for a while could I tell that it included many things that would never be English words. Here was an example of the very early acquisition of a very large part of the gestural aspects of speech.

I might suggest that the acquisition of mannerisms through trial-and-error learning by human example is by no means confined to early life. The number of chronologic adults who are big chunks of mimicry, particularly regarding the gestural aspects of speech, is amazing. Psychiatrists often find that patients begin to sound like them; even though the phonemes they use, if analyzed, would prove to be quite different, the tonal gesture, melody, and so on, come to resemble theirs. In one instance, I could no longer tell which of two people was speaking to me on the telephone, although they once were quite easily identified by what came over the telephone. As a particular instance, I have one old friend who, for some reason that I have never felt free to investigate, fairly early in his professional career acquired the habit of turning on his smile for a moment as if a switch were operating it, and then suddenly switching it off. I have watched among some of his colleagues the acquisition, well along in professional life, of certain degrees of skill at this flashlight smile. Thus I suggest to you that what begins here in the very last stage of infancy doesn't stop then.

Even before the era of childhood, learning of the gestural aspects of speech, and so on, is already manifest; and this business of picking up more and more of the nonverbal, but nonetheless communicative, aspects of speech behavior is well established by that time and continues to be one of our manifest abilities, even if unnoted, for a very long period thereafter. In other words, before speech itself is actually possible—that is, literally during what I consider infancy—a great deal of learning can not only be incorporated into speech behavior, but is actually quite clearly manifest in those infants who are not especially handicapped by anxiety. The first thing which the infant unquestionably picks out from the verbal performances of the mother is the progression of tones and silences—and remember that silence is as much a part of speech as sound is; this progression is more or less the rhythmic tonal pattern to which all domestic animals are apt to show quite specific sensitivity. I trust that I have given some little notion of how early the various components appear that finally add themselves up to language behavior—the remarkably early abilities to catch on to vocal melodies and grosser sound patterns, and to perfect—by trial-and-error learning from the human examples around one—the refined little patterns or subpatterns of sound which make up the phonemal stations used by the language of the home.

The Roles of Reward and Indifference in the Learning of Language

Now I want to invite your attention to effects that the responses of the mother and other significant persons have on these abilities. Quite early, I suppose by the eighth or ninth month, the infant is spacing things like "da" so that it comes out "da-da-da" and presently "da-*da*-da." This means that the element of melodic repetition, the rhythmic tonal business, is already being caught on to by the infant. In this process some things like "dada" happen to be said at an appropriate time, so that an enthusiastic parent is apt to wonder if it isn't an attempt to say "mama" or "papa" or something else, and there is a certain amount of response. If by any chance "mama" is said, that is considered proof that the child has learned to call mother something (which I think is almost infinitely improbable), and there is a strong tender response. I think this is about all there is to it, although I am sure it won't endear me to parents. Thus out of the infant's mere repetitive syllabic experimentation, those experiments which happen to come somewhere near what is supposed to be appropriate baby talk get themselves stamped in, and so meet with much response, reiteration, and attention from the mothering one. When the learning has progressed to the point where different syllabic forms, different combinations of phonemes, and some vague attempts to imitate what is heard get said, there actually appears the beginning of the extremely rich development of sounds, tonal patterns, rhythms, and what not that make up the various great and small languages of the world, including the baby's private language. It is at this time, when the baby is saying things other than mere dada's and caca's and mama's, that the element of learning by reward enters in, so that the child's satisfaction in making vocal noises and hitting, by trial and error, on things that he has heard is now augmented by the tenderness of the mothering one. In addition, there comes in another great teaching influence, which I have not previously stressed—teaching by, of all things, *indifference*. Although it has been there all the time, it takes on particular significance only when the element of teaching by the reward of additional tenderness becomes a conspicuous part of the infant's life. This teaching by indifference is the paradigm of one of the most powerful influences to which man is subjected in later life, which I will, at the cost of getting entirely off the beam, mention as the fear of ostracism.

The very important element in the development of the baby's language is that while a lot of his vocal inventions receive reward, a great many of them do not provoke any response in the mother —and, needless to say, the busier she is and the less imagination she has, the greater will be the proportion of vocal inventions which receive no response. These latter are good only for what little zonal satisfaction there may have been in the hearing of them, and so they tend to drop out, for they don't accomplish anything—they get no special returns. Therefore, perhaps to an extraordinary extent, from the twelfth to the eighteenth month, the vocal efforts which in the presence of the mothering one do not happen to hit the right area fail of frequent repetition. As inter-personal relations grow, this element of socialization under the influence of indifference—which is a case neither of reward by tenderness nor of anxiety, but just a case where nothing happens —becomes pretty powerful.

Autistic Language

In the stage where this learning is well under way the baby develops a language, not the mother's language, not English (I am assuming that it is an English-speaking home), but the baby's own language. It is pertinent to note Edward Sapir's statement that ". . . the elements of language, the symbols that ticket off experience, must . . . be associated with whole groups, delimited classes, of experience rather than with the single experiences themselves." [4] And it is under this interpretation of language—which incidentally is the only interpretation that I have ever heard that made any sense—that we find the baby developing a language in which there is a certain amount of consensus that a particular sound refers to a particular class of events—that is, to a particular class of experience. For example, let us suppose that when the mother brings the nursing bottle or the bowl of food or whatever year-olds use, the baby, by sheer accident, were to say "ha." Now, under certain circumstances, which I cannot possibly discuss, a situation might be set up so that the next time this happens he again would say "ha," whereupon the mother would become much impressed by the probability that "ha" refers to food. And very quickly "ha"—a perfectly good word—does refer to food. It doesn't happen to be very useful in talking to Aunt Mary, who is a rare visitor in the house, but she can be told about it. The point is that it is in a sense a perfectly good language—and such language grows rather rapidly—but it has exceedingly little widespread communicative power. It is what we will later come to name *autistic;* [5] it is rather dangerous to describe it as the baby's private language, for its evolution is not private at all. Certain sound combinations have come, through the influence of the mother, to mean certain types of events. Needless to say, if there are nurses and the like running around the place, this baby language will not have even approximate communicative power to any one of them. In any case, the communicative power of this language is limited because it is all a language of nouns; incidentally, when it comes

[4] [Edward Sapir, *Language: An Introduction to the Study of Speech;* New York: Harcourt, Brace and Co., 1921; p. 11.]

[5] [*Editors' note:* Sullivan says that autistic is ". . . an adjective by which we indicate a primary, unsocialized, unacculturated state of symbol activity, and later states pertaining more to this primary condition than to the conspicuously effective consensually validated symbol activities of more mature personality" (*Conceptions of Modern Psychiatry;* New York: W. W. Norton & Company, 1953, second edition; p. 17).

Patrick Mullahy has described Sullivan's "autistic" as a "subspecies of the parataxic . . . . a verbal manifestation of the parataxic" ("A Theory of Interpersonal Relations and the Evolution of Personality," the same reference, p. 126).]

to verbs, the learning is much more deliberate, in the sense that the mothering one tries to teach their use.

I have discussed the baby's inventing words by establishing connections between a particular enunciated tonal pattern and a particular event or object, and the baby's learning to approximate particular words taught it by the mothering one. Now here are two classes of words that are being built into the baby's vocabulary, so to speak, both of which are autistic, in that only rarely is there a clear relation between a word and the really significant denotation of that same word in language used for communicative purposes among adults. Furthermore, in many, many instances the mother has satisfied some need that I do not understand very well by exposing the infant for a long time, even before the appearance of an autistic language, to sundry distortions of the communicative speech of the society in which she lives, which are called "baby talk." Some of this baby talk has taught the infant the significant approving and forbidding melody patterns of speech. Some of it is imagined to be of educative value because it is supposed to be the sort of speech that the baby can himself manage. However, I am afraid that there is very seldom any correlation between the amount of baby talk the baby hears and his abilities for learning words.

Language as Syntaxic Experience

Insofar as there happens to be a coincidence between the dictionary meanings of words and the infant's prehension and organization of experiences and activities by nouns and verbs—to that extent the language of the very young is beginning to manifest what I shall henceforth discuss as *experience in the syntaxic mode*. In fact, the first unquestionable organization of experience in the syntaxic mode is in the realm of the two great genera of communicative behavior, gesture and speech. And since the syntaxic, as we will later show it, is closely related to such things as the illusion of volition, I should stress that syntaxic symbols are best illustrated by words that have been consensually validated. A consensus has been reached when the infant or child has learned the precisely right word for a situation, a word which means not only what it is thought to mean by the mothering one, but also means that to the infant. Incidentally, an enormous amount of difficulty all through life arises from the fact that communicative behavior miscarries because words do not carry meaning, but evoke meaning. And if a word evokes in the hearer something quite different from that which it was expected to evoke, communication is not a success.

As I have indicated, the first instances of experience in the syntaxic mode appear between, let us say, the twelfth and the eighteenth month of extrauterine life, when verbal signs—words, symbols—are organized which are actually communicative. Of course, a vast deal of what goes on during this period of life is not in the syntaxic mode: there is uncommunicative action by the mother—and wholly uncommunicative behavior as far as the infant's zonal satisfactions are concerned; and there is even the beginning of his avoidance of forbidding gestures, which is the initial manifestation of the infant's self-system.

Reverie: Nonverbal Referential Processes

As the baby's true autistic language develops—which I endeavored to illustrate with my example of "ha" meaning food—we begin to observe evidences of something generically identical with the great body of processes later called *reverie*. And reverie shows at this early stage somewhat of the relationship of the covert and overt, in that the baby carries on, with or without an audience, a certain amount of exercise in his language, first audibly, that is, overtly. Gradually, the language becomes more and more covert, by which I do not mean that he tends to be more and more silent. But his behavior begins to show the process of delay, even with respect to vocalization, so that we are able to presume that there is a change, as it were, from audible to perhaps silent speech. I hope, however, that you will be more-or-less magically protected from translating my remarks into Watsonian psychology and from assuming that I mean a gradual transition from overt to implicit laryngeal behavior. As a matter of fact, I think that speech is very much more a function of the ears that it is of the larynx, and I imply absolutely nothing about moving muscular tensions, and so on, when I talk about the internalization, if you please, or the becoming-covert of processes which have been overt. Certainly we all know that the reverse can be true and that quite often processes which for a long time have been covert can manifest themselves overtly.

As I have said, even in the first half of the second year of life, there is some evidence of what can properly be called the reverie process, which will continue throughout life. The infant is now provided with a baby language—an autistic language, since it has arisen out of coincidences, and so on, in the actual experience of the infant, and has only to a very limited extent been subjected to precise language teaching. In the second year of life such reverie processes as go on must be presumed to be in this purely autistic language. So far as language process is concerned, reverie continues all through life to be only infrequently and in special circumstances of a type that, if it were expressed, would be clearly meaningful and communicative to a hearer. Only those reverie processes which are in preparation for the expression of something, for the communication of something, take on the attributes which we at least hope our spoken and written thoughts will show. Reverie continues to be relatively untroubled by grammatical rules, the necessity for making complete sentences, and so on.

Incidentally there are people who seem completely staggered when one talks about nonverbal referential processes—that is, wordless thinking; these people simply seem to have no ability to grasp the idea that a great deal of covert living—living that is not objectively observable but only inferable—can go on without the use of words. The brute fact is, as I see it, that most of living goes on that way. That does not in any sense reduce the enormous importance of the communicative tools—words and gestures. It is probable that, up to the age of—let us say—three or four, words, mostly still of the child's special language, are used very much as pictures might be used in a book; they decorate, concentrate, or illuminate, referential processes which are not verbal but which are the manifestation of experience in the parataxic mode organized at various times earlier, such as the identification of good and useless nipples, and so on, that I have already talked about.

The Symbolic and the Nonsymbolic

I would like at this point to take up a type of abstract separation of things, supposed to be helpful in thought, which has developed considerable hold in the field of social-psychological theory: namely, the separation of all activity, overt or covert, into the symbolic and the nonsymbolic. I once thought it could be usefully added to this presentation of psychiatric theory, but now I think that it is not relevant. The distinction between the covert and the overt is self-evident when once made; and as long as one is dealing only with the first eighteen or twenty months of life, it is quite easy to make this second abstraction of symbolic and nonsymbolic, which can then be projected into later life. The idea is roughly this: the infant behaves nonsymbolically when he is taking nourishment from the breast; and the child behaves symbolically when he calls an inanimate toy "kitty." Now, I have no inclination whatever to argue the fact that there are activities provided for by the organization of central nervous and muscular tissue, and so on, at birth, such as the elaborate apparatus which actually makes sucking a fact and swallowing a fact. Perhaps the first time that anything happens it is nonsymbolic. But from the very beginning the cooperation of older people is necessary for infantile survival; and from the very beginning the potent influence of anxiety permits the organization of experience, prevents the organization of experience, or gradually shoos the direction of experience into approved channels. Thus it is quite obvious that a great deal of what goes on by the time one is a year old, even if it is inborn, is very highly symbolic. I have emphasized from the beginning that recall and foresight are conspicuous even, according to Jennings, at the level of the amoeba. Wherever the phenomenon of recall and foresight is clearly manifested in the human being so that something can be extracted in the way of communication about it, one finds this very definite anticipation of some achievement connected with it. I am afraid that, for practical purposes, all human behavior so purely and unquestionably manifests the organization of experience into what are in effect signs— whether signals or symbols—that an attempt to discriminate intelligibly in human behavior between what is symbolic and what is nonsymbolic is far more misleading than it is helpful. Therefore, without denying that there may be purely nonsymbolic performances in human beings, I would say that for the purposes of psychiatric theory I am concerned exclusively with covert and overt symbolic activity—that is, with activity influenced by the organization into signs of previous experience in terms of satisfaction, or in terms of avoiding or minimizing anxiety.

CHAPTER
12

Childhood

The Role of Language in the Fusion of Personifications

WE SHALL now more or less depart from our prolonged stay in infancy. In my discussion of language behavior, I hope it was made clear that the infant's success in the field of language behavior carries a very, very high premium so far as favorable, tender response of the significant elder figures is concerned. The extraordinary value that comes to invest verbal behavior, especially as it manifests itself in the school years, is one of the important factors which make it difficult for us to be aware of reverie processes that are in a relatively simple parataxic mode of experience, or even of some reverie processes that are in highly developed forms of the parataxic mode. Verbal behavior takes to itself, in the case of all those who are not born deaf-mutes, qualities bordering on the really magical; for instance, a good many of us, even though we are properly invested with the degree of doctor of this or that, show quite often and quite clearly that we depend on really magical potencies in certain of our verbal behaviors. And in psychiatric practice, we encounter chronological adults whose unearthly dependence on the potency of verbal behavior is, quite clearly, the outstanding characteristic of their difficulty with others.

Now among the things brought about in the very early phases of childhood largely by the peculiar power of language behavior is a fusion of personifications. So far as awareness is concerned, this fusion is final and absolute; but, so far as personality is concerned, it need not be anything like so complete. I am speaking now of

what has, up to this stage, been the double personification of the
mothering one, or the collection of mothering ones—the personifications of the good mother and of the bad or evil mother. Thanks
in no small part to the incredible power which verbal behavior
seems to exercise in interpersonal situations, and to the great
energy devoted by the more mature people around the very young
child to equip him with this most important of all human tools,
language, it becomes quite impossible for the child to carry forward any striking surviving evidence of his earliest impression of
two mothers—one who gives tenderness and cooperation in the
satisfaction of needs, and one who carries anxiety and interferes
with the satisfaction of needs. Although this dichotomy pertaining
to one real person can go on at the lower strata, you might say,
of personality, it can scarcely survive very long the high-pressure
acculturation which makes one person "mama," and possibly another person "sister," or something like that. Thus no matter how
thoroughly organized the two separate personifications of the good
mother and the bad mother were, their individuality is lost or fused
into a later personification, in the process of learning language.
But this fusion is not to be taken to be comprehensive. In other
words, all the attributes organized in infancy in the personification
of the bad mother are not necessarily or probably present in the
personification of mother as it begins to be conspicuous in childhood; and it is scarcely possible under any circumstances that all
the attributes of the good mother of infancy can be fused into the
childhood personification of mother. Under certain circumstances,
we see evidence which makes this last statement practically beyond doubt; that is, in later life the person seeks, and can quite
clearly be proven to be seeking, someone who will fit fairly
closely the personification of the good mother, in aspects which
are not shown in the personification of the 'real' mother. The
peculiarly complex way in which personifications of one stage of
personality enter into personifications at a later stage of personality
—although very seldom totally—is, to a considerable extent, due
to the unique power of vocal verbal behavior, and to the very high
premium that is put on the acquisition of verbal behavior in childhood and the succeeding developmental eras, as long as one is in
organized educational situations.

The Theorem of Escape

I want now to carry further the development of the self-system, which I began to outline a while back, and to present what I have formulated as the *theorem of escape*. The self-system, unlike any of the other dynamisms posited to organize knowledge about interpersonal relations, is extraordinarily resistant to change by experience. This can be expressed in the theorem that *the self-system from its nature—its communal environmental factors, organization, and functional activity—tends to escape influence by experience which is incongruous with its current organization and functional activity.* This peculiarity of the self-system must be grasped if one is either to comprehend personality in terms of this system of psychiatry, or to engage in the types of therapeutic intervention which this system implies. When last I touched on the self-system, I spoke of its being of purely experiential origin, and I said that, unlike the dynamisms of needs, it did not rest on peculiarities of the physicochemical communal existence of the underlying human animal. The self-system is derived wholly from the interpersonal aspects of the necessary environment of the human being; it is organized because of the extremely unpalatable, extremely uncomfortable experience of anxiety; and it is organized in such a way as to avoid or minimize existent or foreseen anxiety.

But I want to repeat that the character of situations which provoke anxiety is never completely to be grasped. It is quite clear that since anxiety in the mother makes the infant anxious, we cannot expect the infant to understand very much about what caused anxiety; what is perhaps a little harder to see is that, in chronological adults, there is this same fringe of the simply undiscoverable about circumstances which cause anxiety. As we get older we like to feel that we can name or explain things and this conceals from us, in part, this never-completely-to-be-graspable character of situations which provoke anxiety. There is an old story about how sick the patient feels when he has a bad pain and how much more comfortable he feels when the doctor says, "Oh, it is only appendicitis." That is a small instance of how much better we feel when we have a verbal tag by which, it seems, a novel set of facts is made familiar—if only to somebody else. So it is with a great many of the things that we recurrently do inefficiently and inappropriately—we feel much better, more worthy, if we can rattle off a string of words, which is often about as effective as the traditional woman's explanation of the mysterious: "I did it *because*." Actually, in a very long psychiatric career I would say that I have come to have more and more affection for the rationalization which ends with "just *because*"; the more words that follow, the harder it is to figure out how much is personal verbalism—rationalization, as it is called—and how much is an important clue to something that one ought to see.

Thus, however much we as adults may be able to talk about situations which provoke anxiety, we almost never grasp the character of such situations—certainly the child never grasps them. Hence all additions to the self-dynamism are either *imperfect observations* of the circumstances that have caused anxiety, and of the successful interventions of the self-system to minimize or avoid repetition of these circumstances; or certain *definite inventions* by which more complex operations are built out of simpler ones, new things are made by recombining the old—a concept which I shall discuss shortly. Furthermore, the culture itself is based on no single great general principle that can be grasped even by a genius, but is based instead on many contradictory principles. And it is in education for life in the culture that we have all experienced a great deal of our anxiety.

Whereas any recurrent experience will quite soon be added to, and will modify, the manifestations of any dynamism in the satisfaction of needs, the particular structure and functional activity of the self-system is such that a person can go through a whole series of consistent failures of what we call security operations— which is the typical performance when the self-dynamism is the central motor of activity—without learning much of anything. In fact, the chances are that self-system activity will come in *more* readily at the faint hint of anxiety-provoking situations, but still without showing the type of profit from failures that would appear in connection with the satisfaction of more biologically conditioned needs. We can see, when we study this curious insensitivity to experience, that the patterns of experience which are not profitable are all characterized by not being understandable or analyzable in terms of the tendencies already incorporated in the self-system.

Needless to say, the lifelong tendency of the self-system to escape profit from experience is not absolute. But I want to emphasize this general tendency of the self-system. I have gone to the trouble of formulating a theorem about it in order to emphasize that we are being perfectly irrational and simply unpleasant if we expect another person to profit quickly from his experience, as long as his self-system is involved—although this is a very reasonable anticipation in all fields in which the self-system is not involved. This does not make the self-system rigidly incapable of change in central characteristics from infancy onward; quite the contrary. Because of the general effect on personality which accompanies every newly matured need or capacity in the early stages of each developmental phase, the functional activity of the self-system invariably does change somewhat in direction and characteristics; and it is at those times that the self-system is peculiarly open to fortunate change. The self-system, so far as I know, can, in any personality system, be changed by experience; but the experience, or rather the set-up in which such change can be expected, often has to be very elaborate and very considerably prolonged. The resistance of the self-system to change as a result of experience is in large part the reason why, in therapy, we find it profitable to think in terms of complexly organized, rather prolonged, therapeutic operations by which we gradually build up a series of situations which requires the self-system to expand —that is, to take in experience which had previously, because of selective inattention or otherwise, had no material effect on the patient's susceptibility to anxiety, in particular interpersonal situations.

Sublimation

To return to our discussion of very early childhood, I now invite attention to what happens with regard to the young child's activity concerned with the pursuit of the satisfaction of *needs*— activity which by now is both covert and overt. These needs are by now not only those clearly concerned with the necessary communality with the physicochemical world—needs for food, water, oxygen, and the elimination of waste products—but also include an ever-increasing complement of zonal needs. This latter category includes the need to manifest every capability that matures—what we see as the child's pleasure in manifesting any ability that he has achieved. The refinements of behavior patterns and of covert processes—which were earlier a matter of inference but which now become objectively verifiable—arise from the maturation of new capacities and from past experience; and these refinements can in some cases now be categorized as improved information about 'reality,' as it is commonly shorthanded. All this leads to the invention of new patterns from old, and to the learning of data from interpersonal situations with the acculturating adults, in the fashions I have described already.

Among these inventions there is one pattern of behavior change—a refinement of behavior patterns and covert processes—which is, according to my definition, of very broad significance. As usual, I have been too lazy or inefficient to find a term for this pattern of behavior change, or referential process change; and so I will again, with the same discontent that I have experienced for at least ten years, say that I am talking about my variant on *sublimation*. As I have already indicated, when I talk about sublimation I am not discussing exactly what Freud had in mind when he set up the terms; my thinking about sublimation makes it a very much more inclusive process than a study of classical psychoanalysis might suggest. The manifestations of what I shall continue to call sublimation, for want of a better term, appear in late infancy, become conspicuous in childhood, and become very conspicuous indeed in the succeeding period. Since this is the label of a very important manifestation of changes in behavior and referential pattern, let me make a somewhat precise statement about it:

Sublimation is the unwitting substitution, for a behavior pattern which encounters anxiety or collides with the self-system, of a socially more acceptable activity pattern which satisfies part of the motivational system that caused trouble. In more fortunate circumstances, symbol processes occurring in sleep take care of the rest of the unsatisfied need.

Now this is the first time that I have laid particular stress on the *unwitting*. I hope that I have prepared the way for it by my discussion of covert living in all of us. In the infant, these covert processes which can be inferred to go on certainly cannot be conceived to be within the infant's awareness, his clear recognition or grasp. As I have already suggested, I believe that in both the more distinguished and the more commonplace performances of each of us in our living, all but the last step—or all but the last few steps —usually goes on quite exterior to anything properly called the content of consciousness, or awareness. Thus by unwitting, or unnoted, I refer to the great congeries of covert referential processes which must have occurred, but whose occurrence is completely unknown to the person concerned, and is only to be inferred from the evidence of what the person does know and does notice— in other words, from what occurs within his so-called field of consciousness. To use the term sublimation in the sense that I use it, one must keep track of the fact that it occurs exterior to the field of conscious content; the reason for that is intricate but nonetheless important, and will perhaps be made clear when we come to discuss particular patterns of so-called mental disorder. What happens in the kind of sublimation that I am now trying to describe is that a need collides with anxiety at the behest of the social censor or acculturating person; a notable example of this—although, of course, no example is perfect—is the very young child who wants to put his thumb in his mouth but his thumb is soiled with, say, feces. If we find that this very young child, when his fingers are soiled in this particular way, always or very frequently picks out a particular toy and sucks it, then we may actually feel with reasonable certainty that there has been a 'substitution' of the experience of sucking this toy, in place of the experience of putting this particular type of soiled thumb in the mouth. When something like this happens in late infancy, we can scarcely presume that it is the result of much thinking on the part of the infant, and for this reason it seems to be a peculiarly good instance by which to call attention to the way sublimation occurs all through life. The person never figures it out. It occurs and is continued, but it is unwitting. And what occurs, and what is continued, is a partial satisfaction of the needs; and this partial satisfaction has been substituted for the satisfaction of the need which has collided with anxiety, which is being prohibited by forbidding gestures of the significant people around. What has been substituted, what appears in lieu of this particular need-satisfying behavior, will be something which is not disapproved, or not so much disapproved—something which is not a target of self-system activity, however primitive this activity may be.

This sublimation, or peculiar substitution of goal may be, and in fact is, in a notable proportion of all instances, almost completely satisfying, so that there is very little leftover, unsatisfied need. In my illustration, in which the finger soiled with feces is not to be gotten anywhere near the mouth, the substitution of a toy cannot satisfy the need concerned, because that need includes the combination of sucking satisfaction and being-sucked satisfaction, whereas the toy is insensate. Now what becomes of the excess need which is not satisfied by these long-circuited, socially approved techniques? In many instances the excess need can be discharged by covert operations. In the adult who leads a fairly busy life, the great time for covert operations of that kind is during sleep; although it doesn't have to be, it very commonly is. In childhood this covert satisfaction does not have to be pushed into sleep, and in later childhood the unsatisfied components of some forbidden activity in the satisfaction of needs can be found to be faithfully reflected in expressed fantasy performances. The point is that the excess of need which is not satisfied by the sublimation is discharged by covert or overt symbolic performances which do not collide particularly with social censure—that is, which are not particularly associated with anxiety. Needless to say, there are some patterns of behavior and covert process in the pursuit of satisfactions that can scarcely be subjected to this process. When we discuss adolescence, we will discover that this is true of lust, at least in my view. Certain zonal needs which form part of the lust pattern may be sublimated, but if one depends on such processes for handling the whole thing, trouble is right around the corner, if not already present.

A great deal of what is called learning is made up of the refinement of behavior, and the change of covert referential processes, which are accomplished by this relatively simple process of sublimation—by combining activity in partial satisfaction of a need with other patterns of action—perhaps purely in the pursuit of security, perhaps partly in the pursuit of other satisfactions—so that anxiety is successfully avoided. But, while this sort of thing makes up an important part of learning, one cannot expect that the person who learned it will know all about how it was learned. When the so-called substitution is undertaken clearly within awareness, the educative process very rarely works effectively, if it works at all. I hear every now and then that the young child should be given every opportunity to understand just why certain things are required. If this were necessary, we might possibly reach maturity anywhere from sixty to a hundred and forty years of age, and I doubt that many people would put up with the tedium. So it is that a very important part of education for living in an essentially irrational culture is found in this type of refinement of behavior and covert process which occurs exterior to awareness, but which has the pattern of giving up immediate, direct, and complete satisfaction of a need, and of utilizing instead some partially satisfying, socially approved pattern, discharging any excess need in sleep or in some other way.

The Disintegration of Behavior Patterns

In less successful child-training projects—that is, in family groups that are not estimable in the skill, ingenuity, and understanding with which they try to discharge their social responsibilities—the first instances of the *disintegration* of behavior patterns and patterns of covert process under the force of anxiety occur quite early in childhood. This, which is somewhat different from sublimation, gets somewhere near the area of the not-me personification which I spoke of earlier. I am now considering a situation in which a pattern of behavior in the pursuit of satisfaction, and the exercise of recall and foresight in connection with this satisfaction, are *stopped* by the mothering one; then, depending on the character of the need—which in turn depends somewhat on the evolutionary stage of the personality concerned—either there is a great deal of trouble, in the sense that the behavior is, in fact, not abandoned by the child, and more and more anxiety piles up in the personality, so that one might say the *whole of living* is rather disorganized; or this *particular pattern* of behavior and covert process is disintegrated. But what is disintegrated does not, in that process, cease to be; it does not, like a coin in the magician's palm, vanish without a trace. And what becomes of patterns of behavior and covert process which have been disintegrated by frontal application of anxiety—which come into complete collision with the self-system so far as it is developed? Since the recombining of activities in this very simple pattern of sublimation presumably has not come off this time, there may be a recombining of activities in more complex patterns of activity—a number of which are best revealed in the mental disorders which we shall presently consider—or there may be *regression*, so-called, to earlier patterns.

Now the conception of regression is often utilized as a pure verbalism; that is, psychiatrists often use the term to brush aside mysteries which they do not grasp at all. I do not want anyone to think, when I use the term regression, that it is some great abstruse whatnot that can be used to sound intelligent about the mysterious. And the notion that regression is something rare, something highly morbid, and so on, can be dismissed on the strength of one very easy observation: that in the course of the life of any child, you can observe, practically at twenty-four hour intervals, the collapse, when the child gets thoroughly tired, of patterns of behavior which are not very well stamped in. Quite commonly before sleep, the child resumes earlier patterns of behavior that are no longer shown in the more alert periods of his life. When the patterns of motivational systems are, however, well established, then such diurnal disintegration is either very much less conspicuous or not in evidence at all. For example, a child who has otherwise entirely desisted from sucking his thumb quite commonly resumes sucking his thumb just before falling asleep. The zonal needs which were concerned in sucking the thumb have in various ways been refined, expanded, and so on; but with the supervention of the state called fatigue, the more complex, more recently evolved patterns of satisfaction-giving behavior, and incidentally security-protecting behavior, fall apart, as it were, and an earlier stage of direct satisfaction of the particular zonal need concerned reappears. Now that is genuinely an example of regression of behavior pattern, and from it, I believe, you can deduce the limits to which this particular conception can rationally be pushed.

The Theorem of Reciprocal Emotion

I want next to take up the vicissitudes in early childhood of the group of personifications which are presently to be fused in the personification of the self—namely, the personifications called good-me and bad-me, and the vestigial, vague personification of not-me. Since at this time there is a steady increase of the socializing influence by the more adult environment, the experiences which can be incorporated into the personification of bad-me grow through these earlier stages of development, and the 'naturalness' of good-me becomes much more open to exception.

In connection with the vicissitudes of the personifications which presently will culminate in the personified self, I would like to refer to a formulation which carries forward, and greatly modifies, the initial theorem of tenderness. My initial theorem stated, approximately, that the evidence of needs, as manifested by the infant, calls out tender cooperative behavior on the part of the mothering one. This is true of the period of the infant's complete dependence, but in childhood the social responsibility of the mothering one begins to interfere with it. Thus *from early childhood onward another general statement might be applied to interpersonal relations*, which, for want of a better name, I once called *the theorem of reciprocal emotion*, or reciprocal motivational patterns: *Integration in an interpersonal situation is a reciprocal process in which (1) complementary needs are resolved, or aggravated; (2) reciprocal patterns of activity are developed, or disintegrated; and (3) foresight of satisfaction, or rebuff, of similar needs is facilitated.*

When I state here that complementary needs are resolved or aggravated, you will observe that this is a change from the theorem of tenderness, in which the complementary needs were definitely resolved. But for the more general purpose—that is, in interpersonal situations from early childhood onward—we find that while there are complementary needs, the fact that a person needs tenderness may bring tenderness, or it may bring a denial of tenderness, or frank anxiety which aggravates the need for tenderness. The second part of my theorem is that reciprocal patterns of activity are developed or disintegrated. We saw, when we discussed the infant, that there was a steady growth on the part of the infant of nursing behavior, and so on, and on the mothering one's part there was certain cooperation with this extending pattern of nursing behavior. But from the more general standpoint, just the reverse may be true; previous patterns of cooperative activity in an interpersonal situation may now be disintegrated, because the mother supposes that the growth of the infant permits of his being educated away from things that she tolerated earlier. And the third part of my theorem is that the foresight of satisfaction, or rebuff, of similar needs is facilitated. The facilitation of the foresight of satisfaction is a particular instance of the continued improvement of behavior in the pursuit of satisfactions, which takes place when the interpersonal situations encourage such improvement. And the facilitation of foresight of rebuff is an instance where self-system processes are called out to interfere; what is foreseen is not the satisfaction of needs, but the forbidding gestures and the anxiety which will attend the direct manifestation of the needs.

So far as the positive aspect of this theorem manifests itself, complementary needs are resolved in the interpersonal relations one lives through; reciprocal patterns of activity are developed, refined, made more perfect; and there is foresight of how satisfaction can be gained more quickly, or continued longer, by improved performance. Now all of that gives rise to experience which is naturally entirely congruous with the personification of good-me, and is manifested, as we can sometimes observe from the vocal and other expressions of young children, as their happiness and pride —to miscall it in traditional terms—in the use of their abilities. But with the increase of pressure toward socialization of the young, naturally the negative side of this reciprocal process appears; needs are aggravated because they are thwarted, and patterns of activity have to be sublimated or disintegrated, and in certain cases rebuff —the probability of unfavorable outcome of behavior—is clearly foreseen as a part of the process of getting rid of those patterns.

Further Developments in the Self-System

Now all the experiences which arise from these situations tend naturally to fit into the personification of bad-me. And in addition, thanks to the general pattern of childhood training in this culture at least, certain peculiar additions to the self-system are cultivated. You recall that all that is the self-system arises in interpersonal relations, and from the elaboration of experience in interpersonal relations. And the peculiar additions I refer to are the development of a presumably biological reaction which we call *disgust*—which represents an elaboration of something that is always present, the capacity to empty the stomach in a reverse direction—and a still further elaboration of part of the experience of being disgusted in what is called the emotion of *shame*.

To go on with the growth of the still tripartite personifications of what will later be the personified self—good-me, bad-me, and not-me—I should like to discuss how a variety of elements in the teaching of language interfere with the more satisfactory development of the personified self. This interference occurs when the behavior of the acculturating older people teaches the young child that certain vocal processes can have a propitiatory effect with respect to items of bad behavior which otherwise are strongly associated with anxiety—that is, which are generally so forbidden that they would be as much as possible sublimated, or they would be disintegrated.

To some extent, I suppose, every one of us in our very early formative years—perhaps all through childhood, and certainly later in the juvenile period—had opportunities to learn that certain combinations of words and gestures would minimize, if not remove, the danger of anxiety which we could clearly foresee in connection with certain behavior, since we had already learned that this behavior endangered our feeling of interpersonal security—that is, was definitely disapproved. Now insofar as a verbal statement by a child is taken by the acculturating adults to have a superior quality of reality to other of his behavioral acts, the child is being trained to be incapable of dealing with life. That is just all there is to it. Yet in a good many homes, the following kind of statement is a conspicuous ingredient in the alleged education of the young: "Willie, I told you not to do that. Now say you are sorry." This is a classical instance of what I mean by propitiatory gesture. If Willie dutifully says he is sorry, that is supposed to markedly mitigate the situation, although it is something that Willie is almost absolutely incapable of understanding—if, in fact, anyone can understand it. The effect of this sort of thing is that it interferes with and delays the fusion of good, bad, indifferent, and unknown aspects into the personified self, and it continues, beyond a reasonable term, the maintenance of the tripartite personification with respect to *my body*. And so you will hear these same children telling you later on, "Oh, I didn't do that, it was my hand," or "Oh, mama, I've been bad," and so on, which are not particularly fortunate evidences of education.

During childhood something striking comes to happen to one of the components of the generic need for tenderness, which characterizes the infant from very early. This component I have referred to, in theoretic explanation of certain later idiosyncrasies, as the need for physical contact. In childhood an elaboration of this need is manifested, first, as a need for participants and, later, as a need for an audience. Late infants and young children like most emphatically to play with mother, to engage in certain exercises with mother which satisfy certain zonal muscular needs, and so on; and at a later stage they have a definite preference for putting on their performances in the presence of the tenderness-giving, approval-giving elder person. But if there are too many demands of other kinds on the mother, or if she has too many other children or is too ignorant of what it is all about, or if there are a variety of other circumstances, including mental disorder on her part, or crazy ideas about the child's will or spirit or what not—then, quite frequently, the child encounters such consistent rebuff of his expressed needs for tenderness that his behavior and covert processes concerned with the expression of the need for tenderness have to be subjected to change. Quite a bit of this can fit into the conception of sublimation, because the more fortunate of these children discover that when sublimations occur, tenderness is again forthcoming, and everything is fine. But a good many of them do not have that experience, and are literally compelled to disintegrate the behavior patterns and covert operations which would manifest themselves as the need for tenderness, because they foresee—on the best grounds possible, namely, frequency of occurrence—the rebuff of any need for tenderness that they manifest. In that case, after a certain time, a pattern of behavior develops which is as if bad-me had become the central part of the picture; there is literally the substitution of malevolent—"mischievous" is usually the word mother uses to tell Aunt Agatha about it—behavior when there is a need for tenderness. I shall discuss this development further, because it is very important in understanding many of the difficulties we have with our patients and others in later life.

CHAPTER 13

Malevolence, Hatred, and Isolating Techniques

Required Behavior and the Necessity to Conceal and Deceive

I NOW want to discuss further the very interesting phenomenon of one's becoming malevolent, and we will see if we can approach a consensus. The gross pattern of a great many things that happen in childhood, as compared with the infantile phase of personality, includes two conspicuous elements. One, as has been emphasized, is the acquisition of not only private but communicative language, with the great returns which the learning of this vitally important human tool always carries with it. But the second element, so far as actual development of interpersonal relations goes, is the more significant difference between the two epochs; it can be stated in terms of required behavior. At birth the infant can do practically nothing to assure his own survival. During infancy, he learns only the grossest culture patterns about zonal and general needs. But throughout the era of childhood there is an increasing demand for his cooperation. The child is expected to do things which are brought to his attention or impressed on him as requirements for action by the authority-carrying environment —the mother, increasingly the father, and perhaps miscellaneous siblings, servants, and what not.

In childhood—in contradistinction to at least the first two-thirds of the infantile period, and, one rather hopes, the whole infantile period—a new educative influence, *fear*, is brought to bear; we touched on this earlier, but we have not given it very much attention, since it has not so far had remarkable significance with respect to personality development. The discrimination between fear and anxiety is a vital one. Very severe fear and very severe anxiety, so far as I know, feel the same—that is, the felt component is identical—but the discrimination between these two powerful disjunctive processes in life is at times vital. Anxiety is something which I believe is acquired by an empathic linkage with the significant older persons, whereas fear is that which appears when the satisfaction of general needs is deferred to the point where these needs become very powerful. And of these general needs, the need which we particularly want to deal with here is the need to be free from painful sensations. Pain is here defined, not figuratively, but in its most obvious central meaning, hurt—that which occurs, for instance, as a result of sufficient pressure on, or incision into, the actual physical organization, or from misadventures in the internal function of some of the vital organs.

In childhood, perhaps not universally nowadays, but still with great frequency in almost all cultures I think, the child, in contradistinction to the infant, is presumed, at certain times, to deserve or require punishment; and the punishment I am talking about is the infliction of pain. Such punishment can be practically free from anxiety, or it can be strongly blended with anxiety. A parent who very methodically feels that a certain breach of the rules calls for a certain more or less specified form and amount of pain can administer it with no particular anxiety, although possibly with some regret, or possibly with singularly neutral feelings as one might have in training a pet. Many parents, however, for a variety of reasons subject the child to anxiety as well as pain. But insofar as punishment, the causing of pain, is used in its own right as an educative influence, this means a new type of learning—namely, learning enforced by a growing discrimination of the connection between certain violations of imposed authority and pain.

Frequently the child is subjected to punishment—pain with or without anxiety, but almost always with anxiety in this case—where he could have foreseen it except that the pressure of a need, zonal or otherwise, made the foresight ineffective in preventing the behavior. In a much more significant, although necessarily quite infrequent, group of circumstances, there comes punishment —pain with, almost invariably in this case, plenty of anxiety— under circumstances which are such that the child could not possibly have foreseen such an outcome from the behavior. This is particularly likely to happen with irritable, ill-tempered parents who are afflicted by many anxiety-producing circumstances in their own lives, and who tend rather strikingly to take it out on the dog or the child or what not.

Thus we see in childhood a new educative influence which shows up very definitely as actual fear of the capacity of the authority-carrying figure to impose pain. It is a peculiarity of the difference between anxiety and fear that, under fortunate circumstances, the factors in the situation in which one was hurt can be observed, analyzed, identified, and incorporated in foresight for the future, while in the case of anxiety that is only relatively true, at best; and if anxiety is very severe, it has, as I have said before, almost the effect of a blow on the head. Thus one has very little data on which to work in the future—we might almost say there is nothing in particular to be elaborated into information and foresight.

In childhood, the increased effort of the parents to teach, to discharge their social responsibility, and—I regret to say—to discharge a good many of the more unfortunate peculiarities of their personality produces, in many cases, a child who is "obedient" or a child who is "rebellious," and this outcome may appear fairly early. Of course the pattern may alternate in the same child, and have a very definite relationship to the existent personifications of good-me and bad-me; in reasonably healthy circumstances, good-me tends fairly definitely to be associated with obedience—but still with a considerable measure of freedom to play and so on—and rebelliousness tends to be part of the personification of bad-me.

In this stage of development—when the parents are making increasing efforts to teach the child, when his abilities are maturing, and when he is organizing past experiences and exercising his fantasy, his covert processes in play and make-believe—there is invariably, from very early, a beginning discrimination by the child among the authority-carrying figures, and later, but still quite early, a beginning discrimination of authority situations. In other words, almost all children learn certain indices that stand them in reasonably good stead as to when it is extremely unsafe to violate authority and when there is some chance of 'getting away with it.' This is, I think, a healthy discrimination which provides useful data, although under certain circumstances, of course, when the parental figures are overloaded with inappropriate and inadequate ways of life, it can be very unfortunate in the way of experience for later life. As the presumed relationship of more-or-less complete dependence of the infant on the mothering one is suspended and the father gets more and more significant, this discrimination by the child of different authority figures and authority situations, insofar as it succeeds—that is, gives information that proves reasonably dependable in foreseeing the course of events—contributes definitely to the growth of and importance of foresight in interpersonal relations. But insofar as the authority figures are confusing to the child and insofar as the authority situations are incongruous from time to time so that, according to the measure of the child's maturing abilities and experience, there is no making sense of them —then, even before the end of the thirtieth month, let us say, we see instances in which the child is already beginning to suffer a deterioration of development of high-grade foresight. In such cases it is quite probable that, in later stages of development, conscious exercise of foresight, witting study of how to get to a more-or-less recognized goal, will not be very highly developed.

Among the things that almost always attend the training of the child to take part in living, to 'cooperate' with the parent, to carry out instructions, to do chores and so on, is very frequently the imposition on the child of the concepts of duties and responsibilities. That is certainly good preparation for life in a social order; but again in cases where the parents are uninformed or suffering from unfortunate peculiarities of personality, this training in concepts and responsibilities includes as a very important adjunct (adulterant perhaps) a great deal of training—that is, experience which is presumed, erroneously I think in a great many cases, to be educational—in which the idea of *ought* is very conspicuous.

When it comes to putting into words an adequate statement of the cultural prescriptions which are generally required in the socialization of the young, one really is confronted by a task which requires most remarkable genius. Had culture grown as the work of a single person or a small group of greatly gifted people, almost crushed under their responsibility for their fellow man, then it is quite possible that one could build up a great structure of statements of what principles govern under all sorts of situations, and the result would be a coherent and rationally understandable social system. But that has been nowhere on earth, that I know of, very strikingly the case; possibly the nearest approach to such a social order is to be found in the regimented groups which have characterized various people at various times. For example, there is at least an attempt to embody often subtly contradictory requirements in such things as army regulations; but people who are really diligent students of army regulations frequently discover that it requires only a minor effort to discover a little conflict in authority, and such a conflict provides room for interpreting a situation according to which of the conflicting authoritative statements apply. But, as I was saying, such regulations do provide a rough approximation to this ideal of a rational culture, in that pretty ingenious people, many of them actively interested in maintaining the peculiar social organization of the military, have done their damndest to put plain statements of *ought* and *must* into words which could be understood by the comparatively uninitiated.

But when it comes to imposing the prescriptions of the culture on the child, these prescriptions are often most glaringly contradictory on different occasions, so that they require complex discrimination of authority situations. Moreover the child is incapable for a good many years of comprehending the prescriptions in terms of their possible reasonableness. And more important than anything else, out of the irrational and impulse-driven type of education by anxiety, and by reward and punishment—that is, tenderness and fear—a great many children quite early begin to develop the ability to conceal what is going on in them, what actually they have been doing behind someone's back, and thus to deceive the authoritative figures. Some of this ability to conceal and to deceive is literally taught by the authority-carrying figures, and some of it represents trial-and-error learning from human example—that is, by observing and analyzing the performances, the successes and failures, of siblings, servants, and the like.

Verbalisms and 'As If' Performances

Now these growing abilities to conceal and to deceive tend very early to fall into two of the important patterns of inadequate and inappropriate behavior—considered from the broad point of view —which become troublesome in later life and get themselves called mental disorders or processes in mental disorder. I hope that I have communicated by this time a very firm conviction that no pattern of mental disorder which is purely functional, as it is called—that is, which is an inadequate and inappropriate way of living with other people and with one's personifications—includes anything which is at all novel as to human equipment. Everything that we see in the symptomatology of these nonorganic—that is, nondefect—situations has its reflection in kind, if not in degree, in the developmental history of every one of us. And so, when we get to, let us say, mid-childhood, it is not uncommon to discover that the child has become fairly skillful at concealing what might otherwise bring anxiety or punishment—at deceiving the authority-carrying figures as to the degree or nature of his compliance with their more-or-less recognized demands.

The first of these two patterns we touched on previously—namely, verbalisms which are often called rationalizations, in which a plausible series of words is offered, regardless of its actual, remarkable irrelevancy, which has power to spare one anxiety or punishment. The degree to which verbalisms constitute elements in inadequate and inappropriate living which we call mental disorder, whether mild or severe, is truly remarkable. If you think that this is not a very powerful tool, you overlook its amazing significance in the service of the self-system, in the very striking characteristic of the self-system which makes favorable change so difficult—namely, the self-system's tendency to escape from experience not congruent to its current directions.

But the second pattern is even more impressive than verbalisms: it is the unfortunate—in the sense of being concealing and deceptive—learning of the value of *as if* performances. There are two grand divisions of these. One of them, far from being necessarily troublesome in personality development, is an absolutely inevitable part of everybody's maturing through childhood; and this is the group which perhaps may be called *dramatizations*. A great deal of the learning which the child achieves is on the basis of human examples, and these examples are at this phase authority-invested. The child will inevitably learn in this fashion a good deal about the mother, and, as the father personification becomes more conspicuous, about the father; and this trial-and-error learning by human example can be observed in the child's playing at *acting-like* and *sounding-like* the seniors concerned, and, in fact, playing at *being* them. Probably the progression literally is that one tries first to *act like* and one tries then to act *as if one were*.

In the earlier half of childhood, this inevitable part of one's learning to be a human being becomes a rather serious concern—in terms of what may show up later—only when these dramatizations become particularly significant in concealing violations of cooperation and in deceiving the authority-invested figures. In these latter cases, for a variety of reasons, some of which we will touch on briefly, these dramatizations tend to become what I could perhaps safely call sub-personifications. The roles which are acted in this way that succeed in avoiding anxiety and punishment, or that perhaps bring tenderness when there was no performance based on previous experience to get tenderness, are organized to the degree that I think we can properly call them *personae;* they are often multiple, and each one later on will be found equally entitled to be called *I*. To describe this type of deviation from the ideal personality development, I long since set up the conception of me-you patterns, by which I mean often grossly incongruent ways of behaving, or roles that one plays, in interpersonal relations with someone else. And all of them, or most of them, seem just as near the real thing—the personification of the self—as can be, although there is no more making sense of them from the standpoint of their representing different aspects of durable traits than there is of translating Sanskrit before you understand language. While these dramatizations are very closely related to learning to be human, they can even in these early days begin to introduce a very strikingly irrational element in the personification of the self.

The other group of these *as if* performances to which I wish to refer is perhaps best considered under the rubric of *preoccupations*. I would like to say a few words about one of my cocker spaniels, because it perhaps makes the point better than anything else I can think of now. This particular dog has always been the most diminutive in a litter of six; she has been kept with two others in this litter to the present time. The two others are a rather large male and a very shrewd and, shall I say, domineering female. The little bitch whom I am attempting to discuss was quite often the butt of the unquestionably painful vigor of the male and the unquestionably clever domineering of the female. Probably as a result of this, this little dog very conspicuously indeed took to remaining apart from her brother and sister, and could be observed very diligently digging great holes and trenches in the environment. This was literally quite a complex performance, in that each scoop of dirt that was flung out between her hind legs had to be examined carefully lest it contain something edible or otherwise interesting; the little dog would dig furiously in one of these mammoth excavations, rush around, examine the dirt thrown out, go down and get another shovel full—a tremendous activity for literally hours at a time. Somehow there seemed to be a stipulation that as long as she was so hard at work, the other two would leave her alone most of the time. But time has passed; she has been rescued from her unhappy submersion in the bigger siblings; and nowadays she treats them very roughly when she meets them. Now the trash man is outstanding around our place as a stimulus for provoking fear in the dogs—they are all quite upset when he shows up and to some extent are afraid of the mammoth truck and the din and so on that goes on about it. But when he is around, this little dog, alone out of the whole family, goes out and barks furiously at him. But she stops, after almost every third bark, to dig frantically, and to rush around and examine the dirt again, and then she goes back and roars furiously at him again. It is not, I think, too much to infer that this dog is really very timid, having had excellent reasons for being afraid in the past, but that she became so accustomed to being saved in the past by being preoccupied with her digging that the excess of fear in this situation leads to the reappearance of her preoccupation with digging.

In the human being, preoccupation as a way of dealing with fear-provoking situations or the threat of punishment, and of avoiding or minimizing anxiety appears quite early in life. And quite often the irrational and, shall I say, emotional way in which parental authority is imposed on the child, teaches the child that preoccupation with some particular onetime interesting and probably, as it turns out, profitable activity is very valuable to con-- tinue, not because it is any longer needed for the maturation of abilities or for satisfaction in new abilities, but as a preoccupation to ward off punishment and anxiety. Now if these performances are not only successful in avoiding unpleasantness, but also get positive reward by the child's being treated tenderly and approved, that naturally sets him on what will later be a strikingly complex way of life—that to which we refer as the *obsessional.*

Anger and Resentment

I have touched previously on learning by doing certain things in play *like* mother or *like* father, and by playing at *being* mother and father. There is one particular phase of this type of learning which is very evident in our ordinary contact with our fellow being, as well as in the psychiatrist's contact with the patient or vice versa. This is learning, from authority figures, a peculiar way of avoiding or neutralizing a fear-provoking situation. You may remember that earlier we spoke of how behavior that could be called, generically, rage behavior arose even in the extremely young when certain types of physical restraint were imposed which produced terror, particularly restraint that might interfere with the breathing movements. Now in punishment situations where pain is to be inflicted, there is invariably an element of restraint of freedom of movement—a particularly deliberate attempt on the part of the punishing person to interfere with the child's escaping the actual physically enforced pain. This, I believe, would, in any very young child who had missed disastrous experience up to then, lead to a movement in the general direction of such fear that rage behavior would be called out. But rage behavior doesn't have any particular value in this situation. And so, since the possibility of analysis and discrimination, and the exercise of foresight are already fairly well under way by now, instead of rage itself occurring as a frequent eventuality, what might be described as a version of its felt component—namely, anger—comes to be quite important. Especially in circumstances in which children are punished by an angry parent—but in all cases sooner or later, if only from improving discrimination of the progression of forbidding gestures in the authority-invested adults—everyone learns the peculiar utility of anger; I think that this statement is probably precisely true, although some people also learn that anger itself can bring a great deal of punitive treatment. But children invariably—or so nearly invariably that we don't need to pay a vast deal of attention to the exceptions—in their play are angry with their toys; and later they are angry with their imaginary companions. And the patterns of the child's being angry, the circumstances when it is suitable, and so on, are pretty much profits from his experience with the authority-carrying adults among whom he lives; what the child tends to show, in general, is that his toy, or whatever, has violated his authority in connection with the business of his *being* mother or *being* father. From this beginning, almost everyone—at least almost all the more fortunate of the denizens of our world—come to use anger very facilely, very frequently; and they use it when they would otherwise be anxious. In other words, it comes to be the process called out by mild degrees of anxiety in a truly remarkable number of people. But when one is around the age of thirty months, it may or may not be that one is well trained in the use of anger with the authority-carrying adults; in the more unhappy parental situations, one does not get very much encouragement that way, in partial result of which it comes about that in certain unhappy homes, children well into the school years have tantrums, which are in essence unmodified rage behavior.

In a great many other unfortunate homes children develop a complex modification of this rather simple use of anger. This more complex modification is the classical outcome of a situation in which the child is going on his way perfectly all right, so far as he can see, whereupon punishment, almost always with anxiety, is discharged upon the child for activity the forbidden aspect of which could not have been foreseen by the child—where there is no possibility of his understanding what the punishment is for. Or the punishment may be for activity so attractive that the possibility of punishment, even though foreseen, was ignored. In those circumstances, a great many children learn that anger will aggravate the situation, and they develop what we properly call *resentment*. Thus resentment is the name of the felt aspect of rather complex processes which, if expressed more directly, would have led to the repressive use of authority; in this way resentment tends to have very important covert aspects. In the most awkward type of home situation, these covert processes are complicated by efforts to conceal even the resentment, lest one be further punished; and concealing resentment is, for reasons I can't touch on now, one of our first very remarkable processes of the group underlying the rather barbarously named 'psychosomatic' field. In other words, in the concealing of resentment, and in the gradual development of self-system processes which preclude one's knowing one's resentment, one actually has to make use of distribution of tension in a fashion quite different from anything that we have touched on thus far. And these processes, which have nothing to do with activity such as a tantrum or something of that kind, are utilized for getting rid of tension so as to avoid activity which would otherwise be revealing, be noticed, and bring punishment.

The Malevolent Transformation

All these generalities about childhood acculturation are background for the circumstances under which the child develops in the direction, not of being obedient or being rebellious, but of being malevolent. Now the ways that malevolence shows in childhood may be numerous. Thus there are so-called timid children whose malevolence shows by their being so afraid to do anything that they just always fail to do the things that are most urgently desired. The great group is the frankly mischievous, and from there we may progress to the potential bully, who takes it out on some younger member of the family, and on the pets, and so on.

But under what circumstances does so remarkable and, may I say, so ubiquitous a thing as malevolence appear as a major pattern of interpersonal relations in childhood? A great many years of preoccupation with this problem has eventuated in a theory which is calculated to get around the idea that man is essentially evil. One of the great social theories is, you know, that society is the only thing that prevents everybody from tearing everybody to bits; or that man is possessed of something wonderful called sadism. I have not found much support for these theories—that man is essentially a devil, that he has an actual need for being cruel and hurtful to his fellows, and so on—in the study of some of the obscure schizophrenic phenomena. And so as the years passed, my interest in understanding why there is so much deviltry in human living culminated in the observation that if the child had certain kinds of very early experience, this malevolent attitude toward his fellows seemed to be conspicuous. And when the child did not have these particular types of experience, then this malevolent attitude was not a major component.

And the pattern that appeared was approximately this: For a variety of reasons, many children have the experience that when they need tenderness, when they do that which once brought tender cooperation, they are not only denied tenderness, but they are treated in a fashion to provoke anxiety or even, in some cases, pain. A child may discover that manifesting the need for tenderness toward the potent figures around him leads frequently to his being disadvantaged, being made anxious, being made fun of, and so on, so that, according to the locution used, he is hurt, or in some cases he may be literally hurt. Under those circumstances, the developmental course changes to the point that the perceived need for tenderness brings a foresight of anxiety or pain. The child learns, you see, that it is highly disadvantageous to show any need for tender cooperation from the authoritative figures around him, in which case he shows something else; and that something else is the basic malevolent attitude, the attitude that one really lives among enemies—that is about what it amounts to. And on that basis, there come about the remarkable developments which are seen later in life, when the juvenile makes it practically impossible for anyone to feel tenderly toward him or to treat him kindly; he beats them to it, so to speak, by the display of his attitude. And this is the development of the earlier discovery that the manifestation of any need for tenderness, and so on, would bring anxiety or pain. The other elaborations—the malevolence that shows as a basic attitude toward life, you might say, as a profound problem in one's interpersonal relations—are also just an elaboration of this earlier warp.

A start in the direction of malevolent development creates a vicious circle. It is obviously a failure of the parents to discharge their social responsibility to produce a well-behaved, well-socialized person. Therefore, the thing tends to grow more or less geometrically. Quite often the way in which the parents minimize or excuse their failure to socialize the child contributes further to his development of a malevolent attitude toward life—and this is likely to be on the part of the mother, since it is difficult to picture a malevolent transformation's occurring at all if the mother did not play a major part in it. A particularly ugly phase of this is found in cases in which the mother is very hostile toward the father, and has exceedingly little sympathy or satisfaction with him; so from very early in the child's life, she explains the increasingly troublesome character of his behavior, his manifestation of as much malevolence as is safe, by saying that he is just like his father in this particular, or just like his father's younger brother, or something of that kind. While the initial references of this kind communicate very little information, their continuation for long enough does tend to warp the child's personification of himself in the direction of something detestable, to be avoided and so on, thereby making very important contributions to his conviction that he will always be treated thoroughly badly.

And in the long course of development, even more subtly destructive are the instances where malevolence has come about because the mother is malevolent toward the child, in which case quite frequently, from very early, there is a good deal of verbal reference which takes the curious form of saying to aunts, uncles, neighbors, and others, "Yes, he has a bad temper just like me," or, "Yes, he is rebellious just like me." One should keep in mind that the mothering one is bound to be significant in all personality evolutions—she can't be otherwise; now when the child gets so that he doesn't think it safe to live among people because he is just like the person that he has to live with, and he gets punished a lot for it, the situation becomes a bit difficult, to say the least. The question arises: If it is all right for mother, why not for me?

Let me conclude by saying that the general conception of malevolence is of very considerable importance. It is perhaps the greatest disaster that happens in the childhood phase of personality development, because the kind of 'ugly'—as it is often called—attitude which it produces is a great handicap to the most profitable experience one could have in subsequent stages of development. It is from the second stage of personality development that a good deal of the foundations of one's attitude toward authoritative figures, superiors, and so on, is laid. So one often learns costly ways of getting around anxiety-provoking and fear-provoking situations—costly in the sense that one never feels exceedingly good or worthy; and these ways of avoiding such situations are not greatly contributory to one's useful information and foresight about living. Thus there can occur this very serious distortion of what might be called the fundamental interpersonal attitude; and this distortion, this malevolence, as it is encountered in life, runs something like this: Once upon a time everything was lovely, but that was before I had to deal with people.

CHAPTER 14

From Childhood into the Juvenile Era

The Meaning of the Arrest of Development

So FAR we have only touched on much that is often discussed as an arrest of development, a term which is much bandied about in discussions of psychiatry, but which needs more than the mere utterance of the words for some of its implications to become clear. I refer to our discussions of the *as if* performances and the transformation of attitudes and interpersonal relations in the direction of malevolence. These may not be immediately evident as an arrest of development. But, as I said before, the transformation toward malevolence might very easily prevent a great deal of profit from subsequent developmental experience. And the use of dramatizations, obsessional preoccupations, and so on, to avoid anxiety and punishment does actually very seriously interfere with the undergoing of subsequent experience, with analysis and synthesis; if the child is encouraged by various influences to make use of a good deal of obsessional substitution and dramatization, there is literally a slowing down of healthy socialization in lieu of the customary useful unfolding of the repertory of interpersonal motivation and behavior patterns. Arrest of development does *not* imply that things have become static, and that from thenceforth the person will be just the same as he was at the time that development was arrested. The conspicuous evidence of arrest and deviation of personality development is, at first, delay in the showing of change which characterizes the statistically usual course, and later, the appearance of eccentricities of interpersonal relations, which are often anything but self-evident signs of the developmental experience which has been missed or sadly distorted. Thus there is nothing static about arrest of development; but the freedom and the velocity of the constructive change are very markedly reduced. Sometimes, from quite early, the persistence of certain characteristics of the self-system strongly suggests a static condition. But that is not as real as it may seem; even if the self-system seems to be quite unchanged from year to year—or very slightly changed from year to year—nonetheless, experience does occur and is elaborated in personality. Thus, the so-called arrest of personality really means that the returns from opportunity are very markedly reduced. As we go on, it will become more and more impressive to notice the consequences, in subsequent stages of development, that attend unfortunate interferences in particular stages.

Gender as a Factor in the Personification of the Self

Certain influences in childhood make for the growth of the personified self, the personifications "me" and "we," along what I choose to call *gender* lines—and I use this term to avoid too easy a confusion between what I am about to discuss and the notion of sexuality, which becomes highly meaningful only much later in life. At this point I want to call attention to an ancient observation of mine which I think has been rather widely accepted in some related fields: that the child is influenced by the fact that the parent who is of the same sex as the child has a feeling of familiarity with the child, of understanding him; while the parent of the other sex has a surviving, justifiable feeling of difference and of uncertainty toward him. Thus, with boys the father feels more comfortable than with girls; and so he is convinced that he is right in his expectations of his sons, and he is less inclined to think twice, perhaps, in reaching a judgment of disapproval or the like. And the contrary is the case with the mother. The result is that each authority figure treats the child of the other sex in a way which is somewhat favorable to the, shall I say, more rational, more insightful education of the child. This is one of the ubiquitous factors that can be misconstrued as having something to do with a conception such as that of the Oedipus complex, which has enjoyed very great vogue in the fairly recent past of psychoanalytic theory.

The additions to the personified self on the specific basis of whether one is a boy or a girl are advanced notably by two influences: One is the child's play at being the authority figure of his own sex. And the other is the influence of so-called rewards and punishments—particularly interest and approval, in contrast with indifference and disapproval—and sometimes the influence of shame and guilt, which in many ways is the obverse of the *ought* business that we talked about previously, with respect to the roles that the child is playing, is observed to be playing, or later, says that he is playing. These influences tend to educate the child with peculiar facility in the social expectations of his particular sex, in the sense of gender, and to inculcate many of the cultural prescriptions. Thus when the girl catches on in play to something that seems very feminine, this play gets a certain amount of applause, interest, and support from the mother—at least it does if the mother happens to still endorse the feminine. In this way, as the result of the authority figure's attitude toward particular items of play, many of the cultural prescriptions of how one behaves when one grows up are transmitted to the child. The play is, in truth, to a considerable extent trial-and-error learning by human example. But this influence of approval, disapproval, praise, blame, appeal to shame, and the inculcation of guilt are worth mentioning.

The Learning of Cultural Prescriptions for Overt Behavior

There is another strong influence in transmitting certain of the cultural prescriptions to the child, which brings about more rapid transition in the personifications of the child than would occur simply from play and maturation, and so on. This is the very widespread practice of telling or reading stories to the child. These are in general of two types: They may be socially approved moral tales which have become ingrained in the culture because they set forth complex ethical ideals in a fashion that can be grasped by a child. Or they are inventions of the authority figure which may be actually pretty far from the socially approved moral stories and a very special function of the parental personality; the child is apt to be particularly impressed by long-continued stories in which a parent takes the trouble to carry the imaginary protagonists night after night through new adventures. A study of the influence of both kinds of stories has, so far as I know, never been made very rigorously. But certainly their influence on the young, early in childhood, or perhaps all through childhood, often appears in personality studies which are made many, many years later.

In this way, children get the impression that they should be governed by certain influences which we call social values, or judgments, or the ethical worth of certain types of behavior. These notions, since they are primarily in the parataxic mode, do not necessarily have much of anything to do with the observed behavior of the parents, or the child's opinions of the parents. Often these values continue to exist in notable magic detachment from the actual living experience of the child himself. They are apt to be particularly rich soil for the production of verbalism; and these verbalisms, for the very reason that they are derived from moral stories or the like which are part of the cultural heritage, have an effect in impressing the other person which is quite magical.

This is a special aspect of a very important discrimination which grows in the child between what can be expressed, demonstrated, shown, or said, in contrast to what goes on but must be treated as if it did not—which amounts in the last analysis to that which can be overt behavior and that which must remain covert in the presence of authority figures. A special instance of this process is the pointless question, which is the bane of many parents at times and is the kind of process that is commonly encountered in the history of those people who do not come to have adequate ways of living. This occurs when the child has caught on to the fact that certain things about which he needs some information are taboo for any demonstration or discussion; whereupon the child begins to ask questions which do not express what is being sought in the way of information. Of course, at the stage I'm discussing, speech itself is not particularly communicative, so that it is never too wise to assume that what a child says means what those words would ordinarily be taken to mean. But what I'm driving at is the situation in which the child *could* indicate the need for information much more clearly, but is prevented by anxiety and the threat of punishment. Therefore, he begins another kind of indirect behavior, which is not to be confused with obsessional preoccupations or dramatizations: he asks the question, but he adds an autistic element to take the place of that which cannot quite be inquired about. The older the child gets, the nearer these autistic elements are to word combinations that actually refer to something, so that the child may make perfectly rational, diligent inquiries about why mother and father are always doing this and that in the morning when he really wants to know why mother and father do not say a word to each other when they wake to join the day. In other words he really wants to know why they're both morose and have nothing to do with each other except possibly in putting the food on the table and getting it eaten, and that sort of thing. This is a field which is actually quite mysterious to the child, first, because the child is scarcely capable of being morose, and therefore has no particular aptitude for understanding the demonstrations of moroseness; and secondly, because he is under such a necessity for participant play—of play with parental audience and so on—that it would scarcely be possible for him even to imitate morose behavior most of the time. So here is something puzzling and disturbing to the child; but any poking around in this field brings anxiety or the actual threat of punishment by a strong forbidding attitude. And so in an attempt to catch on to something which is ununderstandable, the child begins to ask questions that are beside the point. Now they aren't beside the point to the child, but the anxiety element requires that the child shall use words to *conceal* what is being inquired about, if you want to put it that way. Thus in the child's apparently pointless and sometimes tediously repetitive questions, the question is actually an autistic combination of words which refers to what the child wants to know, and not to what the parent supposes the question pertains to. Toward the end of childhood, as the development proceeds, this process becomes more complicated. The element of questioning for questioning's sake, which may be a form of malicious mischief, may actually become quite rational—that is, the child may ask an immense number of questions about things about which he is really questioning, but he may still do it because there is some very puzzling and disturbing element in the interpersonal relations around him which he is, or feels, prohibited from investigating.

Throughout childhood, as I've already hinted, there is what is often called very active imagination—that is, all sorts of toys are used for temporary investiture with traits of personality, traits of humanness. There is gradually a capacity to do this entirely by referential process—in other words, the child doesn't need anything concrete, but can have a perfectly 'imaginary' plaything. As I have indicated, a good deal of learning is attendant upon the parents' interest in these imaginary plays, imaginary conversations, and so on.

In this connection, an element is introduced to the child which often crops up over the years as an exceedingly disturbing sort of experience. At this stage, while the distinction between overt and necessarily covert processes may be fairly clear at times, it sometimes happens that what is supposed to be covert—that is, what the child knows ought not to be revealed—quite simply gets itself revealed, because of the child's very limited grasp on many things. For example, without intending to communicate anything to the authority figures, the child may speak aloud, just because this is exercise of his vocal abilities and part of his imaginary play; the child's ideas, or rudimentary ideas, are picked up by the parent who hears this, and rewards or punishments, particularly the latter, are poured out on the child, to his quite profound mystification. This is likely to give the child the idea that there is something violable about his covert processes, so that the authority figures know things that he is attempting to conceal, that he does not wish to exhibit, that he knows are dangerous to show. Under some circumstances, this kind of experience begins a group of processes in recall and foresight which literally amounts, in later life, to a feeling at times that one's mind can be read, or can at least be wonderfully accurately suspected. And along with this feeling—I think purely because of cultural artifacts—the child is very apt to get the notion that somehow or other this ability is connected with the eyes, a conception which later appears in the hackneyed and, so far as I am concerned, profoundly erroneous notion that one's eyes are in some curious fashion the windows of one's soul, through which people can observe evil within one, and all that sort of thing. If this sounds a little odd to you, you are rather fortunate, because it is one of the survivals of childhood experience which is regarded as a very remarkable delusion when it appears in the content of a psychosis in later life. And incidentally, it's quite essential, if I am to achieve what I am gunning for in this discussion, that you realize that anything that seems to you to be very remarkable indeed in the content of a psychosis is just something that you haven't placed in your own developmental history.

The Growing Necessity for Distinguishing between Reality and Fantasy

There is, as I have said before, a very considerable need for participation of the parents in the child's play, at least as an attentive audience and if possible as people who perform a role, unless there are siblings who serve this purpose. In a good many instances, circumstances do not permit very much of this audience behavior of the authority figures, and the child is actually lonely; and loneliness at this stage is a foreshadowing of the loneliness which we will be discussing later. The 'lonely' child, the child who cannot obtain the presence and participation, however passive, of elder folk, inevitably has a very rich fantasy life—that is, he makes up for the real deficiencies by multiplying the so-called imaginary personifications which fill his mind and influence his behavior.

Of course, it is necessary to remember that the young child probably does not recognize fantasy as such. The young child knows a lot about the "reality" of a cup, a spoon, or of certain toys which are actually experienced. But with the exception of objects which he has actually experienced, he has only very limited ability to distinguish between fantastic objects and objects which have aspects of what we ordinarily call reality. Thus, a good many things which have no 'reality' but which are built up in the child's mind from the example of the authority figures, or from the maturing needs of the child himself, are of approximately the

same reality as the perfectly real things—at least as long as they
continue to be effective in covert process and play. As a matter of
fact, the perfectly real things—that is, 'real' to the adult—are
very heavily invested by the child with [autistic] [1] referential
process, so that this kind of 'reality' and his fantasy are indistinguishable to him. And in turn the things which we as adults come
to take so very seriously—like policemen, and traffic signals, and
all that sort of thing—of course have none of the significance to
the child that they have to us. Toys are useful to the very young
child for the purpose of discharging newly matured abilities: they
do not have any of these relationships which cause us to carry
collision damage insurance on automobiles. In other words, the
distinction between what anyone would agree was real and what
is unutterably the child's own is of no particular moment in this
very early stage. The only exception to this is in the field of anxiety-
provoking phenomena. But, in general, I believe that if the child
under thirty months, for example, considers that performances
of the mothering one which did not occur are valid, this is no
particular evidence of oncoming difficulty in later life. If the
needs and the security operations of the child of this age happen
to result in remarkable 'falsifications' of what really happened, I
see no reason why this should imply anything more than that
the child is alive.

By the end of childhood, the pressure toward socialization has
almost invariably fixed a big premium on carefully sorting out
that which is capable of being agreed to by the authority figure.
This is the first very vivid manifestation in life of the role of consensual validation, by which I mean that a consensus can be established with someone else. Consensually validated symbols underlie
almost all operations in the syntaxic mode; what distinguishes
syntaxic operations from everything else that goes on in the mind
is that they can under appropriate circumstances work quite precisely with other people. And the only reason that they come to
work quite precisely with other people is that in actual contact with

[1] [*Editors' note:* Autistic has been inserted, since Sullivan seems to be
contrasting here the autistic referential processes of the child with the
referential processes of the adult—processes which are in the adult more
syntaxic in regard to "reality."]

other people there has been some degree of exploration, analysis, and the obtaining of information. The business of socializing the child so that what the parents call purely imaginary events are not reported as true, as actually having happened, is so important as an introduction to the next phase of socialization that, as I say, it is enforced by the end of childhood on practically everyone. The lonelier the child has been, the more striking may be the child's need of effort—need of continuous recall and foresight—to fix these distinctions between what, as we say, actually happened and what was part of fantasy process.

In the next phase of development one can make shocking mistakes and get oneself laughed at, punished, and so on, for reporting what we call lively fantasy as real phenomena. If only because that in itself can be so disconcerting, a 'lonely' child has a natural bent toward social isolation, which is one of the relatively unfortunate outcomes of the next era of development. Here is another of these rather circular processes, approximating a vicious circle: already the child has had to develop a very rich fantasy life to make up for the lack of audience and of participation by the authority figures, and from this lack the child is apt to be relatively undeveloped in the very quick discrimination of what is his private fantasy and what may be consensually validated; that in turn exposes the juvenile to ridicule, punishment, and what not, and so tends to give the feeling of risk in life. This feeling of risk is quite distinct from what I discussed before in talking about the transformation of personality toward malevolence. Risk suggests danger of injury and of anxiety; and malevolence is a peculiar transformation which comes from a convinced foresight of these things. The risk that I am now talking about is not so much a transformation of personality as a partial arrest in the socializing process. It is this which makes people around you not so much enemies as unpredictable sources of humiliation, anxiety, and punishment with respect to what you communicate; and that naturally tends to reduce the freedom and enthusiasm of your communication.

The Change in the Role of Playmates in the Juvenile Era

Perhaps I can illustrate the egocentric nature of much of childhood by an example which may for the moment seem tangential but which really supports much of what I have been saying. Nowadays children are not infrequently put in a formal educative situation before they are quite through with this era of childhood. I believe nursery schools often have members who, according to my schematization, would be children. In these nursery-school situations there is a commonly observed phenomenon—so-called egocentric speech. You see, by late childhood, speech has become a great field for play and a very considerable aid in one's fantasy life. A child in a nursery-school setting will talk a blue streak, apparently to another child; but his talk is not at all influenced by, for instance, the other child's starting to talk, or the other child's going away.

As childhood progresses, a time is reached when there is very rapid acceleration of change in the character of fantasy; and this change is in the direction of burying, losing interest in, forgetting, or modifying what may in very early childhood have been truly incredibly fantastic imaginary playmates, and toward a direction of attempting to personify playmates very like oneself. Where circumstances do not contradict the possibility, there is a beginning of truly cooperative action with other people of about the same age. But even in the case of children who have grown up with no possibility of playing with other children, who are born on remote farms, or in other isolated places, this change in play or change in imagination appears. The child now begins to have rather realistic imaginary playmates, while before a great deal of his imaginary accouterments, his imaginary toys, and so on were strikingly fantastic. Now they begin to be as like him as can be, rather than to be things like the pictures in the *Wizard of Oz* or something of that sort. I refer to all this as the maturation of the need for compeers, which ushers in what it seems best to call the *juvenile era*, which is particularly the period of formal education, as required by law, in this nation at least.

CHAPTER
15

The Juvenile Era

I NOW want to give a hurried sketch of the exceedingly important juvenile era. Much of what I will be talking about is actually accessible to all of us—namely, a good many of the factors which contributed to the growth and direction of personality in the years between entrance in school and the time when one actually finds a chum—the last landmark which ends the juvenile era, if it ever does end. In the succeeding phase of preadolescence, in the company of one's chum, one finds oneself more and more able to talk about things which one had learned, during the juvenile era, not to talk about. This relatively brief phase of preadolescence, if it is experienced, is probably rather fantastically valuable in salvaging one from the effects of unfortunate accidents up to then.

But the importance of the juvenile era can scarcely be exaggerated, since it is the actual time for becoming social. People who bog down in the juvenile era have very conspicuous disqualifications for a comfortable life among their fellows. A vast number of important things happen in the juvenile era. This is the first developmental stage in which the limitations and peculiarities of the home as a socializing influence begin to be open to remedy. The juvenile era has to remedy a good many of the cultural idiosyncrasies, eccentricities of value, and so on, that have been picked up in the childhood socialization; if it does not, they are apt to survive and color, or warp, the course of development through subsequent periods.

It is in general true that, as one passes over one of these more-or-less determinable thresholds of a developmental era, everything that has gone before becomes reasonably open to influence; this is true even in the organization of the self-system, which, as I suppose I cannot stress too much, is remarkably inclined to maintain its direction. The changes which take place at the thresholds of the developmental eras, as outlined here, are far-reaching; they touch upon much of what has already been acquired as personality, often making it somewhat acutely inadequate, or at any rate not fully relevant for the sudden new expanding of the personal horizon. Thus the beginning phase of a developmental era may considerably affect those inappropriate aspects of personality which emerge from what the person has undergone up to then. People going into the juvenile era are all too frequently very badly handicapped for acquiring social skill. Take, for example, the child who has been taught to expect everything, who has been taught that his least wish will be of importance to the parents, and that any obscurities in expressing what he is after will keep them awake nights trying to anticipate and satisfy his alleged needs. Now picture what happens to that child when he goes to school. Or take the petty tyrant who rules his parents with complete neglect of their feelings. Take the child, on the other hand, who has been taught to be completely self-effacing and docilely obedient. These are just a few of the many greatly handicapping patterns of dealing with authority which the home permits or imposes on the child. All these children, if they did not undergo very striking change in the juvenile era, would be almost intolerable ingredients, as they grew up, in a group of any particular magnitude.

In this culture, where education is compulsory, it is the school society that rectifies or modifies in the juvenile era a great deal of the unfortunate direction of personality evolution conferred upon the young by their parents and others constituting the family group. There are two contributions to growth in the juvenile era, the experience of social subordination, and the experience of social accommodation.

In considering *social subordination*, it should be noted that in the juvenile era there is a great change in the type of authority, and in the kind of subordination to authority. The social order, by requiring formal education, provides a succession of new authority figures who are often fortunate in their impersonality. Thus the child is exposed to such variegated authority-carrying figures as

the schoolteachers, the recreational directors, the crossing policemen, and so on. Some of these new authority figures have pretty
highly stereotyped limitations on the authority they may exercise;
in every case, they are almost certainly quite different from the
figures in the home, in their exercise of authority and their regard
for and interest in the young juvenile. In his relations with his
teacher and the various other adult authority figures who now
appear, the juvenile is expected—as the child had begun to be by
his parents—to do things on demand; and he is given rewards,
punishments, and so on, with respect to compliance, noncompli-
ance, rebellion, and what not. But there are more-or-less formally
enforced limits to each of these new authorities. At the same time,
there is the possibility for the juvenile to see the interrelation of
the behavior of his compeers to success or failure with the new
authority figures. And in addition to the adult authorities, there
are in almost every school situation malevolent juveniles—bullies.
Part of the incredible gain in ability to live comes from one's finding a way of getting by under the episodic and destructive exercises
of authority by such compeers.

Occasionally some figure in the home is of such great social
importance that the new authority figures are intimidated and
treat the child as exceptional. For example, the psychiatrist may
see an adult in treatment who is the son of an important politician,
and may discover that the potency of this politician-father had
so altered the freedom with which corrective authority could be
imposed on his son that to an extraordinary extent the person as
an adult continues to suffer from warp acquired at home as a child.
But even under extraordinary circumstances of birth and rank,
there occurs some correcting of the more eccentric aspects of
adjustment to authority as soon as the child leaves the home.

In almost all cases, however, the more emphatically effective
contribution of the juvenile era is that of *social accommodation*—
that is, a simply astounding broadening of the grasp of how many
slight differences in living there are; how many of these differences
seem to be all right, even if pretty new; and how many of them
don't seem to be right, but nonetheless how unwise one is to attempt to correct them. This arises from the contact with, and necessity for a certain amount of accommodation to, people of about

the same age with a great variety of personal peculiarities. Some of these juveniles are treated with the utmost crudeness by other juveniles. At this stage—if only because the juvenile has just come from the home situation and his previous experience has been with older and younger siblings, or with really imaginary play-mates—there is a truly rather shocking insensitivity to feelings of personal worth in others. Thus the school years are a time when a degree of crudeness in interpersonal relations, very rarely paral-leled in later life, is the rule. But, in spite of this, the opportunity which is laid before the young juvenile for catching on to how other people are looked upon by authority figures and by each other is an exceedingly important part of the educative process, even though it is one to which no particular attention is convention-ally given. A great deal of this educative experience, which tends to correct idiosyncrasies of past socialization, is never discussed as such. Ten, fifteen, or twenty years after one has left the juvenile era, the experience is extraordinarily inaccessible to ready recall, if, for instance, one is undergoing an intensive study of personality.

The rate of growth of personality through all these earlier phases is truly amazing. We realize this more and more as we be-gin to analyze the enormous number of rather exquisite judgments which one uses in directing one's life in an incoherent culture among people with many specific limitations and individual abili-ties and liabilities. And the amount of education for life that comes from the juvenile era is immensely important. The juvenile can see what other juveniles are doing—either getting away with, or being reproved for—and can notice differences between peo-ple which he had never conceived of, because previously he had had nothing whatever on which to base an idea of something dif-ferent from his own experience.

Authority Figures as People

Perhaps the most startling aspect of the juvenile acculturation, and the last of the enormous accessions to personality in the juvenile era, is the beginning differentiation of the childhood authority figures—parents and their homologues—as simply peo-ple. Failure in this very discrimination of parents as people is often strikingly reflected much later in life. This discrimination is, to a considerable extent, first gained by discovering merits in particular teachers and then discovering demerits in certain other teachers, with or without communication of these experiences to the authority figures at home. But if there has been anything like a healthy development up to this time, these observations *are* discussed in the home. As a result of all this, if it works right, the juvenile gradually has an opportunity to pare the parents down from godlike figures to people. Another great tributary to this type of learning, which appears in most juveniles probably when they are well on in the second grade, is that they learn from other juveniles about their parents. The story most often heard of these earlier school years is, "My father can lick your father"; but it is more important to note that there is simply an amazing amount of checking on the relative virtues and weaknesses of one's parents, especially if there has been no major disaster to development this far. There is no reason in the world why a juvenile should not come out of this period convinced that few people have parents as good as his—that can happen. But if he comes out of the juvenile era with no freedom to compare his parents with other parents, with teachers, and so on—if they still have to be sacrosanct, the most perfect people on earth—then one of the most striking and important of the juvenile contributions to socialization has sadly miscarried.

Competition and Compromise

Now, it is traditional to say—and the tradition is well justified by our observations on inadequate and inappropriate living in chronological adults—that there are two genera of learning which are practically the special province of the early school situation —competition and compromise. They are sufficiently important that certain provisions for them are made in the primary education of all cultures that value these things at all. Unfortunately, competition is the one that gets far more encouragement, although it is perhaps the one that is beginning to sink in importance. The juvenile society itself encourages competitive efforts of all kinds, and in the juvenile himself, I should say, such competition is natural. In addition, the authority figures encourage competition—that is, they do in any culture that values competition. There are some cultures that do not value competition; in those cultures, the tendencies of juveniles to compete appear, but are subjected to inhibitory influence by the authority figures. In our culture, these tendencies are rather vigorously encouraged, so much so, in fact, that if one is physically handicapped or, for some other reason, very bad at competitive performances that are *de rigueur*, then one is practically taught that one is not really fit to be around—that there is something rather profoundly wrong with one.

The other of this pair of elements, compromise, is also invariably enforced by the juvenile society itself, and to a certain extent is encouraged by the school authorities or the juvenile authority figures. Both competition and compromise, while very necessary additions to one's equipment for living with one's fellows, are capable of being developed into outstandingly troublesome traits of the personality. In what I call chronically juvenile people one sees a competitive way of life in which nearly everything that has real importance is part of a process of getting ahead of the other fellow. And if there is also a malevolent transformation of personality, getting the other fellow down becomes the outstanding pattern in the integration of interpersonal relations. This is another of these instances of arrest of development, which is not to say that a chronic juvenile continues in a great many ways to be strikingly like a person, let us say, in the fifth grade of grammar school; it merely means that there are warps in the freedom for interpersonal relations which relate back to the juvenile developmental phase and to particularly unfortunate experiences there. Now under some circumstances compromise also becomes a vice, so that we find people going on from the juvenile era who are perfectly willing to yield almost anything, as long as they have peace and quiet, as they are apt to put it. And that is another unfortunate outcome of juvenile socialization.

Control of Focal Awareness

Thus the juvenile era is the time when the world begins to be really complicated by the presence of other people. The full educational effort, insofar as that effort is formalized by the school curriculum, by the teaching, and so on, is addressed to the extinction of the autistic from the expressed thought and other behavior of the juvenile. And this learning of successful ways of expression and successful types of performance covers so much ground and receives so much encouragement from all sorts of educative influences—all the way from anxiety to carefully awarded prestige with one's fellows—that by the end of the sixth, seventh, or eighth grade, a person of normal endowment has given up a great many of the ideas and operations which, in childhood, and in the home, were all right. This, I believe, is the principal factor entering into the so-called latency period, which was one of the important early psychoanalytic concepts. The effect of the juvenile era is, literally, to make it hard to recall what went on in childhood unless it turns out to be perfectly appropriate and easily modified to meet the strenuous attempt by the society to teach the young to talk, to read, and to "act right."

This giving up of the ideas and operations of childhood comes about through the increasing power of the self-system to control focal awareness. And this in turn comes about because of the very direct, crude, critical reaction of other juveniles, and because of the relatively formulable and predictable manifestations of adult authority. In other words, the juvenile has extraordinary opportunity to learn a great deal about security operations, to learn ways of being free from anxiety, in terms of comparatively understandable sanctions and their violations. This is quite different from anything we have discussed up to now. And insofar as the sanctions and the operations which will avoid anxiety make sense, can be consensually validated, the self-system effectively controls focal awareness so that what does not make sense tends to get no particular attention. That is, effective manifestations of awareness are sternly shepherded by anxiety to be more or less in the syntaxic mode—the mode of experience which offers some possibility of predicting the novel, and some possibility of real interpersonal communication.

This control of focal awareness results in a combination of the fortunate and the unfortunate uses of selective inattention. The sensible use is that there is no need of bothering about things that don't matter, things that will go all right anyway. But, in many cases, there is an unfortunate use of selective inattention, in which one ignores things that do matter; since one has found no way of being secure about them, one excludes them from awareness as long as possible. In any case, the self-system controls, from well on in the juvenile era, the content of consciousness, as we ordinarily call it—that is, what we know we're thinking about—to a very striking extent.

Sublimatory Reformulations

A part of the educational effort, of course, pertains to the acquiring of rote data and information which is not in any particular sense personal; thus juveniles are taught a great many things that seem to have nothing to do with them, but which they have to know in order to get by the teachers. But I am concerned here with the juvenile educative process which is tributary to success in living. Insofar as it is tributary, it is very largely a manifestation, not of rational analysis and valid formulation, but of the sublimatory reformulation of patterns of behavior and covert process. As I have said before, this reformulation occurs when a way of behavior that is socially approved is unwittingly substituted for a part of the motivational pattern that is not acceptable to the authority figures and is not tolerated or regarded with esteem by one's fellows; and when this happens there is some remainder of unsatisfied need which is worked off in private reverie process, especially during sleep.

A very great deal of one's education for living, unfortunately, has to be this sort of sublimatory, strikingly unwitting 'catching-on to' how to get a good deal of satisfaction, although not complete satisfaction. Since it is unwitting, it is not particularly represented in useful understanding of one's behavior. But insofar as it is not overloaded, this process gives one great surety in what one is doing; and one's certainty is not even disturbed by the fact that somebody else may reason better to a different end. Thus when a juvenile acquires a pattern of relating himself to someone else which works and is approved, he simply *knows* that what he is doing is right. And this certainty comes about because there is, in the juvenile era, an increasing power of the self-system to control the contents of awareness, and because the acquisition of the pattern is itself unwitting. Since there is no particular reason for anyone to try to bring into the juvenile's awareness how he arrived at these reformulations of behavior, most of us come into adult life with a great many firmly entrenched ways of dealing with our fellow man which we cannot explain adequately. Even in adult therapy, it is fairly difficult for the psychiatrist to attract enough of the patient's attention to one of these sublimatory reformulations to get him to realize that there's something about it quite beyond explaining. People are not even particularly vulnerable to inquiry in this area, because, by the time anybody is apt to be investigating it, they have a whole variety of devices for heading off awkwardness.

Of the learning which goes on in the juvenile era, a very great amount of it, as I have said before, pertains to competitive and compromising operations to preserve some measure of self-esteem, a feeling of personal worth. As the juvenile era progresses—as one gets into fifth, sixth, seventh, and eighth grades—one has to notice, from this standpoint of the competitive and the compromising operations in which the self-system is involved, the other person concerned. And the other person will be in one of the three groups of significant people that make up the world of the juvenile—the family, the nonfamily authorities, and the other juveniles. The nature of our social system is such that the juvenile alternates between immediate contact with the family group—no juvenile is apt to be able to throw off the influence of the family group— and immediate contact with the school, in its double aspect of authority carriers and other juveniles.

Ostracism

But as the juvenile era goes on, one of its enormously forceful social implements is generally manifest in a segregation into groups within the juvenile society itself—that is, the other pupils in the school—which is a reflection of a good deal of the sickness of the larger society in which juvenility is set. An inevitable outcome of differences in background, differences in abilities, differences in speed of maturations, differences in health, and so on, is the establishment of more-or-less in-groups and out-groups. There are often in-groups with respect to one group of things and in-groups with respect to another; and there are often corresponding out-groups in these various areas. But in most juvenile societies there are a certain number of juveniles who definitely are excluded from very much association with those other juveniles who certainly seem to stand high in the esteem of the school authorities, or in the esteem of the juvenile society in general. The segregating influence which makes some people get along fine together, and apparently rate high with the teachers and with the crossing policemen, or which makes them very important to other juveniles even if they rate very low with the authorities—this segregating influence is sharp, and, to the unfortunate juvenile, quite mysterious. One's experience with these people who are in the right place, who have prestige as a group of juveniles—a very loose group, but still a numerical group at least—is apt to make one feel what can now be perfectly correctly called *ostracism*. Thus juveniles, unless fortunate, can feel ostracized; and if they're quite unfortunate, they get a liberal education in how they are kept ostracized.

In any large group of school children habitually in contact with each other, some of the juveniles will definitely suffer from ostracism by a considerable number of others; but these relatively ostracized out-group youngsters have interpersonal relations one with another. Although these relations to some extent take the curse off the ostracism, they usually do not show enough ingenuity or magical potency to make this unlucky group an in-group. And insofar as these associations with other unfortunate juveniles fail, this experience is not tributary to good self-esteem. In other words, members of out-groups, even if they are fairly successful in maintaining internal competition and compromises, usually show pretty durable evidences of their having been in an inferior position with respect to other compeers whom they were compelled to respect, however painfully and unwillingly, because of their social preferment.

Stereotypes

In the juvenile era, one of the additions to acquaintance with social reality which is almost always encountered is the growth of patterns of others' alleged personalities, which, in a great many cases, amount to actual stereotypes. It is apparent that a great many of us make practical use of stereotypes when we say, "He acts like a farmer." This does not usually mean that we have made a great many observations of farmers and have segregated from all these observations a nuclear group of durable and important traits which are found only in farmers; more probably we are really referring to a stereotype, which may be completely empty of any validifiable meaning. In the juvenile era, the growth of stereotypes which will later disfigure one's ability, or interfere with one's ability, to make careful discriminations about others goes to really lamentable lengths in some instances. These are the stereotypes of persons never encountered in reality, or—perhaps next most troublesome—stereotypes of large groups of humanity on the basis of a solitary instance or a very few instances. Thus, for example, in my own early years, by a series of irrelevant accidents, I heard things said about Jews, but I didn't know any Jews. Because of an extremely fortunate accident of what seemed to be otherwise a very unpleasant developmental history, I did not have very much interest in these vague rumors that I'd never seen exemplified, and so I did not adopt this stereotype. Therefore I emerged into the adult world with some curiosity about these people, whom I thought of as extraordinary, since my own acquaintance with them resulted almost entirely from perusing Holy Writ. I am glad that I did not fix in my mind some of the alleged attributes of Jews which I might have found lying around in certain juveniles, which in turn they, having no actual experience with them, had taken over from parents and other authority figures. Otherwise, I am quite certain that I would have been richly supplied with stereotypes. And these would have been much harder to correct later than was my curiosity as to what the devil the people who wrote the Old Testament must have been like.

Stereotyping can be a source of very real trouble in later life, especially if one is going into a field of work like psychiatry, where the extremely important thing to do is to observe participantly what goes on with another person. If you have a number of implicit assumptions that have not been questioned by you for twenty or twenty-five years about the alleged resemblance of the person before you to some stereotype that you have in your mind, you may find yourself greatly handicapped, for these stereotypes are often viciously incomplete and meaninglessly erroneous.

A great deal of this stereotyping is stamped in, in the juvenile era. Since there is so much to be done in this era and so much pressure on the juvenile to take over any successful patterns for doing it, in our type of school society at least, one of the conspicuous outcomes is that a great many juveniles arrive at preadolescence with quite rigid stereotypes about all sorts of classes and conditions of mankind. One of these stereotypes is about people of the opposite sex. Unless something fortunate intervenes, juveniles pretty nearly have to adopt gross stereotypes of juveniles of the other sex. If you think back to your experience in, say, the first grade, with a particularly attractive playmate who happened to be of the other sex, you may remember how that relationship changed as you went on in juvenile society. And you may realize that, in spite of all experience which was contrary to the stereotype, you almost had to adopt, by the time you were on the verge of preadolescence, what might be described as the juvenile stereotype of the "girls" or the "boys"—whichever the other sex was—and govern yourself accordingly—publicly at least.

Sometimes there are stereotypes about teachers which are all too easy to accept because of previous unpleasantness with authority figures. Quite often there are stereotypes of juveniles' relations to teachers; and if one is actually teacher's pet, or simply for some reason the teacher is especially interested in one, one has to act under the aegis of the juvenile stereotype of the teacher's pet, and cannot therefore derive any simple profit from what would otherwise be a fortunate accident. I suppose, if only because of the speed with which the awesome varieties of people and behavior are impressed on the juvenile, it's hard indeed to avoid organizing—accessible to awareness—crude classifications of people, performance, and so on, which really are irrational and which later become troublesome stereotypes.

Supervisory Patterns

Stereotyping, to a striking extent, also characterizes the evolution of the juvenile's own self-system, insofar as the personifications of the self are concerned. An almost inevitable outcome of the most fortunate kind of juvenile experience is the appearance of what I call *supervisory patterns* in the already very complex system of processes and personifications that make up the self-system. These supervisory patterns amount in certain instances to subpersonalities—that is, they are "really" imaginary people who are always with one.

Perhaps I can make my point by mentioning three of these supervisory patterns that everyone knows most intimately from very prolonged personal experience. When you have to teach, lecture in public, as I am doing, or do any talking in which it's quite important that the other fellow learns something from you, or thinks that you're wonderful, even if obscure, you have as a supervisory pattern a personality whom I might call your *hearer*. Your hearer is strikingly competent in judging the relevancy of what you are saying. This hearer patiently listens to all your harangues in public and sees that the grammar is stuck together and that things that are too opaque are discussed further. In other words, it is really as if a supplementary, or a subordinate, personality worked like thunder to put your thoughts together into some semblance of the English language. My hearer—my particular supervisory pattern—has a certain rather broad composition, which is built out of a great deal of experience in being an essentially solitary, overprivileged juvenile, surrounded by numerous people who were not free from envy. Thus my supervisory pattern is such that I often adjust my remarks fairly well to the needs of, let us say, fifty percent of my audience. Some people's hearers seem to have been even more singularly uninformed about other people than mine, and these hearers let pass, as adequate and proper, expressions which communicate to very few indeed of those that hear them. But in any event, it is as if there were two people—one who actually utters statements, and another who attempts to see that what is uttered is fairly well adjusted to its alleged purpose.

All of you, whether or not you have a diligent hearer, have now long had, as a supervisory pattern, the *spectator*. The spectator diligently pays attention to what you show to others, and do with others; he warns you when it isn't quite cricket, or it's too revealing, or one thing and another; and he hurriedly adds fog or camouflage to make up for any careless breach. And if any of you write seriously, or even write detective stories, you have another supervisory pattern of this kind—your *reader*. I have been very much interested in the character of my reader, never quite interested enough to conduct an extended investigation to discover his actual origin; but enough to know that he's a charming pill, practically entirely responsible for the fact that I almost never publish anything. He is bitterly paranoid, a very brilliant thinker, and at the same time an extraordinarily wrongheaded imbecile. Thus when I attempt to use the written language to communicate serious thought, I am unhappily under constant harassment to so hedge the words around that the most bitterly critical person will be unable to grossly misunderstand them, and, at the same time, to make them so clear that this wrongheaded idiot will grasp what I'm driving at. The result is, as I say, that I write almost nothing. I usually give it up in the process of revising it.

These supervisory patterns ordinarily come into being in the juvenile era and persist, with some refinements, from then on. Their presence in the self-system may well be stressed from another standpoint: They are only a small part of this very elaborate organization, which we all come to have, for maintaining our feeling of personal worth, our self-respect, for obtaining the respect of others, and for insuring the protection which positions of prestige and preferment confer in our particular society.

Social Judgments and Social Handicaps

In the course of the juvenile era, particularly toward the close of it, one is invariably exposed to judgments and suspected judgments which can be called one's reputation as a juvenile. And in a good many cases, there are very great discrepancies—often quite worthy of inspection in the course of later study of personality—between one's reputation with nonfamily authorities, with other juveniles, and with the family society. With other juveniles, one's reputation is particularly determined by the in-groups and by those juveniles who are manifesting what is called leadership in its more rudimentary form—another of the phenomena of juvenile society as it gets on.

Now, the sorts of things that make up one's reputation in these three areas of the social world may be suggested if I run over only a few of the contrasts that are, I suppose, with one through life. A person is popular, is average, or is unpopular. In juvenile society, being average has special qualities; for instance, people who can't be popular are much happier being average than being unpopular. Another one of these contrasts is being a good or a bad sport, particularly for males in this culture. Or again, a person is unquestionably bright, or average, or dull. One is assured, or average, or socially diffident. One is superior, or average, or unfortunately inferior with respect to the progress of one's development in interpersonal relations—that is, as we ordinarily say it, in personality development. One is, in other words, outstanding in one's capacity for understanding and invention of new interpersonal patterns, and so on; or one is below average—that is, literally backward in the evolution of interpersonal relations. There can be very real foundations for a juvenile's being backward in this area, if, for example, ill health comes at critical periods and cuts him out of school recurrently, or if something prevents his participation in games which enjoy great prestige in that particular school group. It can come about because of social handicap; this social handicap may be the reputation of one's father as the neighborhood drunkard—things of that kind, which one was not fortunate enough to discover a way to get around. In the good old days, it might be nothing more fatal than the fact that your mother had divorced and remarried. All these things may literally provide such a handicap that one is pretty slow in developing social accommodation. And some of these social handicaps are very real indeed. One of the things which time and time again has shown itself to have been quite disastrous in the history of patients was the social mobility of the parents, which took the juvenile from one school to another at frequent intervals, so that he was always being introduced as a stranger to another group of juveniles. Other things being equal, if one is getting on at all fortunately in juvenile society, it's a very good thing to stay in that group of juveniles throughout the period, or certainly until near the end of the juvenile era. Otherwise one will actually show considerable inferiority in acquiring the complement of interpersonal aptitudes which the juvenile era, at its best, confers. Of course, if one is in a very unfortunate position in a group of juveniles, it is perhaps fortunate if one can get out of it. But continuous upheaval in schooling—and this is strikingly true with service personnel—is apt to leave a very considerable handicap in this and subsequent phases of development.

The Learning of Disparagement

In addition to all this, there are certain more obscure factors which may make one backward, as it were, in growing up. With respect to one's reputation, and particularly with respect to one's superior profit or inferior profit from the juvenile era, there are rather important influences which may be exerted by the parental group. The particular one that I shall use as an instance is only one of many unfortunate influences which the parents may exercise, which tend to reduce profit from the juvenile era. This is a parental morbidity of security operations, such that the juvenile is taught to disparage others—a common phenomenon on the American scene. It may be the way, for instance, that the significant figure in the home handles a juvenile "misfortune," such as being average instead of superior. It may occur because the parental figure has always disparaged all people who made her or him uncomfortable. It may occur because one or both parents feel threatened by the revealing nature of juvenile communication and so disparage teachers and other people with whom they feel compared. This disparaging business is really like the dust of the streets—it settles everywhere. It is perhaps not so disastrous in the juvenile era as it is from then on; but it is very disastrous at any time. If you have to maintain self-esteem by pulling down the standing of others, you are extraordinarily unfortunate in a variety of ways. Since you have to protect your feeling of personal worth by noting how unworthy everybody around you is, you are not provided with any data that are convincing evidence of your having personal worth; so it gradually evolves into "I am not as bad as the other swine." To be the best of swine, when it would be nice to be a person, is not a particularly good way of furthering anything except security operations. When security is achieved that way, it strikes at the very roots of that which is essentially human—the utterly vital role of interpersonal relations.

In the juvenile era this kind of security operation, literally and very significantly, interferes with adequate analysis of personal worth. In other words, if another boy does well and little Willie reports it to mother, and mother promptly knocks the spots off the other boy and his family, that tends to indicate that little Willie's impression of how the other fellow was behaving was groundless, or that the rewards which the other fellow's behavior got from teachers, and so on, were undeserved. In other words, one is encouraged to feel incapable of knowing what is good. Learning from human examples is extremely important, as I have stressed; but if every example that seems to be worth emulating, learning something from, is reduced to no importance or worth, then who are the models going to be? I think that this is probably the most vicious of the inadequate, inappropriate, and ineffectual performances of parents with juveniles—this interference with a sound development of appreciation of personal worth, by universal derogatory and disparaging attitudes toward anybody who seems to stand out at all. It is in this way that parents are apt to very markedly handicap the 'sane' development of standards of personal worth in their young. To that extent—barring great good fortune in subsequent eras of personality development—they literally guarantee that their children will be barely better than the other swine.

The Conception of Orientation in Living

By the end of the juvenile era, with any good fortune, one has gotten to the point at which it is quite proper to apply the conception of *orientation in living*, as I use the term. *One is oriented in living to the extent to which one has formulated, or can easily be led to formulate (or has insight into), data of the following types: the integrating tendencies (needs) which customarily characterize one's interpersonal relations; the circumstances appropriate to their satisfaction and relatively anxiety-free discharge; and the more or less remote goals for the approximation of which one will forego intercurrent opportunities for satisfaction or the enhancement of one's prestige.* The degree to which one is *adequately oriented* in living is, I believe, a very much better way of indicating what we often have in mind when we speak about how "well integrated" a person is, or what his "character" is in the sense of good, bad, or indifferent.

The juvenile actually has an opportunity to undergo a great deal of social experience, in contrast to the child, who cannot have any orientation in living in the larger world. To the extent that the juvenile knows, or could easily be led to know, what needs motivate his relations with others, and under what circumstances these needs —whether they be for prestige or for anything else—are appropriate and relatively apt to get by without damage to self-respect, to this extent the person has gotten a great deal out of his first big plunge into socialization. If this comes off successfully, he inevitably has established some things which we can really call his values, from the pursuit of which he will not be deflected by other things that come along and might be obtained; in other words, a striking aspect of good orientation in living is the extent to which foresight governs the handling of intercurrent opportunities.

To the extent that a juvenile has been denied an opportunity for a good orientation in living, he will from henceforth show a trait which is a lamentable nuisance: he will be so anxious for the approval and unthinking immediate regard of others that one might well think he lived merely to be liked, or to amuse. And in some cases, that, I fear, is about true.

So, if one has been fortunate in the juvenile era, his orientation in living among other people is fairly well organized. And if his orientation in living is not well organized, his future contributions to the human race will probably be relatively unimportant or will be troublesome, unless he has very good fortune in the next succeeding phases of personality development.

CHAPTER
16

Preadolescence

Need for Interpersonal Intimacy

JUST AS the juvenile era was marked by a significant change—
the development of the need for compeers, for playmates rather
like oneself—the beginning of preadolescence is equally spectacularly marked, in my scheme of development, by the appearance of
a new type of interest in another person. These changes are the
result of maturation and development, or experience. This new
interest in the preadolescent era is not as general as the use of language toward others was in childhood, or the need of similar people as playmates was in the juvenile era. Instead, it is a specific new
type of interest in a *particular* member of the same sex who becomes a chum or a close friend. This change represents the beginning of something very like full-blown, psychiatrically defined
love. In other words, the other fellow takes on a perfectly novel
relationship with the person concerned: he becomes of practically
equal importance in all fields of value. Nothing remotely like that
has ever appeared before. All of you who have children are sure
that your children love you; when you say that, you are expressing
a pleasant illusion. But if you will look very closely at one of your
children when he finally finds a chum—somewhere between eight-
and-a-half and ten—you will discover something very different in
the relationship—namely, that your child begins to develop a real
sensitivity to what matters to another person. And this is not in the
sense of "what should I do to get what I want," but instead "what
should I do to contribute to the happiness or to support the prestige
and feeling of worth-whileness of my chum." So far as I have
ever been able to discover, nothing remotely like this appears be-

fore the age of, say, eight-and-a-half, and sometimes it appears decidedly later.

Thus the developmental epoch of preadolescence is marked by the coming of the integrating tendencies which, when they are completely developed, we call love, or, to say it another way, by the manifestation of the need for interpersonal intimacy. Now even at this late stage in my formulation of these ideas, I still find that some people imagine that intimacy is only a matter of approximating genitals one to another. And so I trust that you will finally and forever grasp that interpersonal intimacy can really consist of a great many things without genital contact; that intimacy in this sense means, just as it always has meant, closeness, without specifying that which is close other than the persons. Intimacy is that type of situation involving two people which permits validation of all components of personal worth. Validation of personal worth requires a type of relationship which I call collaboration, by which I mean clearly formulated adjustments of one's behavior to the expressed needs of the other person in the pursuit of increasingly identical—that is, more and more nearly mutual—satisfactions, and in the maintenance of increasingly similar security operations.[1] Now this preadolescent collaboration is distinctly different from the acquisition, in the juvenile era, of habits of competition, cooperation, and compromise. In preadolescence not only do people occupy themselves in moving toward a common, more-or-less impersonal objective, such as the success of "our team," or the discomfiture of "our teacher," as they might have done in the juvenile era, but they also, specifically and increasingly, move toward supplying each other with satisfactions and taking on each other's successes in the maintenance of prestige, status, and all the things which represent freedom from anxiety, or the diminution of anxiety.[2]

---

[1] [Editors' note: Sullivan's use of the terms "collaboration" and "cooperation" should be kept in mind throughout this section. By cooperation, he means the usual give-and-take of the juvenile era; by collaboration, he means the feeling of sensitivity to another person which appears in preadolescence. "Collaboration . . . is a great step forward from cooperation—I play according to the rules of the game, to preserve my prestige and feeling of superiority and merit. When we collaborate, it is a matter of we." (Conceptions of Modern Psychiatry, p. 55.)]

[2] [Editors' note: Up to this point, this chapter is taken from 1944–1945

Psychotherapeutic Possibilities in Preadolescence

Because of the rapidly developing capacity to revise one's personifications of another person on the basis of great interest in observation and analysis of one's experience with him, it comes about that the preadolescent phase of personality development can have and often does have very great inherent psychotherapeutic possibilities. I believe I have said earlier that it is at the developmental thresholds that the chance for notable favorable change tends to segregate itself. Although the structure of the self-system is such that its development in general is rather powerfully directed along the lines it has already taken, it is much more subject to influence through new experience, either fortunate or unfortunate, at each of the developmental thresholds. The fact that the self-system can undergo distinct change early in each of the developmental stages is of very real significance. For it is the self-system—the vast organization of experience which is concerned with protecting our self-esteem—which is involved in all inadequate and inappropriate living and is quite central to the whole problem of personality disorder and its remedy. And it is this capacity for distinct change in the self-system which begins to be almost fantastically important in preadolescence.

During the juvenile era a number of influences of vicious family life may be attenuated or corrected. But in the Western world a great deal of the activity of juveniles is along the lines of our ideals of intensely competitive, invidious society; only recently—and, I fear, still quite insularly—has there been any marked social pressure toward developing the other aspects of the same thing, the capacity to compromise and cooperate. Because of the competitive element, and also because of the juvenile's relative insensitivity to the importance of other people, it is possible that one can maintain throughout the juvenile era remarkably fantastic ideas about oneself, that one can have a very significantly distorted personification of the self, and keep it under cover. To have a very

lectures, rather than from the series on which this book is primarily based, since this portion is missing in the latter series because of failures of recording equipment. The material corresponds, however, to the outline in Sullivan's Notebook.]

fantastic personification of oneself is, actually, to be very definitely handicapped. In other words, it is a misfortune in development.

Because one draws so close to another, because one is newly capable of seeing oneself through the other's eyes, the preadolescent phase of personality development is especially significant in correcting autistic, fantastic ideas about oneself or others. I would like to stress—at the risk of using superlatives which sometimes get very tedious—that development of this phase of personality is of incredible importance in saving a good many rather seriously handicapped people from otherwise inevitable serious mental disorder.

I may perhaps digress to the extent of saying that for some years I have had no negative instance to the following generalization: As a psychiatrist and a supervising psychiatrist, I have had occasion to hear about many male patients who find all relationships with other men occasions for considerable tenseness and vigilance, and who are uncomfortable in all their business, social, or other dealings with other men; of this group, I have found without exception that each one has lacked anything like good opportunities for preadolescent socialization. (I am confining my remarks to male patients here because the female picture is more complicated and I have less material on it.) These male patients may have what they call very close friends of the same sex, may even be overt and promiscuous homosexuals; but they are not at ease with strange men, they have much more trouble doing business with other men than seems to be justified by the factual aspects of the difficulty, and they are particularly uncertain as to what members of their own sex think of them. In other words, I am practically convinced that capacity for ease, for maximum profit from experience, in carrying on the conventional businesses of life with members of one's own sex requires that one should have been fortunate in entering into and profiting from relations with a chum in the preadolescent phase of personality development.

It is self-evident, I suppose, that I am conspicuously taking exception to the all-too-prevalent idea that things are pretty well fixed in the Jesuitical first seven years. This idea has constituted one of the greatest problems for some anthropologists who have tried to translate psychiatric thought into anthropologically useful ideas. The anthropologists have noised at them from all sides the enormous importance of infantile experience—meaning experience certainly under the age of eight. Yet one of the most conspicuous observations of an anthropologist working anywhere is that children of the privileged, who are raised by servants, do not grow up to be like the servants. That is a little bit difficult for an anthropologist to reconcile with the tremendous emphasis on very early experience. My work has shown me very clearly that, while early experience does a great many things—as I have been trying to suggest thus far—the development of capacity for interpersonal relations is by no means a matter which is completed at some point, say, in the juvenile era. Very far from it. And even preadolescence, which is a very, very important phase of personality development, is not the last phase.

Preadolescent Society

Except in certain rural communities, there occurs in preadolescence the development of at least an approach to what has long been called by sociologists "the gang." I am again speaking rather exclusively of male preadolescents, because by this time the deviations prescribed by the culture make it pretty hard to make a long series of statements which are equally obviously valid for the two sexes. The preadolescent interpersonal relation is primarily, and vastly importantly, a two-group; but these two-groups tend to interlock. In other words, let us say that persons A and B are chums. Person A also finds much that is admirable about person C, and person B finds much that is admirable about person D. And persons C and D each has his chum, so that there is a certain linkage of interest among all of these two-groups. Quite often there will be one particular preadolescent who is, thanks to his having been fortunate in earlier phases, the sort of person that many of these preadolescent people find useful as a model; and he will be the third member, you might say, of many three-groups, composed of any one of a number of two-groups and himself. At the same time, he may have a particular chum just as everybody in this society may have. Thus these close two-groups, which are extremely useful in correcting earlier deviations, tend at the same time to interlock through one person or a few people who are, in a very significant sense, leaders. And incidentally, let me say that many of us are apt to think of leadership in political terms, in terms of "influence" and the "influential." We overlook the fact that influence is exerted by the influential in certain conspicuous areas other than that of getting people to do what the leader wants done. The fact is that a very important field of leadership phenomena—and one that begins to be outstandingly important in preadolescence—is opinion leadership; and understanding this and developing techniques for integrating it might be one of the few great hopes for the future.

Thus some few people tend to come out in leadership positions in preadolescent society. Some of them are the people who can get the others to collaborate, to work with understanding and appreciation of one another toward common objectives or aims, which sometimes may be crimes, or what not. And others are the leaders whose views gradually come to be the views of a large number in the group, which is opinion leadership. This kind of leadership has certain fairly measurable and perhaps some imponderable aspects. One of its reasonably measurable aspects is that people whose development, combined with their intellectual abilities, has given them the ability to separate facts and opinions, tend to be considered by the others as well informed, right in their thinking about things of interest at that particular stage, and thus tend to do the thinking for a good many of the others because of the latter's unfortunate personality warp. And the time when these leaders in opinion do the thinking almost exclusively is when there are serious problems confronting the members of the group. The level of general insecurity about the human future is high at this stage of development, and in any case probably increases when serious problems arise, whether they occur in the preadolescent gang or in society as a whole. It is at those times that perhaps far more than half of the statistical population—handicapped by lack of information, by lack of training, and by various difficulties in personal life which call out a good deal of anxiety, which in turn interferes with practically everything useful —has to look to opinion leadership for anything like reassuring views or capable foresight. Thus an important part of the preadolescent phase of personality development is the developing patterning of leadership-led relationships, which are so vital in any social organization and which are, theoretically at least, of very great importance in relatively democratic organizations of society.

I have suggested that an important aspect of the preadolescent phase is that, practically for the first time, there is consensual validation of personal worth. Now it is true that some children are fortunate, indeed; through the influences to which they have been subjected in the home and school, they are about as sure as they can be that they are worth while in certain respects. But very many people arrive in preadolescence in the sad state which an adult would describe as "getting away with murder." In other words, they have had to develop such remarkable capacities for deceiving and misleading others that they never had a chance to discover what they were really good for. But in this intimate interchange in preadolescence—some preadolescents even have mutual daydreams, spend hours and hours carrying on a sort of spontaneous mythology in which both participate—in this new necessity for thinking of the other fellow as right and for being thought of as right by the other fellow, much of this uncertainty as to the real worth of the personality, and many self-deceptive skills at deceiving others which exist in the juvenile era, may be rectified by the improving communication of the chums and, to a much lesser extent but nonetheless valuably, by confirmatory relations in the collaboration developed in the gang.

Types of Warp and Their Remedy

We might next look at a few of the warped juveniles who can receive very marked beneficial effect from the maturation of this need for intimacy and from preadolescent socialization, who can at this stage literally be put on the right road to a fairly adequate personality development. For example, there are egocentric people, who go from childhood through the juvenile era and still retain literally unlimited expectations of attention and services to themselves. Some of these people you know as those who sulk when something doesn't suit them; some of them are people who have tantrums under certain circumstances. If the families of these juveniles are so influential that the more adult members of the school community hesitate to "break" the juveniles of these undesirable "habits," then about the last chance they have of favorable change is based on their need for getting along with a chum in preadolescence. As juveniles, they have been classified quite uniformly by other juveniles as thoroughly bad sports; there is a distinct tendency for other juveniles to avoid them, to ostracize them, in spite of some necessity for accommodating to them which is imposed by the influence of the family. It is quite possible that in preadolescence such a person will establish his chumship with some other ex-juvenile who is more or less on the fringe of ostracism, and who had been in the out-group of the juvenile society. That looks as if it wouldn't be too good; and in some instances it is not so good, as I will note later. But it is very much better than what was going on before. Not infrequently people of this kind go through the comparatively brief period of preadolescence and come out very much less inclined to expect unlimited services from others, very much nearer the ideal of a good sport who can "take it," and who doesn't require very special treatment. In other words, two unfortunate juveniles thrown together by their unfortunate social status as juveniles may, under the influence of this growing need for intimacy, actually do each other a great deal of good. And as they show some improvement they will become less objectionable to the prevailing preadolescent society and may actually get to be quite well esteemed in the gang. But the risk is that these bad sports, these self-centered or egocentric juveniles, now formed into two-groups, may carry their resentment and misery from the ostracism they have suffered to the length of seeking out and identifying themselves with the most antisocial leadership which can be found.

However, the notion that preadolescence readily consolidates a criminal, antisocial career is the most shocking kind of nonsense, which overlooks almost all instances which happen to be negative. It happens that there is more literature on antisocial gangs than there is on the vastly favorable aspect of preadolescent society. I believe that a study of preadolescent society in the very worst neighborhoods would reveal tendencies other than those leading toward becoming minor criminals. And in some very bad neighborhoods, while there are gangs which are antisocial, there are also gangs which are very much less antisocial, if not actually constituting a constructive element in the neighborhood. In any event, the socialization is bound to happen; and if the setting is bad enough, it's quite possible that the organization will be against the world and will tend to implant that attitude as a reasonable purpose for social action.

Some juveniles arrive in preadolescence strikingly marked with the malevolent transformation of personality which I have discussed previously at some length. All too many of them, because of this malevolent transformation, take their time in establishing a chumship, or may actually fail to do so. But the drive connected with this need for intimate association with someone else is so powerful that quite frequently chumships are formed even by malevolent people. And the entrance into one of these two-groups, which in turn is integrated into the preadolescent gang, provides experience which definitely opens the mind anew to the possibility that one can be treated tenderly, whereupon the malevolent transformation is sometimes reversed, literally cured. More commonly, it is only ameliorated, because the malevolent transformation is apt to have quite a cramping effect on the very easy amalgamation of malevolent two-groups into larger organizations.

There is a variety of other peculiarities that more or less survive the juvenile period. For example, there is the person who feels that something is wrong with others if they don't like him—in other words he really feels perfectly entitled to being universally liked. This kind of person never learns, in the juvenile era, that that is not a reasonable attitude toward life. In the school society, such a person ordinarily has to handle his disappointments by derogatory rationalizations and disparagement of others, for which he generally is set an excellent example in his home. These folk, getting into the preadolescent socialization, quite often gain enough in security from the intimacy with their chums to enable them to really open their minds and discuss these other unpleasant people who don't seem to like them, in a fashion that is illuminating, both as to the real worth of the others and as to some of their own traits which may not be very endearing. Thus preadolescence tends actually to correct to a notable extent one of our most vicious forms of morbidity—the tendency to pull people down because one isn't quite big enough to be comfortable with them. Needless to say, preadolescence does not always cure this, but it tends to mitigate it.

Isolated juveniles, people whom one would expect to go on indefinitely in a rather 'schizoid' way of life, sometimes, by very fortunate preadolescent experience, come out remarkably well able to handle themselves, to develop the social accommodation which did not really reach them in the juvenile period; and this is because of the peculiarly intimate consensual exchange which goes on in preadolescence. On the other hand, social isolation may make it very difficult to establish the type of intimacy which preadolescence calls for; and it may often delay preadolescence so that there is only a brief time, before the puberty change, in which to consolidate the benefits of the preadolescent period.

One of the more warped kinds of juveniles is the one who will not grow up. He is sometimes popular, but often he is unpopular. In any event, he is apt to become increasingly unpopular as the juvenile era wears itself out. This kind of person can properly be called irresponsible. He doesn't want to take on anything that he can avoid; he wants to remain, if you please, juvenile. He wants to be as young as possible, in that he has a real unwillingness to bend the knee to our society's necessities with respect to others. Here again maturation of the need for intimacy sometimes has very marked beneficial effect; on the other hand, it may not work out that way, and he may get into an irresponsible gang. But I do not want you to think that antisocial gangs are in any notable proportion of instances made up of people who were irresponsible juveniles. Whether the gang activity is constructive or destructive in its relationship to the larger society which houses it has nothing in particular to do with the types of warp in the personalities involved in it, but is more a function of what is acceptable as leadership.

In summing up these various warps, one might say that, as long as the warp is not so great as to preclude any undergoing of the preadolescent era, the formation of these new intimacies will provide some consensual validation for all of the warps—that is, one gets a look at oneself through the chum's eyes. To the extent that that is accomplished, the self-system concerned is definitely expanded, and its more troublesome, inadequate, and inappropriate functions are reduced to the point that they become unnecessary.

I should like to mention a few more things that are not quite warps but which might come to be the basis for inadequate and ineffectual living, were it not for the preadolescent influence. Some people go through the juvenile phase with a very favorable record; they are wonderful in sportsmanship, they are very skillful in compromise, or they are just so bright that everybody in the juvenile society profits. Now comes the preadolescent need for intimacy. Any one of these people is apt to be integrated in a two-group with a more average person. And in this interchange in the preadolescent society, some of these very successful juveniles get the first great clue to the fact that they are not going to be carried through life on a silk cushion, and they learn to accept this fact. They discover that if they are lucky enough to have gifts, these gifts carry responsibilities; and that insofar as gifts are used for the discharge of social responsibilities, one is to a certain extent spared the great evil of envy and all the destructive practices which envy carries in its wake.

A somewhat similar group of juveniles are those who have very high intelligence and rate well with teachers, but who are unpopular and unsuccessful with other juveniles—a fact which teachers seldom notice, since they are mainly preoccupied with their pupils' learning. In preadolescence, the drive of the need for intimacy may turn this high intelligence to good use, and literally provide the ex-juvenile with an opportunity for using his intelligence to learn how to be one with others.

Finally, perhaps, I should touch on those who, because of illness or social handicaps or what not, have hung behind all through the juvenile era. Here too the preadolescent intimacy may literally give them, as it were, so much of a helping hand that they come near to catching up with what they have missed in the juvenile era in the way of competition, compromise, and socialization.

The factors that count in the two-groups of preadolescence are: the personal suitability of the people thrown together and then tied together by their need for intimacy; the intensity of the relationship which is achieved; and the durability of the relationship, or the progressive direction of change in those instances in which the relationships have not proved durable throughout preadolescence. This last might result from change of residence of the parents; or there might be factors in the two-group itself that make for disintegration, each of the components then becoming integrated with someone else.

I want particularly to touch on the intensity of the relationship, because it is easy to think that if the preadolescent chumship is very intense, it may tend to fixate the chums in the preadolescent phase, or it may culminate in some such peculiarity of personality as is ordinarily meant by homosexuality—although, incidentally, it is often difficult to say what is meant by this term. Actual facts that have come to my attention lend no support whatever to either of these surmises. In fact, as a psychiatrist, I would hope that preadolescent relationships were intense enough for each of the two chums literally to get to know practically everything about the other one that could possibly be exposed in an intimate relationship, because that remedies a good deal of the often illusory, usually morbid, feeling of being different, which is such a striking part of rationalizations of insecurity in later life.

Perhaps I can illustrate this point by telling you how, by an extraordinary concatenation of events, I was once able to find out something about the adult lives of a onetime preadolescent group who had attended school together in a small Kansas community. I first had access to this information through a man who had been one of the preadolescents in the school, and I was later able to follow this up and get rather complete information on the group. This particular man was an overt homosexual. During his preadolescence, he had been distinctly in the out-group, if only with respect to so-called mutual masturbation and other presumably homosexual activity which went on in this group of boys as preadolescent pals; that is, he had not participated in any of the mutual sexuality which went on in the terminal phase of preadolescence in this group. There was one other preadolescent who had not participated in it, and I was able to track him down. I found that he also had become an overt homosexual. Those who had participated in mutual sexuality were married, with children, divorces, and what not, in the best tradition of American society. In other words, relationships of what might be described as 'illegitimate' intimacy toward the close of the preadolescent period had not conduced to a disturbed type of development in adolescence and later; the facts showed something quite different.

The great remedial effect of preadolescence occurs not only by direct virtue of the intimacy in the two-group, but also because of the real society which emerges among the preadolescents, so that the world is reflected in the preadolescent microcosm. The preadolescent begins to have useful experience in social assessment and social organization. This begins with the relationship which the two-groups come to have to the larger social organization, the gang. The chums are identified as such, and are literally assessed by all other two-groups—and this is not in terms of who they are, but of how they act, and what you can expect from them in the social organization. This is an educative, provocative, and useful experience in social assessment. The fact that one looks out for oneself and is regarded as incredibly individual and what not begins very strikingly to fade from the center of things; and that is an exceedingly fortunate experience to have had. And the gang as a whole finds that it has a relationship to the larger social organization, the community, and that it is assessed by the community. Community acceptance of the gang is likely to depend on whether or not the gang is antisocial, and it may also depend on how widely representative the gang is.

Within the gang, experience in social organization is reflected in how closely integrated the gang is, how stable its leadership is, and how many leaders for different things there are. Sometimes there are preadolescent gangs in which you would find, if you made a careful study, that the members maintain subordination to a number of different leaders, each for different circumstances, which is really pretty refined social organization in miniature.

Disasters in Timing of Developmental Stages

As the preadolescent goes on toward the puberty change, the effect of previous experience on rate of maturation becomes peculiarly conspicuous. The time of the puberty change may vary considerably from person to person—in contrast to the time for the convergence of the eyes in infancy, for instance, which can be predicted almost exactly. This difference in time of puberty maturation may occur partly because of certain biological and hereditary factors; but I know, from considerable data, that factors of experience are also involved. Certain peculiarities of earlier training are so extraordinarily frequent in cases of so-called delayed puberty that one suspects that this training has literally delayed the maturation of the lust dynamism.

One of the lamentable things which can happen to personality in the preadolescent society is that a particular person may not become preadolescent at all promptly—in other words, he literally does not have the need for intimacy when most of the people of about the same age have it, and therefore he does not have an opportunity of being part of the parade as it goes by. But then this person, when preadolescence is passing for most of his contemporaries, develops a need for intimacy with someone of his own sex and may be driven to establishing relationships with a chronologically younger person. This is not necessarily a great disaster. What is more of a disaster is that he may form a preadolescent relationship with an actually adolescent person, which is perhaps more frequently the case in this situation. This does entail some very serious risk to personality and can, I think, in quite a number of instances, be suspected of having considerable to do with the establishment of a homosexual way of life, or at least a 'bisexual' way. And, as I have already hinted, there is definitely a possibility of going no further than preadolescence. The fact that one can be preadolescent for perhaps two years longer than others in one's particular group of young people is nowadays frequent enough to be a study in itself. The number of instances of schizophrenic disorder which are precipitated by one of the chums' getting well into adolescence while the other remains preadolescent is, in my experience, notable.

If adolescence is delayed, it would not have any particular importance, and might actually be somewhat advantageous, as long as one were sure of having a reasonable number of equally delayed people with whom to maintain the type of intimacy which characterizes preadolescence. It is only when chumships are broken up, and the preadolescent society is disorganized by the further maturation of nearly all the members, that great stress may be applied to the personalities which are not able to move on the same time schedule. Sometimes these people who are delayed in puberty have a progression of chums from people of their own age to younger ones, which is somewhat hard on the status of both in the preadolescent organization, tending to exclude both from what would normally be the society of the younger. I suppose the best thing that can happen—next to having a number of confreres who are also slow in maturing—is to be able to take the early stage of adolescence before one has really gotten to it, which is sometimes possible; that is, the adolescent change means a moving of an interest toward members of the other sex, but one can often find an eccentric member of the other sex who also has not undergone the puberty change, but is glad to go through the motions. That reduces the stress on one's feeling of personal worth and security which delayed adolescence may otherwise bring. The delayed completion of the preadolescent phase of personality, together with a shift from the group with which the preadolescent has been developing to marginal groups of adolescents, is, I think, apt to be pretty hard on this younger person; that is, he is, in a sense, the victim of marginal groups of adolescent people, who are actually having plenty of trouble themselves and who are apt to develop a very lively interest in sexual operations with this preadolescent whose adolescence has been delayed. In certain instances, at least, these operations are very costly to the personality when finally the puberty change and the phases of adolescence begin.

In a given person, the beginning of adolescence, as far as personality development is concerned, takes place at an indefinite time; that is, although it does not take place overnight, it is observable at the end of a matter of months, instead of years. Early adolescence, in my scheme of development, is ushered in by the beginning of the array of things called the puberty change, by the frank appearance of the lust dynamism. And the frank appearance of the lust dynamism is, in a great many instances, manifested by the intrusion, into fantasy or the sleep-life, of experience of a piece with the sexual orgasm; in other instances, where there has been preliminary genital play, and so on, it is manifested by the occurrence of orgasm in certain play. Lust is the last to mature of the important integrating tendencies, or needs for satisfaction, which characterize the underlying human animal now well advanced to being a person.

In our society, the age when early adolescence appears varies within three or four years, I think. This remarkable developmental discrepancy which is possible among different people of the same chronological age—a vastly greater discrepancy than occurs in the maturing of any of the previously discussed needs—is one of the important factors which makes adolescence such a time of stress. And incidentally, only by studying a different social organization from ours could one see how much less a time of stress the period of adolescence might be. In certain other societies, where the culture provides a great deal more real preparation for adolescence than ours does, the extraordinarily stressful aspect of adolescence is not nearly so conspicuous. There are, however, certain elements of the puberty change and its associated adolescent phase of personality organization that are not to be overlooked in any social order; those are the ones associated with the remarkable speeding up of certain growth factors which, for example, makes people clumsy and awkward who were previously quite skillful and dexterous. Thus there are always, or almost always, some stresses concerned with this very rapid maturation of the somatic organization which is ushered in by the puberty change. But so far as the psychological stresses are concerned, they are more apt to result from disasters in timing than from anything else.

The Experience of Loneliness [3]

Before going on, I would like to discuss the developmental history of that motivational system which underlies the experience of loneliness.

Now loneliness is possibly most distinguished, among the experiences of human beings, by the toneless quality of the things which are said about it. While I have tried to impress upon you the extreme undesirability of the experience of anxiety, I, in common apparently with all denizens of the English-speaking world, feel inadequate to communicate a really clear impression of the

[3] [Editors' note: Several times, in the series of lectures which has been used as the basis for this book, Sullivan has made reference to a later discussion of loneliness. Yet this discussion does not appear in this particular series, probably through an oversight. We have therefore included here a discussion of loneliness from a 1945 lecture.]

experience of loneliness in its quintessential force. But I think I can give you some idea of why it is a terribly important component of personality, by tracing the various motivational systems by developmental epochs that enter into the experience of loneliness. Of the components which culminate in the experience of real loneliness, the first, so far as I know, appears in infancy as the need for contact. This is unquestionably composed of the elaborate group of dependencies which characterize infancy, and which can be collected under the need for tenderness. This kind of need extends into childhood. And in childhood we see components of what will ultimately be experienced as loneliness appearing in the need for adult participation in activities. These activities start out perhaps in the form of expressive play in which the very young child has to learn how to express emotions by successes and failures in escaping anxiety or in increasing euphoria; in various kinds of manual play in which one learns coordination, and so on; and finally in verbal play—the pleasure-giving use of the components of verbal speech which gradually move over into the consensual validation of speech. In the juvenile era we see components of what will eventually be loneliness in the need for compeers; and in the later phases of the juvenile era, we see it in what I have not previously mentioned by this name, but what you can all recognize from your remembered past, as the need for acceptance. To put it another way, most of you have had, in the juvenile era, an exceedingly bitter experience with your compeers to which the term "fear of ostracism" might be justifiably applied—the fear of being accepted by no one of those whom one must have as models for learning how to be human.

And in preadolescence we come to the final component of the really intimidating experience of loneliness—the need for intimate exchange with a fellow being, whom we may describe or identify as a chum, a friend, or a loved one—that is, the need for the most intimate type of exchange with respect to satisfactions and security.

Loneliness, as an experience which has been so terrible that it practically baffles clear recall, is a phenomenon ordinarily encountered only in preadolescence and afterward. But by giving this very crude outline of the components that enter into this driving impulsion, I hope I have made it clear why, under continued privation, the driving force of this system may integrate inter-personal situations despite really severe anxiety. Although we have not previously, in the course of this outline of the theory of personality, touched on anything which can brush aside the activity of the self-system, we have now come to it: Under loneliness, people seek companionship even though intensely anxious in the performance. When, because of deprivations of companionship, one does integrate a situation in spite of more or less intense anxiety, one often shows, in the situation, evidences of a serious defect of personal orientation. And remember that I am speaking of orientation in living, not orientation in time and space, as the traditional psychiatrists discuss it. I have already given my conception of orientation in living in discussing the juvenile era. Now this defective orientation may be due, for instance, to a primary lack of experience which is needed for the correct appraisal of the situation with respect to its significance, aside from its significance as a relief of loneliness. There are a good many situations in which lonely people literally lack any experience with things which they encounter. . . .

Loneliness reaches its full significance in the preadolescent era, and goes on relatively unchanged from thenceforth throughout life. Anyone who has experienced loneliness is glad to discuss some vague abstract of this previous experience of loneliness. But it is a very difficult therapeutic performance to get anyone to remember clearly how he felt and what he did when he was horribly lonely. In other words, the fact that loneliness will lead to integrations in the face of severe anxiety automatically means that loneliness in itself is more terrible than anxiety. While we show from the very beginning a curiously clear capacity for fearing that which might be fatally injurious, and from very early in life an incredible sensitivity to significant people, only as we reach the preadolescent stage of development does our profound need for dealings with others reach such proportion that fear and anxiety actually do not have the power to stop the stumbling out of restlessness into situations which constitute, in some measure, a relief from loneliness. This is not manifest in anything like driving force until we arrive at the preadolescent era.

CHAPTER
17

Early Adolescence

THE EARLIER phase of adolescence as a period of personality development is defined as extending from the eruption of true genital interest, felt as lust, to the patterning of sexual behavior which is the beginning of the last phase of adolescence. There are very significant differences, in the physiological substrate connected with the beginning of adolescence, between men and women; but in either case there is a rather abrupt change, relatively unparalleled in development, by which a zone of interaction with the environment which had been concerned with excreting waste becomes newly and rapidly significant as a zone of interaction in physical interpersonal intimacy. In other words, what had been, from the somatic viewpoint, the more external tissues of the urinary-excretory zone now become the more external part of the genital zone as well. The change, from the psychological standpoint, pertains to new needs which have their culmination in the experience of sexual orgasm; the felt tensions associated with this need are traditionally and quite properly identified as *lust*. In other words, lust is the felt component of integrating tendencies pertaining to the genital zone of interaction, seeking the satisfaction of cumulatively augmented sentience culminating in orgasm.

There is, so far as I know, no necessarily close relationship between lust, as an integrating tendency, and the need for intimacy, which we have previously discussed, except that they both characterize people at a certain stage in development. The two are strikingly distinct. In fact, making very much sense of the complexities and difficulties which are experienced in adolescence and subsequent phases of life, depends, in considerable measure, on the clarity with which one distinguishes three needs, which are often very intricately combined and at the same time contradictory. These are the need for personal security—that is, for freedom from anxiety; the need for intimacy—that is, for collaboration with at least one other person; and the need for lustful satisfaction, which is connected with genital activity in pursuit of the orgasm.

The Shift in the Intimacy Need

As adolescence is ushered in, there is, in people who are not too much warped for such a development, a change in the so-called object of the need for intimacy. And the change is from what I shall presently be discussing as an isophilic choice to what may be called a heterophilic choice—that is, it is a change from the seeking of someone quite like oneself to the seeking of someone who is in a very significant sense very different from oneself. This change in choice is naturally influenced by the concomitant appearance of the genital drive. Thus, other things being equal and no very serious warp or privation intervening, the change from preadolescence to adolescence appears as a growing interest in the possibilities of achieving some measure of intimacy with a member of the other sex, rather after the pattern of the intimacy that one has in preadolescence enjoyed with a member of one's own sex.

The degree to which the need for intimacy is satisfied in this heterophilic sense in the present-day American scene leaves very much to be desired. The reason is not that the shift of interest toward the other sex in itself makes intimacy difficult, but that the cultural influences which are borne in upon each person include very little which prepares members of different sexes for a fully human, simple, personal relationship together. A great many of the barriers to heterophilic intimacy go back to the very beginnings of the Western world. Just to give a hint of what I am talking about, I might mention the so-called double standard of morality and the legal status which surrounds illegitimate birth. One can get an idea of the important influence of cultural organization and cultural institutions on the possibilities of relationships in adolescence which are easy and, in terms of personality development, successful, by studying a culture very significantly different from our own in this respect. For some years I have recommended in this connection Hortense Powdermaker's *Life in Lesu.*[1] There, the institutions bearing on the distinction between the sexes are very significantly different from ours, and the contrast between our institutions and theirs perhaps sheds some light in itself on unfortunate aspects of the Western world.

But to return to our culture: The change in the need for intimacy—the new awakening of curiosity in the boy as to how he could get to be on as friendly terms with a girl as he has been on with his chum—is usually ushered in by a change of covert process. Fantasy undergoes a rather striking modification—a modification almost as abrupt and striking as the sudden acceleration of somatic growth which begins with the puberty change and leads, for instance, to the awkwardness which I have mentioned. And there may also be a change of content in overt communicative processes, both in the two-group and in the gang. That is, if the preadolescents are successfully progressing toward maturation and uniformly free from personality warp, this interest in members of the other sex also spreads into the area of communication between the chums, even though the one chum may not be quite up to the other and may be somewhat opposed to this new preoccupation with girls. In the more fortunate circumstances, this is presently a gang-wise change, and those who are approximately ready for it profit considerably from this last great topic of preadolescent collaboration—the topic of who's who and what's what in the so-called heterosexual world. If the group includes some members whose development is delayed, the social pressure in the group, in the gang, is extremely hard on their self-esteem and may lead to very serious disturbances of personality indeed. As I have previously hinted, it is not uncommon for the preadolescent phase to fade imperceptibly into the early adolescent phase, and for gang-wise genital activity to become part of the pattern of the very last stage of preadolescence or the verge of adolescence. Thus one not uncommonly finds at this point that the lust dynamism is actually functioning and governing a good part of group activity, but this

[1] [Hortense Powdermaker, *Life in Lesu: The Study of a Melanesian Society in New Ireland;* New York: W. W. Norton & Co., Inc., 1933.]

is very definitely oriented to that which is to follow with members of the other sex.

In this change from preadolescence to adolescence, there has to be a great deal of trial-and-error learning by human example. A considerable number of those at the very beginning of adolescence have some advantage in this learning by virtue of having already acquired data from their observation of and experience with a sibling of the other sex not very far removed from them in developmental age; these data which had been previously unimportant are now rapidly activated.

I believe that according to conventional, statistical experience, women undergo the puberty change somewhat in advance of men; in a great many instances, this leads to a peculiar sort of stutter in developmental progress between the boys and the girls in an age community so that by the time most of the boys have gotten really around to interest in girls, most of the girls are already fairly well wound up in their problems about boys. From the standpoint of personality development, it would be convenient if these things were timed slightly better; but I suppose that in the beginning when everything was arranged—I've never had any private information on the subject, by the way—procreation was fully as important as a feeling of self-esteem is now in a highly developed civilization. And so women get ready for procreation quite early; in fact one of the important problems of adolescence is how to avoid the accident of procreation.

Various Collisions of Lust, Security, and the Intimacy Need

After lust gets under way, it is extremely powerful. In fact, if one overlooks his experience with loneliness, he may well think that lust is the most powerful dynamism in interpersonal relations. Since our culture provides us with singular handicaps for lustful activity rather than with facilitation, lust promptly collides with a whole variety of powerful dynamisms in personality. The most ubiquitous collision is naturally *the collision between one's lust and one's security;* and by security I mean one's feeling of self-esteem and personal worth. Thus a great many people in early adolescence suffer a lot of anxiety in connection with their new-found motivation to sexual or genital activity—and I use those words interchangeably. Besides the puzzlement, embarrassment, and so on, which the culture practically makes certain, there are lamentably too many instances of people who already have a rather profound warp with respect to the general area of the body which is concerned. I have called this the primary genital phobia, which is not entirely to be interpreted on the basis of the usual ideas about phobia. By primary genital phobia I refer to an enduring warp of personality which is often inculcated in late infancy and early childhood and practically converts that area of the body into something not quite of the body. In discussing the excretory function and the exploratory power of the hand, I have commented on the incredible efforts made by certain parents to keep the young child from handling the genitals, from exploring and getting sensations from them. In cases in which this is successful, that area of the body becomes distinctly related to that area of personality to which I long since referred as the not-me. It is almost impossible for the adolescent who has this type of warp to arrive at any simple and, shall I say, conventional type of learning of what to do with lust. Therefore, as that person becomes lustful, he has the energy of the genital dynamism added to loneliness and other causes for restlessness; thus his activity with others becomes comparatively pointless, which almost certainly is humiliating and is not a contribution to his self-esteem. Or he may actually have some fairly serious disturbance of personality because of the outstanding power of the lust dynamism and the comparative hopelessness of learning how he, in particular, can do anything about it. Thus a person in this era may know a good deal about what other people do, but if he finds he can't do it himself, he doesn't feel quite up to the average.

Not only does lust collide with the need for security, but *the shift in the intimacy need may also collide with the need for security*. In early adolescence, the need for intimacy, for collaboration with some very special other person, reaches out toward, and tends to settle on, a member of the other sex. Now the ways in which this may collide with self-esteem are numerous, but there are a few particular instances that I want to bring to your attention. Quite often we discover that the young reach adolescence very much to the discontent of their elders in the home. In those situations it is not uncommon to find that there has been no serious taboo by the family group against the development of a chum relationship or even against membership in a gang; but now as the interest begins to move toward members of the other sex, there does begin to be strong repressive influence brought to bear on the adolescent by the family group.

One of the most potent instruments used in this particular is ridicule; many an adolescent has been ridiculed practically into very severe anxiety by parents who just do not want him to become, as they think of it, an adult interested in such things as sex, which may get him diseased or what not, or may result in marriage and his leaving home. Ridicule from parents and other elders is among the worst tools that are used on early adolescents. Sometimes a modification of ridicule is used by parents who are either too decent to use ridicule or are unaware of its remarkable power; and this modification takes the form of interfering with, objecting to, criticizing, and otherwise getting in the way of any detectable movement of their child toward a member of the other sex. This can go to the point of being a pathological performance which we call jealousy, in which the parent literally gets incredibly wrapped up in the rudimentary two-group that the adolescent is trying to establish with some member of the opposite sex. We will touch on jealousy again when we get around to discussing the particular group of difficulties in living which are called paranoid states. It should merely be noted at this point that jealousy is invariably a matter of more than two people, and that very often everyone concerned in jealousy is pretty fantastic—that is, there are a great many parataxic processes mixed up in it. Sometimes the third person concerned is purely a parataxic delusion on the part of the jealous person. So much for merely a few high spots on the type of collisions between the feeling of personal worth and the change in the direction of the need for intimacy.

There are also *collisions between the intimacy need and lust*. In establishing collaborative intimacy with someone, four varieties of awkwardnesses are common, of which the first three—embarrassment, diffidences, and excessive precautions—make up one group. The fourth represents one of our magic tricks of swinging to the other extreme to get away from something that doesn't work, which I call the *not* technique. In other words, you know what an apple is, and if you were under pressure enough you could produce an imaginary truth, *not apple*, made up entirely of the absence-of-apple characteristics. Thus, one of the ways of attempting to solve this collision between the intimacy need and lust is by something which is about the opposite of diffidence—namely, the development of a very bold approach in the pursuit of the genital objective. But the approach is so poorly addressed to the sensitivities and insecurities of the object that the object is in turn embarrassed and made diffident; and so it overreaches and has the effect of making the integration of real intimacy quite improbable.

A much more common evidence of the collision of these two powerful motivational systems is seen among adolescents in this culture as the segregation of object persons, which is in itself an extremely unfortunate way of growing up. By this I refer to the creating of distinctions between people toward whom lustful motivations can apply, and people who will be sought for the relief of loneliness—that is, for collaborative intimacy, for friendship. The classical instance is the old one of the prostitute and the good girl. The prostitute is the only woman who is to be thought of for genital contact; the good girl is never to be thought of in that connection, but only for friendship and for a somewhat nebulous future state referred to as marriage. When this segregation has been quite striking, this nebulous state takes on a purely fantastic character. Nowadays, the far more prevalent distinction is between sexy girls and good girls, rather than this gross division into bad and good women. But no matter how it comes about that the other sex is cut into two groups—one of which can satisfy a person's loneliness and spare him anxiety, while the other satisfies his lust—the trouble with this is that lust is a part of personality, and no one can get very far at completing his personality development in this way. Thus satisfying one's lust must be at considerable expense to one's self-esteem, since the bad girls are unworthy and not really people in the sense that good girls are. So wherever you find a person who makes this sharp separation of members of the other sex into those who are, you might say, lustful and those who are nonlustful, you may assume that this person has quite a cleavage with respect to his genital behavior, so that he is not really capable of integrating it into his life, simply and with self-respect.

These sundry collisions that come along at this stage may be the principal motives for preadolescents or very early adolescents getting into 'homosexual' play, with some remarkable variations. But a much more common outcome of these various collisions—these difficulties in developing activity to suit one's needs—is the breaking out of a great deal of autosexual behavior, in which one satisfies one's own lust as best one can; this behavior appears because of the way in which preadolescent society breaks up, and because of the various inhibitions which have been inculcated on the subject of freedom regarding the genitals. Now this activity, commonly called masturbation, has in general been rather severely condemned in every culture that generally imposes marked restrictions on freedom of sexual development. That's very neat, you see; it means that adolescence is going to be hell whatever you do, unless you have wonderful preparation for being different from everyone else—in which case you may get into trouble for being different.

Incidentally, problems of masturbation are sufficiently common, even among the wise, so that a word might be said here regarding what seems to be a sound psychiatric view of the matter. The question sometimes arises as to whether masturbation is good or bad. Now whenever a psychiatrist is confronted by such a question, he may well take it under advisement to see whether he can reformulate it into a question that he can, as a psychiatrist, deal with; psychiatrists don't dispense these absolute qualifications of good or bad. The nearest we can approach such values is to decide whether a thing is better or worse in terms of the interpersonal present and near future. From this approach, one can note that in this culture the developmental progress in connection with the adolescent change is handicapped by both lack of preparation and absolute taboos on certain freedoms; but lust *combined with* the need for intimacy frequently does drive the victim toward correcting certain warps in personality and toward developing certain facilities, certain abilities, in interpersonal relations. There is no way that I know of by which one can, all by oneself, satisfy the need for intimacy, cut off the full driving power of loneliness, although loneliness can be manipulated or reduced to a certain extent. But through autosexual performance one can prevent lust from reaching tension sufficient to break down one's barriers. For that reason, the entirely exclusive use of autoerotic procedures can contribute to the prolongation of warp, which in turn contributes to the continued handicap for life of the person concerned. It is from this viewpoint alone that I would consider that masturbation, as the *only* solution for the sundry collisions that lust enters into, is worse than almost anything else that is not definitely malevolent. Needless to say, such an argument becomes meaningless if, as is so often the case in genital behavior, the autoerotic performance is not fixed and exclusive but is incidental or occasional. Arguments against masturbation based on anything other than this particular reason seem to me to smack more of unanalyzed prejudice on the part of the arguer than of good sense.

Fortune and Misfortune in Heterosexual Experimentation

My next topic is the rather important one of the fortune and misfortune which the early adolescent has in his experimentation toward reaching a heterosexual type of experience. In the olden days when I was distinctly more reckless than now, I thought that a good many of the people I saw as mental patients would have been luckier in their adolescence had they carried on their preliminary heterosexual experimentation with a good-natured prostitute —that is, this would have been fortunate in comparison to what actually had happened to them. Not that I regard prostitutes as highly developed personalities of the other sex; but if they happen to be in the business of living off their participation in genital sport and are friendly, they at least will know a good deal about the problems in this field that earlier adolescents encounter, and will treat them with sympathy, understanding, and encouragement; but unfortunately, a great many of these experiments are conducted with people who are themselves badly, though differently, warped. The number of wretched experiences connected with adolescents' first heterosexual attempts is legion, and the experiences are sometimes very expensive to further maturation of personality. If there has been a lively lustful fantasy and little or no overt behavior with respect to the genitals—which incidentally will tend very strongly to characterize everyone who has this primary genital phobia I have spoken of—then it is almost certain that on the verge of an actual genital contact, precocious orgasm will occur in the man; and this precocious orgasm suddenly wipes out the integration and just leaves two people in a practically meaningless situation although they had previously made immense sense to each other. Such an occurrence reflects very severely on the self-esteem of the man concerned and thereby initiates a still more unfortunate process which is apt to appear as impotence. The recollection of so disastrous an occurrence, which has been in terms of anxiety pretty costly, is quite apt to result in either of two outcomes: there may be an overweening conviction that that's the way it's going to go, that one just hasn't any 'virility,' that one's manhood is deficient; or there may be frantic attempts to prove otherwise, which, if they were kept up long enough, would work. Unless there has been some genital activity, or unless the woman is quite expert in reducing the anxiety of the male, or even his sexual excitement, this precocious orgasm is very apt to be a man's introduction to heterosexual life. Needless to say, it has about as much true significance as drinking a glass of water—that is, if one could accept it in perfectly calm and rational fashion, it would prove absolutely nothing except that it had occurred once, and one could subsequently see whether it was going to be typical behavior or whether it was an accident. It usually isn't typical unless its effects are disastrous, in which case it can be stamped in as a sort of morbid way of handling one's incapacity to integrate true lustful situations, or as a channel for various other things which I shall discuss presently.

In other instances in which there is a lack of experience and considerable warp in the personalities concerned, lust may carry things through to orgasm, usually of only one partner; but immediately upon the satisfaction of the lust dynamism and the disintegration of the situation as a lustful situation, the persons concerned may become the prey of guilt, shame, aversion, or revulsion for each other, or at least this may be true for one of the people concerned. And this experience is not a particularly fortunate addition to one's learning how to live in the world as it is. A much less usual, but also unfortunate, event in this initial experimentation in genital activity is that if it has gone pretty well it may become a high-grade preoccupation. This is usually to be understood on the general theory of preoccupation and is just as morbid as any other preoccupation. Since lust has a peculiarly strong biological basis, and, in some people, may be an ever recurrent and very driving force in early adolescence, this preoccupation with lust can lead to serious deterioration of self-respect because of the unpleasant situations one is driven into, because of the disapproval one encounters, and because this type of preoccupation literally interferes with almost any commonplace way of protecting one's self-esteem. A great many people whose self-esteem has been somewhat uncertain, depending on scholarship only, find their standing as students rapidly declining as they become completely preoccupied with the pursuit of lust objects. Thus they become the prey of severe anxiety, since their only distinction is now being knocked in half.

With truly distressing frequency, these sundry problems connected with early adolescence cause the persons concerned to turn to alcohol, one of the great mental-hygiene props in the culture, with unfortunate results. I sometimes think alcohol is, more than any other human invention, the basis for the duration and growth of the Western world. I am quite certain that no such complex, wonderful, and troublesome organization of society could have lasted long enough to become conspicuous if a great number of its unhappy denizens did not have this remarkable chemical compound with which to get relief from intolerable problems of anxiety. But its capacity for dealing with those problems naturally makes it a menace under certain circumstances, as I scarcely think I need argue. Like a good many other props which temporarily remedy but do not in any sense favorably alter cultural impossibilities, it is costly, not to all, but to too many. A peculiarity of alcohol is that it interferes very promptly with complex, refined referential operations, particularly those that are recent—that have not been deeply and extensively involved in the whole business of living—while it does not particularly disturb the older and more essential dynamisms of personality. It definitely poisons the self-system progressively, beginning with the most recent and most complex of the self-system's functions. So personality under alcohol is less competent at protecting itself from anxiety, but practically all the anxiety is experienced later, retrospectively. Since the self-function, which is, of course, very intimately connected with the occurrence of anxiety, is inhibited and disturbed by alcohol, but one's later recall is not, one experiences the anxiety in retrospect, you see. And the problems that get one all too dependent on alcohol are, I think, the problems ·of sexual adjustment, which hit hardest in early adolescence.

The Separation of Lust from Intimacy

I want next to discuss misfortunes of development in early adolescence in which there is, as the outstanding characteristic, a separation of those interpersonal relations motivated by lust from those based on the need for intimacy—that is, motivated by loneliness. This sharp division is merely a very much more extensive and enduring deviation of personality than the kind of classification of heterophilic objects—for example, into good women and bad women—which I previously mentioned. The need for intimacy has been gradually developing along its own lines from very ancient roots, while lust has only recently and vividly appeared. The complex outcomes of these developmental interpersonal relations which are scarcely parallel and are actually divergent are a very rich source for problems which concern the psychiatrist. Some people are unfortunate enough to sublimate, as we still have to call it, their lust—that is, to partially satisfy it while connecting it with socially acceptable goals. This is, as I would again like to remind you, an extremely dangerous overloading of possibilities, which is very apt to collapse in a lamentable way. I am postponing a discussion of what happens to lust under these circumstances. But the intimacy need sometimes shows itself as follows: A member of the other sex who is in a good many ways like the parent of that sex may become invested with full-fledged "love" and devotion. Another, not so striking instance, is the pseudo-sibling relation. There are, of course, many jokes in the culture about the girl who is willing to be a sister to you. But I wonder if you realize how many unfortunate early adolescents get by with the appearance of personality development by striking up one of these pseudo-sibling relationships, which can be mistaken by others for a satisfactory move toward developing a solution for the problems of lust and loneliness. Another change of this kind is, we might say, a prolongation and refinement of the separation of good and bad girls: All women are good—too good; they are noble, and one cannot approach them for anything so something-or-other as genital satisfaction. And there is the alternative of that, in which all women are regarded as extremely unattractive, unsuited to anything but a particular kind of hateful entanglement which becomes practically official business.

In the process of trying to separate one's need for intimacy from one's need for genital integration, certain peculiarities of personality appear which we will later discuss as *dissociation*. Among the people with these peculiarities of personality pertaining to the need for intimacy, there is the one who feels pursued by the other sex and actually spends a lot of time in trying to avoid being hounded by the other sex. There is also the true woman-hater—that is, the man who literally feels the most strenuous antipathy to any but the most superficial relation with members of the other sex. When lust is dissociated—and components in lust are quite frequently dissociated—such things occur, even from early adolescence, as the celibate way of life, in some cases with accessible lustful fantasies, and in other cases with no representation of lustful needs in awareness. This latter can go so far that actually there are no recollections of any content connected with what must have been the satisfaction of lust in sleep; in other words, there are nocturnal orgasms, but there is never any recollectable content at all. When one encounters that sort of thing, one thinks immediately that something has gone very radically wrong with the personality. Another manifestation in this field is what I call, in terms of a man's viewpoint, horror of the female genitals; even though the man considers that women are all right, and in fact, in many instances, may make a very good approach to them, the actual attempt at a physical intergenital situation causes the man to be overcome with a feeling which is literally uncanny, which is quite paralyzing. As I have already hinted, all these uncanny feelings refer to the not-me, and are, by this stage of personality, practically always signs that there is serious dissociation somewhere in personality. Another solution of this kind is to fall into a homosexual way of getting rid of lust; this is accompanied either by liking, by indifference, or by aversion toward the partner, or by revulsion or by fascination for the whole type of situation.

In this special group of disturbances of development, there are also the instances in which the genital drive is discharged with infrahuman or nearly infrahuman participation—that is, some of the lower animals are used as genital partners, or people are used whom the person has so much prejudice against that he scarcely considers them to be human. Very occasionally human ingenuity leads people who suffer from primitive genital phobia to invent what are called masturbating machines. This is a phenomenon that gets a good deal of attention, more than it deserves, and is, supposedly, very interestingly connected with paranoid states. As a matter of fact, it does coincide more than occasionally with later paranoid states, but this relation has been vastly overaccentuated.

The Isolated Adolescent

Finally, I want to mention here the misfortune of isolation in early adolescence, which is quite different from the developmental disturbances I have just discussed. This misfortune of isolation in adolescence has affected quite a number of the people whom you meet in ordinary life, or whom the psychiatrist encounters in his practice. Perhaps because the community is very small, or perhaps because of peculiar home circumstances or something of the sort, the isolated adolescent does not have other adolescents with whom to fraternize, is not thrown into contact with members of the other sex of approximately the same developmental phase. Such people are, from a theoretical standpoint, rather interesting because of the progression of their reverie processes; as they go from preadolescence into adolescence, the chief characters in their long-continued fantasies shift toward the other sex. The extent to which lustful covert processes are added to their fantasies depends, to an extraordinary degree, on the extent to which mediate educational influences have provided some basis for covert processes. Sometimes one finds people who, simply because of their

isolation, have not reached the point of having particularly lustful reverie processes, so that when the lust dynamism comes along,
it discharges itself largely in sleep; and this in itself may not represent a grave disturbance of personality. If we could study some
of these isolated people—or rather if they were, in spite of entire
lack of experience, clever at communication, which is almost un-
heard of—it would be interesting to see what the nocturnal development of covert processes connected with the satisfaction of
lust is like. Some of these isolated early adolescents suffer a particular handicap from this reverie substitution for interpersonal experience, in that they develop quite strongly personified imaginary
companions; and the singularly personal source of the idealized
characteristics may be a severe barrier later on to finding anybody
who strikes them as really suitable for durable interpersonal relations.

Failure to Change the Preadolescent Direction of the Need for Intimacy

I have said that, along with the maturation of the lust dynamism,
but by no means in absolute temporal coincidence with it, there
is, in the fortunate, a shift in the intimacy need toward seeking
friendship with a person who is different, a member of the other
sex. But I now want to consider the accidental development in
which the *lust dynamism matures but there is no change in the
preadolescent direction of the need for intimacy*. In this case
there is added to the impulse which makes for the cultivation and
cherishing of a friend of the same sex, all the force of the lust dynamism with its drive for genital interaction with someone or something. And in these instances transient or persisting homosexual
organization of the interpersonal relations is usual, with the genital
drive handled in a variety of ways. The first of these ways is by
known homosexual reverie processes that are surrounded by precautions which protect the self-esteem, at least partially, of the
person who entertains them. This is generally accompanied by
autogenital discharge of lust, coupled with an avoidance of, or an
indifference to, members of the other sex, and social distance
toward members of the same sex. Thus, while there is a movement
toward satisfying lust in the isophilic or monosexual two-group,

there is either no encouragement for mutual genital satisfaction or no capacity to recognize such encouragement—or in some cases there is even such great fear of the perineal area that mutual genital satisfaction would be impossible. Thus the coincidence of lust with the continuing preadolescent direction of the intimacy need leads to fantasies of what we can call a homosexual character, coupled with various guarding operations, security operations, to prevent their being discovered or suspected. But in order that this may succeed, there must be some satisfaction of lust; and the way that almost all people find for that is self-manipulation. Along with this there is, in boys, usually either an active avoidance or a definite indifference toward girls, although one of the best precautions invented by these delayed people is finding an accepted woman who gives the social appearance of normal development, but who has no expectations of the man. And almost invariably, in these solutions, we see an increase in the social distance between the person concerned and certain boys other than the chum who is the object of the reverie processes. And incidentally, while I have been discussing this largely from the viewpoint of boys, the parallel is perfectly possible in women.

Another of the ways by which the genital drive is handled in this situation is by known—that is, conscious—homosexual reveries which are associated with inadequate precautions to conceal them and with severe anxiety as a result of rebuffs, fancied or real. This often leads to hateful behavior, or to "masturbation-shame," and to a variety of other miseries which are hard for the person to express; but he knows, or can very readily come to know, that these miseries are associated with his homosexual reverie practices.

A third of the difficulties to which man is heir at this juncture and under these circumstances is a situation in which there are covert processes not accessible to awareness—in other words, unconscious processes, to use the old-fashioned term—which are attended by pseudo-heterosexual practices with or without an attenuation of the contact with members of the same sex. This sort of thing is often a precursor of a lifelong course of searching for the 'ideal' woman—or the 'ideal' man, if the person concerned is a woman—with the recurrent discovery of serious imperfections in each candidate for this ideal role. And this type of situation is the classical field for the appearance of the extremely unpleasant tension of jealousy. Jealousy is, I think, in some ways even less welcome than anxiety; and when I say that, I am almost engaging in hyperbole, because anxiety, if at all severe, is *utterly* unwelcome. But jealousy, in my experience with people who really suffer it, seems to come very close to providing an adequate picture of the now old-fashioned Christian hell.

Yet another solution of this failure of the intimacy urge to change its objective to the other sex is the turning to homosexual ways of life which are either so anxiety-ridden as to be scarcely distinguishable as achieving lustful satisfaction, or are definitely admixed with hateful, malevolent motivation, so that while lust may be satisfied more-or-less incidentally, what is most vividly remembered is the malicious mischief connected with the thing. And finally, as an outcome of this continuation of the isophilic intimacy need, a satisfying and relatively secure homosexual way of life may be established, sometimes by trial-and-error learning, quite often from example.

Any of these five typical outcomes which I have mentioned may come presently to include unsatisfactory, but security-giving, heterosexual performances. The outcome which is least apt to culminate in this sort of elaborate masking operation is the anxiety-ridden and hateful homosexual practice. But there are plenty of instances in which these people also finally either set up housekeeping with a common-law wife, or go through the motions of marrying, and even have children, but mostly for security reasons.

Maturation of the Lust Dynamism in the Chronic Juvenile

In addition to these situations in which there has been no change in the preadolescent need for intimacy as the lust dynamism has matured, the situation arises in which there is *maturation of the lust dynamism in those not yet preadolescent*. In other words, a person who is chronically juvenile reaches the time when the lust dynamism matures and goes into action. Arrest in the juvenile era is not by any means an extraordinarily unusual developmental disorder among people in this culture and in these times. The striking instance of this, as seen later in life, is what I call the juvenile ladies' man. You probably are familiar with the story of Don Juan and know how much the conception of Don Juanism has appeared in some of the psychiatric literature; to the extent that I have studied such people, they have proven to be these lustful juveniles. I might describe another outstanding manifestation of this kind by the use of slang terms—women who are customarily called "teasers" and men whom I call "hymen hunters." These people in general engage in more or less refined boasting, frequently have an insatiable interest in pornography, and have simply an overweening necessity for being envied for their women or their men. In fact, I have known some of them who really kept something very like a stable, for different occasions using different people, some of whom were supposed to be appropriate for public appearance. This is the sort of thing which happens when lust matures in a person whose preadolescent expansion of personality has simply been foredoomed and thus has failed to occur. In the sort of outcomes I have described, the person has done something with lust other than falling rather gravely ill—which, incidentally, is not an uncommon outcome of adolescent maturation in those who have serious warp of personality.

The Lust Dynamism as a Psychobiological Integrating Apparatus

I have already discussed some of the more or less typical outcomes that occur in people whose difficulties in development become very seriously complicated, in early adolescence, by the addition of the lust dynamism, although they have not passed into grave disturbances of personality. Now at this point, because we shall presently be moving into the area of difficulties of living rather than of difficulties in development, I should like to review lust as a dynamism, hoping that you remember something of our now fairly distant discussion of the concept of dynamism. Lust is in many ways a peculiarly illuminating example of a dynamism, partly because it comes along when so much of one's referential apparatus, so much of one's capacity to think and to communicate, is pretty well established and pretty well perfected. You may recall that in discussing the concept of dynamism we said that human dynamisms are relatively enduring patterns which manifest, in some cases at least, postnatal origin by maturation and, in all cases, change by experience in the occurrence of which they are significant factors. We then said that these dynamisms can be conceptualized from two viewpoints: first, with primary reference to the sundry recurring tensions manifesting as integrating, disjunctive, and isolative tendencies; and second, with primary reference to the energy transformations characteristic of the particular zones of interaction involved.

The lust dynamism—the last and the most conspicuous and illuminating of all the dynamisms, but nonetheless probably a model of every one of them, may most simply be considered as an organization of apparatus provided by the underlying human organism. This is a purely psychobiological consideration, but nonetheless important. We find that, considered solely as the property of an organism—that is, from the standpoint of psychobiology—lust can be broken up immediately into three kinds of *integrating apparatus*. By integrating apparatus I refer to organizations of tissue and function which hold the psychobiological organism in an organic unity. These three kinds of integrating apparatus are the autacoid system —that is, the endocrine or ductless gland system; the vegetative nervous system; and the central nervous system.

The first, the autacoid system, provides a tying together of the whole, by the simple device of pouring potent chemicals into a circulating fluid. In the lust dynamism, the pouring of this potent chemical into the blood stream determines whether you can have outward manifestations of lustful excitement, or whether you will fail therein. Thus the autacoid element is such that the administering of testosterone propionate, which is a synthetic chemical closely related to some of the testicular hormones, produces the appearance of something very like lust in a man; and a corresponding native hormone can be isolated which, injected into a woman, produces something very like lust. Now a person who was not at all given to very minute study of his interpersonal impulses would report to you, if he were a male, that testosterone made him lustful. However, the autacoid mechanism is not the whole thing; these very powerful chemical agents circulated in the blood stream and lymph are not all there is to being lustful.

The next great integrating apparatus involved in the lust dynamism is the vegetative nervous system, consisting of what is often referred to as the autonomic and the sympathetic nervous systems. Thus, in men, by the time the seminal vesicles are sufficiently distended there is restlessness, and, other things being equal, lust will appear; and somewhat comparably in women, at or around the time of the menstrual change, quite frequently lust will appear. If there is any difficulty with the vegetative part of the incredible integrating apparatus concerned in lust, one might feel lust, but one cannot demonstrate to a partner the necessary preliminaries for the discharge of lust, such as moistening of the vagina or erection of the penis.

And the third great integrating apparatus concerned in the dynamism of lust is the central nervous integrating apparatus. Everyone has probably, at some time, had the experience of gazing at certain art objects and promptly feeling lustful excitement. And it is not so awfully difficult to provoke lust by an appropriate series of remarks, which again reflects the intervention of the integrating apparatus of the central nervous system and includes a vast deal of symbol operations—a pretty far cry from, say, the administration of testosterone. Without the participation of this apparatus, a person would never know that lust was appropriate, unless something seized, or penetrated, the genital apparatus. If the other two integrators were active at that time, he would, after a fashion, respond, but he would not particularly enjoy it.

The Lust Dynamism as a System of Zones of Interaction

Now I pass to a field much more appropriate to psychiatry—that of considering the *lust dynamism as a system of zones of interaction*. When we touched on zones of interaction before, we suggested that all zones of interaction with the environment, considered in the borderline area of psychobiology and psychiatry, were characterized by three significant groups of characteristics: their receptor aspects, their eductor aspects, and their effector aspects. And now let me throw out only a few hints of the aspects of the lust dynamism—the late-comer among the great dynamisms of life—that fit into this frame of reference as zones of interaction with the environment.

In the receptor aspect of the lust dynamism there are the genital-tactile, the genital-visceral, and the aspect pertaining to the "erogenous areas." The peculiar *tactile* sensitivities of the genitals are such that if something touches the delicate mucosa of the genitals—whether it be the hands of a partner, a fly, or merely microscopic organisms like Trichomonas—there is an acute central awareness of specially marked sensations very clearly associated with the genital area. Although such sensations begin at an early age, in some cases practically in late infancy, they become part of the lust dynamism itself only later, when the two other types of receptor function mature.

In addition to the genital-tactile influx, there is the *genital-visceral* influx, which is carried over entirely separate channels, but is just as apt to provoke lust as the other. That is, lust, as experienced, is as often a result of tensions in unstriped muscles as it is of the stimulation of local tactile units. For example, a man can be excited, with lust as a result, by tension suffered by either the seminal vesicles or the prostate or both; or a woman, by tension suffered by the Fallopian tubes, the uterine mucosa, and the vaginal mucosa.

Quite exterior to these two fields of influx to the central nervous system, there are, after the maturation of the lust dynamism, very important influxes from other areas—the so-called *"erogenous areas"* of the body, some of which are fixed by the structure of the organism, and some of which are fixed by the experience that one has had earlier in life. In everyone, this erogenous zone is rather diffusely spread over the region of the perineum. In women, the nipples are quite generally erogenous zones. In other words, anything moving about on the surface of the nipples is apt, just like stimulation of the genitals or tension in the viscera, to be accompanied by the activation of the lust dynamism. But in either sex, any area of the body may be involved, although 'individual' variation is wide and depends on previous experience. So much for the receptor aspect of the zones of interaction.

Next we shall discuss briefly the *eductor aspect* of this system of zones of interaction called the lust dynamism. It was Spearman [2] who formulated the eduction of relationships from the data that

[2] [See Chapter 5, footnote 1.]

flow into the mind as the basis for *knowing*—one of the most profound observations, so far as the needs of psychiatrists are concerned, of the nature and manifestations of human intelligence. When I speak here of the eductor aspect of the zones of interaction, I am referring to the *knowing*—the understanding, interpretation, recognition, and contemplation of goals—which is involved in the lust dynamism considered from the standpoint of a system of zones of interaction. There are three grand divisions of what happens in the region that we call our "mind," by which we ordinarily refer to our capacity to grasp what is the case, and what should be done about it. These are facilitory, precautionary, and inhibitory referential processes. The first of these processes facilitates the identifying of situations which might be appropriately integrated by the lust dynamism. And incidentally, most people seek diligently to cultivate their facilitory symbol operations with respect to achieving lustful integrations. Precautionary measures have been taught us by the difficulties of dealing with tenderness and other motivation which calls for the kindly intervention of others. Precautionary activities enable us to conceal the fact that we are motivated by lust, and tend to protect us from very brutally making fools of ourselves. And frankly inhibitory processes make it difficult or impossible to add up the activities of the receptor apparatus into a statement that lust is present. Any denizen of the Western world has plenty of elaborate apparatus for inhibiting integration in the interest of lust, when such integration would collide with the self-system, or with particular aspects of it. I think that everyone, carefully searching his past, may remember times when he was singularly restless and uncomfortable, which, in retrospect, he will see meant the unrecognized presence of lust; and this lust was unrecognized not because it is hard to know lust, but because there was some powerful impulse active to inhibit its recognition.

And we finally come to what one is more likely to know about from personal experience—the *effector* aspects of the zones of interaction concerned in the lust dynamism. The effector aspects of the zones of interaction connected with lust—to offer the crudest kind of an analysis, leaving out unnumbered interesting aspects —are five in number. The first is the vasomotor-erectile effector aspects of the urethro-genital zone of interaction with the environment, which is often first manifest at birth—but perhaps not consciously—and which is manifest recurrently, from birth onward. This is a complicated performance of obstructing venous return and increasing blood supply, which is illustrated not only in the genitals but also in the nose and sundry other parts of the body —the genitals and the nose being the most troublesome, in this climate at least. Besides the vasomotor-erectile—and appearing very much later, around the time of the puberty change—are the purely secretory effector aspects of the urethro-genital zone of interaction and its system of zones, consisting in the male of such things as the production of a dense but highly lubricant mucus by the Cowper's glands, the production of an anything-but-dense albuminous fluid by the prostate, and the production of a complex nutritive albuminous fluid by the epididymis and probably the seminal vesicles. In the female, there is the secretion of mucus and the hydrogen ion concentration proper for the spermatozoa.

As another very important aspect of the effectors, there are those massive patterns of skeletal behavior which we lump scientifically under the rubric "copulatory posture and movement." The copulatory posture and movements are very complicated. They are one of the few things which faintly support the notion that the concept of instinct is not utterly irrelevant to human beings, for they come without calling, almost as if a little instinct still survived in our incredibly culture-ridden life.

Among the effector apparatus there is also the orgasmic complex of integrated movements, which, again, matures in the puberty change; to some extent this existed before as parts, but these are now suddenly integrated. The orgasmic movements are built up, in men, primarily on the capacity for clonic spasm in the prostatic urethra, with which a man is born so that he is able to expel urine. But this becomes, suddenly in the puberty change, very closely and emphatically (from the sensory or receptor standpoint) coordinated with spasm of the walls of the seminal vesicle, which had not previously occurred. So here we find movements of unstriped muscle, which earlier were used only to expel the last drops of urine, suddenly integrated with the expulsive activity of the container of semen in the male—a coordination which had not been present at all before the puberty change. This is accompanied by the most vivid central representation, comprising that extremely strongly marked experience which represents the satisfaction of the lust dynamism.

But there are still further effector aspects of the zones of interaction which make up the lust dynamism. If the lust dynamism is successfully satisfied, a series of changes restores the apparatus to, shall I say, a resting condition which is called, traditionally, detumescence. There seems to be evidence that in women detumescence is a somewhat longer process, but here too the women's erogenous zones, including the breasts, also shrink and come to rest in comparative insensitivity after the orgasm. In both men and women, after the apparatus has been restored to a resting condition, the lust dynamism, under external or internal provocation, can again become a very powerful organizer of a remarkable part of our capacity for contact with external events.

The Lust Dynamism as a Pattern of Covert and Overt Symbolic Events

Now I wish to consider the lust dynamism neither as an integrating apparatus nor as a system of zones of interaction, but as *a pattern of covert and overt symbolic events*—that is, events meaning something, if you please, which are either inferable or observable. The covert and overt symbolic events which are included in manifestations of experience with respect to the lust dynamism include experience in the prototaxic, the parataxic, and less often in the syntaxic modes. Experience in the prototaxic mode, while it is particularly obvious in the instance of primary genital phobia, is present in any case. The parataxic mode is perhaps more apt to be the major element in the symbol operations connected with lust than it is with any one other dynamism, because the culture is so very hard on consensual validation and syntaxic operations with respect to lust. Experience of covert and overt symbolic events is concerned with six major rubrics. The first rubric is the *observation and identification* of the following: (*a*) the felt aspects of the integrating tendency—that is, lust per se; (*b*) the interpersonal situation as including an 'object'—presumably another person with whom a lustful situation can be integrated, if only in fantasy; (c) the interpersonal situation as otherwise characterized —that is, not merely as to the other person, but with respect to the suitability of the situation for probable satisfaction, the collateral factors which may make lustful excitement strangely irrelevant (for example, the unwisdom of getting intensely sexually excited about your opponent in the traffic court); and (d) the interpersonal situation as characterized with respect to anxiety, which is very important indeed in the lives of most of us.

Now these aspects of observation and identification are, in fortunate situations, supplemented by *foresight*, which is the second of these six rubrics. That is, after observation and identification, there comes foresight, although it is sometimes only rudimentary, and is often by no means extended. And, following the foresight, which is in a sense my way of referring to decision, there comes, third, *activity in pursuit of or in avoidance of the goal*, which is the discharge of lust. At the same time, there are in all real situations—and this is my fourth rubric of experience—sundry, often seemingly irrelevant, *covert accompaniments* of the last-mentioned —that is, processes which can be detected only by inference, which accompany action in pursuit of or in avoidance of the goal. In other words, I refer to a good deal that is going on in the 'mind.'

Regardless of whether integration by the lust dynamism has been effected or avoided, and regardless of the extent of the discharge of lust, there is, later on, *retrospective and prospective, witting and unwitting analysis* of this particular experience, which is my fifth rubric. That is, there is analysis of what has happened recently, with a view to what may happen again. And incidentally, if, in the days of the Puritans, everyone's development of acquaintance with experience regarding lust had depended on *witting* analysis, I think that lust might have disappeared, along with the human race. How much is witting and how much is unwitting depends on one's cultural background, and not on anything else. Thus whether one has pursued the goal of lustful satisfaction, or avoided it, there is always in the experience concerned with any particular episode some review and prospective analysis, with the idea of improving one's capacity for achieving contentment and success in this field of life. Finally, and this is my sixth rubric, in some instances—and, fortunately, this is not always the case—

there are *more complex processes* concerned in the experience, which may replace the retrospective and prospective analysis, or may just complicate it. And these reflect, however obscurely, the personality warp of at least one person concerned in the situation in which the lust dynamism is the principal system of integrating tendencies.

The Lust Dynamism as a System of Integrating Tendencies

And this brings me to my next and more important point. Having reviewed the lust dynamism as a system of covert and overt symbolic events, I should now like to discuss it as a system of integrating tendencies—that is, as an integration of those characteristics of people which integrate situations with other people. In other words, this is an elaborate system of motives which get us involved with others or lead us to avoid them.

The lust dynamism is a *system of integrating tendencies:*

(1) of which the unanalyzable elements have *matured in earlier stages of development* and have *been modified by experience of satisfaction* or *experience with anxiety*, or both, and in some cases with signs of *disintegrative change* or *elaboration in dissociation.*

(2) in which the *anxiety-marked components are widely varied* from person to person, because of inadequacies in the culture complex and their accentuation by resulting family-society and school-society peculiarities.

(3) of which some components are almost always, in this culture, *unrepresented in focal awareness*, whether their lack of representation be due to selective inattention, to masking processes, to misinterpretation, or to the manifestation of a dissociative process in the self.

(4) which is often related to acute or persisting *disorientation in living*, and to the disastrous disturbance of self-esteem.

(5) which, in the handicapped, may come to channel the partial satisfaction of a variety of other integrating tendencies—and thus may come to seem preternaturally important.

(6) of which the recurrent partial satisfaction leaves residual motivation to be discharged in sleep and in waking reverie processes in a way that may undermine self-esteem, or may call for precautionary processes or social distance—which in turn seriously reduce the chances of fortunate experience in life.

Statement (1) is the simplest of these possible views of the lust dynamism. In other words, the integrating tendencies which are systematized in the lust dynamism have matured over various stages of one's past, and have, since maturation, been subjected to experience and to the various characteristics of experience which we have considered thus far, such as change to avoid anxiety, disintegration to avoid anxiety, or actually development in dissociation.

Statement (2) reflects the fact that our culture is the least adequate in preparing one for meeting the eventualities of sexual maturity, which is another way of saying we are the most sex-ridden people on the face of the globe. In (4), I suggest that the lust dynamism is *the* system of integrating tendencies often related to acute or persisting disorientation in living.

When I mention the handicapped in statement (5) I refer to those people who have had disasters in the stages of development before adolescence. I might illustrate this rubric by saying that if your resentment at authority should find in lustful activities a discharge which, though only partial, was better than nothing, then, insofar as you suffered authority, lust and lustful activities would come to be unreasonably, extravagantly important in your life. Thus in those who have had serious warp in personality, the lust dynamism is a system of integrating tendencies which may provide a channel for the obscure and unrecognized satisfaction of many thwarted integrating impulses having no direct connection with lust. The persistently juvenile person who finally reaches genital maturity advertises this fact to the high heavens to those who investigate him. Psychiatrists have tended to overlook the very rich source of data on this particular point because of the seeming essential dullness of the persistently juvenile person and the social insignificance of his life with others.

Patterns of Manifestation of the Integrating Tendencies of the Intimacy Need and Lust

Now I have given you, with a feeling of deep apology for the condensation that has characterized it, something like a theoretically justifiable, if not definitive, variety of approaches to the meaning of the lust dynamism. It is important to realize that everything said of the lust dynamism applies to every dynamism; but because the lust dynamism happens to come along so late in life, it is a particularly informative example of dynamisms in general. I shall presently try to suggest the rich variety of human life with respect to every dynamism by some cold mathematical adumbrations of the possible patterns of adjustment called out in part by the lust dynamism. But first, since these things do not stand alone, I would like to go back to the idea of orientation of living and to defects therein as they are related to the two very powerful integrating tendencies that characterize adolescence—lust and the need for intimacy. In discussing disturbed or inadequate orientation in the later phases of adolescent living and thereafter, one cannot, except for purposes of clarity of thinking, separate the manifestation of these two very powerful motivating systems of human life. But though these systems are intricately interwoven, at the same time they are never identical.

I have already tried to suggest something of the broad basis, in the developmental history of everyone, for the feeling ordinarily called loneliness, which is the exceedingly unpleasant and driving experience connected with inadequate discharge of the need for human intimacy, for interpersonal intimacy. Since it seems to me that no amount of emphasis will be extravagant in this connection, let me again comment on the major integrating tendencies which gradually come to be concerned with the experience of loneliness. It begins in infancy with an integrating tendency that we know only by inference from pathological material later, but which we nonetheless accept unhesitatingly—a need for contact with the living. And its next great increment is a need for tenderness—for protective care delicately adjusted to immediate situations. This need continues into childhood. But in childhood a need for adult participation is added—that is, a need for the interest and participation of significant adults in the child's play. This activity takes the form of expressive play necessary to provide the child with equipment for showing what he feels, in manual play necessary for the coordination of the very delicate and intricate relationships of vision and the prehensile hands, and so on, and in verbal play, which is the basis of all the enormously important acquisitions to personality which are reflected by verbal behavior and abstract thought. All of these activities become more pleasure-giving to the child because of the adults' participation. By the juvenile era, there is added the need for compeers, as indispensable models for one's learning by trial and error; and this is then followed by a need for acceptance which is perhaps to most of you known by its reverse, the fear of ostracism, fear of being excluded from the accepted and significant group. And added to all these important integrating tendencies, there comes in pre-adolescence the need for intimate exchange, for friendship, or for —in its high refinement—the love of another person, with its enormous facilitation of consensual validation, of action patterns, of valuational judgments, and so on. This becomes, in early adolescence, the same need for intimacy, friendship, acceptance, intimate exchange, and, in its more refined form, the need for a loving relationship, with a member of the other sex. Now this is the great structure which is finally consolidated, made meaningful, as the need for intimacy as it characterizes late adolescence and the rest of life.

I have now reviewed the history of one powerful integrating tendency—the need for intimacy—and I have already given my views of lust, the other of these major integrating tendencies. At this point I shall endeavor to give some idea of the possible varieties of intricately interwoven patterns of these tendency systems.

The theoretical patterns of manifestation of the two powerful integrating tendencies, the need for intimacy and lust, may be classified:

(1) on the basis of the intimacy need and the precautions which concern it—as autophilic, isophilic, and heterophilic;

(2) on the basis of the preferred partner in lustful integrations,

or the substitute therefor—as autosexual, homosexual, heterosexual, and katasexual;

(3) on the basis of genital participation or substitution—as orthogenital, paragenital, metagenital, amphigenital, mutual masturbation, and onanism.

In creating the rubrics with respect to the need for intimacy (1), I have turned to the old Greek term *philos*, meaning "loving," since the need for intimacy in its highest manifestations is unquestionably love—and while love has been many things to many people, the common denominator pertains to interpersonal intimacy. All the manifestations, morbid and successful, of this need for intimacy, may be grossly classified under the three rubrics of *autophilic*, *isophilic*, and *heterophilic*. We will use these three rubrics to describe a 'person'—and I use person here in the sense of that which we hypothesize to account for what we see or experience. In the autophilic person, there has been no preadolescent development; or such preadolescent development as took place has been disintegrated because of profound rebuff, and he has been returned to a state before preadolescence in which the capacity to love is, if manifest at all, concentrated within his personification of himself. The autophilic is always a misfortune and a deviation of development. An isophilic person has been unable to progress past preadolescence, and continues to regard as suitable for intimacy only people who are as like himself as possible, in significant fashions—that is, members of his own gender. A heterophilic person has gone through the preadolescent period and made the early adolescent change in which he has become intensely interested in achieving intimacy with members of what, in this culture, is most essentially different—the other sex. The isophilic is, for a period of two-and-a-half to three-and-a-half years, a normal phase of every successful development; but this phase may continue through life. And the heterophilic represents the last stage of development of the need for intimacy; many achieve this phase even though they are unable to leave late adolescence.

Now I invite you to consider (2) and (3), which underlie all that I have already said of the lust dynamism. The first of these refers to the gross characteristics of integrations which seek the discharge of the lust dynamism, which are directly related to recognized lust and its satisfaction; for these I use the term *sexual* —and do not confuse this with the term "erotic." In my classification of sexual behavior on the basis of the preferred partner, the *homosexual* and the *heterosexual* are obviously related to preadolescent and early adolescent phases of development. The *autosexual* represents an earlier stage—that is, although lust has matured, the preadolescent and adolescent eras have not been reached. The *katasexual* refers to passing beyond the confines of the human species—that is, the dead or infrahuman creatures are the preferred lustful partners—and this represents a very complex substitution for things which one experiences as impossible to want.

And finally, I would like you to consider the lust dynamism in terms of (3) the participation of the *genitals* in covert and overt, witting or unwitting, lustful performances; and here I am talking about a region of the body. Situations principally integrated by lust are sexual situations; but at the same time the patterning of this behavior depends on the part played by the genitals, as well as the lustful character of the situation. On the basis of one's genital participation with another, or with a substitute, I have named six rubrics, most of which are neologisms of my own invention. *Orthogenital* situations are characterized by a preferred integration of one's genitals with their natural receptor genitals—genitals of the sexually opposite type. In *paragenital* situations, one uses the genitals as if they were seeking an appropriate opposite type of genitals, but does so in behavior which is not related to the procreation of one's kind. A common example is being masturbated by someone else, in which case the hand is the paragenital receptor of one's genitals; other examples are the passive role in fellatio or the active role in pederasty. In *metagenital* situations, one's genitals need not be involved at all, but the other person's genitals are involved. The most obvious example is masturbating someone else; other examples are taking the passive role in pederasty or the so-called active role in fellatio. In *amphigenital* situations, for which the French have adopted the term "soixante-neuf," either homosexual or heterosexual groups of two people take a singularly analogous if not identical relationship to the genitals of each and the substitutes of each. Besides these, there are the relatively primitive performance of *mutual masturbation* and the quite primitive performance of *onanism.*

Now I do not like to coin freak terms, but what these terms represent is terribly significant. And the terrible significance is this: In this culture the ultimate test of whether you can get on or not is whether you can do something satisfactory with your genitals or somebody else's genitals without undue anxiety and loss of self-esteem. Therefore the psychiatrist who has to consider the life problems presented by people who come to him has to have some way of organizing thought regarding this last phase of interpersonal adjustment. To accomplish that I have had to set up what are, so far as I know, unique inventions: the resolute separation of the need for intimacy from the lust dynamism; and the distinction between the *general interpersonal objective* of the lust dynamism, and the *particular activities* which the genitals— the center of the lust dynamism, one might say—have in preferred adjustive effort.

Since I have set up three classifications of intimacy, four classifications of the general interpersonal objective of the integration of lust, and six classifications of genital relationship, this results in seventy-two theoretical patterns of sexual behavior in situations involving two real partners. As a matter of fact, there are only forty-five patterns of sexual behavior that are reasonably probable; six are very highly improbable, and the rest just aren't possible. From this statement, I would like you to realize, if you realize nothing else, how fatuous it is to toss out the adjectives "heterosexual," "homosexual," or "narcissistic" to classify a person as to his sexual and friendly integrations with others. Such classifications are not anywhere near refined enough for intelligent thought; they are much too gross to do anything except mislead both the observer and the victim. For example, to talk about homosexuality's being a problem really means about as much as to talk about humanity's being a problem.

The reason why I attempt to set up careful classifications in this field is this: It is almost always essential for the psychiatrist, when he ventures into remedial efforts for serious developmental handicaps, to pay attention to the place of lust in the difficulties of the person. And let me make it clear that lust, in my sense, is not some great diffuse striving, 'libido' or what not. By lust I mean simply the felt aspect of the genital drive. And when I say that the psychiatrist must usually pay attention to this, I do not mean that problems in living are primarily or chiefly concerned with genital activity. But I am saying, of people in this culture who are chronologically adult, that their problems in interpersonal relations quite certainly will be either very conspicuous in, or exceedingly well illustrated by, the particular circumstances governing their handling of the emotion of lust. While this statement is, I believe, strikingly true of Northwestern European culture, I would say, although I have no evidence on the matter, that it is not true of certain other cultures.

By the time a person has plunged into early adolescence, he has either largely overcome all the crippling handicaps to personality that he has encountered, or his development in adolescence will be badly warped. And since lust cannot be eliminated from personality any more than hunger can, data on personality warp as seen in a person's sexual behavior is bound to be useful to the psychiatrist, for instance; I mean here the broad conception of sexual behavior, including reverie processes and any evidences of dissociated processes, which I shall discuss presently. But to think that one can remedy personality warp by tinkering with the sex life is a mistake, even though it is a very convenient doctrine for psychiatrists who are chronic juveniles. It may provide them with fees for enjoying their interest in pornography; but if one is a serious psychiatrist, it is apt to be the hardest possible way to tackle one's task. When difficulties in the sex life are presented by a patient as his reason for needing psychiatric help, my experience has demonstrated rather convincingly that the patient's difficulty in living is best manifested by his very choice of this as his peculiar problem. In other words, people don't go to psychiatrists to be aided in their sexual difficulties; but they do sometimes present this as their problem, and such problems show, when properly understood, what ails their living with people. It is only an exceptional person who is able to have his sex life as his major interpersonal activity; only such a person could correctly present to a psychiatrist, as his greatest difficulty in living, a sexual problem. Thus let me warn my fellow psychiatrists: If you want to do psychiatry that can well be crowded into a lifetime, see if you can't find something besides the sexual problem in the strangers that come to you for help. Quite frequently it is no trick at all to find something very much more serious than the sexual difficulty; and quite often the sexual difficulty is remedied in the process of dealing with the other problems. You may notice that there is a slight difference here between my views and some of the views that have been circulated in historic times.

CHAPTER 18

Late Adolescence

THE MARK which, to my way of thinking, separates early adolescence from late adolescence is not a biological maturation but an achievement. Such a discrimination as that between early and late adolescence would not be needed in a social organization in which the culture provided facilitation and capable direction for the achievement of adequate and satisfactory genital activity. But in our own and allied cultures, every taboo from the religious to the political is applied to this last of our developmental achievements.

Late adolescence extends from the patterning of preferred genital activity through unnumbered educative and eductive steps to the establishment of a fully human or mature repertory of interpersonal relations, as permitted by available opportunity, personal and cultural. In other words, a person begins late adolescence when he discovers what he likes in the way of genital behavior and how to fit it into the rest of life. That is an achievement of no mean magnitude for a large number of the denizens of our culture. The failure to achieve late adolescence is, in fact, the last blow to a great many warped, inadequately developed personalities. Because this kind of experience is such an all-absorbing and all-frustrating preoccupation, it often constitutes the presenting difficulty which precedes the eruption of very grave personality disorder in a large number of people; it is of course by no means the actual difficulty.

The Importance of Opportunity

The outcome of late adolescence is so much a matter of accident that whether one continues to be, dynamically, a late adolescent throughout life, or actually achieves something that might reasonably be called human maturity, is often no particular reflection on anything more than one's socioeconomic status and the like. Opportunity, as I have used it in my definition, is now a matter of other people and of the institutional or gross social facilitation and prohibition. A psychiatrist sees people who could have gone much further had they had a chance at the educational experience which others at this time of life are able to undergo.

We cannot escape the fact that many people who have had excellent developmental opportunity are caught, perhaps chiefly because of the culture, in circumstances in which there are exceedingly restricted opportunities for further growth. For example, suppose that the eldest son in a rather large family in the lower economic cadres finds himself suddenly in the position of wage earner for the family because of the death of the father. Now if this eldest son has had excellent developmental opportunity up to that point, it becomes practically certain that he will take over a large measure of the responsibility for giving the younger siblings opportunities. Along with his taking over of the responsibilities previously carried by his father, there will be a corresponding very marked reduction of his opportunities to live and learn. Thus there is no gainsaying the 'real' factors entirely outside of the developmental history of the person concerned.

Yet at the same time there are people who, with all the educational opportunities in the world, simply do not have the capacity to adequately observe and analyze the opportunities which come to them, because of inherent defect or because of various types of warp which they have not been able to correct in time. The only chance that such a person has then—except by an act of God—is through psychiatry. And how small that chance is has become more and more overwhelmingly apparent to me the longer I live.

Growth of Experience in the Syntaxic Mode

Insofar as the long stretch of late adolescence is successful, there is a great growth of experience in the syntaxic mode. Consider, for example, a person from a fairly well-knit community and a pretty good home, who has fortunately achieved a patterning of his genital behavior. If he then goes to a university, he is given several years of truly extraordinary opportunity to observe his fellows, to hear about people in various parts of the world, to discuss what has been presented and observed, to find out, on this basis, what in his past experience is inadequately grasped, and what is a natural springboard to grasping the new. In other words, for the fortunate, the educational opportunity provided by living at a university is very great.

But this is also the time when people who are not that fortunate, or who are not interested in further education, are attempting to establish some way of making a living, as wage earners, or exploiters of their fellow man, or something or other. Within limits, the kind of experience obtained is much the same as at a university, except for the probable lack of the broad, cultural interest which we trust characterizes all higher formal education. But the education in how to make a living, how to get on with people in the same line of work, is similarly a source of a great deal of observational data, and provides great possibilities for interchange of views, for expanding of one's limitations, and for the validating of one's hunches. Thus, once a person who is not very seriously warped has got the sex problem settled reasonably well, whatever he does is bound to broaden his acquaintance with other people's attitudes toward living, the degree of their interdependence in living, and the ways of handling various kinds of interpersonal problems—much of which is learned by trial and error from human example. In other words, in late adolescence one refines relatively personally-limited experience into the consensually dependable, which is much less limited. Just as in preadolescence a very remarkable, if sketchy, social organization develops on the basis of the people actually available for social organization, so in late adolescence everyone is more or less integrated into society as it is. Some of those whose opportunities are great are potentially able to integrate literally with the world society—to be at home in the world. Those who are working as apprentices in machine shops, for example, have, needless to say, vastly less opportunity in terms of geographical and cultural scope. But still they are now, from the viewpoint of society, going concerns in every way—provided with the franchise, expected to pay income tax, and the like. In general, late adolescents are adults in the eyes of the law, and have all the benefits and handicaps thereunto appertaining. Thus they have to take on a good many responsibilities which are written into the culture; they may have evaded these responsibilities thus far, but now they have to develop ways of at least giving the appearance of meeting some of them. If they are fortunate, their growth goes on and on; they observe, formulate, and validate more and more; and at the same time, their foresight continuously expands so that they can foresee their career line—not as it inevitably will be, but in terms of expectation and probability, with perhaps provisions for disappointment.

Inadequate and Inappropriate Personifications of the Self and Others

Now the fact that a great many people don't seem to get very far in this phase of personality development is to be understood primarily from the consideration of the role of anxiety in their living, which is, in turn, a way of referring to self-system functioning within the personality. Long since, I mentioned the peculiar tendency of the self-system to govern 'witting' experience, so that one tends to be strangely unchanging in spite of what might be called objective opportunities for observing and analyzing, and learning and changing. And when it comes to finding out why people do not profit from experience and why people get so short a distance toward maturity in long stretches of time, one has primarily to consider the nature and functional activity of the self-system in the person concerned. At the level where communication is fairly easy, this critical opposition of anxiety, of self-system function, is manifest as inadequate and inappropriate personification of the self. People have come to hold views of themselves which are so far from valid formulations that these views are eternally catching them in situations in which the incongruity and inappropriateness are about to become evident, whereupon the person suffers the interference of anxiety. And as I have said before, when anxiety is severe, it has almost the effect of a blow on the head; one isn't really clear on the exact situation in which the anxiety occurred. A phenomenon which is very much more important in the later phases of personality development is that people become extremely agile at responding to minor hints of anxiety. By that I don't mean that the person warns himself, "You will be anxious presently if you are not careful"—not at all. But nevertheless the appearance of just a little anxiety serves to deflect living away from the situation, just as the amoebae are deflected away from the hot water, as I have mentioned much earlier.

Thus the most accessible aspects of the self-system in many late adolescents show such superficially incomprehensible falsifications in the person's view of himself that he is not apt to learn very much in this field unless somebody goes to a great deal of trouble to put him through educative experience. And this kind of experience is fraught with relatively severe anxiety which—as I hope you will grasp by now—people put up with only when they can't help themselves. When the imperative necessity for change is recognized through psychiatric or similar experience, then most people are able to stand some anxiety, although I suppose this varies on the basis of individual past experience. To say that a person is able to stand some anxiety is another way of saying that he is able to observe previously ignored and misinterpreted experience in such fashion that his formulation of himself and of living can change in a favorable direction. One might suppose, then, that anybody who has had considerable anxiety ought to have made wonderful progress in development. But the joker to that is that the overwhelming conviction of the necessity for change is, in other than special circumstances, utterly lacking in people who suffer a great deal of anxiety. In fact, they expect to go on indefinitely as they are; they can't do anything about it; and when you attempt to show them what might be done about it, they get still more anxious and know that you are bad medicine and avoid you. What I am attempting to suggest at this point is that there is a very considerable difference between being very much in the grip of anxiety, mild or severe, and, as it were, 'coming to grips' with a source of anxiety, mild or severe.

Now I shall have to digress long enough to remove any shadows of voluntaristic meaning from my use of such expressions as "coming to grips" with anxiety and "confronting" anxiety. There seems to be very little profit in psychiatry from dependence on any such idea as the mysterious power of the will. I think I have touched on this before in discussing the evil effects of the doctrine of the will on development. In a society in which people are usually quite proud of their will and are noisy about it, I would like to warn psychiatrists that the less voluntaristic their language, and the more utterly free their thinking from convictions about the will, the further they will be able to get in understanding and perhaps favorably influencing their patients. So when I speak of the confronting of anxiety, I do not mean that a psychiatrist asks a patient to pull himself together and exert his will so that he will not so easily yield to the threat of anxiety. What the psychiatrist does, if he accomplishes anything in this particular, is to so nurture in the patient correct foresight of the near future that it becomes intolerable to be always running away from minor anxiety. The appearance of anxiety is in no sense connected with any mythological or real will; it is connected with experience which has been incorporated into and become a part of the self-system and with the foresight of increasing anxiety in connection with the self-system. The problem of the psychiatrist is more or less to spread a larger context before the patient; insofar as that succeeds, the patient realizes that, anxiety or not, the present way of life is unsatisfactory and is unprofitable in the sense that it is not changing things for the better; whereupon, in spite of anxiety, other things being equal, the self-system can be modified.

In addition to inadequate and inappropriate personifications of the self, there are, attendant upon that, and in congruity with it, inadequate and inappropriate personification of others. Such inadequacy and inappropriateness of secondary personifications—secondary because to most people they seem less important than a person's personification of himself—may apply broadly to everyone, or specifically to stereotypes of certain alleged people. A person cannot personify others with any particular refinement except in terms of his own personification of himself and in terms of more-or-less imaginary entities related by the 'not' technique to his personification of himself. If you regard yourself as generous, then you tend to assume that others will be generous; but since you have a good deal of experience not in keeping with that, you personify many people as ungenerous, *not* generous. Now that doesn't give you any particularly good formulation of what they are; they are just different and opposite from you in one of your better aspects. Thus, to a remarkable degree this limitation in the personification of others is based on inappropriate and inadequate personification of oneself. Particularly troublesome are the inadequate and inappropriate personifications by what I have referred to as stereotypes, which again reflect the limitations in the personification of the self. We often encounter the most accessible part of such things as prejudices, intolerances, fears, hatreds, aversions, and revulsions that pertain to alleged classes of people. Now these stereotypes may concern newsboys, the Jews, the Greeks, the Communists, the Chinese, or what have you. They are, needless to say, not based on adequate observation, analysis, and consensual validation of data about the people concerned.

Stereotypes reflect inadequate and inappropriate elements in one's own self-system; thus all the special stereotypes are either poor imitations of ingredients in the personified self, or—even more inadequate in terms of providing a guide in life—they are *not* elements from the personification of the self. For example, the view that the Irish are all politicians can be held with perfect impunity and peace of mind either by people who show remarkable political gifts, or by those who show remarkable political imbecility. That is, if you are a good politician you can stereotype a whole ethnic group or biethnic group with this characteristic, and if you are a rotten politician you can simply stigmatize a group with a *not* variant of yourself.

Incidentally—to continue a little further with the subject of prejudice and stereotypes—I am myself inclined to think that the Irish are pagans. Now there is no shadow of doubt in my mind that any sort of searching study of the current residents of Ireland would toss up a great many instances in which the term pagan would be irrelevant, in any meaningful sense. What I have in mind is that in many ethnic groups or ethnic communities which are vigorously Christian in their protestations, one can find, as soon as one gets into actual informative interchange with their members about their religious convictions, a truly wonderful survival of types of attitude toward transcendental power and so on which have very little indeed to do with Christian prescriptions. The Irish, who happen to be my ancestral people, are a little better known to me than are, for example, the Chinese; and so I feel—

after the best modern pattern—perfectly free to make a wisecrack about the underlying religious attitude of my people. But, thank God, I know that it may or may not make any sense; I wouldn't think of staking anything on it. It is all right for parlor conversation with good friends, preferably Irish. But if I say it often to other people, I may very unhappily present them with an opportunity to clinch an uninformed prejudice, which is usually done by nailing it onto a preceding one. Whether such remarks are amusing wisecracks which may be used for little prestige purposes, and so on, as doubtless my comment about the pagan Irish is, or whether they are a device for avoiding any growth of intelligence, information, and consensual agreement about whole huge sections of the human race, largely depends on the extent to which the prejudice expressed reflects a serious limitation in the personification of the self.

The purposes served by these stereotypes are many. But the alleged purpose which almost any unsophisticated person will immediately produce under suitable circumstances is one of the saddest commentaries on the misfortunes of personality in our world and time: namely, that they are very useful guides for dealing with strangers. Quite simply, they are not. They are, insofar as they are important, exactly the opposite of guides for dealing with strangers; they are inescapable handicaps in becoming acquainted with strangers. And to that extent they are chiefly effective in denying one any opportunity for spontaneous favorable change in the corresponding limitation in one's personification of oneself.

Parataxic Processes to Minimize Anxiety

In further commenting on the critical opposition of anxiety and the self-system to favorable growth in late adolescence, I would like to call attention to the parataxic processes concerned in avoiding and minimizing anxiety. These processes extend from selective inattention—which to a certain extent covers the world like a tent —through all the other classical dynamisms of difficulty, to the gravest dissociation of one or more of the vitally essential human dynamisms. And incidentally, while I once liked the rubric, dynamism of difficulty, it has lost its charm over my years of attempting to teach psychiatry, because the conviction grew among some of the people who encountered this usage that these dynamisms represented peculiarities shown by the morbid. On the contrary, I believe that there are no peculiarities shown by the morbid; there are only differences in degree—that is, in intensity and timing—of that which is shown by everyone.[1] Thus whenever I speak of dynamisms I am discussing universal human equipment, sometimes represented almost entirely in dreadful distortions of living, but still universal. And the distortions arise from misfortunes in development, restrictions of opportunity, and the like. Thus the interventions of the self-system which are striking in this late adolescent phase—that is, in chronologic maturity—cover the whole field of what we like to talk about as being psychiatric entities—mental disorders, if you please.

Restrictions in Freedom of Living

Another way of approaching the general topic of the self-system's prevention of favorable change in the late adolescent phase is to consider restrictions in freedom of living, with their complex processes for the discharge of the integrating tendencies that are restricted. This is a different approach to what we have already discussed and is an attempt to highlight certain things which we have not noticed before.

By restrictions in freedom of living, I refer here to the limitations that arise 'internally,' because of handicaps in one's past, and not to the restrictions which come under the broad classification of opportunity, which I have touched on before. Restrictions in freedom of living are attended by complex ways of getting at least partial satisfaction for what one's restrictions prevent and by further complex processes, in the shape of sleep disorders and the like, for discharging dangerous accumulations of tensions. These restrictions may be usefully considered from the standpoint of restricted contact with others and of restrictions of interest. Restricted contact with others may range from the early develop-

---

[1] I am always in these remarks eliminating the organic; in other words, if someone shoots away half of a person's skull, he will not be thereafter in the central field of my psychiatric interest—not that psychiatry might not grow from studying him.

ment of a strikingly isolated way of life, with such great social distance that one has to continue to deny oneself a great deal of useful, educative, and consensual validating experience with others, to circumscriptions of oneself on the basis of factors such as prejudice, caste, and class, if one happens to be in a very small minority.

But in a great many instances, the restrictions in freedom of living are very much more striking in the sharp circumscriptions of interest; large numbers of aspects of living are, as it were, taboo— one avoids them. Sometimes a compulsory restriction of living growing out of warp in the past is masked in the shape of pseudo-social rituals and interests which look like something quite different from a restriction. And these rituals seem to raise the person concerned above the level of the common horde and take on great distinction, at least to him and his ilk. The example I am going to give concerns *devotion to games,* and in this instance devotion to bridge. Since I got into quite serious trouble with a very distinguished and greatly respected anthropologist by this example of bridge, I judge that it has some power to fix interest, and so I will use it again. Now I have never played much of anything well; I think probably my vulgar taste is well handled by casino or hearts; certainly it isn't anywhere near up to bridge. My example concerns a very select group of women in New York who have great socioeconomic opportunities. They do little each day but get out of bed and prepare for the bridge club, to which they repair with minimum talk to their husbands or chauffeurs and there spend many hours in a very highly ritualized interchange with their fellows, whereupon they are content with life and repair to bed again. I hope that you begin to get a notion of what I mean by pseudosocial ritual; in this case, each person is busily engaged with people, but nothing particularly personal transpires. I believe that most of these people would be willing to agree that it would be rather better—aside from considerations of displaying their clothing, and so on—if they could sit in cubicles with one-way screens directed toward the cards. There would be less distraction from people coughing and sneezing and so on, and they could therefore perform their function in life more comfortably. While this is an extreme example of pseudosocial ritual, there are a remark-

able number of people who have ways of being social as the devil
without having anything to do with the other people concerned.
They live by very sharply restricted rules.

Another of these restrictions in living is the development of
ritual avoidances and ritual preoccupations. Regardless of your
political leanings, you have probably all experienced with your
confreres ritualized avoidance in matters of political thought. For
example, this kind of avoidance might appear if you talked to your
banker about the necessity for further New Deal legislation. To
give a personal example, on the rare occasions that I get to a barber
shop, I am duly shorn by a good fellow veteran of the First World
War whom I cherish both because he is a very public-spirited citi-
zen who does a great deal of welfare work, and because he is a
good barber and keeps quiet. I so detest the business of having my
hair cut that I wish to at least approach dozing, and conversation
is extremely unwelcome. But one day as I was getting my hair cut,
the radio had some tweet on about Henry Wallace, and the barber
denounced Henry Wallace very succinctly. I remarked that,
well, I knew the man and liked him very much. I feel that, like
some of the rest of us, he is not always possessed of the most
brilliant and far-reaching foresight, but he has occasionally had
some remarkably good ideas, which is enough to give a person
standing with me. It was not difficult after that to repose during
the time I was in the barber chair. Five or six months later, when
Henry Wallace was boosted out of the Department of Commerce,
the subject came up again; in other words, it was an important
matter. Now this barber has no real desire to quarrel with me
about anything, but my comment about Wallace had disturbed
part of his ritual avoidance machinery; and this disturbance was
attached to me, since he's got good enough recall to know how I
disturbed him. And so the topic was developed further. But we still
patronize each other for all that.

Now all these ritual avoidances and preoccupations give one a
feeling that one is making some sense in an important area of living. Actually one is not making any sense at all, because one is
completely inaccessible to any data. Besides the political, there is
the 'society' aspect; here again great sections of life are closed off
by supposedly rational definitions which, on careful scrutiny, turn

out to be simply ritualistic avoidances. The same is true in the world of art; and those who have dealt with natural and unnatural sciences may have noticed much the same thing at annual meetings and the like. And God knows the world is filled with ritual avoidances and preoccupations under the name of religion.

Of course, I can quite respect a person for being clear as to what he is interested in and what he is not particularly interested in. For instance, there is no earthly reason why I should be frantically interested in the theory of money. There is no reason on earth why I should labor to develop an aesthetic appreciation of painting, or of unnumbered other things in which I have only vestigial interest. I could not conceivably be adequately interested in anything like the whole field of internal medicine. But if no one can even *talk* to me about Dadaism, for instance, or the Baptists, or the theory of money, it is not because my life course has concentrated a great deal of my satisfaction and security in a particular field; it is because my security depends on *avoiding* a particular field or a particular subject. Life, I suppose, has never been all equally interesting to any one person or within the capacity of any one person. I am quite sure that as the primal horde came out of prehistory there was some specialization among the denizens; certainly there was specialization in the bearing of children, and such a specialization as that would surely call for further specializations. Ritual avoidances and preoccupations may superficially look the same as specializations, but they actually mean that you cannot enter a certain field; any interest moving toward that field immediately arouses anxiety which prohibits any further movement in pursuit of information.

Self-Respect and Human Maturity

From all that I have suggested you may see that it is no extraordinary use of inference to presume that self-respect is necessary for the adequate respect of others. There are many people who respect many people they don't know, but that isn't what I am talking about. It is safe to say that people who respect no one except people they don't know do not respect themselves. And people who are very high in self-respect—that is, whose life experience has permitted them to uncover and demonstrate to their own satisfaction remarkable capacity for living with and among others—are people who find no particular expense to themselves connected with respecting any meritorious performance of anyone else. One of the feeblest props for an inadequate self-system is the attitude of disparaging others, which I once boiled down into the doctrine that if you are a molehill then, by God, there shall be no mountains. In a good many ways one can read the whole state of a person's self-respect from his disparagement of others. The disparagement is built of two ingredients, that which one 'despises' about oneself, and a great many *not* operations. Thus the person who greatly respects himself for his "generosity," which is probably always of a very public character, finds an incredible number of people ungenerous, stingy, mean, and so on. I think it has been known from the beginning of recorded thought that a person who is very bitter toward others, very hard on his fellow man for certain faults, is usually very sensitive to these particular faults because they are secret vices of his own. Insofar as self-respect has been permitted to grow without restrictions, because of comparatively unwarped personal development or because warp of personal development has been remedied, there is no expense, no feeling of impoverishment, no hints of anxiety connected with discovering that somebody else is much better than you are in a particular field. It is lamentably true that in so highly specialized and intricate a social organization as almost any extant culture is, it is virtually certain that there are very few top figures in any complex operation. Most people are not as good as the very few, and many people are much worse than the average. But there is such an enormous field for living that one does not have to depend on what one is not good at, and therefore one has no particular need for keeping a bookkeeping record on how many people are worse in a field in which one is bad. But some people, because of certain warps in personal development, make this an outstanding operation, in order to reduce anxiety from invidious comparisons with others.

I should like now to say a few words about human maturity—a subject I always treat extremely casually, partly because it is not a problem of psychiatry, although it could be extrapolated from psychiatry. But the actual fact is that an understanding of maturity eludes us as psychiatrists who are students of interpersonal relations, for the people who manifest the most maturity are least accessible for study; and the progress of our patients toward maturity invariably removes them from our observation before they have reached it. Thus a psychiatrist, as a psychiatrist, doesn't have much actual data. But one can guess a few things. I would guess that each of the outstanding achievements of the developmental eras that I have discussed will be outstandingly manifest in the mature personality. The last of these great developments is the appearance and growth of the need for intimacy—for collaboration with at least one other, preferably more others; and in this collaboration there is the very striking feature of a very lively sensitivity to the needs of the other and to the interpersonal security or absence of anxiety in the other. Thus we can certainly extrapolate from what we know that the mature, insofar as nothing of great importance collides, will be quite sympathetically understanding of the limitations, interests, possibilities, anxieties, and so on of those among whom they move or with whom they deal. Another thing which can quite certainly be extrapolated is that, whether it be by eternally widening interests or by deepening interests or both, the life of the mature—far from becoming monotonous and a bore—is always increasing in, shall I say, importance. There is no reason to entertain for an instant the notion that it would be too bad to become mature, because then one might get bored to death; quite the contrary. It is certain that no person, whether mature or terribly ill, is proof against any possibility of anxiety or fear, or against any of the needs that characterize life. But the greater the degree of maturity, the less will be the interference of anxiety with living, and therefore the less nuisance value one has for oneself and for others. And when one is mature, anything which even infinitesimally approximates the complexity of living in the world as we know it today is not apt to become boring.

PART
III

Patterns of Inadequate or Inappropriate Interpersonal Relations

The Earlier Manifestations of Mental Disorder: Matters Schizoid and Schizophrenic

I AM now beginning a discussion of the patterns of inadequate or inappropriate interpersonal relations which are ordinarily referred to as mental disorders, mild or severe. By adding "mild or severe," I wish to indicate that the topic of mental disorders covers all sorts of things, from minor accidents, such as unhappily being unable to remember an important person's name when you are about to request a favor from him, to the most chronic psychosis in the mental hospital. And so—as nearly as I can discover —if the term, mental disorder, is to be meaningful, it must cover like a tent the whole field of inadequate or inappropriate performance in interpersonal relations.

To begin with, I must make it clear that I am not dealing with all those disorders of living which arise primarily because of more-or-less clearly biological defect. On these I will have nothing in particular to say, although I believe that this theory of psychiatry will make evident to the more thoughtful how primary biological defect can influence the developmental course and the necessary preparation for living as a person among persons. Primary biological defect can be either inborn and manifest from the beginning, as in the case of the very unfortunate imitations of human beings called idiots; or it may be as recondite as a particular vulnerability to life, which manifests itself, for instance, in premature old age or premature senile deterioration (Alzheimer's disease), or in the arteriosclerotic changes and the senile psychoses. All these things refer much more to the innate constitution of the living matter that makes up the human body than they do to life experience, although, as I have indicated from time to time, life experience may have some influence on the timing of the manifestation of the defect. But it is quite clear that there are people so well endowed by heredity that they can survive very, very stressful circumstances for many years without marked destructive elevation of blood pressure or serious deterioration of the walls of the blood vessels such as occurs in arteriosclerosis; such people can go on into their eighties, perhaps even past the middle of the eighties, with no material senile changes, such as we see in the senile psychoses. Thus there is a large body of phenomena ordained by heredity which probably have fundamentally important bearing on the course of life. But what I am discussing is the difficulties of living which arise far more from misfortunes in developmental history than from any innate endowment.

Developmental Events Tributary to the Not-Me

To open this discussion of 'mental disorders'—or patterns of inadequate and inappropriate action in interpersonal relations—I want to take up more fully the 'natural history' of the conception of *not-me*, which I could only hint at in connection with late infancy and early childhood. The not-me is literally the organization of experience with significant people that has been subjected to such intense anxiety, and anxiety so suddenly precipitated, that it was impossible for the then relatively rudimentary person to make any sense of, to develop any true grasp on, the particular circumstances which dictated the experience of this intense anxiety. As I have said, very intense anxiety precipitated by a sudden, intense, negative emotional reaction on the part of the significant environment has more than a little in common with a blow on the head. It tends to erase any possibility of elaborating the exact circumstances of its occurrence, and about the most the person can remember in retrospect is a somewhat fenestrated account of the event in the immediate neighborhood. If, for example, a parent has had a subpsychotic fear of the infant's becoming a lustful monster and has gone off the deep end whenever the infant was discovered to be holding the penis or fondling the vulva—then we expect that the personality of the infant as it develops will show a sort of hole in that area, in the sense that any approach to the genitals will ultimately lead to the appearance of a feeling which has scarcely evolved beyond sudden, intense, all-encompassing anxiety. All this almost undifferentiated, sudden, violent anxiety is experienced as *uncanny* emotion; that is, if a person had a good grasp on the word, he would say, in trying to describe what was happening to him, that he felt uncanny. In later life, this all-encompassing anxiety shows some slight elaborations, which are hinted at by four words in our language—awe, dread, loathing, and horror. Although these four words suggest the possibility of discriminating between various uncanny emotions, actually the experiences are pretty much indistinguishable, which is borne out by the descriptions offered by highly articulate people.

While there is an awfulness connected with all of the uncanny emotions, *awe* itself is one of them. From it, of course, we get our term "awful," although the connection has been lost in the history of English. Awe is perhaps the least oppressively sudden and the least paralyzing of these uncanny emotions; in fact, it is in many adults called out only by unexpected, stupendous manifestations of nature, or of man's works, stirring some of the more fantastically autistic reveries of the past. Thus upon entering certain buildings which have great architectural beauty, one may feel awe, which, if the building happens to be a church, may carry with it curiously early thinking about the nature and actual presence of the deity, for example. And many people, when they first climb the hill and look into the Grand Canyon, have a paralyzing emotion which is anything but really an attractive experience, but yet is not horrible. One is, as it were, lifted utterly out of the context of life and is profoundly impressed.

The other three terms connected with the uncanny emotions speak very much more of the dreadful character of the experience; they are dread itself, loathing, and horror. Loathing is that peculiar combination of physical illness and other extremely unpleasant things which some not particularly articulate people have described to me as an intense desire to vomit without the capacity to even feel nauseated—which in its way is rather impressive. And horror is the uncanny emotion that all of you have known at least once, probably in your sleep. Horror is a simply paralyzing combination of what I like to call revulsion—a feeling of almost total desire to be elsewhere and away from all this sort of thing—coupled again with a great desire to vomit, and perhaps a tendency to have diarrhea and one thing and another; and at the same time there is literally a sort of paralysis of everything, so that nothing really goes on except this awful and—if it can possibly be avoided—never-to-be-repeated experience.

All these things seem to be rather of the essence of sudden attacks of all-paralyzing anxiety; and this anxiety can be induced very early in one's life by the sudden outburst, in a significant person, of extremely unpleasant emotions. And this is the foundation, if you please, of certain experience structures in personality that can be for practical purposes, because of their later manifestations, referred to as the not-me—in contrast to good-me and bad-me. Good-me and bad-me, as I have said, are the basis of lifelong ingredients of consciousness—that is, there is no person who is not, in the privacy of his own covert operations, perfectly clear on the fact that he has a number of unsatisfactory and undesirable attributes which he is busily engaged in concealing, or excusing, or what not, and that he also has some good traits, among the others; and these are the outgrowths of the initial dichotomy of good-me and bad-me. But only under exceptional circumstances are there any reflections in consciousness—that is, in awareness—of that part of one's life experience which I have called not-me—a sort of third rudimentary personification.

Evidences of Dissociation

In addition to every other form or process elaborated into the self-system for the avoiding or minimizing of anxiety or for the concealing of anxiety, the self-system has, in practically every instance, some aspects which can be said to be—and this is highly figurative language—directed to keep one safe from any possibility of passing into that extremely unpleasant state of living which can be called the uncanny emotions; and these aspects of the self-system can only be inferred, except in case of disaster. Depending on one's distant past, this group of self-processes may be fairly extensive or may be minor indeed. The manifestations of such self-functions, as experienced by practically everyone, are actually called out by progressions of processes in sleep which become so explicit, in some allegedly impossible aspect of personality, that they suddenly call into action self-system processes which are ordinarily in abeyance at night. The result is that one suddenly awakes with a more-or-less shivery feeling of having been in the presence of something dreadful. Now the nightmare, as it is ordinarily encountered, may or may not represent matters actually touching upon the not-me component in personality. But in a good many ways the smaller the content of the nightmare and the more tremendous the emotion—the more utterly shattering the recollection of the emotional state—the more you may surmise that some process in sleep has all too emphatically connected with this particular component of personality, which is ordinarily only inferentially evident, and which is the result of the most disastrous contacts with sudden and violent anxiety in the early years.

In later childhood, the basis provided by the not-me experience of early childhood may either grow or may be more or less stationary, depending on the experience at that time. In that era, the more fortunate people develop precautionary and propitiatory processes concerned with manifestations of what was previously bad-me, and disintegrate those motivational systems that get them into very serious trouble, with either reorganization—sublimatory or otherwise—of the disintegrated motivational system, or regressive reactivation of earlier patterns of behavior for such components as are not reorganized. But in the later childhood of more fated people who, for instance, lose a parent in childhood and get instead a very bad imitation, or are sent to an inferior institution, or something like that, there may begin to be very clear evidences of this exceedingly important system of processes to which we refer as *dissociation.*[1]

In dissociation, the trick is that one shall carry on within aware-

---

[1] Dissociation is unfortunately made rather too important in *Conceptions* [Sullivan, *Conceptions of Modern Psychiatry; op. cit.*], in which I did not take enough time to emphasize all the other things that go on besides dissociation.

ness processes which make it practically impossible, while one is awake, to encounter uncanny emotion. You see, dissociation can easily be mistaken for a really quite magical business in which you fling something of you out into outer darkness, where it reposes for years, quite peacefully. That is a fantastic oversimplification. Dissociation works very suavely indeed as long as it works, but it isn't a matter of keeping a sleeping dog under an anesthetic. It works by a continuous alertness or vigilance of awareness, with certain supplementary processes which prevent one's ever discovering the usually quite clear evidences that part of one's living is done without any awareness. I am practically ready to say that the dissociating components of self-system processes have their most classical manifestation in obsessive substitution for difficulties in living. Certainly there seems to be no clear line between people who have, as their prevailing ineffective, inappropriate, and inadequate interpersonal process, substitutive processes of the obsessional type, and those who, under certain circumstances, suffer episodes of schizophrenic living. And so, while it would be rather unreasonable, at this point, to say that the great wealth of substitutive processes found in this culture are all clear evidences of serious dissociations, I believe that when our theoretical formulations have progressed a little further on the basis of better study of data, we will find that that may be just the case. In any event, there is such a close parallel between the difficulties of working with really important substitutive processes and the difficulties in working with schizophrenic processes that the distinction again becomes minor. And when I say really important substitutive processes, I mean the use of substitution in very important areas of living. Quite strikingly, in this day and age, substitutive processes are used to conceal extreme vulnerability to anxiety at the hands of practically anyone. One finds in a great many of the more severe obsessional people, as we call them in the vernacular, a great degree of what they call hatred, but what actually, on more close scrutiny, proves to be their shocking vulnerability to almost anybody with whom they are integrated. And the obsessional substitutions which make up such conspicuous and troublesome aspects of their lives are simply all-encompassing attenuations of contact which protect them from their abnormal vulnerability to anxiety.

Thus one should look upon obsessional substitution as perhaps an outstanding instance of what goes on in the self-system in order to keep something utterly excluded from awareness, so that there is no possibility of its eruption into awareness.

Whenever dissociated systems of motives are involved, we find a relative suspension of awareness as to any effects that these motives have. That suspension of awareness may be as minor as the relatively trifling and almost ubiquitous disturbance of awareness to which I give the term *selective inattention*, in which one simply doesn't happen to notice almost an infinite series of more-or-less meaningful details of one's living. But even selective inattention is very impressive when one observes that it could not possibly act so suavely, and so eternally at the right times, unless there was continuous vigilance lest one notice what for some obscure reasons one is not going to notice. Selective inattention is, more than any other of the inappropriate and inadequate performances of life, the classic means by which we do not profit from experience which falls within the areas of our particular handicap. We don't *have* the experience from which we might profit—that is, although it occurs, we never notice what it must mean; in fact we never notice that a good deal of it has occurred at all. That is what is really troublesome in psychotherapy, I suppose—the wonderfully bland way in which people overlook the most glaring implications of certain acts of their own, or of certain reactions of theirs to other people's acts—that is, what they are apt to report as other people's acts. Much more tragically, they may overlook the fact that these things have occurred at all; these things just aren't remembered, even though the person has had them most unpleasantly impressed on him.

I'm going to digress for a moment to give an instance of the circumvention of selective inattention, which involves one of my more gross acts of unkindness. There is a drugstore at which I frequently have to purchase this and that; and during the war years it had among its clerks at the soda fountain a person who, I am quite sure, would be shown by intelligence tests to be a low-grade moron. Not only was he quite lacking in intelligence, but also—in which I sympathize with him, as I do with everyone who deals with the public—he showed a very rare collection of hostilities to customers, so that whatever you asked for, he would dutifully, when he got around to it, bring you something else. Having suffered from this repeatedly, I was extremely unpleasant on one particular occasion and said, "What is that, huh?" And he said, "Water. Didn't you ask for it?" And I said, "*Get me what I asked for!*" Whereupon the poor bird tottered off under the unpleasantness and got me what I had asked for. But the great joker is that the next time I saw him he grinned at me and immediately got me what I asked for. Now, that humbled me, because his inattention was not as complete as I had thought. He profited from an unpleasant experience, and, by God, that's more than some of us do. If he had acted as I expected, it would have been a classical instance of selective inattention; he would never have noticed that almost always he brought people things they didn't want. And therefore, of course, any occasion such as I provoked would be utterly novel, inexplicable—just an instance of deviltry on my part. The great joker was that it didn't seem to be. This story to the contrary, I hope I have given you a notion of how suavely we simply ignore great bodies of experience, any clearly analyzed instance of which might present us with a very real necessity for change.

Among the other evidences of dissociation—in addition to selective inattention and the dissociative processes such as obsessional substitution—there are certain relatively uncommon marginal observations which go on in awareness in unusual interpersonal situations; and these observations have a touch of the uncanny about them. And the uncanny in this very mild sense is what I call revulsion. Revulsion is a certain sort of chilled turning away from things, quite different from chronic detestations, such as I have for yolk of egg—a detestation in which there is no shadow of anything except a realization that were I to taste it again it would be as unpleasant as ever. Revulsion is something else: you have a little disturbance in your belly and so on, and you aren't at all inclined to think what would happen if you had gone further. And in the course of average living, evidences of dissociation may also appear as certain disturbances at night, from which one is awakened with nothing except uncanny emotion— a feeling that one was having a damned unpleasant dream which was lost in the process of awakening. Much more occasionally one recalls fragments of dreams which were clearly associated with horror, dread, or what not. These are almost invariably uninterpretable as they are ordinarily reported. Only when psychotherapy becomes fairly well established can a person ordinarily stand the strain of having fairly clear dissociated processes revealed in his dreams.

Along with these detectable ingredients of awareness, there are, when there is dissociation of major motives, certain gross items of behavior which we call *automatisms*. And while I say that this happens when there is dissociation of major motives, I presume that this is true in any instance of dissociation, although it is very much harder to see when the motives are not major. Automatisms can be very massive performances under certain circumstances, although they are minor movements in general; and sometimes they are such extreme things as tics, convulsions of certain muscle groups, and so on, which seem about as far removed from meaningful behavior as possible. A graphic instance of these automatisms can be frequently seen in the more populated areas such as Manhattan. Those of you who are men may have discovered, as you're walking down the street, that quite a number of other men look at what is called the fly of your pants, and look away hastily. Many of them raise their eyes to yours—apparently, insofar as you can interpret, to see if they have been noticed. But the point is that some of them, if they encounter your gaze, are as numb and indifferent as if nothing had occurred. Others of them blush and are obviously very much disturbed. In the latter, it has not been an automatism; if being detected in this act is very embarrassing to the person who manifested it, then the act has had meaning to him. But when such an act is automatic—the manifestation of dissociated motivation—it is not embarrassing to be detected. Even if it were brought emphatically to the attention of the person who manifested it, his natural inclination would always be to deny that it had occurred. If, perhaps with a photograph, you could demonstrate that it had occurred, the person would still feel completely blank as to what on earth it could have arisen from, what it could mean. Thus major systems in dissociation—and I presume all dissociated experience—manifest themselves in certain disturbances of behavior, or certain gross behavioral acts, whose single distinction is the fact that their occurrence is either unknown, or at least meaningless, to the person who shows them.

In more major automatisms, one 'finds oneself,' with very considerable disturbance, in very awkward situations into which one has apparently walked with one's eyes shut, so to speak; and this discovery leads to uncanny emotion. Sometimes one realizes that one has been in a really curious state of mind during the time that one got into this awkwardness; and this state of mind might be labeled *fascination*. When fascinated, one is actually engaging in molar behavior which gets one into a situation where the manifestations of a dissociated impulse would be appropriate. That seldom happens; instead one 'finds oneself' with thoroughly disagreeable fringes of horror, dread, revulsion, or something of the kind, and extricates oneself, usually with a distinct feeling of being badly shaken by the experience.

Possibility of Reintegration of Dissociated Systems

Dissociated systems are founded in early life; their greatest chance of automatic remedy, and also their greatest contributions to danger to the personality, occur in the preadolescent and adolescent phases of development. Many people have come out of preadolescence and early adolescence in distinctly less risk, so far as their future is concerned, than when they began these eras. But at the same time, anyone familiar with mental-hospital admission rates knows that very grave disturbances of personality often occur in the instance of the delayed preadolescent or during the phases of adolescence. In general, important aspects of personality existing in dissociation are not reintegrated except under extremely fortunate circumstances. One of these fortunate circumstances is found in preadolescence, as I have already said, when the development of the need for intimacy can lead to very considerable improvement of the partition of energy between the not-me component and the other components of personality. And at the same time that this new integrating tendency is being called out by maturation, certain eventualities are likely to occur which may have favorable influence in reintegrating a dissociated tendency system. Among these fortunate eventualities of preadolescence and adolescence are the reintegration by what I call "deliberate fugue"; the reintegration "as if by misadventure while asleep"; and the reintegration by "adjustment to the uncanny."

To begin with, perhaps I should explain what I mean by fugue. A fugue, in the sense in which I use the term, is literally a relatively prolonged state of dreaming-while-awake—that is, one acts a dream with every conviction that one is awake, and one actually is awake, as far as a bystander can tell. Fugues sometimes occur in the perhaps partially organic, if not wholly organic, state of epilepsy, although fugues, in the sense I'm now discussing, are by no means restricted to the epileptic. Fugues are part of the onset of some very serious mental disorders, although sometimes the occurrence of a fugue is all that is needed to avoid the onset of very serious mental disorder. But in any case, when one is in a fugue, as I am trying to describe it, one *believes* that one is awake, one *acts as if* one were awake in many important particulars, and everyone else *presumes* one is awake. But the relationship with circumambient reality and with the meanings to which things attach from one's past is, to a certain extent, as fundamentally and as absolutely suspended as it is when one is asleep. And there are certain absolute barriers to recall, which are to be understood only on the basis of their being minor indications of a very prolonged state of sleep.

Now preadolescents and adolescents sometimes approach situations in what I call *deliberate fugues*: that is, a person braces himself with an attitude of "Well, hell, let's take a chance on anything once." He then plunges into some situation, with a sort of tightening up of everything, often keeping his eye on something irrelevant—that is, preoccupying himself with things really tangential to what he is after. This has striking resemblances to an active fugue state, although without the literal cutting-off of certain aspects of past history that a true fugue shows. In this state one has experiences which under other circumstances would precipitate a psychosis. And by a sort of attenuating process, by which the whole thing adds itself to conscious experience slowly, one survives it and is the better for it.

I have mentioned that reintegration of dissociated tendencies may be initiated, as it were, by misadventure, particularly in connection with the relative abeyance of security operations as if one were asleep. That is, one gets into situations primarily motivated by the dissociated system, as if one were asleep. This, again, is a very tricky business, and it is a mistake to accuse a person of having falsely claimed to be asleep in such situations. The longer we deal intimately with personalities in this very risky area, the more we realize that we have no absolute criterion for sleep and that there are unquestionably a number of levels of sleep. The true fugue, for example, is of the essence of sleep, but no criterion that we could ordinarily apply would show it to be anything remotely like what we think sleep is. Thus one may hear of a youngster who has found himself in some presumably very disturbing experience because he had fallen asleep, although he knows all about it; one may think this a little bit curious and be inclined to doubt it, but one should proceed cautiously. I'm not sure he isn't simply telling the truth. In other words, these misadventures, when one may or may not have been asleep, are perhaps the next step between the "deliberate fugue," where one decides to pull ahead and take the consequences, and the true fugue, where one has no more clarity on what has happened to one than if one were profoundly asleep.

The last method by which dissociated systems may be reintegrated—and one I have difficulty putting into words—is what I call the "adjustment to the uncanny." This is probably in some ways a function of the mythology that has been incorporated in one's earlier experience. In other words, to a certain extent, one acts a part in a relatively cosmic drama—that is, one literally steps out of the world as it is into the world of some mythological system and for a while plays a role in that. In some very serious disturbances following the failure of dissociation, people fight out, with tremendous expenditures of energy, dramas virtually on a cosmic scale; for example, one of my patients at one time exhausted himself in the battle of the nuns and the fathers. Adjustment to the uncanny is doing this with a feeling that *you* do it instead of its being forced upon you by transcendental powers. A few people have had experiences in their developmental years of meeting situations actually characterized by these extremely disquieting and extraordinarily repelling uncanny emotions, in which, for a while, they acted as if they were one of the demigods or the demidevils or what not, and got through it, and so from then on knew more about life on the far side of it.[2]

The Schizophrenic Way of Life and Possible Outcomes

All things connected with dissociated systems are risky. The act of dissociation is perhaps the most magnificently complex performance of human personality, and it is certainly the riskiest way of dealing with any of the very major motivations in life. Even in adolescence and preadolescence—as the very high schizophrenia rate of these eras indicates—the risks are anything but nominal. And after these developmental thresholds have been passed, continuing risks—that is, if there are major systems in dissociation—are really pretty ominous.

But let me now discuss the dramatic manifestations of risk—that is, the disasters that come from having major systems in dissociation, or major components of motivational systems in dissociation. These disastrous failures are most likely to occur in the age group from fourteen to twenty-seven, roughly. Of the very, very risky things that can happen, perhaps the least disastrous in outcome is the 'displacement,' with very serious disturbance of consciousness, of the conventional personified self by behavior patterns, and so on, concerned with the dissociated pattern. This is the real fugue. One may come out of the fugue in a very sad state indeed; or the fugue may suddenly clear up after possibly a year and a half's duration, and one then seems to be all right. Fugues occurring in this adolescent era are quite frequently not as successful as some of the so-called hysterical fugues, in which a person who is not really crooked embezzles a lot of money and wakes up in a strange city with an assumed personality.

[2] [Editors' note: In another lecture, in 1945, Sullivan described the "adjustment to the uncanny" as follows: "After an uncanny experience there then supervenes a total state of personality, one might say, in which one says, 'Well, this is it; for good or evil, for better or worse, it is so.' And this acceptance of something—even though one cannot think of it, cannot analyze it—as being so, to be survived or not as the case may be, is what I mean by the peculiar expression, adjustment to the uncanny."]

The fugue might be called a very massive change of personality. Another, somewhat less massive, disturbance of personality is what I call the eruption into awareness of *abhorrent cravings*. In my view the term "craving" doesn't need the adjective "abhorrent," but I wish to indicate by this term the entrance into personal awareness of increasingly-intense-because-unsatisfied longings to engage in something which is abhorrent—that is, the picturing of engaging in it is attended by uncanny emotion such as horror, dread, loathing, or the like. The classic instance of this eruption of cravings is the eruption of 'homosexual' desires—desires to participate in what the patient feels, classically and outstandingly, to be homosexual performances. I think I can illustrate this, perhaps without misleading you too badly, by mentioning one of my patients, an only boy with five sisters, who had led as sheltered a life as that situation would permit. Shortly after getting into uniform in World War II he was prowling around Washington, and was gathered up by a very well-dressed and charming dentist, who took him to his office and performed what is called fellatio on this boy. The boy felt, I presume, a mild adjustment to the uncanny, and went his way, perhaps in some fashion rewarded. But the next day he quite absent-mindedly walked back to the immediate proximity of the dentist's office, that being in some ways, you see, an untroubled fugue—whereupon, finding himself so very near what had happened the day before, he was no longer able to exclude from awareness the fact that he would like to continue to undergo these experiences. This is a classical instance of an abhorrent craving in that it was entirely intolerable to him. The day before it had been a kind of new experience, but when it burst upon him in this way, it was attended by all sorts of revulsions and a feeling that it would be infrahuman, and what not, to have such interests. And he arrived at the hospital shortly afterward in what is called schizophrenic disturbance.

The eruption of abhorrent cravings may or may not precipitate immediately a change for the much worse, but in a good many cases fugues or the eruption of abhorrent cravings in the adolescent days soon precipitate a state which is so completely disorganizing that it may be called, with certain reservations, *panic*. I think it very rarely approximates the panic which occurs when something that one has utterly trusted collapses—the sort of mixture of terror and absolutely blindly disorganized inactivity, which one some-times hears of in theater fires, and so on. Panic does not lead to action; panic leads to nothing. One is disorganized. Terror usually follows panic, and terror very often includes blind frantic activities which can be very destructive to oneself or others. The panic that quite often is the outcome of fugue or the eruption of abhorrent cravings is a very brief complete disorganization. In this case, the most significant of the things which are disorganized is the struc-ture of one's beliefs and convictions as to the guarantees and securities and dependable properties of the universe in which one is living. And the far side of these panicky instances may be any-thing from terror to great religious exaltation. In any case, the personality is partly torn from its moorings and has moved from what was actually its developmental level into a state which we call the schizophrenic way of life.

In the schizophrenic state, very early types of referential process occur within clear awareness, to the profound mystification of the person concerned. And since many of these referential processes are literally historically identical with the composition of the not-me components in personality, their presence is attended by uncanny emotions, sometimes dreadfully strong. These referential processes seem so bizarre to people who have not had them that the schizophrenic way of life is often described as unpsychological and completely beyond understanding. The justification for such reckless language is that those schizophrenic processes which we encounter represent attempts on the sufferer's part to communicate types of processes that most of us ceased to have within clear awareness by the time that we were two-and-a-half. There is a possibility that a dissociated system which has broken cover in this way can only very briefly continue to be free from being greatly complicated by what remains of the security apparatus, the self-system; and this possibility completes the picture of why the schizophrenic illnesses give one a feeling of the utter futility of human thought to understand what is going on. If the eventu-alities of a fugue, or the eventualities of the eruption of abhorrent cravings, are followed by experience which is able to terminate the association of a major part of the particular motivational system with these uncanny emotions, and associate it with the main trends of personality development, then we would have achieved the integration of a previously dissociated motivational system with the rest of the personality; and there would then be none of this dreadful spectacle of the schizophrenic way of life, with its exceedingly ominous probable outcomes. People can actually suffer recurrent—and they can recur as frequently as several times an hour—waves of schizophrenic process, or seem actually to remain continuously in schizophrenic process for a matter of years, and quite suddenly effect a reintegration of personality, make a very quick recovery, and go on for the rest of their life with no major disturbances.

But a great many of the people who get involved in schizophrenic disturbance proceed through it to one of two very unfortunate outcomes. One we call the paranoid maladjustment, in which sundry elements of blame and guilt in the personality are attached to other people round about, with such disastrous effects on the possibility of intimacy and simple relation with anybody in the environment that there is no way back. In the other outcome, people literally disintegrate so much under the force of horror in this schizophrenic business that they become examples of something scarcely noticed in the developmental years—namely, relatively satisfactory preoccupation with the simple pleasures of the zones of interaction provoked by one's own manipulations, which seems to be about the essence of what we call the hebephrenic change, or the hebephrenic dilapidation of personality. These illnesses are not to be regarded, according to my light, as part of schizophrenia, but as very unfortunate outcomes of schizophrenic episodes; and they are not so successful but that for many, many years after these unfortunate outcomes have been instituted, episodes of schizophrenic processes may still occur. That is not always the case; some people make stable paranoid maladjustments which are singularly free from schizophrenic processes, which actually insure them from occasions where they will have schizophrenic processes. And I am sure that some people dilapidate in such a fashion that they are very little troubled by schizophrenic processes. But a great many of the people who have undergone these very unfortunate developments have not solved life to the point where they can be happy though psychotic.

CHAPTER 20

Sleep, Dreams, and Myths *

Sleep as Relief from Security Operations

IN DISCUSSING the comparatively neglected topic of sleep, dreams, myths, and the related disorders of living, I shall refer to sleep only briefly. It is a phase of living which is very important indeed, in that—aside from all the biological factors involved—it is the part of life in which we are almost by definition relieved from the necessity of maintaining security. In other words, while we are asleep, we have a comparative dearth of security operations, because the movement into the state of sleep in itself requires a situation more or less routinely known to be free from dangers to one's self-esteem. When anxiety is severe, sleep is practically impossible, although as one gets tired enough, the need for sleep becomes impossible to fight off; under those conditions, sleep is cut up into very brief periods of deep sleep and relatively long stages of very light sleep, which are hard to tell objectively from waking. In certain other situations, deep sleep tends to be an insidious incident in periods of such light sleep that the patient not uncommonly reports that he has not slept at all; although there does not seem to be any obvious danger to one's self-esteem or any very striking sources of anxiety in such situations, on deeper study it is found that something characterized by anxiety does exist in the realm of reverie processes, such as dealing with difficult people, or the like. I used to have a fairly critical feeling about patients who reported that they had had no sleep and were utterly exhausted,

* [*Editors' note:* The illustrative material from myths that Sullivan has used in this lecture has not been changed, although the stories are not in precise agreement with the legends and stories that we know: for instance, the published version of Mark Twain's *The Mysterious Stranger* has a different setting, characters, and events.]

when it was perfectly obvious, from the report of dispassionate observers, that they had slept a good part of the night; I thought that this was some type of substitutive operation which should be dealt with as such. But on one occasion when I was aroused regularly at brief intervals throughout the night, I discovered that the very expense of maintaining the processes of preparing myself for being aroused, and of trying to avoid all the processes thereunto pertaining that would tend to waste time in my getting back to sleep, amounted actually to my sleeping so superficially most of the time that I did not enjoy relief from security operations, relief from processes all too closely related to the stressful aspects of waking life. I began very rapidly then to understand why people who, during a night, have never fallen profoundly asleep nor stayed asleep as long as they needed to—though they may have slept, at intervals, a total of even five, six, or seven hours—are inclined to think that they haven't had any sleep at all, and, in fact, have certainly not derived any benefit from what they have had.

As I have said, the functional importance of sleep, from the psychiatric standpoint, is that there is a very great relaxation of security operations. As a result of this, many unsatisfied needs from the day, and unsatisfied components of the needs satisfied during the day—which cannot be satisfied in waking life because of the anxiety and security operations associated with them—are satisfied, insofar as may be, by covert operations, symbolic devices, which occur in sleep. This is difficult to demonstrate directly but is a fairly probable inference made on the basis of the state of people when they are denied sleep; in such a situation, a person's previous handling of unwelcome, disapproved motivations, and so on, deteriorates fairly rapidly, with serious impairment of his apparent mental health.

Although I have suggested that security operations are inconspicuous in sleep and that the sleep situation is actually defined by the possibility of relaxing self-system functions, I have not said that the self-system is absolutely relaxed, or that it has no effect whatever. Evidences of its actual state of functional activity are perhaps most vividly demonstrated in the relatively frequent occurrence of the onset of schizophrenia during sleep. Quite a number of people who are tense and extremely uncomfortable while awake, have a frightful nightmare, one night, which they cannot awake from, even though they objectively 'wake up'; and not very long after that such people become unquestionably schizophrenic throughout their apparent waking life. Now, that which awakens one from certain covert operations in sleep must be, clearly, a manifestation of the self-system. In other words, we maintain our dissociations, despite recurrent periods of sleep, by maintaining continued alertness, continued vigilance of the dissociative apparatus in the self-system. As a derivative of that, it may be said that the more of personality which exists in dissociation, the less restful and more troubled will be the person's sleep. Thus, depth of sleep is in a certain sense really a direct, simple function of the extent to which the activity of the self-system can be abandoned for a certain part of the twenty-four hours; and when powerful motivational systems are dissociated, it is impossible to abandon enough of the self-system function so that one can have deep and restful sleep.

The Significance of Dreams in Psychotherapy

I now want to present the comparatively direct evidence for my statement that sleep is a period of life during which covert operations deal with the unsatisfied needs which waking life does not take care of, although my evidence is pretty far from the kind obtained with a caliper or a measuring telescope in the natural sciences. The best evidence is in the shape of the reports of remembered dreams. I believe most of us will agree that we dream, and that we remember something of what we have dreamed on certain occasions. But what we can recall of dreaming is never any too adequate, unless the dream is very brief and marked by tremendous emotion. My point is that there is an impassable barrier between covert operations when one is asleep and covert operations and reports of them when one is awake. If the barrier is passable at all, it is only by the use of such techniques as hypnosis, which are so complex as to produce data no more reliable than the recalled dream, so that in essence the barrier *is* impassable. In other words, for the purposes of my theory, one never, under any circumstances, deals directly with dreams. It is simply impossible. What one deals with in psychiatry, and actually in a great many other aspects of life, are recollections pertaining to dreams; how closely, how adequately these recollections approximate the actual dreams is an insoluble problem, because as far as I know there is no way to develop a reasonable conviction of one-to-one correspondence between recollections of dreams and dreams themselves.

Many of us probably have had the experience of having a dream of the night before so much in mind that we just had to tell somebody what we recollected of it. This feeling of urgency about reporting and discussing a dream is the mark that these covert operations are of very material importance in keeping us going as social beings in human society. An important part of intensive psychotherapy consists in recognizing that if a patient, without encouragement, recalls something that has occurred in the sleep component of his current living and is impelled to report it, then that is a valid and important part of his relation with the psychiatrist. In intensive psychotherapy there need never be any question of what actually was dreamed; but the psychiatrist can have many reasonable questions about the completeness of the report and its communicative value. I have heard accounts of dreams which impressed me as definitely truncated, as very highly improbable accounts of what had happened. In many accounts of dreams there are areas that are as foggy and uncommunicative as are many of the statements of persons utilizing substitutive processes in reporting on their current living. At those points in a reported dream where the psychiatrist has a definite feeling of improbability or of unnecessary obscurity, there is no reason in the world why he should not make the same efforts to obtain completeness and to clear up obscurities as he would for an account of the patient's waking life. I do not mean by this that one person will be able to follow lucidly another person's dream; such an expectancy is at best a very pleasant delusion. But when a psychiatrist feels that he is hearing, in the report of a dream, an obscured account of living—perhaps so obscured that it is impossible to distinguish whether one of the critical figures in this account of living was a man or a woman, a wolf or a bear—I think that there is no reason against inquiry, and that there is much benefit to be derived from clarifying whether the dreamer really cannot make any discrimination between these relatively dissimilar possibilities. Establishing such a point is important, for such lack of discrimination is a valid, presumably important, part of a person's current living. The psychiatrist's merely accepting without question the unclarity of a person's report of a dream is very much like merely accepting the general unclarity of every obsessional neurotic—it means that the psychiatrist will never quite discover what is being discussed, but will just go on in a comparatively useful semisocial relationship.

In the intensive study of personality, the psychiatrist works with these curious survivals from the dream life, which is always cut off from the waking life. In most of the dreams that the patient feels more or less compelled to report, one frequently encounters massive evidences of security operations that have gone into action on awakening. Although the fragments of these dreams which are reported might be very helpful if they could be preserved in meaningful detail, they have quite insidiously and unwittingly been woven into great textures of dramatic action in which everything which met the real utility of the dream has been almost hopelessly confounded into what Freud called secondary elaborations. But these elaborations are actually interventions of the self-system which simply foredoom the possibility of using these reports meaningfully. Certain other dreams that the psychiatrist hears have as their most obvious characteristic the fact that they are rather simple statements of dramatic action; they are very vivid, very strongly colored, very succinct statements of something. In some of these simple statements which occur at the most critical times in a person's life, there is some strong feeling, although that feeling may be as vague as a mere feeling of urgency and importance connected with the dream. For instance, a person may come to his friend or his therapist, more or less preoccupied with the necessity of reporting the dream; but as he reports the dream, he is swept into the feeling of the dream, which may be terror or any of the uncanny emotions such as dread. That particular experience I have to mention, not because it is frequent, but because it is of such dangerous importance that it's very sad for a psychiatrist not to realize what a critical situation has suddenly shown up in his office.

In some particularly unfortunate people, we discover that from very early in life something has apparently been going terribly wrong in the part of their life which is partitioned to sleep—that is, they have night terrors. Night terrors sometimes show up in very early childhood—conceivably in very late infancy—and can continue, so far as I know, indefinitely, although with any increase in competence at being a person, night terror usually passes over into nightmares. The term, night terror, applies to the situation in which one awakens from some utterly unknown events in practically primordial terror; in this state, one is on the border of complete disintegration of personality—in other words, there are almost no evidences of any particular competence and one is almost disorganized, since one is actually in a state of panic. By the time the personality has pulled itself together to the point where anything like interpersonal relations could be manifested, the curtain has descended—that is, there has been a separation from consciousness of any trace of what was going on at the time of the primordial terror. Thus night terrors are empty in terms of any recollection of what they were about. Night terror is distinguished from nightmare by the fact that the content in night terror is more completely obliterated, since night terror appears very early when the process of becoming a person is terribly threatened. But nightmare—dreadful dreams, with recollectable content—represents a grave emergency in personality at a time when the personality is more competent to deal with it; that is, the personality can make use of interpersonal relations in a curious attempt to validate the nature of the threat, or to overcome the terrible isolation and loneliness connected with the threat.

Some of you will recall having had occasionally an extremely unpleasant dream which awakened you, but did not awaken you completely; in other words, it moved you from deep sleep to very light sleep. The evidence of your still being in light sleep is that while you have every feeling of being awake, and certainly have perfect freedom of voluntary motion—which is rather strikingly curtailed in anything like deep sleep—you cannot get what you know to be reality to behave. In this connection, I will mention fragments of two or three dreams which come to my mind. One was a dream which I had to undergo very early in my study of schizophrenia, in order to realize that I had some grave barriers to the task which the gods had brought me. To give some background on this dream, I should say that in my very early childhood it was discovered that I was so repelled by spiders that the body of a dead spider put at the top of the stairs would discourage my ambulatory efforts, which had previously often resulted in my falling downstairs. Now, of course, if one considers that the spider is a mother symbol, and that this occurred around the age of two-and-a-half to four, one can picture what profound problems I had in repressing my hostility to the mother, or something of the sort. But I prefer to say, simply, that I didn't like spiders, and I disliked them so much that I wouldn't pass one. As the years rolled by, I never got fond of spiders. I haven't very much objection to most living things, but I have never appreciated spiders and other predatory creatures of that kind, and I fear I never shall. I had the following dream at the time when it became possible, finally, for me really to start on an intensive study of schizophrenia, partly by my own efforts and largely by accident; and I had decided on this study and all the arrangements were satisfactory. You all recall the geometric designs that spiders weave on grass, and that show up in the country when the dew's on the ground. My dream started with a great series of these beautiful geometric patterns, each strand being very nicely midway between the one in front of it and the one behind it, and so on—quite a remarkable textile, and incidentally I am noticeably interested in textiles. Then the textile pattern became a tunnel reaching backward after the fashion of the tunnel-web spiders, and then the spider began to approach. And as the spider approached, it grew and grew into truly stupendous and utterly horrendous proportions. And I awakened extremely shaken and was unable to obliterate the spider, which continued to be a dark spot on the sheet which I knew perfectly well would re-expand into the spider if I tried to go to sleep. So instead, I got up and smoked a cigarette and looked out the window and one thing and another, and came back and inspected the sheet, and the spot was gone. So I concluded that it was safe to go back to bed. Now, I'm not going to tell you all about what that meant, because only God knows what I dreamed; I've just told you what I recalled. I'm trying to stress the hang-over, the utter intrusion into sensory perception, which required the shaking off of the last vestige of sleep process, the definite reassertion of me and mine, Washington, and what not, in order to prevent the thing from going on. Fortunately, with some assistance, I guessed what might be the case, and thus escaped certain handicaps for the study of schizophrenia. I might add that spiders thereupon disappeared forever from my sleep—so far as I know.

To go on to another dream: At one time I had a really marvelous assistant—one of those people without any particular formal education whose gifts and life experience had produced the sort of person who automatically reassured terrified people. He possessed no suitable hooks that panicky young schizophrenics could use to hang their terror on, and he reflected in many other ways the naturally estimable personality structure that would be required for dealing with schizophrenics. In those days there was a great deal I didn't know about the risks attendant on dealing with human personality, and this young man rapidly became not only my left hand, but, I suppose, most of my left upper extremity. After the pattern of the-good-if-they-do-not-die-young, he became of great interest to a bitterly paranoid woman. Thanks to the eternal vigilance which we do preserve, however blindly, he was worried about this relationship, and talked to me about it. And I talked to him and talked to her, and counseled delay, because she seemed to be suffering frightfully from his very casual heterosexual life away from her, and I thought that such worries would grow if they were legitimatized, and so on. And also I didn't want him upset—he was too valuable. Whereupon he dreamed a dream. Some of you may have been in the environment of Baltimore and have seen Loch Raven. Loch Raven is one of those monolithic concrete dams which produce very beautiful artificial lakes behind them. And this monolithic dam is quite impressive—very high, with a wide sluiceway. This dream is set at the foot of the Loch Raven dam. There is an island, very small, very green—a lovely island—not far from the shore, on which this assistant of mine and I are walking, engaged in conversation. He gazes up at the dam and sees his fiancée at the top of it, and is not particularly distracted in his conversation with me. Then he observes that the area of water between the island and the shore, over which we had stepped, is rapidly widening. He awakens in terror, finding himself leaping out of bed into a pool of moonlight in the bedroom.[1]

The two illustrations I've given—and studiously refrained from interpreting—show how a good deal of waking activity—that is, activity we ordinarily associate with being awake—can actually carry into it surviving referential processes from the period of sleep, and that these processes take precedence over the capacity to actually perceive reality. Thus when a psychiatrist hears a patient report a dream and the patient is thoroughly undone by the reappearance of the uncanny emotion or the terror associated with the dream, the psychiatrist has to assume that he is seeing in this very situation grave peril to the maintenance of full awareness while one is nominally awake; in other words, the psychiatrist is literally seeing a mild schizophrenic episode right there in the office. In the same way, any of us who have difficulties in asserting our knowledge of reality on awakening from certain types of unpleasant dreams are, at least for a few minutes, living in a world completely of a piece with the world in which schizophrenics live for hours. In the practice of psychiatry, it is really up to the psychiatrist to observe the imminence of any such very serious upheaval of personality, and then to do something besides listening and preparing to hear free association in pursuit of the latent content. It is not possible here to do more than suggest what should be done in this kind of situation. But I will say that when the patient's anxiety is becoming, in the reporting of a dream, utterly unmanageable and very dangerous for the continuity of useful work, the psychiatrist should intervene. Intervention in this situation is but a special instance of intervention whenever the patient experiences such anxiety. Thus the psychiatrist should treat reported dreams, I believe, in the same way that he treats everything else that seems to be extremely significant: the psychiatrist reflects back to the person what has seemed to him to be the significant

---

[1] One might compare here somnambulistic performances in which people have complete freedom of locomotion—that is, complete control of their skeletal musculature and so on—but cannot discover what they were doing when they crawled around in their sleep, are completely cut off, in the act of being awakened, from whatever was going on, and, in fact, sometimes go back to bed with only accidental observers knowing anything about it.

statement, stripped of all the little personal details, confusions, and obscurities which often protect significant statements, and then sees if it provokes any thought in the mind of the patient.

To give an example: An obsessional neurotic, who is reporting on a highly significant difficulty he is having in living, will usually tell the psychiatrist different instances of much the same thing for perhaps six weeks. The instances gradually become somewhat clearer to the psychiatrist—that is, he can finally guess what the devil's really being reported. He can't possibly do it the first time because the patient deletes, through security operations, everything that would improve the psychiatrist's grasp on the subject. The patient has not lied; but he has neglected to report anything that would be highly provocative of the psychiatrist's grasping what's being reported. After the psychiatrist has delimited the area of the patient's careful deletions so that he can finally catch on to what's probably being reported, he can then say, "Well, is it that you are telling me that you did so-and-so and the other person did so-and-so?" Whereupon, with considerable anxiety the patient says, "Yes," and the psychiatrist has something to work on. I believe that it's the same with the dream, except that it doesn't take so long. The psychiatrist clears up as much as he can of what is irrelevant and obscuring in the reported dream, presents what he seems to hear in terms of a dramatic picture of some important problem of the patient's, and then propounds the riddle: "What does that bring to mind?" And if the psychiatrist has been good at it, it often brings something very significant from the patient.

For example, for many, many months in working with a schizoid obsessional patient, I heard data of how vaguely annoying and depressing his mother had been for several years past. His father was a hellion, to put it mildly, and we didn't have so much difficulty understanding what father did. But about all mother did was somehow to depress and annoy him, discourage him vaguely. Now this patient dreamed of a Dutch windmill. It was a very beautiful scene, with a carefully cared-for lawn leading up to the horizon on which this beautiful Dutch windmill revolved in the breeze. Suddenly he was within the windmill. And there everything was wrack and ruin, with rust inches deep; it was perfectly obvious that the windmill hadn't moved in years. And when the patient had finished reporting his dream, I was able to pick out the significant details successfully—one of those occasional fortunate instances. I said, "That is, beautiful, active on the outside—utterly dead and decayed within. Does it provoke anything?" He said, "My God, my mother." That was his trouble, you see. The mother had become a sort of zombi—unutterably crushed by the burdens that had been imposed on her. She was simply a sort of weary phonograph offering cultural platitudes, without any thought of what they did to anybody or what they meant. Though she was still showing signs of life, everything had died within. We made fairly rapid progress in getting some lucidity about the mother. You will note that I have not discussed the latent content of the dream; but in psychotherapy, as I've come to consider it, one is occupied chiefly in benefiting the patient.

Myths: Dreams That Satisfy the Needs of Many

The types of operations which are recalled, however imperfectly, from sleep are not limited in importance to the purpose they serve in the life pattern of the person who reports them. Some of them not only seem to serve some purpose for the person who had the dream, but come so near to dealing with general problems that they become incorporated into the culture as myths. And to understand the higher level of referential processes which we have named parataxic, there is perhaps no better approach than the study of highly significant dreams and myths which have held considerable force over perhaps centuries, certainly over the stretch of culture eras. And so I am going to mention a few of these myths. I would like to remind you that you will find very little here that is simply and directly explicit statement of fact, since I am now dealing with material that is inferential about parataxic processes in living.

The oldest myth that comes to my mind in this connection is that of Balaam and his ass. Quite recently I came in contact with this survival from the prehistory of the Western culture—that is, the Jewish culture—and I had an experience with it which is perhaps worth taking a little time on. During his long fatal illness, my beloved friend Sapir was reading the Bible in Aramaic and he encountered the myth of Balaam and his ass. He recounted it to me, and it annoyed me, and I made some unpleasant comment as I very often do when I am annoyed. The myth is something like this: Balaam was a very fine character indeed, one of the outstanding merchants and benefactors in a city which was under attack from certain 'barbarians' over the mountains. The city didn't seem to get very far with the 'barbarians,' and so finally Balaam was sent as an emissary—Balaam himself. And he mounted his ass and fared forth toward the mountains. And at a certain point the ass balked, and Balaam spoke gently to the ass, but the ass continued to balk. And so he beat the ass. And then the ass spoke—and this is the sort of thing that annoys me in dreams or myths—and said to Balaam, "Balaam, Balaam, why beatest thou me? Have I not always been thy faithful servant, responsive to your slightest request, patient under your increasing weight, and one thing and another?" Balaam was ashamed because of what the ass presented to him; and as he felt this shame, the scales fell from his eyes and he discovered an angel with a sword standing in the path in front of him, which accounted for the ass's balking. And, as I say, this myth annoyed me; but while I was waiting for a bus later that evening, it occurred to me that way back in this shadowy period some Jewish scholar had presented one of his dreams in this shape, and that it was a very simple statement of the relationship between our proud self-consciousness and our contact with life as a going concern. Balaam and his ass might well be human personality, and only the proud self-respect-pursuing part of personality would overlook the imminent danger—the whole personality would not. The psychiatrist finds unnumbered instances in his work in which people cling, with a certain tense franticness, to certain idealizations of life which get them into a great deal of trouble; but the intensity with which they cling indicates that the ass—the deeper, older part of personality—knows the thing isn't true, knows it isn't so. For the psychiatrist to be taken in by the intensity with which these ideals are presented is merely to fit into the chronic illness of the patient. If the psychiatrist observes the peculiar path in life which the patient is taking—in that the patient gives lip-service and a frantic amount of conscious attention to the ideal, and carefully vitiates it through other interpersonal performances —the psychiatrist will often discover that the patient is living by standards which were inculcated in childhood but which he knows from other experiences are not valid. But since the patient can't formulate what he knows, he goes on in the same old way.

I would like to refer only briefly to the subject of personal myths; many of us have such myths which we can be led to tell when we are tight enough or feeling friendly enough. For example, I sometimes tell the myth of the Stack family, which interests at least me.[2]

I shall now mention a myth which was borrowed from Northwestern European culture by the great musical genius, Wagner, and woven into the "Nibelung Ring"; the myth is of course the Rheingold. The Rheingold represented transcendental power that could be utilized by man. It was protected rather carefully by various beings from falling into the hands of any man, because the Rheingold when seized conferred such terrible powers on its stealers. Moreover, it should be noted that seizing the Rheingold brought doom, the doom being foretold by the weary earth-goddess, Erda. This myth illustrates a practically universal feeling, in all times and among all people, that to seize transcendental power may well be evil.

I am reminded of a story which is very much closer to us than the origins of Balaam and his ass or the Nibelung saga. It is Mark Twain's *The Mysterious Stranger*. After he had finished writing the story, he was moved to suppress it, stipulating that it not be published till after his death. I believe the scene is laid in a very beautiful Swiss village where everybody has known each other for generations. There was almost no evil in this community. Among the estimable young was a fine young boy greatly cherished in the community and with many friends. And this little country hero was out walking, basking in the natural beauties one morning, when he met another very lovely young man—a stranger. This

[2] [*Editors' note:* Sullivan has made scattered references to the legend of his mother's family throughout his published and unpublished writings. In one footnote, he says, for instance: ". . . consider an only surviving child of a proudly professional maternal family not yet recovered from the reduction in status that attended on grandfather's emigration—among the mythological ancestors of which is the West Wind, the horse who runs with the Earth into the future. . . ." "Towards a Psychiatry of Peoples," *Psychiatry* (1948) 11: p. 109.]

stranger seemed to be quite as attractive as our hero, who was a paragon of Swiss virtues. Our hero asked him his name, and he said, "My name is Satan." That startled our hero, so he said, "Well, not the Satan that—" "Oh, no, no, a remote relative, perhaps a second cousin." Well, Satan was taken to the bosom of the youthful community. He excelled in all sports, but also in appropriate humility, and the rest; in fact, he was an enormous addition to the community. Both young and old admired him.

One day, one of the other boys got caught in a whirlpool in one of the mountain rivers, and it was impossible to rescue him. Our hero, who was standing on the bank with Satan and suffering with the impending disaster, said aloud, "I would give almost anything to save John." And Satan said, "What!" And our hero said, "Yes, yes, I'd do anything to save him." And Satan said, "You wish to save him?" And our hero did. The stream suddenly dried up. The boy, of course, walked ashore. Then the account goes on for some time, during which, by a terrible inevitability, the rescued boy comes to a dreadful end, which wrings the heart of everyone ever so much more than would have his sudden death in the whirlpool. But two or three times more, our hero in the midst of his anxiety, terror, and grief over impending disaster expressed his mental state in such a way that Satan, this accommodating new friend, could realize what he wished. Each time Satan was astounded, but each time Satan intervened; and always dreadful, horrible, unutterable consequences flowed from this intervention of human wishes, not through Satan's action, just through the tedious interrelation of events. That myth, as written by Mark Twain, has passed into a certain decline; perhaps it is not hard to guess why. For there is a great distinction between what this myth says of life and of the evils of transcendental power at the disposal of man, and that which is said in the Nibelung myth of the Rheingold and in many other myths to be found in the lore of peoples.

Let me say in brief that both the myth and the dream represent a relatively valid parataxic operation for the relief of insoluble problems of living. In the myth, the problems concern many people, and it is this fact which keeps the myth going and refines and polishes it as the generations roll it around. The dream has that function for a person in an immediate situation; but insofar as he remembers it and communicates it, he is seeking validation with someone else. The schizophrenic illness, the living by the schizophrenic way, is the situation into which one falls when, for a variety of reasons, the intense handicaps of living are so great that they must be dealt with during a large part of one's waking life in this same dream-myth sort of way. Insofar as schizophrenic content, reported dreams, or personal myth are stripped of some decoration in the telling and thus undergo to some extent the general process of consensual validation, the dreamer, the schizophrenic, or the myth-maker has some awareness of aspects of his life problems that have hitherto been utterly prohibited from such awareness by security operation. In these terms, such content can be dealt with in therapy; but to deal with it on the basis that one can convert dreams or myths into consensually valid statements by intellectual operations seems to me such a misunderstanding—such a complete missing of the point of how we got along before we had consensually valid formulae—that I don't know how one can take it seriously. People who feel that they should analyze either a dream or schizophrenic content into what it stands for, seem to me to be in exactly the state of mind of the person who says to a child of two-and-a-half, "You ought to show more respect for your mother because God on Mount Sinai said to Moses, 'Honor thy father and thy mother.'" There are limits to what is practical and practicable. I do believe that the reporting of dreams can be very significant in intensive psychotherapy as long as the patient is not encouraged to waste time by whatever he can build up about his night life; but the importance of dreams lies in that which they obscurely deal with, which the psychiatrist may or may not be able to elicit. Obsessional ideas and schizophrenic content, and so on, are important in the same way, although the less troubled an obsessional is, the less important the content. In all these cases, the psychiatrist is dealing with the type of referential operation which is *not* in the syntaxic mode, and one merely stultifies himself, to my way of thinking, by trying to make this kind of report syntaxic. The fact that it is not syntaxic in no sense alters its validity and importance for the work.

CHAPTER
21

The Later Manifestations of Mental Disorder: Matters Paranoid and Paranoiac *

As I have already noted, failure to achieve late adolescence is the last blow to a great many warped, inadequately developed personalities with low self-esteem. And the usual solution in chronological maturity is to cover over one's chronic defect in self-esteem by disparaging others—a solution which is used by all of us in varying degrees.

Tributary Developmental Difficulties

In childhood, the deviations begin which, unless modified in the subsequent developmental eras, may result in disastrous mental disorder in later life. With the beginning of the emphasis on cooperation, the child undergoes the experience of fear when he does not live up to the required behavior, and the complex anxiety derivatives of shame and guilt are inculcated. Thus the child is presumed to deserve or require punishment at times, and this punishment takes the form of the infliction of pain, which may be accompanied by anxiety. As a result, the child often has to make

* [*Editors' note:* Through p. 348 of this chapter, we have had to rely largely on the Notebook, since no recording of the lecture itself was made. In order to provide the continuity of Sullivan's thinking, we have put into sentence form the topical outline given in his Notebook and expanded this on the basis of related material given elsewhere in this book. Beginning with the section on the Wish-Fulfilling Fantasy, the chapter is from a recorded lecture.]

complex discriminations of authority situations, so that the ability to conceal things from the authoritative figures and to deceive them becomes a necessity which is implemented by the authority-carrying figures themselves. As a part of this comes the development of precautionary techniques and propitiatory activities such as verbal 'excusing,' often with the evolution of techniques for the maintenance of 'social distance.'

A great many children learn that anger will aggravate the situation and they develop instead *resentment;* and resentment has very important covert aspects. Sometimes even the resentment has to be concealed in childhood, and this gradually results in a self-system process which precludes one's knowing his resentment. Again, I have commented on the fact that the manifesting of the need for tenderness toward the significant people around one often leads to one's being disadvantaged, made anxious, made fun of, and so on. And in this way the groundwork is laid for the malevolent attitude toward life in general, in which other people are viewed as enemies, which is the greatest disaster that happens in childhood, in that it may represent a great handicap for profitable experience in the subsequent stages of development.

In the juvenile era, the need for compeers brings about the threat of ostracism. There is a difference in background, abilities, in speed of maturation, and so on, which helps to set up the in-groups and the out-groups. And under this segregating influence, a great many juveniles feel ostracized and suffer a loss of self-esteem. Most people have had in the juvenile period an exceedingly bitter experience with their compeers to which the term "fear of ostracism" might be justifiably applied—the fear of being accepted by no one of those whom one must have as models for learning how to be human. In this era also there is the learning of disparagement, with the possibility for chronic defect in one's self-esteem. This disparagement has its beginning for the most part in influence exerted by the parental group, who teach the juvenile to notice the shortcomings of others. And this necessity of maintaining self-esteem by pulling down the standing of others, if uncorrected in subsequent developmental eras, has unfortunate later outcomes. In the juvenile era this kind of security operation literally and importantly interferes with adequate appraisal of personal worth. Since one has to protect his feeling of self-esteem by noting how unworthy everybody else is, this fails to provide any convincing data on one's having personal worth; one begins to think, "I am not as bad as the other swine."

But one hates one's 'weaknesses'—one's feeling of shame and guilt, one's loneliness—particularly if one believes in the doctrine of the transcendental will. It is clear that a very great number of people suffer from the illusion of voluntary choice and its attendant consequences of transcendentally conditioned guilt and self-blame; and the transcendental element is the supernatural character of the will, whether it is recognized as such or not.

Security Operations for Maintaining Selective Inattention

In some instances, these difficulties, as I have already noted, are remedied at the thresholds of the subsequent developmental eras. But sometimes there is failure to profit from experience. Even though there may be many actual opportunities, various security operations interfere with observation and analysis, and thus prevent the profit one might gain from experience.

We have already discussed the tedious miracle of selective inattention, which is, more than any other of the inappropriate and inadequate performances of life, the classic means by which we do not profit from experience which falls within the areas of our particular handicap. Since the identification of areas of selective inattention is an important part of the therapeutic intervention, I would like now to set up certain gross classifications of security operations which help to maintain selective inattention and which have their beginnings in childhood. For the areas of selective inattention are, like Balaam's ass, actually fields of experience. And these difficulties in living, as I have already mentioned, begin in childhood.

The first security operation for the maintenance of selective inattention is found in the dramatizations of roles which a person *knows to be false*. In other words, these spurious subpersonalities are more or less clearly assumed. Such a person adopts patterns of behaving *as if* he were someone else, although he privately knows he is not. Even though this often overtaxes his abilities, he must ignore his errors, lest he 'give himself away' completely.

Second, a person may use parataxic me-you patterns [1] which are incongruous with the actual interpersonal situation; and in this instance he has no clear realization of the multiple "personalities" involved and of the instability of his behavior. In this connection, we shall presently consider the esteemed psychiatric term "projection."

Third, a person may use substitutive processes running the gamut from 'deliberately' talking about something else, in the sense of changing the subject; through unwitting shifts of 'communicative set,' which can be very subtle (this has possible bearing on states called "excitement," in which people show extreme distractibility, staying on no particular topic for any length of time); to the utmost absorption in intense preoccupation with covert processes. The wish-fulfilling fantasy, which I shall presently discuss, is an example of the last of these substitutive processes. Preoccupation with covert processes may be with or without behavior which is, or borders on being, wholly inexplicable. But when the intense absorption spills over into speech, the speech is clearly uncommunicative. To illustrate these substitutive processes, I shall presently discuss hypochondriacal preoccupations and self-pity.

And, finally, there are transient or enduring "transformations of personality"—and remember that personality is here defined as the *relatively* enduring pattern of one's characteristic interpersonal relations. We have already discussed the malevolent transformation in childhood, in which one acts unpleasantly when one needs tenderness. We have also touched on the more transient transformation under the topic of fugue. We shall have more to say on transformation of personality with respect to the massive transfer of blame, or *paranoid transformation*.

Jealousy and Envy

Before going further, let me discriminate my meaning of the terms, jealousy and envy, which are often tossed around as synonyms. There is a fundamental difference in the felt components of

[1] [*Editors' note:* For a discussion of "me-you" patterns, see Patrick Mullahy, "A Theory of Interpersonal Relations and the Evolution of Personality," in *Conceptions of Modern Psychiatry*.]

envy and jealousy; and there is also a fundamental difference in the interpersonal situation in which these processes occur, for envy occurs in a two-group, with perhaps a subsidiary two-group made up of the person suffering envy and his auditor, while jealousy always appears in a relationship involving a group of three or more. I define envy, which is more widespread in our social organization than jealousy, as pertaining to personal attachments or attributes. It is a substitutive activity in which one contemplates the unfortunate results of someone else's having something that one does not have. And envy does not cease to be envy when it passes from objects to attributes of another human being, for envy may be an active realization that one is not good enough, compared with someone else. Although it involves primarily a two-group situation, one of the two may be a more-or-less mythological person.

Jealousy, on the other hand, never concerns a two-group situation. It is invariably a very complex, painful process involving a group of three or more persons, one or more of whom may be absolutely fantasied. Jealousy is much more poignant and devastating than envy; in contrast with envy, it does not concern itself with an attribute or an attachment, but, rather, involves a great complex field of interpersonal relations. While data are hard to get, apparently jealousy occurs frequently in adolescence, and frequently with real or fancied lustful involvement with someone else. In such cases, the jealous person has a deep conviction of his own inadequacy and unworthiness in participation in lustful involvement, along with the conviction that his partner and the third person could do much better.

Jealousy in malevolent situations often assumes delusional proportions, in which the person tends more or less insidiously to become inaccessible to remedial experience by being secretive and, later, by supplementary processes which make any factual data ineffective. Jealousy becomes properly termed paranoid when the sufferer "sees" that the second person in the threesome—the link—is doing things to make him jealous out of pure malice.

The "Wish-Fulfilling Fantasy"

I would like now to discuss the expression, "wish-fulfilling fantasy," which is, I suppose, still very fashionable. Now, there are, unquestionably, quite witting covert processes which go on in human beings, and there are, undoubtedly, many circumstances in which one, over a long period of time, derives some satisfaction, or freedom from severe anxiety, as a result of these witting covert processes. This is entirely in contradistinction to the type of process that goes on in sleep, or goes on in those waking states of abstraction when one doesn't know what one is thinking of —states to which such terms as "brown study" have been applied. In certain instances, these prolonged witting covert processes, or reverie processes, represent, beyond any shadow of doubt, a partial satisfaction of needs. And among these, the simplest of all are of a compensatory character, with awareness, ranging from vague to clear, of the felt need which is being satisfied by the reverie process. But these quite witting processes include some components which are less witting. Let us say, for example, that after having been rebuffed by a very charming woman met at a cocktail party, one sits at home having a drink later that evening, entertaining a fantasy that is quite the contrary of rebuff by this same charming woman. Even in a reverie of such a simple compensatory character, there are apt to be, in the actual content of the reverie processes, evidences of processes which are *not* simply the need which the fantasy principally satisfies. Furthermore, in a good many so-called wish-fulfilling fantasies, the principal motivating force is not primarily the satisfaction of a need, but is something pertaining to security, or freedom from anxiety. All of you have experienced classical instances of this. For example, let us say that somebody at a party makes a bright and perhaps disconcerting remark to you; later, while you are driving home, you think up the perfect response; this response, unhappily, has to be discharged in your reverie process since it comes after the situation has passed into history. Thus a great many of these so-called conscious reverie processes exist for the discharge of hostility and other disjunctive motivation, and for the relief of anxiety. And not at all infrequently, in the more unhappy type of person, a great deal of the so-called wish-fulfilling fantasy is actually of a very complex compensatory character, arising in various ways from chronic low self-esteem and self-blame.

When reverie processes of this 'witting-fantasy' sort are reported to the psychiatrist, he should carefully study them in order to determine to what extent they are 'mere' partial satisfactions, and to what extent they include elements of foreseeing—in other words, to what extent they are prospective reverie, tending to improve what one does in the next similar situation. Furthermore, the psychiatrist should determine what elements in the reverie are not really understood by the person who has the reverie, and the extent to which these elements reflect aspects of personality of which the patient is relatively unaware.[2]

Customarily Low Self-Esteem

I now want to touch upon a phenomenon that is described rather widely in the psychiatric literature and in the conversation of psychiatrists as "feelings of inferiority." I believe that this phenomenon can better be described as the experience of customarily low self-esteem—that is, the person's personification of himself is not very estimable by comparison with his personifications of significant other people. By low self-esteem, I do not mean accurate self-esteem in a person who has, indeed, had very few opportunities, or perhaps has limited abilities; low self-esteem is the outcome of certain unfortunate experiences. Now if one customarily entertains a low opinion of oneself, a great handicap is imposed on the manifestation of what I call *conjunctive motivations*. By this

[2] Thus the psychiatrist should think twice before too glibly dismissing something reported by the patient as "mere wish-fulfilling fantasy." For it is practically impossible for one to be entirely free from intervention of the self-system—even though one is just entertaining himself with daydreams. The element of partial satisfaction of genuine needs, the element of self-system function—the minimizing or avoiding of anxiety—the actual discharge of hostile disjunctive impulses which are in part anxiety, and the very complex processes necessary for the maintaining of dissociation—all these may be fairly easily discoverable in the structure of fantasies. Yet the psychiatrist often acts as if fantasies were some minor misdemeanor of the patient, or discusses them with colleagues as if they were silly little evidences of immaturity. Sometimes one of these fantasies is actually a manifestation of foresight—an analysis and planning of situations and study of possibilities in case similar situations appear in the future. In such cases it is particularly bad for the psychiatrist to practically denounce the fantasy to the patient as an instance of something not quite respectable. Thus I believe that talking with patients and colleagues about "wish-fulfilling fantasy" is misleading rather than helpful, and actually tends to limit the clarity of the psychiatrist's own thought.

term I refer to those impulses which integrate situations in which needs can be satisfied and security enhanced. The great classic example of conjunctive motivation is love, which, however rare in itself, has its great root tendencies in the many impulses which make up the need for intimacy. But customarily low self-esteem makes it difficult indeed for the carrier person to manifest conjunctive motivation—to find himself comfortably able to manifest good feeling toward another person.

People who have customarily low self-esteem may minimize their anxiety by concealments and social isolation, may channel their anxiety and disjunctive motivations in interpersonal relations by exploitative attitudes and substitutive processes, or may manifest them in dissociative processes.

Concealments and Social Isolation

Many of the people who have this customarily low self-esteem minimize their anxiety by the use of sundry concealments, one extreme of which is *actual* social isolation. In any event, there is usually some degree of social isolation, for these people are unapproachable excepting on certain bases stipulated by them. Perhaps the crudest instance of this is found in the person who conceals by elaborate fictions which have become practically true—that is, the person who uses them has become so accustomed to them and so skillful in their indication or expression that he scarcely doubts them himself. As a general rule, then, a person with customarily low self-esteem has some form or degree of social isolation—that is, some degree of limitations or stipulations on his contact with others.

Exploitative Attitudes

Another aspect of these people with customarily low self-esteem is that anxiety and other disjunctive motivations—many of which, such as hatred, are derivatives of anxiety—tend to be channeled, in interpersonal relations, in a number of ways that are not perfectly obvious. Since conjunctive—that is, tender, friendly—relations with significant others are very difficult for these people, many of them have a *direct exploitative attitude*, to which psychiatric slang has attached the term "passive dependency." Here again, instead of merely making ourselves comfortable by using the words, let us try to think what it would feel like to *live* such a thing. What happens is that a person who has a low opinion of himself develops a relatively suave way of manifesting, if not inferiority to significant people, at least such blatant hints of inferiority that he becomes more or less an object of philanthropic concern on the part of the other person. This represents the development of considerable skill in interpersonal relations—sometimes remarkable skill—although the actual motivation concerned in these interpersonal relations is all relatively unfriendly. Now, since people with chronically low self-esteem are involved in these situations, the situations are apt to be somewhat unpleasant and complex for the other people involved—particularly if the other people are prone to find themselves in relationships in which domineering and vassalizing their fellows is their source of security. Under those circumstances, the passive-dependent people fall very readily into the orbit of these others, and all concerned do a great deal for one another without any particular satisfaction.

More puzzling for the psychiatrist is the *indirect exploitative attitude* for channeling disjunctive motivations, in which this almost explicit admission of inferiority does not appear. Instead, there is a sort of continuous offer that one can be found to be dependent. It suggests to me the expression "come-on"; one offers, but one does not quite deliver. One cannot bear to be regarded as dependent—and this is the reason for the indirection; a person has to have some complications in the business to save what self-esteem he has. In this connection a theory of personality and interpersonal relations has appeared, in the literature of the recent past, that is built up, in striking part, on the notion of masochism; I don't now keep up with all competing theories, so this one may have been laid away in its grave—I would hope so. I think there's probably nothing in the notion of masochism except foggy thinking. Masochism was, I believe, brought over the horizon of psychiatric thought in intimate companionship with another notion, called sadism. And in those estimable days, it was all very simple: People who liked to be hurt, as well as to be engaged in lustful sports, were masochists; and those who liked to hurt the partner, as well as engage in lustful sports, were sadists. But after the habit of a fungus the thing grew and got all sorts of places. And masochism has finally, I think, been attenuated to such a point that if a person keeps quiet while somebody else is talking, it could be called the manifestation of a masochistic tendency. In any event, there is a large number of people who appear to go to rather extraordinary lengths to get themselves imposed on, abused, humiliated, and what not; but as you get further data, you discover that this quite often pays—in other words, they get things they want. And the things that everybody wants are satisfaction and security from anxiety. Thus these people who get themselves abused and so on are indirectly getting the other people involved in doing something useful in exchange.

Another aspect of the indirect exploitative attitude might be termed "preying on sympathy." Actually this way of channeling disjunctive motivation approaches the substitutive activities, which I shall discuss next, and may indeed often be confused with them. Preying on sympathy, as an indirect exploitative attitude, is manifested in a development of interpersonal technique by which, no matter whether the person has done something rather exceptional or has made a very dreary flop, he has to get some audience to feel sorry that he was laboring under such handicaps. This group includes people who after having said, "Good morning," begin to rattle off a long list of current minor disasters and worries that have crushed their spirits completely, simply in the expectation that you will show sympathetic understanding of their woe—whereupon they look for the next person. This is, I suppose, indirect exploitation at its most highly symbolic level; it doesn't seem to be much of anything else. Of course, this preying on sympathy can also serve the much more practical purposes of tying your hands so that you can't criticize the person for something that is really detrimental to you and your interests; and there the indirect exploitative attitude is quite clear.

Substitutive Processes

But it is not always meaningful, in thinking of interpersonal difficulties, to describe such behavior as "preying on sympathy." For instance, it may not be self-evident whether the behavior has anything indirectly exploitative in it or whether it is a part of this vast body of complex performances which we call substitute activity; it is particularly difficult to make this distinction in dealing with a stranger. Substitute activity, in contrast to indirect exploitative attitudes, is not addressed primarily to an audience; instead it is addressed primarily to avoiding certain conscious clarity about one's own situation, one's own motivations, and so on. When this is the case, the apparent "preying on sympathy" actually touches more upon a preoccupation which, for want of a better term, I shall call "self-pity." And this preoccupation is actually in the realm of substitutive processes. It is important to distinguish between two kinds of self-pity in trying to clarify one's thoughts about what sort of problem one has on one's hands. It may be a massive preoccupation—an extraordinary facility at filling up time, in reverie or in conversation, with long series of thoughts which wind up with the speaker practically in tears about how wretchedly he is treated by fate. Or it may be a concomitant of only certain situations in a relatively limited field. People with massive preoccupation—and this is one of the fields of my greatest defeats in therapy—meet almost all interpersonal situations in which they feel inferior to the other person by looking for anything that can be utilized in building up one of these long trains of covert or conversational processes which serve to show what a woebegone and very unhappily used person the speaker is. But in the second group, although the preoccupation is substitutive in the sense that it obliterates something costly to self-esteem, the preoccupation is in a particular context, and does not represent a very unhappy way of life. For example, I sometimes say and feel very deeply that my lectures have not gone very well or been very clear because I was too tired. In any event, preoccupations with one's misfortune which represent pure substitution for something much more disturbing are legion. But it is the psychiatrist's job, when such a preoccupation comes along, to discriminate whether it is exploitative or substitutive—to figure out, to put it crudely, whether he is being put on the spot to do something for the other person, or whether this is a process by which the other person is keeping off the spot with himself. In other words, the substitutive processes are primarily addressed to minimizing or avoiding anxiety, whereas the more exploitative techniques are ways of getting what one wants but feels one could not get on one's face value.

This element of self-pity is within calling distance of a group of substitutive activities which I have already mentioned—that enormously popular business of entertaining envy. Envy perhaps is in no sense self-pity, but certainly it is substitutive activity. It is called out in all sorts and kinds of situations where the person with customarily low self-esteem is disturbed. And it saves one from invidious comparisons which would be anything but uplifting to one's self-regard.

Now, beyond these preoccupations I have mentioned, there are the hypochondriacal preoccupations, a field of substitutive activities which ordinarily channel the anxiety and other unfriendly or disjunctive motivations that are more or less characteristic of people who have chronically low self-esteem—although sometimes they can serve even conjunctive impulses. Hypochondriacal preoccupations, which is the traditional term for great preoccupation with one's health or with the operation of certain parts of one's somatic apparatus, are not devices for preying on sympathy; curiously enough, there are some people who show hypochondriacal preoccupations only in the face of the other person's strong friendly motivation. These preoccupations are a very special group of substitute activities which are to be understood on the basis of one's personifying oneself as customarily handicapped. They are not to be understood as preoccupation with one's health in the sense of always wondering if one might catch a cold, or something of that kind; they are much more specific. For example, I know a very distinguished man who travels a great deal, always equipped with a fair-sized suitcase containing drugs enough to put a country general practitioner to shame in terms of preparation for any form of illness that man might fall heir to. While I am, needless to say, being extravagant, it sometimes seems to me that my friend carries preparations for practically any eventuality from smallpox to pregnancy; and among them he carries treatments for a large series of weaknesses, illnesses, and disabilities which he *has*. He's a very efficient person, by the way; I love to think what he'd be if he did not have all this really dangerous substitute activity going on in him. But time and again, on occasions when I was perhaps within gunshot of being bored, I've seen him suddenly become preoccupied and hurry away; and I know just what he does: he goes home and treats the malady which showed signs of becoming active under the same circumstances in which I became bored. My friend is an unusual instance, however, because the hypochondriacal person ordinarily doesn't manifest extraordinary gifts, broad interests, or anything of that kind. He is, on the other hand, capable of very deep preoccupation with his pulse rate, which is not taken as such, of course, but as evidence of serious risks surrounding the heart; he can give a tremendous amount of attention to his digestive tract, a preoccupation which I think is much more common; and—this is indeterminately common—he is capable of very deep preoccupation with sensations, or the absence of sensations, in the urogenital tract.

Thus in these deep, absorbing preoccupations, in which one loses practically all touch with things outside of oneself short of fire, there is great centering of conscious referential process on tiny little signs, often grossly and dreadfully misinterpreted, of something going on somewhere in the somatic organization of the body. Perhaps an illustration would serve to clarify what I am discussing here. A good many young men who have had very unfortunate experience, who are intensely socially isolated, and who are about to have a schizophrenic episode, show a particular type of hypochondriacal preoccupation with their genitals. This preoccupation has the following substance to it: When one is tense, the urinary bladder wall is tense, which in turn makes for high pressure against the internal urethral sphincter. If then the person is distracted, it is quite possible for the internal sphincter to relax according to the general pattern of getting ready for action. That permits a drop of urine to escape from the bladder into the prostatic urethra, which produces a distinct urgency to urinate. But it is quite possible that this sequence of events may not be completed in the person who has the particular type of hypochondriacal preoccupation with the genitals which I am discussing. So although the drop of urine escapes into the prostatic urethra, the person goes on into new tensions which somewhat distract him from the necessity to urinate. A little while later, the person becomes entirely absorbed in the, to him, awful experience of having seminal fluids sneaking out through the penis; in fact, he may actually inspect the penis, and he may then see a very little visible, palpable moisture at the meatus of the penis. To him, here is proof that he is losing vitality—for semen can take on remarkable symbolic importance. And this was all because he was too distracted and too preoccupied to notice that he might have urinated. Now, this situation gets wound up to the point where it practically becomes a vicious circle: the person is constantly anxious about this loss of vitality by way of the semen; and he loses it any time he's distracted by contact with anybody else or by any idea and so on, because at that time the internal sphincter is apt to relax a little bit; so the drop of urine gets in the prostatic urethra and then gets metamorphosed by this profound preoccupation with further loss of semen. Now this is an instance of hypochondriacal preoccupation which has been of such great interest to me that I've taken the trouble to figure out how a great many instances of it happen. Let me assure you that it is no more complex in its structure than a great many other hypochondriacal preoccupations with which certain desperately unhappy people can occupy practically their whole waking life.

I now want to discuss the special instance in which social isolation is combined with these hypochondriacal interests, in which case the latter are an important part of the dissociative system within the self-system. In this connection, one must remember that in addition to a motivational system which is dissociated—completely cut off from representation within awareness—there is also a complex system composed of dissociative processes which *maintain* this dissociation. In other words, one cannot maintain a dissociation without having a lot of precautionary apparatus, and so on, in the self-system to avoid any sudden crashing of the dissociation. These hypochondriacal interests quite often are part of the dissociative system, in which case one would expect these interests to become extreme and absorbing whenever the interpersonal relation is such that something in dissociation tends to become active. This is often strikingly demonstrable in the group of young men I have just mentioned. It is one of the classical occasions on which the careless psychiatrist might say that the patient 'blocked.' In other words, as a conversation between the psychiatrist and the patient moves into a region which might, by some accident, stir a dissociated tendency in the patient, then the patient becomes profoundly preoccupied with the fact that he is now losing a little more vitality. But since this thought is always fringed with the possibility of uncanny emotion, he doesn't tell the psychiatrist about it. And in any case, the patient feels that it is profoundly irrelevant to what he was talking about. All this is accompanied by such unpleasant emotion and has such preoccupying power that whatever he was talking about is as completely lost as if it had been erased. The psychiatrist has to start all over again, and if he and the patient can get to the same place at which blocking first occurred, blocking will probably occur again at that place. Of course, it is unlikely that they can get to the same point, because the patient will be already warned and will block as soon as that progression barely gets started.

"Being Taken Advantage Of"

The subject that I now want to discuss may seem to be quite removed from what I have just discussed, but actually it is quite closely related. The experience that I will describe is ordinarily called "being taken advantage of." This is probably within the experience of everyone, and very sadly and frequently within the experience of some people. Some of the less significant instances of this experience are, for example, being cheated or outwitted in the realm of real property. But the instances which I am concerned with here occur when someone takes advantage of you in such a way as to lead you to expose a weakness; as a result of this exposure, you suffer real or fantasied ridicule and have a feeling of being humiliated. I am quite sure that most of you can recall at least one person, in your more distant past life, who would now and then, as if by malice aforethought, entrap you into doing or saying something for which he then ridiculed you. In adult life, you may still find yourself occasionally in such situations; but now you probably have so much presence, so much caution and social distance, that the nearest you come to following the earlier pattern is that you wonder if the other person is ridiculing you; at least that's the ordinary attenuation.

A discussion of real or fancied ridicule seems a good place to embark on a discussion of "projection." When we get to the point of wondering whether people are admiring us or ridiculing us, we may have some little difficulty in distinguishing between that situation and what is usually meant by projection. But first I want to comment on the loose use of the term, projection. To begin with, we project in all interpersonal relations. We attempt to foresee action; we foresee it as the activity of embodied others; and that in itself is projection. Thus foresight applies in those situations in which you have put your worst foot forward and you think that the person who led you into the situation will now tell others about it with joy. But the term projection, as it is often used in psychiatry, seems to mean—if it means anything—that we project the wrong thing; for example, when I'm thinking very well of you, you 'project' upon me malice, hatred, and contempt! Well, that's nice—for certain late-evening-alcoholic psychiatric discussions. What I want to stress is that the degree to which foresight can be good, adequate, and appropriate, and the degree to which it can be far beside the point, is a matter which varies in everyone, from occasion to occasion, on such bases as what motivational complex is at work in the one person, what motivational complex is at work in the other, how tired the one or the other is, and, literally, what the recent past has been. I have already suggested the degree to which people with chronically low self-esteem anticipate unfavorable opinions in others; and I do not think that the mechanism of projection accounts for much of anything.

The Failure of Dissociation

I now want to consider a particularly important situation which arises as a special instance in these people with chronically low self-esteem who have advantage taken of them. And this is the situation in which the weakness which is so revealed actually includes some evidences of a dissociative system in the personality concerned. And, in these instances, the experience of being led to reveal one's weakness is, briefly or permanently, attended by some measure of the uncanny emotions—awe, dread, loathing, and horror. These emotions are, in many ways, the nearest that anybody comes to the reality of dissociated components in his personality, unless a person plunges into the sort of waking bad dream of schizophrenia. These, then, are instances of momentary representation within awareness, or of more durable representation within awareness, of the not-me phase of personality, which I can scarcely say is ordinarily personified, but which under certain unfortunate circumstances *can* now become personified. As I have noted briefly before, these situations may be accompanied either by such fascination that the person, despite dreadful feelings, cannot seem to avoid being entangled with this unpleasant person who has taken advantage of him; or else by revulsion, which is an extreme avoidance coupled with an uncanny feeling, so powerful and intense that the person is in the unhappy position of wondering what on earth could have made this particular affair so repulsive—which, in itself, is an unhappy addition to one's self-awareness. Or these situations may be accompanied by the still more chilling *awful suspicion* by which one really begins to build up structures of probability—or improbability—which become more and more uncanny.

And here we approach the experience of *jealousy*. Now jealousy may either be not particularly uncanny; or it may be what older psychiatrists call "delusional jealousy." Its form of manifestation is, in a large measure, determined by the extent to which dissociated systems are involved in its occurrence. That is to say, according to my experience with patients, jealousy is colored by uncanny emotion to the extent that dissociated systems are involved. And the more uncanny—that is, the more pathological—and the more marked the jealousy, the more fantastic one or two of the three people concerned will prove to be. This fantastic character is a complex function of the defense which the self-system exercises against the appearance of dissociated motivation; and insofar as that defense has to be vigorous, the dissociative distortions become striking.

Beyond fascination, significant revulsion, and awful suspicion, the next stage—in this unhappy concomitant of one's having been led unfairly to reveal one's weakness which happens to have something to do with a dissociative system—is the occurrence of what I will call *full-fledged "autochthonous" ideas*. Now, this tedious old word refers to a content of thought, a matter in mind, which seems literally to have come from outside one, as if put there—that is, one has no feeling of ownership or parentage. Thus while the self-system excludes from awareness clear evidences of a dissociated motivational system, that which is dissociated is represented in awareness by some group of ideas or thoughts which are marked uncannily with utter foreignness—they have nothing to do with oneself. And they really have nothing to do with oneself except that they are a kind of compromise.

The next step in this unhappy process is the actual occurrence of *hallucinations*, which with astonishing frequency are auditory. The occurrence of hallucinations means not only that one has something in mind which seems foreign and imposed from outside, but that one experiences events which are uncanny—one hears something which is strongly colored with a feeling of awe, dread, horror, loathing, or something of that kind. The hallucination has, so far as I know, every indication of being a perfectly valid experience, except that it is uncanny. And whether the hallucination needs any external source or not is perfectly irrelevant—in fact, the question is one of the most tedious topics of psychiatric drivel.

The Paranoid Transformation of Personality

Although hallucinations do not necessarily usher in schizophrenic episodes, they very frequently do so. And I would now like to discuss briefly what happens when the schizophrenic episode has occurred, followed—often quite promptly—by what I call a paranoid transformation of personality. In these situations, it is now impossible to maintain reasonable dissociation of previously dissociated tendencies in one's personality which are still, in terms of the personified self, *apart*. As a result, that which was dissociated, and which was in a certain meaningful sense related to the not-me, is now definitely *personified* as not-me—that is, as *others*. And the others carry blame for that which had previously had to be maintained in dissociation as an intolerable aspect of one's own personal possibilities.

Now, at the beginning of this transformation, the only impression one has is of a person in the grip of horror, of uncanny devastation which makes everyone threatening beyond belief. But if the person is not utterly crushed by the process, he can begin rather rapidly to elaborate personifications of evil creatures. And in this process of personifying the specific evil, the transformation begins to move fast, since it's wonderfully successful in one respect: it begins to put on these others—people who are outside of him, his enemies—everything which he has clearly formulated in himself as defect, blamable weakness, and so on. Thus as the process goes on, he begins to wash his hands of all those real and fancied unfortunate aspects of his own personality which he has suffered for up to this time. Under those circumstances, needless to say, he arrives at a state which is pretty hard to remedy—by categorical name, a paranoid state. If the schizophrenic prelude is very inconspicuous—in which case, I might add, the development may be in some ways a little more ominous—the beginning phase of the paranoid state has a curious relationship with what I call moments of 'illumination.' These occur when, by extremely fortunate circumstance, one actually sees, to a considerable extent, a real situation that he had been selectively inattending to previously, so that he is really better oriented. But far more common than these fortunate illuminations is the onrushing of this paranoid transformation of personality—the transfer of blame—in which the person suddenly 'sees it all.' The beginning of this process comes literally as a sudden insight into some suspicion and it comes with a blaze of horror. The suspicion may have hovered around before the sudden insight, and may have been marked by a little uncanniness; but with the insight, one has started living in a world in which not-me has become personified, very active, and very absorptive of one's weaknesses.

Now, the thing that ties all this together is that in some people there is an interweaving and alternation of hypochondriacal preoccupations and paranoid interpersonal relations. Intense hypochondriacal preoccupations often usher in disasters which can emerge from schizophrenia as paranoid transformations. At certain times, in the course of the paranoid way of existence, there can be a recession of all this fearing of enemies and seeing plots, and so on, in favor of a profound preoccupation with disorder of the bodily function—with the idea of disastrous things going on.[3] This

[3] It is interesting to note that hypochondriacal preoccupation is not preoccupation with healthy function, as the hebephrenic deterioration seems to be.

alternation—which many of us have encountered, for it's not too uncommon—is of very considerable importance in suggesting the reality underlying the conceptual structure of not-me.

I think that I can hint at the processes concerned in this interweaving of hypochondriacal preoccupations and paranoid states by mentioning the only very markedly paranoid schizophrenic whom I ever brought to what I felt might imply ultimate recovery. This boy, as he began to really clear up after a very extensive paranoid schizophrenic illness, still complained of his throat. His throat bothered him terribly. It was very difficult to quite discover what symptoms accompanied it, but there was no shadow of doubt that he was profoundly preoccupied with his throat. I sent him to a laryngologist who was both very skillful and quite sympathetic to the problems of psychiatry. The boy's throat was examined very carefully, and at the same time he was given a fine anatomical textbook and was permitted to look at it and to notice how neatly his throat coincided with the skillfully colored anatomical picture. And he went away very deeply touched; it had been a very successful adventure. But the next time I saw him, he came into the office and said, "Look, Doctor, I don't care anything about what ails my throat; I want something cut out."

PART
IV

Towards a Psychiatry of Peoples

CHAPTER

22 *

PSYCHIATRY has come to mean something to a great many people, but, for our purpose, it must be defined. There is a meaning of psychiatry which makes it an art or body of empirical practices pertaining to the treatment or prevention of mental disorder. This meaning of psychiatry is irrelevant, here. Psychiatry, as here to be discussed, is a science and its related technology. The science of psychiatry has been nurtured by work with the mentally ailing, has grown in the milieu of hospital and clinic, but is no more a science of mental illness than geography is a science of Western Europe.

The mentally ill are particular instances of people living among others in localities of more or less uniform culture. The science that has grown from preoccupation with these mentally disordered ways of living has naturally to become a science of living under the conditions which prevail in the given social order. I believe that this statement is simply axiomatic, but it does not imply that a particular psychiatric scientist need concern himself with any and all aspects of man's life in society.

A physicist may usefully concentrate his scientific efforts on particular aspects of the phenomena anciently called *light*. His results, so far as they are good physics, will be meaningful throughout physics. They may be more richly meaningful in, for example, the region of wave motion than in that of gravitation; but here one may recall the confirmation of Einstein's anticipation that light would be found to 'bend' in traversing a gravitational field.

The general science of psychiatry seems to me to cover much

* [*Editors' note:* This chapter is mainly taken from "Towards a Psychiatry of Peoples" (*Psychiatry* 11:105–116). Beginning with the section headed "Whence the Urgency," there appears an excerpt from "Remobilization for Enduring Peace and Social Progress" (*Psychiatry* 10:239–252; p. 244). Most of the chapter has also been reprinted in *Tensions That Cause Wars*, edited by Hadley Cantril (Univ. of Ill. Press, 1950).]

the same field as that which is studied by social psychology, because scientific psychiatry has to be defined as the study of interpersonal relations, and this in the end calls for the use of the kind of conceptual framework that we now call *field theory*. From such a standpoint, personality is taken to be hypothetical. That which can be studied is the pattern of processes which characterize the interaction of personalities in particular recurrent situations or fields which 'include' the observer. Since any one participant observer can study but a finite number of these situations or fields, which, in turn, will be anything but representative of the whole variegated world of human life, not all of the personality of the observer will be revealed and 'what he comes to know about himself' will always be somewhat incomplete and variously contingent on poorly defined or actually unnoticed factors. Generalizations which he can make about "the other fellow" cannot but be even more incomplete and contingent.

The observer, the instrument used in assembling the data of psychiatry, is, then, seen to be an only imperfectly understood tool, some of the results of the use of which may be quite misleading. This conclusion might be taken to forbid any effort toward developing a scientific psychiatry, much less a psychiatry of everyone everywhere in the world. It certainly forbids any conceit about the present state of psychiatry, but one may well notice that every science has been—and, less obviously, still is—in the same position. One may note, also, that ignorance of the principles of the internal-combustion engine has not prevented the expert driving of automobiles, although it might prove costly to anyone who substituted a high explosive for gasoline fuel because he was in a hurry.

Bear with me now in an attempt to outline a position in general psychiatry from which I shall presently undertake to make some temporarily valid generalizations of world scope. What anyone can observe and analyze becomes ultimately a matter of *tensions* and *energy transformations*, many of the latter being obvious *actions*, but many others of which are obscure activities that go on, as we say, in the mind.

What anyone can discover by investigating his past is that the *patterns* of tensions and energy transformations which make up his living are, to a truly astonishing extent, matters of his education for living in a particular expected society. If he is clever, he can also notice inadequacies in his educators' expectations; he finds that he is not any too well-prepared for living in the groups in which he has come to be involved.

If he is philosophically inclined and historic minded, he is apt to conclude that this very element of being ill-prepared has characterized people in every period of expanding world contacts and ensuing accelerated social change.

If he is interested in psychiatry, he is almost certain to come to consider the role of *foresight* in determining the adequacy and appropriateness of the energy transformations, his overt and covert activity, with respect to the actual demands of the situations in which he finds himself involved with significant others.

I touch here on what I believe is the most remarkable of human characteristics, the importance exercised by often but vaguely formulated aspirations, anticipations, and expectations which can be summed up in the term, foresight, the manifest influence of which makes the near future a thoroughly real factor in explaining human events. I hope that you will resist the idea that something clearly teleological is being introduced here: I am saying that, *circumstances not interfering*, man the person lives with his past, the present, and the neighboring future all clearly relevant in explaining his thought and action; and the near future is influential to a degree nowhere else remotely approached among the species of the living.

Note that I have said "circumstances not interfering." It is from study of the interferences which reduce, or otherwise modify, the functional activity of foresight that a great deal of light has been thrown on the nature of man as revealed in his doings with others.

We assume that all biological tensions arise from the course of events "inside" and/or "outside" the gross spatial limits of the organism. Human tensions are no exception to this, but one of their congeries—one very important kind of tension—ensues from a kind of events the experiencing of which is almost unique to the human being.

With this single important exception, tensions can be regarded as needs for particular energy transformations which will dissipate the tension, often with an accompanying change of "mental state," a change of awareness, to which we can apply the general term *satisfaction*.

Thus the particular tension the felt component of which we call *hunger* is pleasantly satisfied by activity which includes the taking of food. Our hunger is *not* the tension, the tension is not merely a "mental state," a phenomenon within awareness, nor is it entirely "within" us in any simple space-time sense. But for practical purposes, I may usually trust this particular once-familiar "mental state" to coincide perfectly with my need for food, and "make up my mind to eat," or "decide to go to dinner," or entertain within awareness some other 'thought' which sounds as if something quite powerful named "I" is directing something else, "myself," to do something about "my being hungry" with reasonable certainty that I shall feel more comfortable, when the performance has been finished.

Whatever pomp and circumstance may go on "in one's head," the need for food reaches into the past in which it has arisen, and on the basis of which its felt component can be said to have 'meaning,' and it reaches into the future in which its tension can be foreseen to have been relieved by appropriate action in proper circumstances.

We share most, if not all, of this large congeries of recurrent needs with a good many other species of the living—even including our recurrent need for contact with others, often felt as *loneliness*, which is paralleled in the gregarious animals.

The single other great congeries of recurrent tensions, some grasp on the nature of which is simply fundamental to understanding human life, is probably restricted to man and some of the creatures which he has domesticated. It arises not from the impact of physicochemical and biological events directly connected with keeping alive and reproducing the species, but from the impact of people. The felt component of any of this congeries of tensions includes the experience of *anxiety*; action which *avoids* or *relieves* any of these tensions is experienced as continued or enhanced *self-respect* or *self-esteem*, significantly different from what is ordinarily meant by self-satisfaction. All the factors entering into the vicissitudes of self-esteem, excepting only man's innate capacity for being anxious, are wholly a matter of past experience with people, the given interpersonal situation, and foresight of what will happen.

There is nothing I can conceive in the way of interpersonal action about which one could not be trained to be anxious, so that if such an action is foreseen one feels anxious, and if it occurs one's self-esteem is reduced. The realm of this congeries of tensions is the area of one's *training for life* at the hands of significant others, and of how much or little one has been able to synthesize out of these training experiences.

One cannot be trained by others in advance of certain biological events; namely, the maturation of appropriate capabilities of man the underlying animal. Training efforts exerted before this time are undergone as something very different from what was "intended" and, if they have any effect, exert thoroughly unfortunate influence on the future development of the victim.[1] This biologically ordained serial maturation of capabilities underlies the currently entertained scheme of stages in human development [infancy, childhood, the juvenile era, preadolescence, early adolescence, and late adolescence to maturity]. . . . Let me discuss the implication of the idea of developmental stages. When, and only when, maturation of capacities has occurred, experience of a valuable kind can occur. *If it does not occur*, if experience is definitely unsuited to providing competence for living with others, at this particular level of development, the probabilities of future adequate and appropriate interpersonal relations are definitely *and specifically* reduced. The reduction of probability is specifically related to the forms of competence which are customarily developed under favorable circumstances in the course of this particular stage.

Seen from this viewpoint, not the earlier stages only, but each and every stage, is equally important in its own right, in the unfolding of possibilities for interpersonal relations, in the progression from birth toward mature competence for life in a fully human world. It is often true that severe warp incurred, say, in

---

[1] They generally contribute to the not-me component of personality, the source of the tension in interpersonal fields elsewhere described as the experience of uncanny emotions—awe, dread, loathing, and horror—felt components of the most strongly disjunctive force of which we have knowledge.

childhood interferes so seriously with the course of events in the succeeding juvenile era that the constructive effects of living with compeers, and under school and other nonfamily authorities, are meager. It also happens, and not infrequently, that quite serious warp from childhood is all but corrected by good fortune early in the juvenile era, so that its residual traces are observable only under circumstances of "intense emotion," severe "fatigue," anoxemia, hypoglycemia, or alcoholic and related "decerebration." [2]

In the course of intensive, guided psychotherapy one may observe, in many instances, a condensed, relatively vicarious, remedying of deficiencies in developmental experience, and this seems to be a successful way of consolidating favorable change in the patient's interpersonal relations.

Thus unremedied misfortune in the preadolescent phase leaves one at a lifelong disadvantage in dealing with important strangers of the same sex. *When this pattern of discomfort has been made clear* by participant observation 'with' the patient, the latter will often develop a belated, transient, preadolescence. Some previously guarded contact will deepen into a very warm friendship; the satisfactions and security of the "buddy" become overwhelmingly important to the patient and his current activities are largely directed to promoting them. At the same time, any strong motivation in the patient-physician relationship is in abeyance, as if he had lost any particular interest in the work. Then, presently, the 'outside' attachment loses intensity and a favorably changed patient is again at work with the psychiatrist, tracking down the ramifications of the disability from which he is now recovering.

This illustrates the meaning of isophilic in my triad: the autophilic, the isophilic, and the heterophilic are those persons, respectively, who can manifest in their interpersonal relations the pattern of field forces properly called *love* for no one, for a person of one's own sex, or for persons of one's own and of the other sex. The ability to love is a factor in the patterning of genital, sexual, behavior; but it is only one of three factors which must be considered in order to 'make sense' of what goes on in that con-

---

[2] Even in these 'reduced' states, the peculiarities of interpersonal relations can sometimes be seen to be a movement as if to remedy ancient deficiencies of experience.

nection. In this culture, many people show the ability to love in advance of the occurrence of puberty. Many others have yet to evolve the ability to love long after a relatively active sexual life of one kind or another has been established.

Much more important, for my present purpose, is the import of the illustration as an example of 'curative' processes in interpersonal fields. It is from prolonged consideration of psychotherapeutic "successes" and "failures"—and of possibilities for increasing the proportion and speeding the achievement of the former —that I have come to feel sure that we may depend on everyone's drive toward more adequate and appropriate ways of living; in a word, toward improved mental health, *if* an improved ability to foresee the future can offer a fair prospect of becoming contented. That "if" is a big one when one has been 'out of life' for years in a hospital for the mentally disordered, when one is advanced in years, or when the prospect appears to entail giving up sources of prestige and income which one's current, however troubled, life is providing.

The often great difficulty encountered in achieving improved ability to live with significant others is considered to arise, then, not from a deficiency of tendency but from something else; something which manifests itself as an equilibrating factor in living, whether the living be fortunate or unfortunate; namely, the extensive organization of experience within personality which I have called the *self-system*.

I think it will suffice for my present purpose to say that anything which would seriously disturb the equilibrium, any event which tends to bring about a basic change in an *established pattern* of dealing with others, sets up the tension of anxiety and calls out activities for its relief. This tension and the activities required for its reduction or relief—which we call *security operations* because they can be said to be addressed to maintaining a feeling of safety in the esteem reflected to one from the other person concerned— always interfere with whatever other tensions and energy transformations they happen to coincide with.

This in no way denies the usefulness of security operations. They are often quite successful in protecting one's self-esteem. Without them, life in an increasingly incoherent social organization would be exceedingly difficult or impossible for most people. We, the people of these United States, in particular, would quite certainly exterminate ourselves before we could devise and disseminate adequate substitutes for our now ubiquitous security processes.

Let us be very clear about the fact that anxiety and security operations are an absolutely necessary part of human life as long as the past is more important in preparing the young for life than is the reasonably foreseeable future.

But for all their indispensable utility to each and every one of us, in these days, security operations are a powerful brake on personal and on human progress—as I can perhaps indicate by referring to a particular one of them which is very frequently to be observed.

I shall use as an example the process called *selective inattention*, something very different indeed from mere negligent oversight. By selective inattention we fail to recognize the actual import of a good many things we see, hear, think, do, and say, not because there is anything the matter with our zones of interaction with others but because the process of inferential analysis is opposed by the self-system. Clear recognition of the implications of matters to which we are selectively inattentive would call for basic change in an established pattern of dealing with the sort of interpersonal situation concerned; would make us either more, or in some cases less, competent, but in any case *different* from the way we now conceive ourself to be. Good observation and analysis of a mass of incidents selectively overlooked would expand the self-system, which usually controls the contents of awareness and the scope of the referential processes that are fully useful in *communicating* with others. The ever iterated miracle of selective inattention explains the faith we have in unnumbered prejudicial verbalisms, "rationalizations," about ourself and others and half explains the characterization of the Bourbon as one who never forgets anything and never learns anything.

While there is some reason to believe that a sufficient degree of novelty will always call out a disjunctive force the felt component of which we know as *fear*, a very great many otherwise illuminating observations, of by no means intimidating novelty and difference, fail entirely to inform us about the world we live in because of the equilibrating influence of the self-system—the tree that all too frequently reflects the way the twig was bent in the developmental years.

The extension of psychiatric theory beyond the confines of the familiar into the world of "foreigners" whose ways of life are alien to us calls for a sharp discrimination between fear and the various manifestations of anxiety and self-system activity, especially those of irrational *dislikes, aversions,* and *revulsions,* and the today so widespread *distrust of others.*

Current theory makes *hate* the characteristic of interpersonal situations in which the people concerned recurrently and frequently 'provoke anxiety in each other,' yet 'cannot break up the situation' because of some conjunctive forces which hold them together. If the conjunctive force acts entirely outside of awareness, uncanny *fascination,* with moments of revulsion or loathing, may appear. If the integrating forces are not very strong; if the situation is 'not very important,' the milder manifestations of 'more or less concealed,' "actually unjustified," dislike and distrust are shown. The "actually unjustified" means that a consensually valid statement of adequate grounds for the dislike or distrust cannot be formulated. The unpleasant 'emotion' arises from something more than what either person could readily come to know about the situation.

Let me illustrate the meaning of these terms by some thoroughly crude examples. A couple make what certainly is a marriage of great convenience. Friends of each notice with increasing discomfort that husband and wife seem more and more bent on humiliating each other in the presence of the friends. This illustrates an increasingly hateful integration.

A mother, taking over the care of her first-born from the nurse, is greatly upset—feels faint, looks pale, trembles severely, and is bathed with perspiration—on first encountering soiled diapers. She is undergoing the uncanny variant on the much more commonplace *disgust,* either of which is mostly a matter of her training for life.

Another mother discovers her fifteen-month-old child holding his obviously "excited" genital. She is filled with a shuddering 'emotion' not unrelated to the fascination *and* horror many people encounter when first thinking about witches' sabbaths, Voodoo rites, or other folk encounters with personified Sexual Evil. Parenthetically, the infant by empathy is filled with the most primitive anxiety, almost as paralyzing and as uninformative as a blow on the head from a hammer; but if the mother's 'reaction' does not change by virtue of habituation or "insight," he will gradually catch on to enough of what happens to come to the juvenile era a person who shows *primitive genital phobia*—a more or less contentless aversion to action or thought about "touching himself" in the perineum; often with a lively, if unwelcome, hope that he may be "touched" by others, and perhaps "touch" them in turn; after which actual experience he would come to "dislike" and avoid them, or, more unhappily, suffer recurrent deeply disturbing revulsion after each of a series of "conflictful" repetitions.

I can perhaps now proceed to the thesis of this paper; namely, that while no one can now be adequately equipped for a greatly significant inquiry into the fundamental "facts of life" of everyone, everywhere, there are many possibilities of greatly constructive efforts in this direction—if, and only if, instead of plunging into the field recklessly "hoping for the best," one prefaces one's attempt with a careful survey of one's assets and liabilities for participant observation.

Every constructive effort of the psychiatrist, today, is a strategy of interpersonal field operations which (1) seeks to map the areas of disjunctive force that block the efficient collaboration of the patient and others, and (2) seeks to expand the patient's awareness so that this unnecessary blockage can be brought to an end.

For a psychiatry of peoples, we must follow the selfsame strategy applied to significant groupings of people—families, communities, political entities, regional organizations, world blocs—and seek to map the interventions of disjunctive force which block the integration of the group with other groups in pursuit of the common welfare; and seek out the characteristics of each group's culture or subculture, and the methods used to impose it on the young, which perpetuate the restrictions of freedom for constructive growth.

The master tactics for a psychiatrist's work with a handicapped person consist in (1) elucidating the actual situations in which unfortunate action is currently shown repeatedly, so that the disorder-

pattern may become clear; (2) discovering the less obvious ramifications of this inadequate and inappropriate way of life throughout
other phases of the present and the near future, including the
doctor-patient relationship and the patient's expectations about it;
and (3) with the problem of inadequate development now clearly
formulated, utilizing his human abilities to explore its origins in
his experience with significant people of the past.

It must be noted that an identical distortion of living common to
doctor and patient makes this type of inquiry, at the best, very difficult. Neither is able to 'see' the troublesome patterns, and both are
inclined to relate the difficulties to the unhappy peculiarities of the
other people concerned in their less fortunate interpersonal relations. Each respects the parallel limitation in the other, and their
mutual effort is apt to be concentrated on irrelevant or immaterial
problems, until they both become more discouraged or still more
firmly deceived about life.

For a psychiatry of peoples, these tactical requirements of good
therapy—which is also good research—have to be expanded into
(1) a preliminary discovery of the actual major patterns of tensions and energy transformations which characterize more adequate and appropriate living in that group; this is a background for
noticing the exceptions—the incidents of mental disorder among
these folk—uninformed study of which would be misleading; (2)
a parallel development of skill at rectifying the effects of limitations
in our own developmental background; in order (3) that it may
become possible to observe better the factors that actually resist
any tendency to extend the integrations of our subject-persons, so
that they would include representatives of other groups relatively
alien to them—a pilot test of which is the integration with ourself—
and (4) thus to find real problems in the foresight of intergroup
living which can be tracked down to their origins in our subject-
people's education for life.

There is good reason to believe that all this is not impossible.
These world-psychiatric inquiries are not at bottom particularly
different from the already mentioned, all too common, instances
where doctor and patient suffer approximately *the same* disorders
in living. Let me say a word about the way in which one may proceed to reduce the handicap of such a situation, at the same time

pointing to the answer to an oft-heard question: "What can I do to help myself?"

My conception of anxiety is in point here. While we may be unaware, at least temporarily, of milder degrees of any one of the other tensions connected with living, we are never unaware of anxiety at the very time that it occurs. The awareness can be, and very often is, fleeting, especially when an appropriate security operation is called out. The awareness can be most variously characterized from person to person, even from incident to incident, excepting only that it is always unpleasant. At the moment that anxiety occurs, one becomes aware of something unpleasant; but whether this seems to be a mere realization that all is not going so well, or a noticing of some disturbance in the activity or postural tone in one of the zones of interaction—a change in one's 'facial expression' or in one's voice, as examples—a feeling of tightening up in some group of skeletal muscles, a disturbance of the action of one's heart, a discomfort in one's belly, a realization that one has begun to sweat; as I say, whether it be one of these or yet another variety of symptoms, one is always at least momentarily aware that one has become uncomfortable, or more acutely uncomfortable, as the case may be.

No matter what may have followed upon this awareness of diminished feeling of well-being, there was the awareness. It best serves in ordinary interpersonal relations to "pay as little attention to it as one can," and to "forget it." But if one is intent on refining oneself as an instrument of participant observation, it is necessary to pay the greatest attention, at least retrospectively, to these fleeting movements of anxiety. They are the telltales which show increased activity of the self-system in the interpersonal field of the moment concerned.

They mark the point in the course of events at which something disjunctive, something that tends to pull away from the other fellow, has first appeared or has suddenly increased. They signal a change from relatively uncomplicated movement toward a presumptively common goal to a protecting of one's self-esteem, with a definite *complicating* of the interpersonal action.

To the extent that one can retrospectively observe the exact situation in which one's anxiety was called out, one may be able to infer the corresponding pattern of difficulty in dealing with others. As these patterns are usually a matter of past training or its absence, detecting them is seldom an easy matter, but, I repeat, it is by no means impossible—unless there is an actual *dissociation* in one's personality system, in which case there will be prohibitively great difficulty in recalling anything significant about the actual situation which evoked the anxiety.

Two things more remain to be said about this, shall I say, self-observation of disjunctive processes in interpersonal relations.

Anxiety appears not only as awareness of itself but also in the experience of some *complex* 'emotions' into which it has been elaborated by specific early training. I cannot say what all these are, but I can use names for a few of them which should 'open the mind' to their nature: embarrassment, shame, humiliation, guilt, and chagrin. The circumstances under which these unpleasant 'emotions' occur are particularly hard to observe accurately and to subject to the retrospective analysis which is apt to be most rewarding.

A group of security operations born of experience which has gone into the development of these complex unpleasant 'emotions' is equally hard for one to observe and analyze. These are the movements of thought and the actions by which we, as it were, impute to, or seek to provoke in, the other fellow feelings like embarrassment, shame, humiliation, guilt, or chagrin. It is peculiarly difficult to observe retrospectively and to subject to analysis the exact circumstances under which we are moved to act as if the other person "should be ashamed of himself," is "stupid," or is guilty of anything from a breach of good taste to a mortal sin. These interpersonal movements which put the other fellow at a disadvantage on the basis of a low relative personal worth are extremely troublesome elements in living and very great handicaps to investigating strange people.

Disparaging and derogatory thought and action that make one feel "better" than the other person concerned, that expand one's self-esteem, as it were, at his cost, are always to be suspected of arising from anxiety. These processes are far removed from a judicious inquiry into one's relative personal skill in living. They do not reflect a good use of observation and analysis but rather indicate a low self-esteem in the person who uses them. The quicker one comes to a low opinion of another, other things being equal, the poorer is one's secret view of one's own worth in the field of the disparagement.

It is rather easy to correct interferences in participant observation of another which arise from one's true superiorities to him. It is quite otherwise with the baleful effects of one's secret doubts and uncertainties. We are apt to be most severely critical of others when they are thought to be showing an instance of something of which we ourselves are secretly ashamed, and which we hope we are concealing.

This must suffice as an indication of the more pervasive of the often unnoticed interferences with participant observation with representatives of somewhat unfamiliar background. I need scarcely discuss the role of linguistic difficulties or that of sheer ignorance of the culture patterns to which remarks make reference. These latter are actually only somewhat more striking instances of similar interferences in getting acquainted with any stranger.

Progress toward a psychiatry of peoples is to be expected from efforts expended along two lines of investigation: (1) an improving grasp on the significant patterns—and on the pattern of patterns—of living around the world; and (2) the uncovering of significant details in the sundry courses of personality development by which the people of each different social organization come to manifest more or less adequate and appropriate behavior, in their given social setting.

Each of these lines of investigation is a necessary supplement to the other. The first, which may be taken to pertain more to the interests and techniques of the cultural anthropologist, cannot be pushed very far, very securely, without data from the second. The second can scarcely produce meaningful data unless it is informed by the provisional hypotheses of the former. The two provide indispensable checks upon each other, without which neither can proceed noticeably without running into increasing uncertainty.

The theory of interpersonal relations lays great stress on the method of participant observation, and relegates data obtained by other methods to, at most, a secondary importance. This in turn implies that skill in the face-to-face, or person-to-person, *psychiatric interview* is of fundamental importance.

While the value of interchange by use of the mediate channels of communication—correspondence, publications, radio, speaking films—may be very great, especially if the people concerned have already become fairly well acquainted with each other as a result of previous face-to-face exchange, it must be remembered that communication in the psychiatric interview is by no means solely a matter of exchanging verbal contexts, but is rather the development of an exquisitely complex pattern of field processes which *imply* important conclusions about the people concerned.

This is scarcely the place for a discussion of current views about what one can learn about the theory and practice of psychiatric interviewing; I wish chiefly to emphasize the *instrumental* character of the interviewing psychiatrist and the critical importance of his being free to observe—and subsequently analyze—as many as possible of his performances as a dynamic center in the field patterns that make up the interview.

Everything that can be said about good psychiatric interviewing is relevant to the directly interpersonal aspects of any work in the direction of a psychiatry of peoples. Every safeguard useful in avoiding erroneous conclusions about 'the other fellow' becomes newly important when the barriers of linguistic and other cultural uncertainties are in the way.

Inquiries into the alien ways of educating the young must be oriented with close regard to *biological time* as it is reflected in the serial maturation of capacities; to *social time* as it is reflected in the series of formulable expectations concerning what the young will 'know how to behave about' from stage to stage of their development; and to the exact *chronology* of presumptively educative efforts brought to bear on the young.

The spread of variations in each of these three fields is of great importance in understanding the people and their relationships, which make up any community. Consider, for example, the effect of delayed puberty on the adequacy and appropriateness of subsequent behavior in many a youth in any of our urban areas. Consider, again, the effects on the living of the outstandingly bright boy from a small town when he enters a great metropolitan university. And, finally, consider the probable effects of early training in venereal prophylaxis in contrast with that of suppression of information in this field.

It is by virtue of an ever better grasp on the significant patterns in these series of events that we help patients to help themselves, at the same time becoming better and better informed about the factors which govern the possibilities of interpersonal action. To the extent that we have useful approximations to an understanding of the actual processes of personality development which have ensued in the people with whom we deal, we become able to 'make sense' of what seems to be going on. This must be the case, whether one is a stranger in Malaya or host to a visiting Malay.

Whence the Urgency

In a world in which time is of the essence, in which we can scarcely defer great constructive changes until we shall have raised a new generation to political power, the most searching scrutiny of the dynamics of favorable change in personality becomes utterly imperative. Even if time were not of the essence, the imperative would be much the same, for we cannot "jump a generation" and *training for life as it is becoming* begins in, and reaches very far forward from, the primary group of the home. The less of parents' work that has to be corrected, the quicker man moves ahead. The surer our aid to parents in preparing their young for life, the more geometrically expanding will be the resulting good to the greater number.

I think it is no longer wise or expedient to talk and think *as if* the great majority of chronologically adult people, here or elsewhere, will ever become well-informed about a great deal that is acutely vitally important to them.

I think that we must recognize explicitly that universal literacy and complete "freedom of information" *in themselves* offer no solution to any of the imperative problems of the times. . . . Freedom of information is meaningless unless it is used for a purpose, namely, to promote the peace and well-being of humanity.

Can anyone who is experienced in dealing with others doubt that it is ever so much easier to replace one prejudice with another

than it is to bring about informed judgment? Do we not actually
have this in mind when we express ourselves to the so-called laity?
Or perhaps better put: *should* we not have this in mind? Consider,
for instance, the effects, detectable even in some psychiatrists'
homes, of disseminating information about the evil effects of parental mismanagement. Some considerable number of parents now
suffer such uncertainty about "frustrating" and "fixating" and
"making dependent" and the like that they themselves need psychiatric help and their offspring will certainly require it. We do
not seem to have done too good a job of public education in this
vital area. Perhaps our information was not adequate; perhaps,
on the other hand, it was not so bad but we used it badly.

I hold that it is self-evident that a very great many chronologically adult people must act on faith with respect to almost
every field of living. The great hope for the future lies not in attempting to change this fact but in so reducing the effectiveness
of certain vicious elements in current faiths that the young who
grow up under the influence of these elders will have much
greater freedom to observe and to understand and to foresee correctly than had their parents and teachers and the others under
whose authority their abilities for interpersonal relations were
molded.

The achievement of this exceedingly desirable goal is anything
but easy and foolproof. The thinking-out of constructive, functionally coherent, revisions of any one of the major cultures of
the world, so that the personal imperatives which derive from it
—whether in the obscure, very early inculcated, patterns of *con-
science* or the subsequently acquired, less recondite, patterns of
acceptable rationalizations and potent verbalisms—shall be less
restrictive on understanding and more permissive of social progress;
that, truly, is a task to which unnumbered groups of the skillful
may well apply themselves.

There will remain the intimidating task of implementing the
better, once it shall have been designed; but for the first time in
the history of man, there is world-wide, if often most unhappy,
realization of the necessity, and at the same time a set of admin-
istrative agencies clearly charged with the responsibility. I say
to you with the utmost seriousness of which I am capable that

this is no time to excuse yourself from paying the debt you and yours owe the social order with some such facile verbalism as "Nothing will come of it; it can't be done." Begin; and let it be said of you, if there is any more history, that you labored nobly in the measure of man in the twentieth century of the scientific, Western world.

Index

Adolescence:
  early, 263–296
    beginning of, 257–260
    defined, 33–34, 263
  late, 297–310
    defined, 34, 297
Adulthood:
  defined, 34
  See also Maturity
Alcohol, use of, 273–274
Amoebae, example of, 152–153
Anal zone of interaction, 126–134,
    143–145, 158–159
  See also Zones of interaction
Anger, 211–213
Anoxia, 49–51
Anxiety, tension of, 113–115, 300–302,
    308, 370, 374
  anger called out by, 212–213
  associated with punishment, 155,
    204–205
  awareness of, 378–379
  in infancy, 8–12, 41–45, 53–61, 70,
    72–75, 80, 85–87, 94–97, 116–122,
    120n, 133–134, 141–145
  theorem of, 41
  learning by gradient of, 152–154,
    159–160
  in lust dynamism, 266–268, 287–289,
    294
  in maturity, 310
  minimizing and channeling of,
    165n, 304–305, 351–359
  psychiatric handling of, 301–302,
    337–338
  relation of, to wish-fulfilling fan-
    tasies, 349–350n
  severe, 144–145, 152, 160–161, 163,
    268, 314–316
  in sleep, 329–331
  See also Disintegration, of inter-
    personal situation; Mother,
    good and bad; Not-me; Self-
    system

Apathy, 55–57, 61, 61n, 71, 121n
"As if" performances, 170, 208–211,
    346–347
Audience, need for, 155, 201, 223
Auditory zone of interaction, 22–23,
    52, 88–91n, 122–123, 148–149
Autacoid system, 281
Authority:
  in childhood, 204–208
  in juvenile era, 228–232
  resentment of, 289
Autistic, the, 181–183, 221–225, 232–
    234
Autochthonous ideas, 360–361
Automatisms, 321–322
Autosexuality, 270–271, 278, 292–293
Awareness, 57, 288, 316, 317–319, 349–
    350, 357, 360
  of anxiety, 378–379
  focal, control of, 232–235
  See also Selective inattention; Un-
    witting, the

Bad-me, 161–162, 164, 168, 170, 198–
    202, 205, 316–317
Bad mother, see Mother, good and
    bad
Balaam, Biblical story of, 339–340, 346
Behavior:
  delayed, 176–177n
  required, 203–208
Benedict, R., 25–26
Blame, transfer of, 328, 347, 361–362
Blocking, 358
Bridgman, P. W., 14, 19

Central nervous system, 281–282
Chagrin, 379
Change, favorable (in personality),
    see Self-system
Childhood, 172–216
  defined, 33
  transition from childhood to juve-
    nile era, 217–226

385

Childhood (*continued*)
transition from infancy to, 172–187
Chum, preadolescent, 227, 245–262, 264–265, 268
Collaboration, 246, 246n
Communal existence with environment, 37, 98, 103, 190
principle of, 31–32
Communication, 239, 374
See also Syntaxic mode of experience
Compeers, need for, 226, 245, 261, 291
Competition in juvenile era, 231–232
Compromise in juvenile era, 231–232
Concealment, 207–209, 213, 221–222, 345, 351
Conjunctive motivation, 350–351
Consciousness, see Awareness
Consensual validation, see Syntaxic mode of experience
Contact, need for, 40n, 155, 201, 261, 290, 370
Cooley, C. H., 16
Cooperation:
in juvenile era, 226, 246, 246n
by mother in infancy, 59, 92, 115–116, 127–134, 158
See also Tenderness, need for
Coordination, see Hands; Zones of interaction
Cottrell, L., 18–19n
Covert processes, 175–180, 184–187, 195, 197, 224, 234, 276–278, 286–288, 330–331, 349–350, 354
Craving, abhorrent, 326
Crying as experience in infancy, 38, 52–54, 62, 66–74, 76–77, 80–81, 83–85, 87–89
Cultural anthropology, 17–18, 25–26
Cultural environment, man's need for interchange with, 31–32, 98–99
Cultural prescriptions, learning of, 206–207, 219–223
Culture, 168–169, 191, 206–207, 260, 264–265, 288–289, 294–295, 297–298

Deception, 207–209, 251, 345
Delusional jealousy, 360
Dependency, 351–353
passive, 351–352

Development, arrest of, 217–218, 232
Developmental eras:
change at thresholds of, 227–228, 247
disaster in timing of, 257–260
heuristic stages, 33–34, 371–372
Differences:
inherent human, 20–30, 32–33
See also Pattern
Differentiation of experience, see Experience
Disgust, 200, 375
Disintegration:
of behavior patterns, 196–199, 317
of interpersonal situation, 92–97
Disjunctive motivation, 351–352, 371n, 376, 379
See also Disintegration of interpersonal situation
Disparagement, 242–243, 253, 309, 344–345, 379–380
Dissociation, 275–276, 288–289, 325, 327–328, 331, 379
evidence of, 316–322
failure of, 359–363
maintenance of, 357–358
reintegration of, 322–325
See also Not-me; Uncanny emotion
Distance receptors in infancy, 85–91, 117–118, 128, 131
Distrust of others, 375
Don Juanism, 279–280
Dramatizations, 209, 346–347
Dreams, 321, 329
incorporated in culture as myths, 339–343
Loch Raven dream, 336–337
significance of, in psychotherapy, 331–339, 342–343
spider dream, 334–336
Dunham, A., 35n
Dynamism:
concept of, 62–109
in psychiatry, 107–109
statement of, 102–103
tributary concepts to, 62–102
of difficulty, 304–305
of lust, 266, 280–290
of self-system, 164–168

Education by parents, 172–175
  See also Juvenile era; Learning
Eduction of relationships, 63n, 156
Eductor, 63n, 63–64, 282–284
  See also Zones of interaction
Effector, 63–64, 145–146, 282, 284–286
  See also Zones of interaction
Ego, 167n
Egocentricity:
  in childhood, 226
  in juvenile era, 251–252
Eldridge, S., 31, 31n, 32n
Embarrassment, 379
Emotion, see Uncanny emotion
Empathy, 41
Energy, 97–98
  transformation of, 35–36, 36n, 103,
    125–126, 368
Envy, 255, 347–348, 355
Epilepsy, 323
Escape, theorem of, 190–192, 208
Euphoria, 34–37
  See also Tension
Evil in man, 213–214
Experience, 26–30, 35–36, 38–39, 52–
    53, 64–65, 107–109
  differentiation of, 66–91, 120–122,
    120n, 136–141
    See also Forbidding gestures;
      Mother, good and bad
  early, review of, 98–102
  generalization of, 83–91
  organization of, see Learning
  role of, in self-system, 190–192
  signs, signals, and symbols in, 75–
    91
    See also Parataxic, Prototaxic, and
      Syntaxic mode of experience;
      Zones of interaction
Exploitative attitudes, 351–354
Eyes, delusion about, 222–223

Facial expression, 145–148
Family group, psychiatric relevancy
  of, 114–115
Fantasy:
  in childhood, 195, 223–226
  wish-fulfilling, 348–350n
Fascination, 322, 375
Fatigue, 197
Fear, tension of, 9, 108, 310, 374

  as educative influence, 203–204
  patterns of dealing with, 49–53
Fellatio, 293
Field theory, 367–368, 376, 381
  See also Operationalism
Fondling of infant, see Contact, need
  for
Forbidding gestures, 86–91n, 118,
    121n, 166
Foreigners, 375
Foresight and recall, 38–39, 69, 71–72,
    75–76, 206, 211, 287, 369
  foresight as projection, 358–359
  lack of foresight in anxiety, 42–44
Freud, S., 16
Fugue, 323, 325–326
  deliberate, 323
Functional activity, 92, 98, 119–121n
  principle of, 31–32, 32n
  of self-system, 166, 190–192

Gallagher, R., 18n
Games, 306–307
Gang, preadolescent, 249–257, 265
  antisocial, 252–254
Gender in personification of self,
    218–219
Generalization of experience, see Ex-
  perience
Genital zone of interaction, see Lust
  dynamism; Phobia, primary
  genital
Genius, definition of, 23
Gesture, 178–180
  See also Forbidding gestures
Goal, 75–76n, 95–97
Good-me, 161–165, 168, 198–202, 205,
    316
Good mother, see Mother, good and
  bad
Guilt, 219, 344, 379

Habits, 154
Hallucinations, 361
Hands, 20
  manual-exploratory training, 141–
    145, 160
  manual-oral coordination, 135–141
  manual-oral training, 159
Hate, 375
  See also Malevolent transformation

Hearing, *see* Auditory zone of inter-action
Hebephrenia, 328, 362*n*
Heredity, 313–314
    See also Differences, inherent human
Heterosexuality:
    adolescent experimentation in, 271–274
    See also Lust dynamism, and intimacy need, patterns of manifestation of
Homosexuality, 248, 256–258, 270, 276–279, 294, 326
    See also Lust dynamism, and intimacy need, patterns of manifestation of
Human similarities and differences, *see* One-genus postulate
Humiliation, 225, 358, 379
Hypochondriacal preoccupations, 355–358, 362–363, 362*n*

Illumination, 362
Imagination in childhood, 222–225
Incorporation, 166, 168
Individuality, unique, delusion of, 140
Infancy:
    anal and urethral zones in, 126–134
    anxiety in, 8–10, 41–51, 53–55
    apathy and somnolent detachment in, 55–57
    beginnings of self-system in, 158–171
    concept of dynamism in, 98–110
    concept of personality in, 110–111
    defined, 33
    differentiation of body in, 135–145
    differentiation of experience in, 66–75
    euphoria and tension in, 34–37
    fear in, 49–53
    integration, resolution, and disintegration of situations in, 92–98
    learning in, 145–157
    needs in, 37–41
    nursing as an interpersonal experience in, 122–124
    organization of personifications in, 111–122
    signs, signals, and symbols in, 75–91
    tension of need for sleep in, 57–61
    transition from infancy to childhood, 172–187
    zonal needs and general needs in, 124–126
    zones of interaction in, 62–66
Inference, use of, in study of personality, 119, 175–176
In-groups, 235–236, 252
Instinct, 21, 146–147, 285
Integration of interpersonal situation, 92–97, 151
    See also Intimacy, need for; Lust dynamism
Interpersonal situation, integration, resolution, and disintegration of, 92–98
Interpersonal theory, history of, 16–20
Intimacy, need for:
    in adolescence, 264–266
    collision of, with other needs, 266–271
    failure to change preadolescent direction of, 277–279
    in preadolescence, 245–246, 258
    separation of, from lust, 274–276
    See also Loneliness; Lust dynamism, and intimacy need, patterns of manifestation of
Introjection, 166, 168
Invention, 191
Irresponsibility, in juvenile era, 254
Isolation, social, 203, 225, 254, 276–277, 305–306, 351, 357–358
    See also Cultural environment, man's need for interchange with; Malevolent transformation

Jealousy, 268, 279, 347–348, 360
Juvenile, chronic, 232
    lust dynamism in, 279–280, 289
Juvenile era, 227–244
    cooperation in, 226, 246, 246*n*
    defined, 33, 226
    transition to, 217–226
    types of warp emerging from, 251–255

Keller, H., 66

Language, 105–106
learning of, 148–149, 156–157, 178–185
role of, in fusion of personifications, 188–189
See also Autistic, the; Communication; Syntaxic mode of experience; Verbalisms
Latency period, 233
Leadership, 240, 250–251, 254, 257
Learning:
by anxiety, 151–154, 159–160
of cultural prescriptions, 219–223
of disparagement, 242–243
eductive, 156
of facial expression, 145–148
of gesture and language, 148–149, 156, 178–185
by indifference, 180–181
as organization of experience, 150–151
by physical pain, 155, 204–205, 211–213
by reward and punishment, 155, 158–159, 180–181
sublimatory, 153–154, 195–196, 234–235
by trial-and-error, 137, 147–148, 155–157, 178–180
by trial-and-success, 154–155
Levy, D. M., 125–126
Lewin, K., 35n, 39
Libido, 295
Loneliness, 271, 370
in childhood, 223–225
developmental history of, 260–262, 290–291
See also Intimacy, need for
Love, 245, 291–292, 351, 372–373
Lust dynamism, 109
in adolescent experimentation, 271–274
in chronic juvenile, 279–280
collision of, with security and intimacy need, 266–271
delay in maturation of, 257–258
first appearance of, 257–260, 263, 265–266
and intimacy need, patterns of manifestation of, 290–296, 372–373

amphigenital, 292–293
autophilic, 291–292, 372
autosexual, 270–271, 292–293
heterophilic, 264, 291–292, 372
heterosexual, 292–293
homosexual, 292–293
isophilic, 264, 291–292, 372
katasexual, 292–293
metagenital, 292–293
mutual masturbation, 292–294
onanism, 292–294
orthogenital, 292–293
paragenital, 292–293
in isolated adolescent, 276–277
as a pattern of covert and overt symbolic events, 286–288
with preadolescent intimacy direction, 277–279
as a psychobiological integrating apparatus, 280–282
separation of, from intimacy, 274–276
sublimation of, 195, 274
as a system of integrating tendencies, 288–289
as a system of zones of interaction, 282–286

Magic, 69–70, 188, 220
Malevolence, in mothering one, 115–116
Malevolent transformation, 201–202, 203–216, 253, 345, 347
Malinowski, B., 18
Masochism, 352–353
Masturbation, see Autosexuality
Maturity, 298, 308–310
Mead, G. H., 16–17, 18n
Meaning, see Sign
Mental disorder, 4, 114–115, 162–164, 174, 208, 223, 305, 367, 373
defined, 313
See also Dissociation; Not-me; Paranoid states; Schizophrenia; Substitutive processes; Warp, personality
Meyer, A., 16, 105–106
Me-you patterns, 209, 347, 347n
Mimicry, 179
Morris, C., 87–88n

Mother, good and bad, 85–91, 111–124, 139, 188–189
Mozart, 104
Mullahy, P., 28n–29n, 347n
"My body," 139–141, 156, 161, 163, 201
Mysterious Stranger, The, 329n, 341–342
Myths:
  Balaam, Biblical story of, 339–340
  as dreams, 339–343
  The Mysterious Stranger, 341–342
  personal, 341, 341n
  the Rheingold, 341–342

Need(s):
  for compeers, see Compeers, need for
  for contact, 40n, 155, 201, 261, 290, 370
  general, 124–126
  for intimacy, see Intimacy, need for
  for sleep, 58–60
  for tenderness, 40, 261
  tension of, 37–45, 369–370
  zonal, 124–126, 145
Nightmare, 164, 317, 334
Nipple (good, bad, evil, wrong):
  classification of, 80
  See also Experience, differentiation of
Nonsymbolic, the, 186–188
Not-me, 145, 152, 161–164, 168, 201, 267, 275, 314–316, 361–363, 371n
  See also Dissociation; Uncanny emotion
"Not" technique, 268–269, 303, 309
Nursing:
  accessory behavior in, 123–124
  as an interpersonal experience, 122–124
  nipple-lips experience in infancy, 66–75, 79–81
  See also Nipple

Obedience in childhood, 205
Observer, see Participant observation
Obsessional substitution, see Substitutive processes
Oedipus complex, 219

One-genus postulate, 32–33, 305
  See also Differences, inherent human
Operationalism, 14–15
  See also Field theory
Opinion leadership, 250
Oral zone, 63–75, 125–126, 135–141, 159–160
  See also Zones of interaction
Organization, principle of, 31–32, 32n, 98–99
  in self-system, 190
Orientation in living, 87
  concept of, 243–244
  defective, 262, 288–290
Ostracism, 155, 181, 235–236, 252, 261, 291, 345
"Ought," training in concept of, 206–208
Out-groups, 235–236, 252
Overt processes, 175–180, 184–187, 286–288

Pain, physical, see Learning by physical pain
Panic, 326–327
Paranoid states, 276, 328, 344–363, 348
  paranoid transformation of personality, 347, 361–363
Parataxic mode of experience, 28–29, 28n, 36, 36n, 38–39, 75, 83–84, 108, 163, 286, 304–305, 339, 342–343
Participant observation, 13–14, 175–176, 368, 372, 376, 378, 380
Pattern:
  defined, 103–107
  in interpersonal relations, 368
  See also Fear, tension of, patterns of dealing with; Lust dynamism, and intimacy need, patterns of manifestation of
Pederasty, 293
Perception, see Experience
Personality, concept of, 110–111
Personification(s):
  complexity of, 167–168
  fusion of, in childhood, 188–189
  of mother (in infancy), 118–122, 139

of not-me in paranoid states, 361–363

of others, *see* Stereotypes

parents', of infant, 174–175

of self:

    in childhood, 198–202, 205, 215, 218–219, 317

    in juvenile era, 247–248

    in late adolescence, 300–304

    rudimentary, in infancy, 161–171, 314–316 (*see also* "My body")

    subpersonifications, 209

Phobia, primary genital, 143–145, 160–161, 174, 267, 272, 276, 286, 314–315, 376

Phonemes, 105–106, 148–149, 156, 180

Powdermaker, H., 265

Powerlessness, experience of, 70–72, 72n

Preadolescence, 227, 245–262, 265–266, 372

    defined, 33

Prehension, 28n, 76–77

Prejudice, *see* Stereotypes; Verbalisms

Preoccupation, *see* Substitutive processes

Projection, 358–359

Propitiation, 200–201, 345

    See also Verbalisms

Prototaxic mode of experience, 28–29, 28n, 36, 36n, 38, 77–78, 84, 286

Psychiatric interview, 381

Psychiatry:

    defined, 13–14, 367–368

    as a developing field, 72n

    developmental approach in, 3–12

    of peoples, 367–384

Psychobiology, 16

Psychosomatic processes, 213

    See also Substitutive processes

Psychotherapy, 114–115, 192, 295–296, 349–350n, 372–373, 376–377

    significance of dreams in, 331–339, 343

Puberty change, *see* Lust dynamism, first appearance of

Punishment, *see* Learning, by physical pain

Rage behavior, 54, 211–213

Rationalization, 113

    See also Verbalisms

Reality, discrimination of, in childhood, 223–225

Rebelliousness in childhood, 205

Rebuff, 198–202

    See also Malevolent transformation

Recall, *see* Foresight and recall

Receptor, 63–64, 282–283

    See also Distance receptors in infancy; Zones of interaction

Reciprocal emotion, theorem of, 198–199

Referential process:

    facilitory, 284

    inhibitory, 284

    nonverbal, 184–185

    precautionary, 284

Regression, 197

Reintegration of dissociated systems, 322–325

Resentment, 211–213, 345

Resolution of interpersonal situation, 92–97, 151

Restrictions in living, 305–308

Reverie, 184–185, 349–350

Reward and punishment, *see* Learning, by reward and punishment

Rheingold, the, 341–342

Ribble, M., 61

Ridicule, 268, 358–359

Ritual, social, 306–307

Ritual avoidances and preoccupations, 307–308

Sadism, 213–214, 352–353

Sapir, E., 24–25, 339

Satisfaction of needs, 37–44, 112, 370

    first invariant experience of, 139–140

Schizophrenia, 68, 258, 313–328, 330–331, 337, 343, 356, 359, 361, 362–363

School society, *see* Juvenile era

Secondary elaboration, 333

Security, interpersonal, *see* Self-system

Security operations, *see* Self-system

Selective inattention, 170, 233–234, 288, 304, 319–320, 346–347, 374
See also Fear, tension of, patterns of dealing with
Self-esteem, low, in interpersonal difficulties, 350–359
Self-pity, 354–355
Self-respect, 308–310, 370
Self-sentience, 136–142
Self-sufficiency, initial venture in, 142
Self-system, 109, 316–317, 373–375
beginnings of, 158–161
development of, in childhood, 59–60
dynamism of, 164–168
favorable change in, 192, 228, 247–248, 302
and loneliness, 262
necessary and unfortunate aspects of, 168–171
security, interpersonal, 42–43, 267–268
security operations, 191, 224, 243, 329–331, 333, 346–347, 373–374, 379
in sleep, 330–331
theorem of escape, 190–192, 208
See also Personifications; Supervisory patterns
Sentience, 27–29
See also Self-sentience
Sex as a presenting problem in psychotherapy, 295–296
Sexual behavior, *see* Lust dynamism
Shame, 200, 219, 344, 379
Sign, 76–79, 86–91, 101, 106, 108–109, 175, 186–187
Signal, *see* Sign
Situation, interpersonal, 92–97, 111
See also Resolution of interpersonal situation
Sleep, 58–60, 289, 323–324, 329–339
Smith, T. V., 17n
Social accommodation, 229–230
Social handicaps, 240–242
Social judgments, 240–242
Social psychology, 16–20
Social responsibility of parents, 113–114, 142–145, 165, 215
Social ritual, 306–307

Social subordination, 228–229
Socialization:
of child, 224–225
of infant, 172–175
of juvenile, 227–232, 244
of preadolescent, 248–259
Socioeconomic opportunity in late adolescence, 298
Somnambulism, 337n
Somnolent detachment, 57
Spearman, C., 27–28n, 63, 63n, 156, 283–284
Stereotypes, 236–238, 302–304
Story-telling by parents in childhood, 219–220
Strangers, 304
Sublimation, 153–154, 192–196, 234–235, 274
Substitutive processes, 318–319, 347–348, 353–358
obsessional, 211, 318–319, 338, 343
preoccupation, 273, 307–308, 354–358, 362–363
example of, in cocker spaniel, 210–211
Sucking, *see* Needs, zonal
Sullivan, H. S., 8n, 36n, 154n, 182n, 367n
Superego, 166, 167, 167n
Supervisory patterns, 238–240
Surrogates, mother, 115–120
Suspicion, 360n, 362
Symbol, 87
See also Sign
Symbolic, the, and the nonsymbolic, 186–188
Sympathy, preying on, 353
Syntaxic mode of experience, 28–29n, 36, 36n, 38–39, 183–184, 224–225, 232–234, 286, 298–300, 343

Taboo, uncanny, 161
Tantrums, 212–213
Tenderness:
in late infancy, 158–159
and malevolence, 214–215
need for, 40, 52–53, 59, 130–134, 201–202, 261, 290
theorem of, 39
modification of, 198–199
Tension, 34–37, 368–369

of anxiety, 41–45, 113–115, 300–302, 308, 370, 374
of fear, 9, 49–53, 108, 203–204, 310, 374
of need for sleep, 57–60
of needs, 37–45, 369–370
Terror, 49
night, 334
Theorems:
of anxiety, 41
of escape, 190–192, 208
of reciprocal emotion, 198–199
of tenderness, 39
Thumb-in-lips situation, 136–141
Tic, 321
Toilet training, 174
See also Anal zone of interaction; Urethral zone of interaction
Training:
in concept of "ought," 206–207
for life, 371, 382
manual-exploratory, 143–145, 160
manual-oral, 142–143, 159–160
See also Education by parents; Learning
Transformation of personality, 347
See also Malevolent transformation; Paranoid states
Twain, Mark, 329n, 341–342

Uncanny emotion, 10, 72n, 160, 163–164, 315–316, 320–322, 326–327, 333, 337, 359–362, 371n, 375
adjustment to the uncanny, 324–325n

See also Dissociation; Not-me
Unconscious, the, 176–177, 193–196, 232–235, 278–279, 316
See also Covert processes; Dissociation; Selective inattention
Unwitting, the, 193–196, 287
See also Sublimation
Urethral zone of interaction, 126–127, 130–134, 285
See also Zones of interaction

Vector, concept of, 95–97
Vegetative nervous system, 281–282
Verbalisms, 191, 208, 220, 374
See also Propitiation
Visual sentience, 80–81, 85–91

Wagner, R., 341
Wallace, H., 307
Warp, personality:
in childhood, 372
remedy of, in preadolescence, 251–257
Whitehead, A. N., 102, 102n
Will, doctrine of, 171, 173, 301–302, 346
Wish-fulfilling fantasy, 348–350n
Work, 92–93, 97–98

Zones of interaction, 62–75, 108–109, 126–134, 158, 282–286
multizonal coordination, 135–141, 148–149
zonal needs, 124–126, 145

Books That Live

THE NORTON IMPRINT ON A BOOK
MEANS THAT IN THE PUBLISHER'S
ESTIMATION IT IS A BOOK NOT FOR A
SINGLE SEASON BUT FOR THE YEARS

W · W · NORTON & COMPANY · INC ·